BISON
BOOKS

MEN *in*

UNIVERSITY OF NEBRASKA PRESS | LINCOLN AND LONDON

EDEN

WILLIAM DRUMMOND STEWART

and SAME-SEX DESIRE *in the*

ROCKY MOUNTAIN FUR TRADE

William Benemann

Library of Congress
Cataloging-in-Publication Data
Benemann, William, 1949–
Men in Eden : William
Drummond Stewart and same-
sex desire in the Rocky Mountain
fur trade / William Benemann.
p. cm. Includes bibliographical
references and index.
ISBN 978-0-8032-3778-0
(pbk. : alk. paper)
1. Stewart, William Drummond,
Sir, 1795 or 6–1871.
2. Homosexuals—Great
Britain—Biography. 3. Fur traders—West (U.S.)—Biography.
4. Fur trade—Social aspects—
West (U.S.)—History—19th century. 5. Homosexuality—West
(U.S.)—History—19th century.
6. Male friendship—West
(U.S.)—History—19th century.
7. Frontier and pioneer life—
West (U.S.) I. Title.
HQ75.8.S74B46 2012
306.76′6097809034—dc23
2012008489

Set in Fanwood by Kim Essman.
Designed by Nathan Putens.

Beanntaichean àrda is àillidh leacainnean,
sluagh ann an còmhnuidh is coire cleachdainnean,
's aotrom mo cheum a' leum g'am faicinn . . .

Acknowledgments

Writing history is often the art of following a slender thread wherever it leads. For anyone writing early gay history the first challenge is finding a thread to follow, and for the thread that led to this book I have to thank Jim Wilke, whose article in *Frontiers* magazine first alerted me to the life of William Drummond Stewart. Wilke in that 1998 article lamented the lack of books on early gay American history and suggested a number of topics that *someone* should write about someday. Here, so very many years later, I answer that call.

My travels in pursuit of Sir William's story led me over many miles and into many archives. Many institutions throughout this country and abroad deserve my gratitude for the numerous ways they aided my research, but a few should be singled out for particular mention. The staff members of the American Heritage Center at the University of Wyoming were beyond question the most accommodating archivists I have ever encountered. They opened Mae Reed Porter's research files to me in a way that made my stay in Laramie phenomenally productive (with the lagniappe of being able to eat my lunch each day surrounded by Alfred Jacob Miller's paintings of Sir William and Antoine Clement). The archivists at the National Archives of Scotland in Edinburgh went above and beyond the call of duty to provide me with the ribbon-tied bundles of Stewart family papers, even when a labor strike intervened at the least opportune time. Closer to home, I gladly make a long-overdue acknowledgment of the staff members of the Interlibrary Borrowing Service at the University of California, Berkeley, who for my last three books have conjured out of the ether the most obscure publications and delivered them swiftly into my hands just at the moment I most needed them. The service they provide to scholars is beyond measure and beyond price.

One individual deserves special recognition: William R. Johnston, emeritus director of the Walters Art Museum in Baltimore. Dr. Johnston not only opened his personal research files to me, he also slipped me in the back door of the building before the museum opened to the public and hosted me to a lunch at which he frankly discussed his views about Stewart's sexuality. He was particularly helpful in volunteering to serve as liaison between the Miller family and me in my attempt to track down the originals of the letters Alfred Jacob Miller wrote from Murthly Castle. My memorable morning at the Walters began with Dr. Johnston quite literally racing through the museum in his excitement to show me Miller's portrait of Antoine Clement. The generosity with which he welcomed me into his busy schedule is very much appreciated.

My trips to the Missouri Historical Society (now known as the Missouri History Museum Library and Research Center) and to the National Archives of Scotland were underwritten in part by a research grant from the Librarians Association of the University of California. The university's commitment to professional development and scholarly research even during these challenging economic times is a mark of how strongly it maintains the lofty goals upon which the University of California was first established. I would not have been able to take advantage of the generous grant without the understanding and flexibility of my employer, the University of California School of Law (Boalt Hall). Moreover, Berkeley Law's unsurpassed collections of Anglo-American and international law were indispensable in my research. As will be demonstrated in the following chapters, much of William Drummond Stewart's life can be documented only through court records.

Once launched, all research projects provide unexpected pleasures. For this particular project it was the magical experience of connecting with a number of people who quite literally carry the DNA of the story I was trying to reconstruct. I am very grateful to Hans-Wolff Sillem of Hamburg, Germany, descendent of Sir William's companion of 1835–36, Adolph Sillem. Herr Sillem provided me with the correct first name of Adolph as well as with a very valuable sketch of his ancestor's life. Jan Wood of Devon, England, provided a similar service, as she is a descendent of another of Sir William's companions, Charles Howard Ashworth. In this case also I started with only a last name and a few brief biographical details. Ms. Wood provided two long contemporary descriptions of Ashworth's visit to America that filled in the sketchy story and revealed Ashworth to be a very colorful character indeed.

For his gracious hospitality, unflagging enthusiasm, and gentlemanly patience I am deeply indebted to Thomas Steuart Fothringham, the current laird of Murthly Castle. He and his wife, Kate, welcomed me and my partner to their estate and into their home, and we will long treasure the memory of a warm May afternoon spent sipping coffee in the garden of Murthly Castle, talking about Sir William's "very odd marriage." Shortly after my return from Scotland I began to launch castleward an assault of inquiring e-mail messages on various arcana having to do with the Stewart/Steuart family. Mr. Steuart Fothringham was unfailingly patient with my pestering, pondered my theories with a bracing curiosity, and generously offered me copies of family portraits and photographs to use as illustrations for the book. Perhaps with this biography I can begin to recompense the family for the unfortunate depredations of that other Yank.

I would like to thank Les K. Wright of the Bear History Project and the Neshoba Institute, and Massimiliano Carocci of the University of London and the Royal Anthropological Institute for their close readings of the manuscript. Their knowledge respectively of queer masculinities and American Plains Indian culture helped to correct some misstatements and guided me along some very specialized exploratory paths. All remaining errors in the text are, of course, my own.

Finally, I happily acknowledge my continuing debt to my partner, Kevin Jewell, who became my legal spouse during the writing of this book. He is my editor, my proofreader, my travel agent, my tech geek, my German and Scots Gaelic translator, my sounding board, and my best friend. In writing of William Drummond Stewart's long and essentially lonely life, I realized anew how profoundly I am blessed.

MEN in EDEN

Introduction

In 1980 art historian Ron Tyler traveled to Scotland in preparation for a major exhibition of the western paintings of Alfred Jacob Miller, an event planned for the Amon Carter Museum in Fort Worth, Texas. The artist had traveled west as far as the Rocky Mountains, engaged by the Scottish nobleman William Drummond Stewart in 1837 to document his journey to the annual fur traders' rendezvous. Miller had subsequently spent many months at Stewart's Murthly Castle in Perthshire producing large oil paintings from his original watercolor sketches of life in the Rockies, among the earliest known images of the region. From the Caledonian Hotel on Edinburgh's elegant Princes Street, Tyler wrote back to his colleague William Johnston in Baltimore: "This trip has proved once again that there is no substitute for on-the-spot research. In addition to the usual gleanings from the archives and dusty tomes, I picked up the real reason for Stewart's disenchantment re his family: he was homosexual, or so a lady in Birnam told me, in a hushed voice and with a raised eyebrow, as if Stewart himself might come around the corner to contradict her."[1]

Since 2006 I have felt very much like that informant in the teashop in Birnam, sensing that Sir William Drummond Stewart was lurking just around the corner — not to contradict me if I revealed that he was homosexual but to correct me if, in sifting through the hints and circumlocutions, I got his story wrong. I have followed Sir William's trail from his birthplace (and his burial crypt) at Murthly Castle to the Wind River Range in Wyoming, from the brisk windswept walks of New York City's Battery Park to the steaming streets of the French Quarter in New Orleans. In the process I have come to realize the wisdom of Ron Tyler's dictum that there is no substitute for on-the-spot research.

As I followed Stewart's story, I ran across a litany of familiar names: explorer William Clark, Baptiste Charbonneau (son of Sacagawea), mountain men Jim Bridger and Jedediah Smith, Marcus and Narcissa Whitman, Kit Carson, Washington Irving, John James Audubon, Senator Thomas Hart Benton, Daniel Boone, John C. Frémont, William Henry Harrison, Daniel Webster, Henry Clay, John Augustus Sutter — a Who's Who of early nineteenth-century America. These were names familiar to me since grade school, and yet I had never heard of William Drummond Stewart. I began to feel as though I had stumbled across an old photograph of a large family gathering, a photograph from which one member of the family had been digitally erased. To restore William Drummond Stewart to his place at the table — with all his virtues and his faults — has been the mission behind the writing of this book.

The current book is not the first biography of William Drummond Stewart. In 1963 historians Mae Reed Porter and Odessa Davenport published *Scotsman in Buckskin*, the first full-length exploration of Stewart's life. Mrs. Porter's involvement with the project began in 1935 when, while visiting a museum in Baltimore, she was shown a series of watercolors by Alfred Jacob Miller. She promptly purchased the entire collection and began investigating their story. This led her to Sir William and to nearly three decades of research into his life.

By the late 1950s Mrs. Porter and her husband, historian Clyde H. Porter, had amassed an impressive file of research material (currently housed at the American History Center at the University of Wyoming and at the Huntington Library in San Marino, California), but the death of Mr. Porter in 1958 and Mrs. Porter's own declining health made the idea of launching a major writing project daunting. She was therefore delighted when she met Odessa Davenport, who had the professional interest and the personal enthusiasm to take on the task of writing the book.

Scotsman in Buckskin presents frustrating obstacles to anyone wishing to use it as source material. The 306-page book does not include a single footnote, and the bibliography is sketchy and incomplete. The central problem of the book, however, is that Porter and Davenport were writing at a time when to many people it was quite literally unthinkable that a vigorous, dashing figure in American history could be a homosexual. It does not appear that either woman ever considered that Stewart might have been gay. They invent a happy marriage for him and insert hints of heterosexual American romances that appear nowhere in the nineteenth-century sources. From my reading of Porter's research files, I do not believe that she actively suppressed evidence of Stewart's homosexuality. I believe it simply never occurred to her.

The only other book to deal in a substantial way with William Drummond Stewart is Bernard DeVoto's Pulitzer Prize–winning *Across the Wide Missouri*, published in 1947. DeVoto's book is a history of the American fur trade in the early nineteenth century, and while Stewart makes frequent appearances in the text, the author discusses his life only in connection with the trade. In his preface he describes Stewart as "the unifying force in the book so far as it has one," but admits that "not much all told can be found out about him; he left exceedingly little record of his seven years in the West." DeVoto explicitly holds back from providing the complete story of Stewart's life, explaining that Mae Reed Porter (who provided the foreword for his own book) was currently working on a full biography. Porter's book would not appear for another sixteen years.[2]

Bernard DeVoto did, I believe, consider the possibility that William Drummond Stewart was a homosexual. While researching at the Missouri Historical Society he uncovered a letter from Stewart to his closest American friend, William Sublette, speculating on whether a clerk in Sublette's store was a "Fairy." DeVoto paused to consider the implications of that word, but decided merely to note the occurrence and move on. The present book will explore the role gay men played in a nineteenth-century mercantile setting, but to DeVoto — again, writing before homosexuality was considered a fit subject for historians — the topic was simply beyond the pale.

The issue of William Drummond Stewart's homosexuality — and the discomfort that evidence of it has produced in historians who cannot bring themselves to acknowledge it — reaches a peak of denial in Marshall Sprague's 1967 work *A Gallery of Dudes*, which devotes a chapter to Stewart. Sprague, who relied heavily on Porter and Davenport's book as his source material, obviously picked up on vibrations that the two women had missed, and as a result he felt it necessary to wrap Stewart in a protective cloak of respectable heterosexuality:

> You will have observed that Sir William spent his life avoiding women and consorting with men. During his Rockies years he always had males in tow, and yet, paradoxically, this preference for men derived from the fact that he liked women very much indeed — Anglo, Indian, Creole or whatever. He avoided them, socially at least, because the alluring Christina had taught him early in life what would happen to him if he didn't — the awful slavery of love, children and dear, dull domesticity. Until his retirement in 1844, he was far too egocentric and adventurous to endure such an existence. The deepening experience of connubial bliss was not for him and, for that reason, he lived and died a limited man. He settled deliberately for half a loaf.[3]

Today we have a greater appreciation of the diversity and complexity of sexual desire, but challenges for historians still remain. Anyone writing about a period of gay history much before the end of the nineteenth century must grapple with the ghost of Michel Foucault. In his monumentally influential 1976 book *The History of Sexuality* (volume 1 of an uncompleted work), the French philosopher presented his theory that homosexuality is merely a socially constructed phenomenon, one created by the medico-legal establishment in the late 1860s. Before that period, men and women did not think in terms of sexual orientation or view themselves in terms of labels such as homosexual or heterosexual. Sexuality was expressed in terms of independent acts, acts that were not viewed by the participants as inherent to their natures. So pioneering and so brilliant was Foucault's work that it has been accepted almost without question by many historians of sexuality. When writing about early same-sex relations these historians strictly avoid employing the term *homosexuality*; the word has become the shibboleth by which the enlightened are distinguished from the hopelessly uninformed.

In the years since Foucault's untimely death in 1984, however, evidence has been mounting that raises doubts about his theories on the development of the concept of homosexuality. Researchers have documented extensive same-sex community building at least as early as the eighteenth century: the establishment of what we would now call "queer space" (in the form of specially designated taverns, clubs, and public meeting areas), the development of specialized slang and jargon incomprehensible to most outsiders, the adoption of secret symbols to reveal membership in the enclosed community, the evolution of staged rituals in which only initiates were allowed to take part, and so on. All of these phenomena are markers of the development of a *group* identity — whether the members of the group chose to call themselves sodomites, sodomists, mollies, perverts, buggers, berdaches, hermaphrodites, androgynes, or (William Drummond Stewart's own choice) fairies. All of these terms were used prior to the late nineteenth century to designate men who habitually preferred to have sex with other men. When in 1730s Paris a young man boasted to a police informant that for the last twenty years he had been proudly active in *la bardacherie*, he was describing not a series of isolated acts but an entire lifestyle based around having sex with other men.[4]

William Drummond Stewart was sexually active with other men at least by the early 1830s, and he died just as the term *homosexual* was being adopted by the medico-legal establishment. In his avoidance of sexual relations with women, in his preference for inhabiting environments where male-male sexuality was an acceptable option, in his extended romantic attachments to other men, Stewart lived his life in a way that a twenty-first-century observer would recognize as unquestionably *homosexual*. But what do we mean when we use that word?

5

As Alfred Kinsey's studies have demonstrated, sexual orientation is a continuum, with all men and women falling somewhere on a gay/straight scale. As a consequence, overt conduct reveals only part of an individual's story. Lack of homosexual activity does not preclude homosexual attraction, marriages do not prove heterosexuality, sexual experimentation does not alter inherent orientation. In order to understand the full implications of a person's sexuality, it is necessary to understand the pressures, choices, and options that that individual faced during his or her lifetime. The gap in our understanding of homosexuality in the early years of American history makes this type of analysis problematic; the sparseness of even the most basic documentation about the 1830s and 1840s makes William Drummond Stewart's life intriguing and significant. Although it would be an overstatement to characterize Stewart as a homosexual pioneer, he *did* spend his years in America living with a degree of candor that many have assumed was impossible during that era. He traveled openly with his partners, never flaunting his sexuality but also never slinking in the shadows.[5]

As I explored William Drummond Stewart's life, I was struck by how frequently the lives of his associates followed the patterns I documented in my previous book, *Male-Male Intimacy in Early America* (2006). My initial reaction was reinforced when I began to explore the Rocky Mountain fur trade beyond those individuals immediately connected with Stewart. Although many participants left behind too little in the way of biographical information to provide significant data about their lives, much can be inferred from the available information. LeRoy R. Hafen, in his exhaustive ten-volume study *The Mountain Men and the Fur Trade of the Far West* (1965–72), compiled biographical essays on 292 men. A statistical comparison of Hafen's findings against national population data for the same period reveals a significantly high percentage of "confirmed bachelors" among the men associated with the Rocky Mountain fur trade.

Because the U.S. Census did not gather information on marital status until 1890, it is difficult to determine exact figures for earlier years. However, historians and sociologists have employed a battery of other sources to come up with reliable estimates concerning marriage patterns in American history. One consistent result of that analysis has been documentation that Americans — first as colonists and then as citizens of a new nation — were more likely to marry, and to marry at an earlier age, than their European counterparts. America was a marrying nation. European visitors such as Chevalier Félix de Beaujour commented on the almost frenetic fecundity of the Republic: "In the United States, more children are necessarily born than among us, because the inhabitants in such an extent of country, finding the means of subsistence more abundant, marry at an earlier age. No human consideration there operates as a hindrance to reproduction, and the children swarm on the rich land in the same manner as do the insects."[6]

The social and economic pressure to marry was intense, so much so that unmarried adults were "almost in the class of suspected criminals." Women were to a great extent trapped in their circumstances, but men who did not want to become anyone's husband could exercise the option of choosing a career in which the expectation of marriage was removed, or at least postponed. As I have described elsewhere, "The professions of soldier, sailor, merchant marine, whaler, riverman, trapper, or itinerant trader provided an unmarried man with a context in which to live his life until he either found a wife or accepted the status of confirmed bachelor." The status of confirmed bachelor — or, as sociologists term it, "permanent non-marriage" — has been defined as people aged forty-five to fifty-four who have never been married. In 1880, the earliest year for which precise figures are available, the percentage of men in a state of permanent non-marriage was 7.8 of the total male American population.[7]

Hafen and his associates were able to determine the marital status of 268 men involved in the fur trade, and they discovered that a full 16 percent remained lifelong bachelors, a figure perhaps twice the national average for the period. Lest it be assumed that the precarious life of a trapper resulted in many dying before the age by which a man would presumably marry, it should be noted that of the 233 men in Hafen's study for whom a complete biography was available, only 3 percent died before the age of forty. To an extent that is statistically greater than would be expected, then, we encounter men in the fur trade who remained confirmed bachelors. If we add to this figure trappers and traders who entered into late-life marriages that were obviously not intended to be companionate (because of the vast difference in the age of the partners or because the husband spent extended periods of time separated from his wife), there is evidence that a significantly large number of men involved in the fur trade absented themselves from the national nuptial frenzy.[8]

Most of the men involved in the Rocky Mountain fur trade — 84 percent in Hafen's study — *did* marry, as might be expected. Of those who married, 36 percent entered into marriages or long-term relationships with Native American women. Most nineteenth-century descriptions of these relationships stress the desirability of white men as husbands (though it should be noted that most of the descriptions were written by white men). These writers believed that Indian women felt they enjoyed a more comfortable life with a white husband, as in many Indian tribes traditional woman's work was arduous and unrelenting. Marrying a white man could raise a Native American woman's status by providing her with an important social role: she might learn enough of a European language to serve as a liaison between outsiders and her own people. There were also very real material advantages that manifested themselves through a display of much-desired status symbols. White men were able to shower their female partners with "gewgaws" and "foofaraw" — ornamental trinkets that were highly valued because they could not be produced in the mountains and were available only through trade with the fur companies.[9]

This is not to say that romance was never a factor in these relationships, but the peripatetic life of a trapper, and the brief encounters that that life dictated, did not lend itself to extended courtships. A combination of immediate sexual attraction and perceived material benefit was of much greater importance. In a pattern that was not unusual in nineteenth-century America, practical considerations trumped romance. Love might follow marriage. Though the historical descriptions of these relationships are unfortunately one-sided, they suggest that almost any white man interested in pursuing a liaison with an Indian woman could find one who felt the partnership would be advantageous to her or to her family. The fact that many men chose not to link themselves in some fashion despite long years away from white women might tell us something about their sexual orientation.

Any man who headed west knew that months or even years might pass before he saw a white woman again, and while many of those men entered into relationships with Native American women that lasted a few minutes or many years, others formed emotional and physical relationships only with other men — white, Indian, and Métis. When they crossed the Mississippi, men who had been reared in communities that taught them that sodomy was the most grievous of unpardonable sins encountered Native American cultures in which homosexuality in the phenomenon of the berdache was not just permitted but ritualized. The American West for these men became the land of the special dispensation, and many who journeyed there discovered a prelapsarian paradise, an Eden filled only with Adams — one whose borders were contracting each spring as "civilization" in the form of wagon trains full of traditional families rolled ever westward. This was the world that William Drummond Stewart entered in 1833.

1

Friedrich Armand Strubberg, having fled Germany after wounding a romantic rival in a duel, was slowly making his way through the rugged wilderness of the Rocky Mountains during the summer of 1843. He and his small party had followed a branch of the Colorado River to the Continental Divide and were now tracing the North Platte. The terrain was vast and craggy, breathtakingly isolated. "From all sides the individual mountains around it sank into green depths," he later wrote, "and out of its middle arose a high, skittle-shaped butte [*Kegelförmiger hoher Fels*], the peak of which had the shape of a ruined fortress." Buffalo could be seen in the distance, grazing on the lower slopes of the butte. Four members of the party grabbed their rifles and soon Strubberg heard the crack of their cartridges and saw puffs of white smoke rise on the still, cold air. One of the buffalo fell to the ground and the hunters descended on him, butchering knives flashing.[1]

That evening their camp was filled with the musky scent of roasting buffalo ribs, and in their frying pans sizzled trout just caught from a nearby stream. Overhead the sky was dark and silent, the stars so brilliant it looked as though one could reach up and pluck them like diamonds. Strubberg felt himself very far indeed from his petty romantic entanglements in Hesse. The hunters, their leather clothing greasy with sweat and crusted with dried buffalo blood, huddled around the flickering campfire in the immense wilderness of that strange and savage land.

"The next morning we were done early with packing our animals and wanted to leave our campground," Strubberg wrote,

> when we saw behind that butte and its mountain ruins a multitude of columns of smoke rising from the valley, which indicated a large Indian encampment. We needed to exercise the precaution of finding out to what tribe they belonged and in which direction they were moving, so we rode down into the valley and hid ourselves to the side in thick woods. The tiger [servant] and I then went to the butte and climbed to the top, from where we could see into the other side of the valley. Who can describe our surprise as we glimpsed at our feet a wide, colorfully laid-out camp, with all the signs of civilization.[2]

Before their amazed eyes spread what appeared to be a rollicking medieval market faire magically transported to the American West. Festive pennants waved above a jumble of colorful tents. Here and there naked men crawled out from beneath striped canvas and ran to a nearby lake, where they hooted and splashed in the morning sunlight. The revelers, around eighty of them in total, were mostly young men in their teens and twenties, and those who were clothed could be seen sporting the most fantastic and colorful costumes.

Strubberg tied the remnants of his handkerchief onto the end of his rifle and, standing on the highest visible peak, fired off both barrels while waving the white flag wildly over his head. A salvo of fifty shots answered his greeting, and the men in the valley brandished their neckerchiefs in the air. Strubberg and his friends galloped down to join the surreal celebration. They were stunned by what they saw.

> Many young dandies from the large, luxurious, eastern cities of this continent, as well as from those of the Old World, reared in salons, cafes, opera and concert halls, had followed their fantasies in the choice of their clothing and appeared in old chivalrous costumes with large plumed hats with rolled-up brims, jerkins with slit sleeves, leather leggings, tall riding boots with enormous spurs, large gauntlets, and they had girded on their ancestral swords; others

had preferred the old Spanish costume and had draped themselves with broad violet-blue and May-green velvet greatcoats, while the hat of an Italian brigand captain with red cock's feathers held their long perfumed locks, and their wide white shirt collar fell over their shoulders. Open sleeves showed the fine linen of the shirts, wide white baggy breeches were forced by tight red bindings into long boots, on which large-wheeled spurs clinked, and a pair of long, silver-inlaid, beautifully decorated pistols alongside a dagger decorated their belts. Yet others had read [James Fenimore] Cooper and chosen his heroes as a model: clothed in leather from head to foot, with wide-brimmed grey hats, a long, heavy hunting knife at the side, and with an enormous rifle, they stood there and appeared to envy me as their ideal in my worn-out clothes stiff with blood, while their suits, barely come from the hands of the tailor, were not yet dirtied by any spots. Still others had remained true to the appearance of the gentleman from Broadway in New York, replacing the top hat with a wide-brimmed one, and went around the fire in comfortable slippers, smoking their Havana cigars.[3]

The visitors were soon engulfed in a thick crowd of curious young gentlemen who peppered them with questions about their journey. Gradually Strubberg made his way to the very center of the camp, where a large striped marquee stood in regal splendor, a white pennant waving from its peak. "A man came toward me whose features appeared familiar to me at the first glance, and in the same moment I read clearly that I had made the same impression on him. Looking at one another searchingly, we reached out our hands, and after the first few words of greeting I recognized an old acquaintance, Lord S., whom I had last seen ten years before in the East of this continent. The happiness of meeting again was increased even more by the very strange circumstances in which it took place."[4]

The circumstances that in 1843 led Sir William Drummond Stewart to assemble a large entourage of fops, dandies, and handsome youths for a costume party in the remote Rockies were indeed strange, and his story reveals much about the lure of the western wilderness for men eager to escape the tightening bonds of Victorian sexual morality. His was an odd variation on a story that was all too familiar in nineteenth-century America: a black sheep dispatched to the New World with a remittance just large enough to keep him from returning to Europe to embarrass his family by his unconventional conduct. In essence, that was how his story started. It would end with a grand party that was the apotheosis of dandified travel through the vanishing American wilderness, one last all-male hurrah before the wagon trains and the families and the plows changed everything forever.

William Drummond Stewart was born the day after Christmas in 1795 in Perthshire, Scotland, the second son of Sir George Stewart (seventeenth Lord of Grandtully, fifth Baronet of Murthly) and Lady Catherine Drummond Stewart. Little is known of his childhood other than that it was spent mostly at the family's primary estate, Murthly Castle. The castle grounds were the home of fabled Birnam Wood, whose approach to Dunsinane foretold the defeat of Macbeth in Shakespeare's play. In Stewart's time only two trees remained of that ancient forest.

Though his young brother George studied at Christ Church, Oxford, William's interests lay in a different direction. In 1813, when William was seventeen, his father purchased him a cornetcy in the Sixth Dragoon Guards at a cost of £735. A coronet was the lowest rank in the cavalry, the usual starting place for a gentleman with no military experience and few influential connections. Stewart found life in the Guards uncongenial and asked his father to purchase for him instead a lieutenancy in the more fashionable Fifteenth Kings Light Dragoons. These officers were better known for their dashing appearance than their military prowess, but a soldier who could obtain a commission would be assured the adventure of actual combat, as the Fifteenth Kings Hussars were already engaged on the Continent. The commission was registered on January 6, 1814, and soon thereafter Lieutenant Stewart joined his regiment on the battlefields of France.[5]

The Fifteenth Light Dragoons was one of the cavalry units fighting

Napoleon during the Peninsular War, and Stewart quickly found himself immersed in battle after battle as the British army pushed toward Paris. A victory at Orthès was followed by engagements at Grenade, St. Germier, Tarbes, Tournefeuille, St. Simon, Gagnac, and Toulouse. With the defeat and exile of Napoleon in April 1814, the regiment was withdrawn to England, and in September it embarked from Liverpool for service in Ireland, where the regiment maintained its headquarters.[6]

Within the year Napoleon had escaped from Elba, and the Fifteenth Light Dragoons was once again ordered into action, landing at Ostend on May 19, 1815. Although the British cavalry was eager to do its part, the Duke of Wellington was far from convinced of the potential value of its contribution. The cavalry's effectiveness as a fighting unit suffered because of the policy of selling commissions, which too frequently attracted wealthy (and/or well-connected) men who were primarily interested in the dashing cut of the uniform, and who looked upon military discipline as an outrageous abridgement of their aristocratic privilege. The hussars, whose extravagantly theatrical military costumes attracted more than their share of foppish mannequins, were particularly prone to this vexing problem. Despite Wellington's misgivings, however, the hussars were dispatched to join the fight against Napoleon. When the Fifteenth arrived its vessel was run ashore on the sands of Ostend and the horses were lowered into the water so they could swim to the beach. Stewart's beplumed shako was soon drenched and his breeches splashed with Belgian mud. It was to rain nearly every day for the next two months.[7]

Napoleon's army was, of course, eventually defeated at Waterloo. Stewart's regiment at first formed part of the army of occupation that remained in France, but in May 1816 it was withdrawn to England and then to its home barracks in Dundalk, County Louth, Ireland. Waterloo had been a momentous victory, and for the first time in history the British government awarded a medal to *all* participants in a military action, officers and men. Though it was called the Waterloo Medal, the award was granted to all who had fought at Ligny, Quatre Bras, or Waterloo, the three battles (June 16–18) that comprised the Waterloo campaign.

The medal was also the first for which a new mechanical process was employed that allowed each soldier's name, rank, and unit to be stamped along the edge. More than forty thousand of the medals were awarded, but each was made unique by the addition of the individual soldier's name. Stewart's Waterloo Medal, on a crimson ribbon with dark blue edges, was stamped, "Lieut. W. Stewart — 15th Kings Hussars."[8]

In the months that followed Stewart found himself in the company of soldiers for whom once again fashionable display was of paramount importance. The regimental history records that in 1817 "an additional quantity of gold lace and embroidery was ordered to be worn on the officers' clothing and appointments." As usual, peace in Europe led Britain to reduce the size of its army and navy. Many officers were furloughed and put on half pay. By April 1821 the Fifteenth Kings Hussars had been reduced to only six troops. Stewart, seeing the end of his military career rapidly approaching, took steps to improve his rank while he could. He persuaded his father's neighbor, Thomas Graham, first Baron Lynedoch, to write to Maj. Gen. Sir Hubert Taylor asking Taylor's support in an effort to gain promotion to captain. The promotion was granted, becoming official on June 15, 1820. Shortly thereafter Stewart retired on half pay. Though he bore the designation for only a few months of active duty, the title "Captain" would serve him well among rank-conscious Americans in the years to come.[9]

After his separation from the army, Stewart assumed the lifestyle of a Regency dandy, albeit one with annoying financial limitations since he was only the second son. For the next decade he divided his time between Murthly Castle and his family's London home at 77 Eaton Place, attending balls and hunts, running up bills at the tailor and the wine merchant, worrying his family with his lack of direction and ambition. There are two physical objects that have survived to provide a glimpse into these otherwise lost years. The first is a letter Stewart received from his close friend Bertram, fourth Earl Ashburnham. Lord Ashburnham wrote to Stewart with the effusive embellishment and assumed ennui of the rich young dandy: "If you can excuse my long silence it is more than I can do," the young lord sighed.

Believe me that often, after passing such a night as men with evil consciences may, it has been my morning resolution to begin a letter to you, but idleness and procrastination have always persuaded me that I had really nothing of interest to tell you, & that I might as well wait in hope of something occuring. . . . You are often remembered in the Smoking room & at Bar[?] time, & Percy [Ashburnham's younger brother] and I always conclude with the very sincere wish that we may see you in your old place before the end of October, & if you do not return then you are a "perfidy man" I guess.[10]

The literary reference is to a comment made by Sophia Western's maid in the Henry Fielding novel *Tom Jones*. The servant asks her mistress if the disreputable Mr. Jones has proved himself to be a "perfidy man," completely abandoning the innocent young maiden he has professed to love.

Ashburnham goes on to mention that he has received a visit from James Gillespie Graham. Gillespie Graham, one of Scotland's finest architects, would produce some of his greatest work on the Murthly estate. He would also assist Stewart on a personal level by smoothing over certain complications arising from Stewart's irregular private life. "You will probably have heard that I had a visit here last May from Goliah of Goth — or as Scots call him Gillespie Graham," writes Ashburnham. "He was I think more pleased with the place [Ashburnham Place, the family's seat in Sussex] than any guest except yourself that I have had. Of the house he pronounced a more favorable opinion than I expected, and yet abused it to my satisfaction. . . . I invited him here to meet Mr. Driver (who is quite *safe*) who I thought might be of service to him, & believe he was." Who Mr. Driver was, and why he was "quite safe," is unknown.[11]

Ashburnham completes his missive by announcing that he would probably go to London, "& if I can pick up materials to fill only one side of a letter to you I will write — at the present I am exhausted." During his lifetime Ashburnham would assemble one of the finest rare book collections in England, though his reluctance to allow access to it frustrated scholars. He married at the age of forty-two, eventually fathering eleven children.[12]

The other evocative physical object surviving from this period is a lithograph from a small pencil drawing of Stewart's younger brother Thomas. The portrait, framed and still hanging on the walls of Murthly Castle, is dated 1828 and signed "Cte d'Orsay fecit." Alfred, comte d'Orsay, was the most notorious dandy of the early nineteenth century. Like his predecessor Beau Brummell, he became famous primarily as an arbiter of fashion, but whereas Brummell favored an elegant understatement in his apparel, the count made his mark with a dazzling peacock brilliance. The scion of a newly ennobled French family, he was able to finance his lifestyle thanks to a fortunate alliance with Charles Gardiner, first Earl of Blessington. Joining the Irish nobleman's household in 1822, the ravishingly handsome d'Orsay became the lover of both the earl and of the countess. When the ménage à trois threatened to become too scandalous even for those of the most worldly sophistication, it was decided that d'Orsay should marry one of Lord Blessington's daughters by his first marriage. Having met neither of them, he chose the younger, and fifteen-year-old Harriet was dispatched from Ireland to join the household in France. Reportedly Lady Blessington insisted that the marriage with her stepdaughter not be consummated for at least four years after the wedding, so that she need share her lover only with her own husband.[13]

D'Orsay was an unusually talented amateur artist (by the 1840s he would be relying on his skill as a portraitist for much-needed infusions of cash), and his sketch of Thomas Stewart is one of the finest of his small pencil portraits. It shows the young man in profile, his tousled hair piled up high in large curls, his starched shirt collar closely hugging his aristocratic jawline. Thomas — and most likely his older brother William also — had obviously fallen under the sartorial spell of the young count. Thomas was the guest of the earl, the countess, and d'Orsay at their Palazzo Belvedere in Naples, and his verses in honor of Lady Blessington were later published.

Another young dandy who fell under the count's spell during this period was Benjamin Disraeli, who would later serve as prime minister under Queen Victoria. Disraeli, too, sat for a pencil portrait. "A portrait by the count became something of a fashion accessory during the 1830s and 1840s," explains d'Orsay's biographer. "The young Disraeli is almost indecently exultant at having his likeness captured by him. From his evident pleasure, it seems to have been a rite of passage, an exclusive club, and, to judge from the tone of his letters about it, something of a peak that any social climber keen to arrive in London Society had to scale."[14]

Disraeli dedicated his 1837 novel *Henrietta Temple* to Count d'Orsay and included him in the novel in the character of Count Alcibiades de Mirabel. Mirabel is a dashing French aristocrat who has become the arbiter of fashion in London, and in Disraeli's description of a member of the count's entourage we see a dandy who could easily have been one of the young Stewart brothers:

> Mr. Bevil was a very tall and very handsome young man, of a great family and great estate, who passed his life in an imitation of Count Alcibiades de Mirabel. He was always dressed by the same tailor, and it was his pride that his cab or his vis-à-vis was constantly mistaken for the equipage of his model; and really now, as the shade stood beside the substance, quite as tall, almost as good-looking, with the satin-lined coat thrown open with the same style of flowing grandeur, and revealing a breast plate of starched cambric scarcely less broad and brilliant, the uninitiated might have held the resemblance as perfect. The wristbands were turned up with not less compact precision, and were fastened by jewelled studs, that glittered with not less radiancy. The satin waistcoat, the creaseless hosen, were the same; and if the foot were not quite as small, its Parisian polish was not less bright.[15]

In the same way that in Disraeli's novel Mr. Bevil is only an imitative flame standing next to the luminous Count de Mirabel, d'Orsay himself was a dim reflection of an incandescent comet. Looming over London during William Drummond Stewart's young manhood was a man who was not even there: George Gordon Lord Byron. By the time

Stewart left the Kings Hussars and joined the London social scene, Byron had already fled to the Continent, driven abroad by rumors of spousal abuse and incest and — far more egregious in the eyes of the English public — sodomitical practices. Byron's poetry became a great passion for Stewart. The only work of literature he is known to have taken with him on his first trip to America was a copy of Byron's play *Sardanapalus*, probably contained in a traveling edition of the poet's *Works*.

Lord Byron presented many attractions for Stewart. In addition to the stirring beauty and sexual daring of his poetry, Byron was a Scot, thanks to his mother's Gordon lineage. Reared in early childhood in Aberdeen, he arrived as a schoolboy at Harrow speaking with a broad Scots accent. Byron was the most notable transgressive figure of the age, famously branded as "mad, bad and dangerous to know," and to a generation of young London swells he represented everything that they secretly longed to be but were too timid to become. To a smaller group of those men — those who, like Stewart, were aware of their sexual attraction to other men — he served both as an idol and as a caution. Byron's homosexual activities were not documented until well after his death, but they were the subject of extensive rumor, and his fate was closely watched by men who wondered if they, like Byron, could have it all: fame, fortune, title, marriage, social position — and an active homosexual life. For a while Byron almost possessed the unobtainable, and his courage in trying gave hope to men for whom the pillory or the gallows were a constant threat. While elsewhere in Europe country after country repealed or reduced its sodomy laws, in England during the first three decades of the nineteenth century sixty homosexuals were hanged in very public displays of civic displeasure, and twenty more were executed aboard ships of the Royal Navy. In 1806 more men in England were executed for sodomy than for murder. To be openly homosexual in Britain during this period was to risk a very ignominious death.[16]

Stewart's sexual behavior during these years is difficult to document, and it is possible that he held back from engaging on an active level with other men. In Stewart's autobiographical novel *Edward Warren* the narrator offers an amazingly frank description of the spark of sexual desire that sometimes passed between himself and other men, and of his determination not to act on those hidden desires: "However I may be alive to surprise or admiration, or to those mysterious sympathies which are electrically conveyed by the touch as well as by the sight, I have never been conscious of betraying it by outward emotion." Edward Warren is finally compelled to express outward emotion toward another man when he meets a seductively handsome American Indian, and indeed it was not uncommon for a European who had carefully repressed his homosexuality at home to find it blossoming — to his dismay and to his wonderment — once he encountered Native Americans so strikingly handsome that it became almost a cliché to compare them to a naked Adonis or Apollo. Stewart may have been very discreetly homosexually active while in London, or it may have been the liberating atmosphere of America that allowed him at last to open himself to homosexual desire.[17]

It is clear, however, that Stewart did his best to follow in Byron's footsteps in other ways. When it came time to make his Grand Tour, he eschewed the more conventional Paris-Florence-Rome itinerary, choosing instead to retrace Byron's route to Greece and Turkey. To Stewart and his contemporaries the Ottoman Empire represented a sexual paradise where homoerotic desire, far from leading to death by hanging in a public square, was celebrated by poets and practiced by kings. Stewart returned from his Eastern voyage perhaps no less virginal than the day he left Portsmouth, but he was completely won over to the ambience of the seraglio. This passion for Orientalia would stay with him for the rest of his life. When he was at last ensconced on the Murthly estate he would decorate his rooms with Persian carpets, crimson damask wall hangings, and pierced silver Ottoman lanterns, and he would sleep on an improvised Turkish divan festooned with brocade cushions. On his final trip to the Rockies two decades later, he would bring with him a fantasy re-creation of a sultan's tent, where he would entertain each evening in Oriental splendor — though with the requisite lithesome harem girls replaced by the sturdy sons of Kentucky farmers.

If Stewart was reluctant to engage his homosexual desires, it was with good reason. At precisely the time that Stewart separated from the army and began an independent life in London, Parliament commenced debate on a bill to abolish the pillory, a popular form of punishment for men convicted of sodomy. The penalty consisted of being locked into a wooden yoke while an enraged public pelted the miscreant with rotten vegetables, offal from butcher shops, and dead dogs and cats. Men who endured the pillory were almost always severely injured, and some were killed by the assault. The parliamentary debates that took place during the winter of 1816 showed significant legislative support for this law reform, but the suggestion that sodomites might be spared the pillory resulted in an increase in anti-homosexual public outrage. In London the people made their will known: if the courts were blocked from handing down the traditional punishment to these depraved men, the public would step in to make sure they received their just deserts.

Sodomy trials in magistrate courts "were treated as a form of popular theatre." Public interest was particularly strong if the accused was a person of high social standing, but even men of less exalted rank could draw the public's ire. Riots might occur if word spread in advance that a sodomite was to appear in court. Often "police escorts of forty or fifty constables were required to conduct these men through the streets, who would otherwise have been in danger for their lives." In April 1830 a newspaper reported: "On Monday afternoon, when the three men who were committed to Tothill-fields prison on a similar charge [indecent assault] were taken down, a large mob assembled in the streets, and they were assailed with missiles of every description. It was with the greatest difficulty the officers could keep them from the fury of the populace. The officers, as well as the prisoners, were covered with mud from head to foot. On getting inside the prison gates, they were in such a dreadful state, that they were forced to strip and wash themselves." This atmosphere of mob hostility led Byron to hide his homosexuality while in England, even to the point of marrying a woman he did not love. When the marriage quickly soured and his wife began making public charges against him — including the revelation of his affair with his half-sister, Augusta — Byron fled England, never to return.[18]

It was in this atmosphere of very public debate about homosexuality — and very vocal and sometimes violent public animosity — that Stewart began to struggle with his own attraction to other men. He had neither the money nor the genius nor the social position of Lord Byron, and if the dashing poet found the onslaught of English anti-homosexual hysteria so daunting that he retreated to the closet, perhaps Stewart can be absolved for deciding not to leave it in the first place.

The risk involved in being openly homosexual increased significantly in 1829 with the establishment of the London Metropolitan Police, whose advent in the criminal justice system coincided with a steep rise in sodomy prosecutions. While the police were willing to turn a blind eye to homosexual acts committed between consenting adults in private, public cruising areas were under nearly constant surveillance and were sometimes the scene of carefully choreographed entrapment. The resulting statistics are startling. In 1826 only thirty-nine men were arrested for sodomy or attempted sodomy in all of England and Wales. Only two years later the number had nearly tripled. In 1829 it was seventy-four; in 1830 it was eighty-two; and in 1832, the year Stewart left for America, seventy-nine homosexual men were taken into custody.[19]

So keen was the public's interest in the prosecution of homosexuals that even the staid *Times* of London carried detailed accounts of the arrests. In the spring and summer of 1830 the august newspaper rivaled the flash tabloids with its exposé of a group it labeled "the Hyde-park Gang." Though the men were probably unrelated individuals and not actually members of any organized group, the newspaper viewed with alarm the apparent increase in the number of men using Hyde Park for homosexual cruising. The increase may have been more apparent than real, reflecting a well-orchestrated program instigated by the London Metropolitan Police of using handsome officers in plain clothes to entice homosexual overtures. The accounts published in the *Times* provide an intriguing window into the world of gay London in the 1830s.[20]

This campaign against male-male sexuality was different from previous efforts, as it focused not on the more outrageous and flamboyant members of the community — mollies and fops — but instead on men who could otherwise pass as average citizens. "Contrary to what might be expected, it was not the male cross-dresser, the debauched aristocrat, or the man already repeatedly engaging in sexual acts with other men who was the primary target of the new systems of regulation. The state and newspapers instead most often drew attention to casual encounters in public space between men of differing class backgrounds who could otherwise present themselves as respectable." As will be discussed in the following chapters, the aristocratic William Drummond Stewart's desire for young working-class men would have made him a prime target for this very public campaign.[21]

Perhaps in an effort to "cure" himself by becoming actively heterosexual, Stewart during one of his stays in Scotland became sexually involved with a young servant girl, Christian Marie Battersby, who became pregnant and in due course bore him a son. (While Christian is an unusual given name for a woman, it was not unique in nineteenth-century Scotland.) Little is known of the circumstances of Stewart's sexual encounter. All that can be said with certainty is that he got a servant girl pregnant, as have many sons of the nobility before and since. Unlike many sons of the nobility before and since, though, he acknowledged the child as his and took full financial responsibility for both mother and son. He did not marry the woman, though in subsequent unofficial documents a marriage was fabricated and dated exactly nine months before the child's birth. Stewart set up Christian Battersby (or Christie, as she is invariably called in surviving correspondence) and the infant William George (called Will by the family) in a flat in Edinburgh, and from then on, though he was conscientious about paying for their living expenses and for Will's education, he kept his distance. The pair never lived under the same roof. Father and son in time grew to be close, but Christie was never a significant part of Stewart's life. It does not appear that they even corresponded with any regularity, despite the geographical distances that frequently separated them. Of the over five hundred letters from the period of the relationship held by the National Archives of Scotland, not one is from William to Christie or from Christie to William.[22]

We know Christie was literate because of a letter the eleven-year-old

Will wrote to his mother from school: "My Dear Mama, I hope you are quite well I told Master that you wished me to write a letter in French But he said I could not write a letter in french yet but he hoped I could write soon." The letter closes with a plaintive postscript: "send me some fruit every Boy has got alls some fruite except me." Five months after his arrival in America, Stewart received a letter from his brother John in which he forwarded a letter that Christie had sent to Murthly Castle — further evidence that though she was perhaps not highly educated, she was at least literate. (Stewart preserved his brother's letter, but not the enclosed letter from Christie.) An exchange of correspondence with the mother of his son was evidently not a high priority for Stewart: before his departure, he made careful arrangements with his banker to make sure that his annuity payments would arrive promptly, instructing the bank to send correspondence to "Post office New York, & put of Grandtully on it, as there may be many of my name there." He had obviously not given similar information to Christie about how to contact him while he was abroad.[23]

Included in the family correspondence over the years are several letters, from friends and later from Will as a young adult, mentioning to Stewart that they have recently visited Christie in Edinburgh and reporting on her health and current activities. The clear implication is that Stewart's knowledge of her daily life came exclusively from this secondhand information. The lack of contact after the birth of their child suggests that Christie was never Stewart's loving mistress, that there was no great affection or perhaps even emotional attachment in their relationship. Other men of his social station maintained separate households for women who were not their wives, and Christie's relocation to Edinburgh would have given Stewart sufficient freedom to carry on an extended affair with periodic discreet visits, if he had so desired. Given the atmosphere of the times, it would also have been very tempting for a man struggling with his homosexuality to use this woman as a convenient "beard." A deliberately poorly concealed affair would have shielded him from much humiliating speculation (at thirty-three he was old enough to have to parry questions about his continued bachelor status), and an aristocrat with a lusty low-born mistress would in many circles be the subject of mirthful envy. To his credit, he refused to take that expedient course.

There are no known photographs or paintings of Christian Battersby. It is possible, however, that a fictional character in an 1840 novel is based on her. Charles Augustus Murray was one of Stewart's cousins, and both of the men traveled around the American West during the 1830s (for several months in 1835 they were even traveling companions). Early in Murray's novel *The Prairie-bird* he introduces a minor character named David Muir, a rough Scotsman who runs a general store on the banks of the Ohio River. Muir is a henpecked husband married to "a tall, powerful woman, whose features, though strong and masculine, retained the marks of early beauty, and whose voice, when raised in wrath, reached the ears of every individual." The decidedly undemure Mrs. Muir's name: Christie. Later in the novel Murray adds: "A sharp attack of fever had subdued for a season the domineering spirit of Dame Christie, and David found himself not only respected by the neighbours, but even enjoyed the sweet, though brief delusion, that he was master in his own house."[24]

Murray's fictional Christie is a woman with a "strong and masculine" demeanor who dominates her husband. Perhaps, like his hero Lord Byron, William Drummond Stewart found it easier to engage in hetero-sexual activity with someone with a somewhat masculine presentation. (Famously, Lady Caroline Lamb used to dress as a pageboy to entice Byron to her bed.) Sexual attraction aside, there is evidence that Stewart admired strong, independent women. In his first novel — written decades before British suffragettes chained themselves to the railings at 10 Downing Street — Stewart has one of his characters, an English nobleman visiting New York, indicate his support for the American abolitionist movement, but then add that "the first slavery that ought to be abolished, is that of English and American wives, indeed, women at large, to the male sex."[25]

Whatever the dynamics of William and Christie's sexual liaison, whatever his reasons for entering into the relationship, their union was brief and unique. Never again would his name be linked with that of a woman.

William Drummond Stewart's father died in 1827, and the son's financial situation took an unexpected turn. Since the estate was entailed, William's elder brother, John, by law inherited the title and the property. While William always knew that the bulk of the family assets would pass to his brother, he hoped that he would inherit enough money to set himself up in a somewhat independent fashion. When his father's will was read, William was sorely disappointed.

Sir George Stewart had created a trust that provided regular payments to the four sons and two daughters who would not inherit his entailed estate. William was left the not insubstantial sum of £3,750, but it was to be paid to him as an annuity of only £150 a year. His brothers received similar amounts (the solicitor's accounting gives no explanation for why the amounts were not equal): Archibald and Thomas received somewhat more, £4,250, while George received slightly less, £3,526. The trust set aside £6,500 for "Miss Stewart," but it is unclear which of the two Stewart daughters is intended, Catherine (born in 1797) or Clementina (born in 1800). Catherine, as the elder daughter, would by custom be accorded the honorific "Miss Stewart," but the will would then appear to exclude Clementina. Perhaps, given the size of the bequest, it was intended for both "Miss Stewarts," neither of whom had yet married at the time of their father's death. In all cases the inheritance was to paid out in £75 increments, twice a year.[26]

In frustration, William asked John to give him the entire amount in a lump sum, and when his brother tried to explain the restrictions on the trust, William threatened to sue. Sir John consulted his solicitor and received assurances that William's demand simply could not be met at that time: "Captain Stewart was unkind to give Sir John trouble & annoyance. I hope you will be able to dissuade him from resorting to any harsh measure, & that you will advise him to permit matters to be arranged under the Trust. He *cannot* make himself better than he is; & he can truly do no more, if he so inclines, than give pain & trouble, while by permitting us to work out the trust all will go on well and creditably."[27]

Undeterred, William decided to give pain and trouble by hiring his own solicitor. The provisions of the will were explicit and unassailable, but William Wilson, Esq., of the firm of Dundas and Wilson, Edinburgh, suggested another tactic: John should *loan* William £3,000, with the annuity as security. John's solicitor, Joseph M. Melville, Esq., replied that that, too, was fiscally imprudent. Wilson fired off a response and a threat: lend William the £3,000 or he would immediately sue for the full amount. Things were beginning to descend into ugly territory. William was finally persuaded that the estate simply could not afford to award him a lump sum payment without reducing capital and endangering the annuities promised to his brothers and sisters. Having given it his best shot, he backed off, accepting the reality that he would not be able to gain his independence by carrying off a portion of the family fortune. Stewart's doled-out annuity was sufficient to allow him to live in reasonable comfort and to travel extensively, but it was also a tether that kept him bound to the family hearth. Though it was a golden chain, it chafed.

In the years immediately following the defeat of Napoleon and extending well into the 1830s, the *Edinburgh Review* published a series of articles extolling America. The articles took the form of book reviews, with a reviewer analyzing the contents of one or more new books exploring various aspects of American culture. The articles provide a fascinating look at what an educated Scotsman might have believed about the raw and vibrant country across the Atlantic. "We have always been strenuous advocates for, and admirers of, America," one article reads, "not taking our ideas from the overweening vanity of the weaker part of the Americans themselves, but from what we have observed of their real energy and wisdom. It is very natural that we Scotch, who live in a little shabby scraggy corner of a remote island, with a climate which cannot ripen an apple, should be jealous of the aggressive pleasantry of more favoured people."[28]

The *Edinburgh Review* articles make much of the liberality and tolerance of the American people, especially in the area of freedom of conscience. England at the time was debating Catholic Emancipation, and various Protestant denominations were jostling for supremacy within the country. "But the wisdom of America keeps them all down — secures to them all their just rights — gives to each of them their separate pews and bells and steeples — makes them all aldermen in their turns — and quietly extinguishes the faggots which each is preparing for the combustion of the other. . . . They are devout without being unjust (the great problem in religion); an higher proof of civilization than painted tea-cups, water-proof leather, or broad cloth at two guineas a yard."[29]

If a former soldier like Captain Stewart worried that the Americans might harbor hostile feelings toward officers of their onetime enemy — occupiers during the Revolutionary War, invaders during the War of 1812 — he could be reassured by the experiences of Lt. Francis Hall of the Fourteenth Light Dragoons: "It might well surprise an English traveller, who had been told, as I had, that the Americans never failed to cheat and insult every Englishman who travelled through their country, especially if they knew him to be an officer. This latter particular they never failed to inform themselves of, for they are by no means bashful in inquiries; but if the discovery operated in any way upon their behaviour, it was rather to my advantage; nor did I meet with a single instance of incivility betwixt Canada and Charleston, except at the Shenandoah Point, from a drunken English deserter."[30]

Lieutenant Hall found American men civil, if perhaps a tad too inquisitive about personal matters, but he was less enthusiastic about the rest of the population. "The travellers agree, we think, in complaining of the insubordination of American children — and do not much like American ladies." The people he met were in general polite and friendly, but they were sensitive about issues of class and would become prickly if an Englishman exhibited the least degree of haughtiness or presumption.

Travellers from Europe, in passing through the western country, or indeed any part of the United States, ought to be previously

acquainted with this part of the American character, and more particularly if they have been in the habit of treating with contempt,
or irritating with abuse, those whom accidental circumstances may
have placed in a situation to administer to their wants. Let no one
here indulge himself in abusing the waiter or ostler at an inn: that
waiter or ostler is probably a citizen, and does not, nor cannot con-
ceive, that a situation in which he discharges a duty to society, not
in itself dishonourable, should subject him to insult: but this feeling,
so far as I have experienced, is entirely defensive. I have travelled
near 10,000 miles in the United States, and never met with the least
incivility or affront.

Well aware that travelers frequently criticized Americans for their vulgar
pushiness, the journal jumped to the former colonists' defense: "Whose
employment is the worst — [the Americans'] successful enterprise — or
the affectation of gaping strangers, come across the Atlantic to quiz the
rustics through an opera lorgnette?"[31]

Among the peculiarities of American culture, *Review* writers single
out the colonies of Shakers and the Harmonites, whose communal form
of living and commitment to a life without sexual relations is seen as
passing strange. "The Harmonites," one writer explains, "profess equal-
ity, community of goods, and celibacy; for the men and women (let Mr
Malthus hear this) live separately, and are not allowed the slightest
intercourse. In order to keep up their numbers, they have once or twice
sent over for a supply of Germans, as they admit no Americans, of any
intercourse with whom they are very jealous."[32]

Since the eighteenth-century Scottish Enlightenment, scholars such
as Thomas Malthus had been intrigued by the perceived sexual con-
tinence of Native Americans. Malthus, Lord Kames, Dugald Stewart,
John Millar, and William Robertson all theorized about the lack of
sexual passion among the Indians, and while they differed at times
in their scientific reasoning, they presented the phenomenon itself as
an unassailable fact. Robertson was particularly insistent about "the
dispassionate coldness of the American young men in their intercourse

with the other sex," pointing to the well-known physical characteristics: "The beardless countenance and smooth skin of the American seems to indicate a defect of vigour, occasioned by some vice in his frame. He is destitute of [even] one sign of manhood and of strength." While their focus was on the Native American and not the European colonist, the implication was that in America relations between the sexes are constrained or even nonexistent. For a man conflicted about his sexual desires, America seemed to hold the promise of a welcome escape from the increasing pressure of heterosexual obligations.[33]

The *Edinburgh Review* built on the traditions established by the Scottish Enlightenment philosophers, presenting America as a land of religious tolerance, hospitality, enthusiastic entrepreneurship, and sexual nonconformity.[34] To this paean the *Review* added a note of urgency, informing its readers that America was changing at breakneck speed, and if anyone wished to experience it in all its glorious newness, he needed to travel *now*.

A broad, deep, and rapid stream of population is running constantly towards the western parts of the Continent; and vast states are forming towards the Pacific Ocean, the growth of which as much exceeds in rapidity what we have been wont to admire on the shores of the Atlantic, as this leaves at an immeasurable distance the scarcely perceptible progress of our European societies. . . . Where is this prodigious increase of numbers, this vast extension of dominion, to end? What bounds has Nature set to the progress of this mighty nation? Let our jealousy burn as it may; let our intolerance of America be as unreasonably violent as we please; still it is plain, that she is a power in spite of us, rapidly rising to supremacy; or, at least, that each year so mightily augments her strength, as to overtake, by a most sensible distance, even the most formidable of her competitors.[35]

As the *Edinburgh Review* was painting such a glowing and seductive portrait of the United States in all its liberality and entrepreneurial energy, both European and American periodicals added their own siren songs with adventure stories of derring-do on the wild frontier, stories that marginalized (and at times completely eliminated) the role of women. In America, they proclaimed, the rugged mountains and the vast prairies were a refuge for uninhibited male bonding. The stories were frequently illustrated with eye-catching graphics that could be subliminally — and at times overtly — homoerotic, showing heroically muscled men stripped for action against the daunting challenges of the American wilderness.

In America the greatest contributor to the myth was James Fenimore Cooper. First with *The Pioneers* (1823) and more vividly with *The Last of the Mohicans* (1826), Cooper inflamed the imaginations of a generation of young European males with his vivid tales about the western margins of the new land. The novels are significant in their appeal not because of their descriptions of an enticing wilderness landscape — the forests and prairies in Cooper are as flat and generic as cardboard stage props — but because at their core they are tales of masculine friendship unambiguously presented as superior to any male-female relationship. In the confirmed bachelor Nathaniel "Natty" Bumppo, Cooper created a character who slowly and perhaps inevitably replaced Byron's Don Juan as the role model for a generation of young British males for whom a flaunted sexuality had become socially unsustainable. For men like William Drummond Stewart, struggling to negotiate the tangled forest of their same-sex desire, Natty Bumppo was indeed the Pathfinder.

In his groundbreaking 1960 critique *Love and Death in the American Novel*, Leslie A. Fiedler was the first to present an in-depth analysis of Cooper's novels demonstrating that homoerotic themes reside deeply and explicitly at the core of his narratives. "Two mythic figures have detached themselves from the texts of Cooper's books," Fiedler wrote, "and have entered the free domain of our dreams: Natty Bumppo, the hunter and enemy of cities; and Chingachgook, nature's nobleman and Vanishing American. But these two between them postulate a third myth, an archetypal relationship which also haunts the American psyche: two lonely men, one dark-skinned, one white, bend together over a carefully guarded fire in the virgin heart of the American wilderness; they have forsaken all others for the sake of the austere, almost inarticulate, but unquestioned love which binds them to each other and to the world of nature which they have preferred to civilization."[36]

In his novels Cooper creates a world in which women represent the stifling straitjacket of society — the imprisoning world of rules and expectations governed by overprotective mothers and domineering wives. As Fiedler explains, "The very end of the pure love of male for male is to *outwit* woman, that is, to keep her from trapping the male through marriage into civilization and Christianity." But to embrace such a worldview the male reader needs to become a boy again, to reenter a space in which sex and death have no objective reality, in which messy details like pregnant serving girls and stingy brothers have no more serious consequences in life than do common boyhood games. "That is why Cooper is so fond of presenting his anti-female alliance of outcast and savage in an atmosphere of make-believe, of 'playing Indians.'"[37]

Playing was in fact the very essence of William Drummond Stewart's sojourn in the American Rockies. In total he spent nearly seven years wandering on horseback through the prairies and the rugged backwoods, through scorching deserts and snow-blocked mountain passes. He earned the unalloyed respect of such hardened mountain men as William Sublette and Tom Fitzpatrick. He learned the craft of tracking and hunting so well that he was placed in charge of operations in which thousands of dollars of the fur-trading industry were at stake. He lived and fought and ate and drank with the wildest, toughest characters the American West had to offer — and yet his actions never lost the aura of playacting. Again and again in the diaries and letters of his contemporaries he is referred to as an English gentleman visiting the Rockies "on a pleasure trip." Something about Stewart kept him always apart in the perceptions of his colleagues, even though they never for a moment questioned his skill and courage. That difference was in fact at the heart of his journey.

In 1827 Cooper published the third of his Leatherstocking novels, *The Prairie*. Though it was the third book to be published, its story falls last chronologically, as it describes Natty Bumppo in his old age. For readers whose imaginations were fired by the adventures of *The Last of the Mohicans*, the novel had the same message as the articles in the *Edinburgh Review*: the America you are dreaming of is changing rapidly. If you are going to seek it, seek it now. Like other Europeans, William Drummond Stewart took that message to heart.

2

William Drummond Stewart wrote very little about the years he spent in America. A few letters written to a friend in New York announcing his return to civilization after his first two years in the wilderness survive, and a few passages in his later correspondence make reference to his experiences in the Rockies. The most extensive discussion of his journeys appears in fictional form in his two novels, *Altowan* (1846) and *Edward Warren* (1854). Both books draw heavily on his personal experiences, and in his introduction to *Edward Warren* Stewart even describes the novel as "a fictitious Auto-biography." Stewart goes so far as to annotate his second novel with footnotes describing the actual events upon which the fiction is based, and many of the characters in the novel are given the real names of their historical counterparts. In scenes in which the action taking place in the novel has been described in other memoirs of the period by other participants in the same event, even the novel's dialogue reproduces closely what was actually said at the time.[1]

Given that the novels so closely adhere to actual events, the question inevitably arises: why did Stewart hold back from writing a straightforward narrative of his American experiences? The decision is particularly puzzling in light of the long tradition that preceded *Altowan* — every European who spent three weeks in America returned home to publish a two-volume treatise explaining the strange new country to an eager population of adventure readers. From the French aristocrat Alexis de

Tocqueville to the German noblemen Prince Maximilian zu Wied-Neuwied and Bernhard, Duke of Saxe-Weimar Eisenach, from Stewart's fussy cousin Charles Augustus Murray to the indefatigable Fanny Trollope, it seems few literate Europeans could resist the temptation to describe at length everything he or she had seen. There was an eager European audience, and no stigma attached to someone of aristocratic birth dabbling in printer's ink. What, then, caused Stewart to follow in that well-trod literary tradition, only to pull back when it came to revealing the full story of his American adventures?

In the "Notice to the Reader" that prefaces *Altowan* (unsigned but perhaps written by Stewart himself) we are told, "The following story has been written for the amusement of some young friends on Long Island. . . . [J]ust as it is, without even a revision, I offer it to those for whom it was intended." Journalist James Watson Webb, the editor of the novel, insisted that it was written for the private entertainment of Webb's own children, and yet the sexually charged subject matter — adultery, desertion, illegitimacy, homosexuality, transvestism, and incest — is hardly the stuff of the *Boy's Own* adventure stories. Webb is not always the most trustworthy of writers. (Historian Bernard DeVoto writes, "It is seldom necessary to believe what Mr. Webb says," and he contends that at least half of Webb's statements about William Drummond Stewart are "flatly wrong.") But if not for the Webb children, then for whom?[2]

Stewart's reasons for writing the novels are particularly difficult to decipher because the books themselves are so very challenging to read. The utter obscurity of their plots may be the result of the author's clumsy attempt to encode a secret narrative — or it may simply be that he was a spectacularly ungifted writer. Both novels are elliptical to the point of opaqueness. Events occur without rational explanation. Characters loom and then disappear completely, or pop up in unexpected places for no reason other than the exigencies of the plot. Heavy hints are dropped portentously — and then completely abandoned. The entire first chapter of *Altowan* consists of an encounter in New York harbor between two nameless men referred to only as "the younger" and "the elder." Again and again in both novels strings of pronouns with ambiguous antecedents make the action almost impossible to untangle without the use of extensive penciled notes.

Given that the books are nearly impenetrable, and were in any case presented to the world as fiction, it would perhaps be best not to rely on them when reconstructing Stewart's life. Unfortunately, the novels are his major autobiographical writings and so, as frustrating and unsatisfactory as they are, they must play a central role in any biography. *Altowan* has been out of print for 150 years, and *Edward Warren*, though reprinted in 1986 with added chapter breaks and brief caption summaries, is no easier to read than it ever was. A plot summary of the books would not be especially helpful since the narratives have no sustaining logic, but perhaps it would be illuminating to focus on a few incidents in the novels that reveal something about Stewart's sexual awakening in America.

In *Altowan* the reader is introduced to two men who are by the end of the novel revealed to be half brothers: the title character (living as a chief of the Blackfeet tribe, he is in realty an Englishman named Walter, son of Lord Daerwold) and Roallan, Lord Daerwold's son by a second marriage. Roallan's reasons for coming to America are obscure — perhaps to murder his half brother and thereby inherit their father's estate? — but in the course of the narrative he seduces and kidnaps Altowan's half sister Idalie (the child of Altowan/Walter's mother and her lover). Roallan is primarily heterosexual in his orientation, but when he meets a handsome young man from Missouri named Joe Henry, they strike up a friendship that is immediate and intimate: "An affection had sprung up between these two young men, nearly of an age . . . which had insensibly ripened into friendship; and they had sought that shady spot where both were in the habit of bathing — each with the hope of meeting the other." It is a repeated theme in both of Stewart's novels: young men drawn to one another and seeking each other out in places where they can be unclothed together.[3]

A more specific reference to homosexuality is made through one of the novel's protagonists, Watoe, a berdache. Berdaches were gender-variant Indians present in many tribes, almost always men who cross-dressed and performed many of the tasks of women, including taking a receptive role in sexual relations with other men. Stewart must have encountered berdaches during his travels, and though he misnames them as "Broadashe," he displays in his writing respect and even affection for them. "The few clothes of Altowan and some extra baggage, were given in charge to a handsome youth, who was attached to the service of the rest. Having refused to take part in the warlike feats of the men, he had previously been consigned, under the name of Broadashe, to the society, the duties, and the dress of the women. There are youths of this description in every camp, resembling in office the eunuchs of the seraglio." Stewart was aware that the berdaches among the tribes he visited held an ambiguous status, "subject to occasional degradation — generally abandoned to reckless debauchery."[4]

Watoe, deeply in love with Altowan, is downcast when he believes that Altowan is about to marry Idalie. With tenderness of gesture and expression, Altowan lets Watoe know that he has nothing to worry about:

> During the foregoing harangue, which was somewhat long for the speaker — whose habits, though dissolute and gay, were seldom verbose — Altowan's eyes were intently fixed on his. The usually downcast look was slowly raised when he answered not at the close his communication, and met the inquiry of the gaze directed upon him by one in which melancholy could not veil the deep interest which lighted their upward glance. Altowan pressed him to his side as he continued. . . . "Watoe," rejoined Altowan, as he parted the thick hair that fell over his brow, "I am about to tell you what Pinatsi knows not, and what you must not reveal. Idalie is my sister; her mother was also my mother; she will not live with me but in the lodge of Perahoe; your eye must watch her, and I will make a brother of you; and he who is my brother is a chief. . . ." The light shone through a vacant space in the foliage above, and a sunbeam fell on them. "Behold, the eye of the Great Spirit looks down upon us!" He took the hand of Watoe, and the compact was sealed.[5]

When the braves ride out to battle, Watoe stays behind with the women, but when the village comes under attack, it is Watoe who leads the defense. Later killed in an ambush, he dies professing his love for Altowan. When Altowan learns of Watoe's death, he retreats into an abyss of grief. "The death of Watoe he heard in silence; and returned to the solitude of his tent, at the door of which, that whole day, Parfin sat, and refused all admittance. M. Deriot alone, in a state of half-intoxication, forced an entrance; but did not stay long. He was often fruitlessly questioned at the time, as to what befell him there; and even in those veins of boasting to which he was habitually addicted, it became common in after times, to silence him by asking how he had fared when he alone had ventured to intrude on the solitude of the unknown chief."[6]

Edward Warren is by far the more interesting of Stewart's two novels. While the plot is no less melodramatic and improbable, there are extended passages of descriptive narrative that give a detailed and vivid picture of life in the Rockies in the 1830s. The plot still galumphs along awkwardly in the background, but if the reader can put on hold a need for logic and coherence in storytelling, the novel offers some literary rewards.

Edward Warren is particularly interesting to the biographer since it, unlike *Altowan*, includes extensive scenes of the author/narrator's youth. Almost nothing is known of William Drummond Stewart's life before he entered the army at the age of seventeen, so the early scenes of the novel take on a heightened interest — particularly in light of Stewart's description of the book as "fictitious Auto-biography." Edward Warren's youth would appear at first to have nothing at all in common with William Drummond Stewart's: Warren is not the second son of a Scottish peer growing up on an estate in Perthshire, he is the only son of a merchant from Yorkshire who attends an idyllic private boys' school. Given that the title character's later years closely mirror the author's own experiences, the reader wonders whether Stewart completely fictionalized the early years or whether he drew on his own real-life experiences but encoded them so that they were not immediately recognizable. The latter is the more probable explanation for a work that is frankly presented as autobiographical, yet one wonders what is real and what is fiction, and why the obfuscation was necessary. Curiosity is focused inevitably on those early parts of the novel in which the action is compellingly odd or completely indecipherable.

Chapter 1 begins with a narrator looking back to a golden period in his life when he hunted in the Rocky Mountains. "In 1833 there was but one man, in all that region of the hunter, who was not there for gain, but the love of sport." The one white man in the Rockies in 1833 who was there strictly for the love of sport was, of course, Stewart himself, who made his first trip to the West that year. The narrator describes the changes to the region in the intervening years, lamenting how "civilization" has ruined what he first knew as a pristine paradise.[7]

The second chapter begins an autobiographical tale told by a first-person narrator named Edward Warren, or Ned. He was, he explains, born in Yorkshire, but he knows very little else about his early life. His mother died when he was young, and his father sent him off to boarding school in Chester. He was called home to Yorkshire only once a year, but as his return visits never coincided with the regularly scheduled school holidays, he often found himself the only student left behind in Chester when the other boys had gone home to the warm embrace of their families. His attempts to bond with the other boys always ended in frustration. "I had formed boyish attachments," he explains, "which had been broken by cruel parents." His was a lonely, isolated childhood.[8]

Fluent in French and German, Ned draws the attention of a young Swiss teacher of modern languages. Ned is at first repelled by the teacher, whom he describes as "without principle" and "without reverence for everything in heaven and earth." Ned has an adolescent crush on the headmaster's daughter who, as the only young female in the closed community of the boarding school, is also the object of desire of the unmarried male teachers. One day Ned sees the young woman walking with the Swiss. He and the teacher begin to mock wrestle, supposedly for the favor of the headmaster's daughter, but Ned accidentally knocks the Swiss into the river, where he hits his head on a rock and nearly drowns. Ned rescues him and vows to nurse him back to health. "I had undressed him and rolled him in a warm blanket, and had examined him all over, to see if there was any other injury, but was relieved to find there was none; I had only remarked that there were some letters tattooed on his back; and, as I examined his muscular frame, felt grateful, for the first time, to the groom at my father's, a sturdy youth from Lancashire, who used to throw me about every day for an hour during my latter years' visits."[9]

In a better novelist, the letters tattooed on the young man's muscular back would be foreshadowing — a hint, a clue of secrets to be revealed. The odd detail cries out for an explanation later in the novel, but unfortunately there is none. We never learn what those words were or why they were inked in such an odd place. Precisely because they are completely unimportant to the plot, they gain significance for what they might reveal about the author himself. In the early nineteenth century, where would Stewart have been most likely to view words tattooed on a muscular back?

Studies of nineteenth-century tattooing practices report that the two groups of men most likely to be inked were sailors and criminals. Stewart's travels placed him no doubt in contact with both groups. The placement of the tattoo, however, argues against its being connected with the men of the sea. An early study of the location of sailors' tattoos documents that the most popular place was the forearm, followed by the arms, chest, shoulders, and hands, then the wrists, legs, and feet. The back was the ninth most likely place to be tattooed; only the face was a less likely place for a sailor to decorate his body. There was, however, another group of men for whom having a tattooed back was not uncommon. Male prostitutes in Germany often sported a scene of a cat chasing a mouse down their back, with the mouse just about to disappear into the man's anus. Also common was a scene of two policemen waiting to arrest someone, tattooed on the lower back just above the buttocks and accompanied by the words *Durch diese hohle Gasse muss er kommen* (Through this hollow path he must come) — a quotation from Schiller's poem about William Tell, the Swiss national hero.[10]

Ned becomes the convalescing Swiss's personal nurse, to the exclusion of everyone else in the boarding school. He even sleeps in the same room with his patient, setting the stage for one of the novel's many strange and highly homoerotic incidents. "The night was hot," the narrator remembers.

> I threw off my clothes, and then gathering a blanket round me, disposed myself to rest. I soon sank into sleep, but it was not sound, and I had that feeling, in my dreams, which it is impossible to describe, that all was not right. The sun was shining through the lattice when I awoke; there were no curtains. I had not, however, moved, so my companion could not perceive that my eyes were open under the shadow of my arm; but I lay as still as a statue. Opposite me lay him whom I know involuntarily watched; his face was alone visible; there was a bandage on his temple, and a slight hectic on his cheek; he was gazing upon me with the full force of his large grey eye. I always, since I can remember, made it a point to look any one down who fixed my eye; and, though unseen, I felt relieved when his eyelid, for a moment, faltered. I cannot tell what feeling of fascination that look brought upon me; but it has never been forgotten.

Two naked men staring each other down in the sweltering heat of a sunlit bedroom is a scene of homoerotic intensity rarely seen in early nineteenth-century novels.[11]

When he is sixteen Ned is called to the headmaster's office and told that his father has ordered him to go to Liverpool. "Among all my leave-takings, that of most pathos was with the Swiss. He had not sought me much since his accident, but when we met, there was more affection in his manner towards me, and that almost uncomfortable influence of his eye, when I found it fixed on me . . . Bernard [the Swiss] threw his arms round my neck, and kissed me on either cheek, and, with a convulsive pressure of the hand, we parted without a word."[12]

When Ned arrives in Liverpool he finds a note from his father directing him to come to London. There he is introduced to "a tall, showy-looking young man, of about twenty" — Lord Fernwold — who offers to introduce his guest to the delights of the city. He takes Ned to Covent Garden (a well-known homosexual cruising area during Stewart's day) but then leaves him for a moment. Almost immediately another man accosts Ned and starts walking off with him, until Fernwold reappears, taps the man on the shoulder with his cane, and sends him scurrying away to hook up with someone else. "There can be nothing so green in the market tomorrow morning as you are," Fernwold chides Ned, "it is most refreshing — early peas, yet in their pod, are stale compared to you." As they walk off together Ned observes that Fernwold "held me fast, as if he intended me for his own prey."[13]

Lord Fernwold takes Ned to a house in fashionable St. James Place, where a secret knock opens the door on a wild drinking party of young men. Ned finds himself inexplicably drawn to the strange company and becomes now completely enthralled with the handsome lord who is obviously their leader. The next day he rushes to Fernwold's flat eager to renew his friendship, but the young lord appears flustered to find Ned unexpectedly at his door and hurriedly ushers him outside to go for a carriage ride. During the ride Fernwold asks Ned to move in with him but is careful to set certain rules: "You can come into my bed-room, which is divided from yours, you know, only by a passage, when the door is not bolted. And if I am asleep, your own good nature will prevent your waking me; if I am occupied or moody, I suppose you will turn and leave."[14]

On a hot night when Ned is lying unclothed on his bed, Fernwold softly enters the bedroom. A scene unfolds very much like the one between Ned and the Swiss: "I again threw myself on the bed; soon after, the door gently opened, and my opposite neighbour looked in, as if to see whether I was awake. I suppose, seeing my naked figure on the bed, and the clothes tossed about, he came forward to see if anything was the matter. I shut my eyes at the first sound, ashamed at being caught more in the position of a lunatic than a sober guest. He came and sat down by me in his wrapper." Fernwold confesses that he feels that somehow Ned is going to be the source of great unhappiness for him. He senses (correctly) that Ned is about to become romantically entangled with a woman, and makes him promise not to marry without first discussing the matter with his new friend.[15]

Lord Fernwold is one of the more convincingly drawn of Stewart's characters, and though the extent of his involvement in the plot is minimal, his speech and his actions are so lifelike (made even more so in contrast to the melodramatic dialogue and histrionic posturing of some of the other characters) that the reader suspects he was based on an actual person. The author even annotates one scene from the novel with a footnote reading, "This incident is faithfully taken from a real occurrence many years ago, and the speech was made by the Earl of ____ at a Silver Hell, in Bury Street." (A "silver hell" was a low-class gambling saloon.) Perhaps Stewart was introduced to homosexual society in London by a young peer who served as model, or perhaps Stewart knew someone to whom he was attracted but whom — like Ned with Lord Fernwold — he kept at a distance, unsure of how to respond to the attraction he was experiencing.[16]

Ned meanwhile has been secretly meeting with a mysterious woman named Isabella whom he encountered one day while riding in the park. He is reluctant to mention her to Fernwold. Ned slips out to meet Isabella, who confesses that she has been engaged by Ned's father to lure him to a deserted place where he will be kidnapped and "shut up in a private madhouse." She has decided to help him escape, but before he can evade his father's henchmen he is captured and taken to an asylum, where he is locked in solitary confinement.[17]

This incident parallels a similar event in *Altowan* in which a character is drugged and kidnapped and awakens in an institution, confined in a straitjacket, and early in *Edward Warren* Ned ties up a captured Indian by binding his arms "something like a straight waistcoat." Was there an event in Stewart's early, undocumented life that he is drawing upon for these similar incidents in his autobiographical novels? In *Altowan* it is Roallan who is confined to prevent him from marrying Idalie. In *Edward Warren* Ned learns that his father has imprisoned him in a madhouse to keep him from marrying the similarly named Isabella. (That his father has engaged Isabella to lure him away from marrying Isabella is a plot inconsistency that the reader is expected to ignore.) Did Stewart's family consider his homosexuality a form of insanity and have him hospitalized against his will? Does the incident have something to do with the pregnant Christie, perhaps a conflict about whether or not he should marry her? The historical record is unfortunately blank.[18]

In any case, Ned's doctor explains that his father will approve his release from the asylum only on the condition that he leave England and sail to America. When he learns Fernwold has already left for Lisbon, Ned agrees. He looks forward to what he will find in that wild Eden so far away:

> I cannot describe with what feelings I looked forward to that land, in which there were so many wonders of nature to be overcome, or utilized by that mighty race, the fusion together of all the energies of other lands. I was to walk in the untrodden forest, and see the original man, uncontaminated by the schoolmaster; I was to be free to prey upon the beasts of these wilds, as they might be to prey upon me. I was to build my own canoe, and sail her upon inland seas, and no one to say me nay. My horse was to seek where he listed the choice of food, and to browse upon plants, a prize for European shews. I was to cull the choicest fruits, the apple, the peach, and the pear, where I found them in my way; and where I sought the haunts of men, waste not the unvarnished welcome, and the sacred salt.[19]

Ned will indeed "see the original man, uncontaminated by the school-master" (he was perhaps feeling uncomfortable about his encounters with the Swiss language teacher), but first he spends a few days in New York City and in Cincinnati before establishing himself in St. Louis. Here his money begins to run low, so he decides to go west with a party of fur traders that is about to leave for the Rocky Mountains. He delays his departure as long as possible, hoping that more money will arrive from England. When the fur traders leave Ned stays on, intending to catch up with them later.

Finally, on the day before he must depart St. Louis or miss the chance of traveling with the traders, he reads in the *St. Louis Republican* a small item picked up from a Chester newspaper: his father is dead. In Ned's reaction to this news we can perhaps see Stewart's complex response to his own father's death: "What affection I had for my father was entirely negative. I could not dislike him; and the sole arbitrary act of his life towards me [the enforced hospitalization] had been forgotten, or might be justified, and could not make a balance against his previous uniform kindness. But what tended to change the nature of my grief, was the neglect with which I had been treated." Ned picks up the newspaper once more and notices another obituary: Lord Fernwold, too, has died. To this death his reactions are unmixed: "It gave me a pang I know not how to describe; and, in the silence of a grief I had never felt before, I laid myself down forlorn in that distant land, and in the darkness of the night yielded to unavailing tears."[20]

Ned sets out after the party of traders, and Stewart for the next 250 pages weaves into the novel incidents of his journey through America in a narrative that is convoluted and elliptical, at times barely comprehensible. As in *Altowan* the novel is laced with homoeroticism, though in *Edward Warren* the atmosphere is much more explicitly charged than in the earlier novel. In particular Ned is envious of the easy physical affection shown among the Native American men he meets along the way. "The chiefs and the braves were riding forth, and often a friend jumped up behind, the more secretly to hold a confabulation, or the more lovingly to enjoy the society of a brother or a companion." He is especially intrigued by a handsome Indian he encounters while on a hunt, an Indian who appears to be flirting with him but who remains frustratingly elusive.[21]

Rejoining the Indian encampment after the hunt, Ned wanders along the banks of a nearby river, searching for his new friend. Stealthily he threads his way among the tall grasses, "sometimes to intercept the secret conferences of lovers, or at my approach to cause a disappointment in some beating heart." He is silently creeping through the bushes when he abruptly meets the Indian he has been seeking.

There was no light to shine on a known face, and no voice to tell on a friendly ear, and yet one of those mystic instincts which communicate between certain persons, told me plainly through every fibre in my frame, that the Indian I sought was before me, and I held out my arms to embrace my wild friend with the ardour of real joy. We had never been, while together, in any state of emotion; there had never occurred any thing to call forth any unusual demonstration of regard; but this meeting, so sudden and unlooked for, had destroyed all forms and reserve, and I strained my friend to my heart with unalloyed delight; neither of us spoke — my heart was full.[22]

Ned discovers at this point that the Indian friend who has so bewitched him is really a woman who has been passing as a man. In a clumsy sleight of hand the author attempts to mitigate the sexual implications of the previous scenes by revealing that Ned was in actuality drawn to a woman. The convenient gender shift would be more convincing as a plot device if Ned had previously expressed any confusion or disorientation about his strong attraction to another man. He had not, and so the inherent homoeroticism of the earlier scenes remains undiluted — and is further strengthened by succeeding scenes in which another object of his desire is indisputably male.

Ned is hunting a bear when he almost literally stumbles over a Blackfeet Indian crouching in the underbrush, stalking the same bear. The Indian expects the white man to shoot him, but instead Ned offers him his hand in friendship. Ned is deeply impressed by what he sees:

In getting up he took this turban of fur from his head, and let the long hair which it had confined fall free upon his neck. His height appeared to be, by several inches, above six feet, though the symmetrical proportion of his figure did not permit him to seem so; his limbs — what of them were naked — were round, though slight; his head was nobly carried, and the neck long and muscular; the countenance was decidedly Indian, and the tint the red brown sometimes seen in the works of Georgoné; the eyes, somewhat depressed towards the nose, were long and almond-shaped; the nose, thick and well formed, without being high, and the nostrils somewhat distended; the mouth large, and the lips rather full and projecting in the middle, but thinning inwards into a curve as they extended towards the cheeks; the eyelashes had been plucked out, as is the fashion with the three great tribes, the Blackfeet, the Crows, and the Snakes, but the lids were thick, and gave a deep and strong shadow, and the lower one was well supported up upon the ball by the oval cheek; beard there was none, nor eyebrows, but their lines were well defined, and the brent brow, though not lofty, was full of power. There was a peculiar thickness in his hands, without breadth, and of the fingers, without preventing their coming to a taper point; the nails, long and oval, both of them and of the toes, for the moccasins had been tied to the girdle which supported the legging thongs and the brayé [breech cloth]; the feet were beautiful and the toes healthily articulated and distinct.[23]

Perhaps feeling that he has strained the credulity of the reader with this detailed paean to the physical beauty of American Indians (right down to their articulated toes), Stewart through his narrator explains how he is able to give such a precise description of the man after only a brief glance: "It is not to be supposed that I had time to note this description down at the moment, but as the impression of the whole was strong to intensity, the traits were not difficult to remember; and I may as well here, as they were first remarked, record the description of a form which I had but too well the opportunity of examining at an after time."[24]

The form that Stewart later had the opportunity of examining was that of Antoine Clement, a Métis (Cree and French Canadian) who enjoyed the reputation of being perhaps the finest hunter in the Rockies during the 1830s. The two men met during Stewart's first trip to the mountains and quickly became lovers, eventually traveling together throughout America, Europe, and the Middle East. Theirs would be a tumultuous relationship with long periods of separation, but Clement would always embody for Stewart all that was wild, free, and sexually liberating about the American West.

When William Drummond Stewart first set foot on American soil in 1832 he was thirty-six years old. He was slightly taller than average for the period, with dark curly hair, a florid complexion, and a thick moustache beneath a pronounced hawk-like nose. He had a somewhat stiff, military bearing, the legacy of his career in the British army, and he spoke with what was described as a typical nobleman's lisp. In social situations he was reserved and somewhat formal, expecting deference but not insisting upon it. In a country that only fifty-six years earlier had declared its independence from England, and among a people who still viewed British aristocracy with a mixture of defensiveness and awe, he had a gift for making himself welcome. He could be charming without being ingratiating, disarmingly unpretentious without forfeiting a whit of his aristocratic cachet.

Stewart had served under the Duke of Wellington and had acquitted himself with honor, albeit with no particular distinction. He still technically held the rank of captain, and now that he was in a country where such honorifics impressed the general public he usually introduced himself as Captain Stewart. Yet for all his elegant bearing and noble lineage he was chronically short of cash. His only source of income was his half-pay stipend from the army and the semiannual payments on the annuity from his inheritance. As the son of a Scottish lord he had been reared with a taste for the finer things in life, but as a second son he was hard-pressed to pay for them. He had little in the way of a formal education and even if he had been qualified to take a paying job, his social position would not allow him to work for wages. Barring another war, it was unlikely that he would be called back to his regiment, and — being a lapsed Presbyterian — a career in the church did not appear to be in the cards. Nor could he hope for a brilliant marriage to fill his coffers. Second sons were not considered worthy quarry for rich heiresses (American or otherwise) who were in the market for crenellated castles and ancient titles.

And there was the cloud always obscuring his horizon: his sexual attraction to other men. If the comments he makes in his autobiographical novels refer to his own life experiences — and there is every reason to believe they do — at the time he landed in America he probably had not yet had sex with another man. He was, however, well aware of what was at stake. He need only open a copy of the *Times* to read of careers ended and lives shattered by a single moment of indiscretion, and so he had perhaps fought back any temptation to reveal the secret he carried within him. Now all that was about to change.

"On an evening near the close of April, 183-," Stewart's first autobiographical novel begins, "a boat having the appearance of a man-of-war's gig, under the care of a single seaman, was dancing on the gentle swell that agitated the water of New York Bay, where the Castle, as it is called, rears its shapeless mass." It was April 1832 when Stewart landed in the shadow of the resort known as Castle Clinton, disembarking from a small rowboat that ferried passengers from their transatlantic ships to the wharves at Battery Park. Stewart was about to undertake a journey, both geographical and psychological, that would leave him profoundly changed. Given that he would return to Scotland seven years later as an active homosexual, thanks to a great extent to his experiences in America, it is particularly appropriate that he landed exactly where he did. In the early nineteenth century Battery Park was the eroticized tip of the island of Manhattan.[1]

Perhaps no one described the lure of Battery Park in the early nineteenth century more eloquently than Herman Melville, who opens *Moby Dick* with a paean to the young men who were drawn, yearning, to the farthest limit of the Manhattan waterfront. "Tell me," Melville wonders about the streams of humanity drawn down Broadway urgently, irresistibly toward the docks, "does the magnetic virtue of the needles of the compasses of all those ships attract them thither?" For many New Yorkers and visitors to the city it was not compass needles that drew them to the Battery, but a much more primal force. Already in Melville's time the promenades of Battery Park were employed extensively as places of sexual encounter. In 1849 E. Porter Belden noted that Battery Park with its boardwalk "draws within its precincts by a more irresistible attraction, the young men and maidens of our own days, whose breasts are heaving with tender emotions." A visitor from Maryland was told "that to walk out after dusk upon this platform was a good way for a stranger to fit himself with a courtesan; for that place was the general rendezvous of the fair sex of that profession after sunset." Some potential sexual partners connected and then retired to private quarters, while others simply concealed themselves within the park's many bushes to complete the encounter. The *Flash*, one of the so-called sporting or flash newspapers dedicated to sex and scandal in the early decades of the nineteenth century, reported one such encounter: "At twelve o'clock, a devil-may-care sort of a fellow entered, and after taking two or three turns through the walks, he pitched upon a victim, and from what I overheard, I soon found that she was yet green in the profession she was following. The rowdy, for such he appeared to be, took her to the end of the public building, where they entered a vacant place, and a transaction took place which for us to name, would not sound well, to ears polite. . . . Such scenes nightly occur in the Park, and it would be well for some of our officers to see it."[2]

New York's flash newspapers were published with the express purpose of furnishing titillating stories of illicit sex, though they were always careful to cloak their stories in the language of a conservative moral crusade in order to avoid prosecutions for obscenity. The intended audience was heterosexual men, who avidly consumed these lurid tales of sexual depravity served up with fabricated outrage. The prostitute, the fallen woman, the adulterer, the rake were all favorite subjects of these tabloids, always spoken of with faux shock and feigned dismay while at the same time providing the most salacious details printable.[3]

Heterosexual prostitution was not the only sexual activity taking place among the trees and bushes of Battery Park. In the opening decades of the nineteenth century the city was overwhelmed by an influx of young unmarried men who were drawn from the surrounding farms and villages by the lure of employment in Manhattan's offices and commercial emporia. Cut loose from the tether of family ties, without enough money to spend on prostitutes, many of these young men turned to one another for sexual release. Most lived in crowded boardinghouses that offered no privacy, so New York's public parks became a convenient locus of homosexual activity.

When the flash newspapers turned their attention to these "sodomites" there was nothing feigned about the fervor of their attacks. In 1842 the *Whip* began publishing a series of articles aimed at exposing men who sought sex with other men, comparing New York City's parks to the Palais-Royal, which for nearly a century had been notorious as one of the major Parisian gathering spots for homosexual cruising. To the editors of the *Whip*, New York was well on its way to rivaling the depravity of the French capital:

> To what is New York come, if this intolerable nuisance is continued much longer[?] Our city within the vicinity of the Park will become a second Palais Royale. Their [sic] the agents of a horror stricken crime are men or rather miscreants, wearing the appearance of the human form also, their [sic] is no difference between the doings of these fiendish agents of the Palais Royale and the brutal sodomites of New York; their diabolical enticements lead to the same end. Fear seizes the mind of the moral man when he is thus accosted and his first impulse is to escape; who would appear at the police office even to prefer a charge against one of the abominable sinners, why no one in the world; yet we have the names of men who have been acted

upon by these fiends, and when we want them, they will be called upon by a tribunal that they dare not refuse to obey — the Law.[4]

It is doubtful that the *Whip*'s editors actually possessed a list of men who had been unwillingly "acted upon" by homosexuals cruising the Battery or City Hall parks. Because the main goal of the flash newspapers was entertainment, the details of any particular story should be viewed skeptically. Still, there was almost certainly some basis of fact behind their inflammatory journalism and at the very least the articles can be said to reflect the general tenor of the times. There is an authentic ring of nativist intolerance behind the declaration "We thank God, that, as yet, among the numerous names of the *beasts* who follow that unhallowed practice of Sodomy, we find no Americans, as yet — they are all Englishmen or French," and a familiar expression of anti-Semitism in the observation "We believe that they are mostly of the Hebrew race — at least, we find no laws, save in Leviticus, to punish them."[5]

A letter to the editor of the *Flash* repeated the accusation that most sodomites were English and gave a detailed description of their modus operandi: "They are continually parading our streets of an evening, watching for their prey, and hundreds of young boys, yes, sir, boys as young as twelve years to eighteen, are victims to their foul and disgusting deeds. I venture to say none of them are married, but hire rooms in various parts of the city for the purpose of bringing their victims to."[6]

The streets and parks of New York were the most popular but not the sole sites of homosexual cruising. For those seeking more athletic partners, or those wanting visual enjoyment without the implication of improper desire, the Battery offered swimsuit-optional public bathhouses where clients could rent one of the private rooms surrounding a large enclosed pool or splash in a "public bath basin." A writer for the *Sportman* described the scene on a typical sultry July afternoon: "We sat, and looked at the great swimming tank at Rabineau's, and saw some twenty men and boys, fat and lean, long and short, all stark naked, without the slightest bathing dress, swimming and standing in all sorts of attitudes, a study for an artist." Bathhouses such as Rabineau's were a favorite haunt of Walt Whitman, who immortalized the young men he came there to gaze upon: "The swimmer naked in the swimmingbath . . . seen as he swims through the salt transparent greenshine, or lies on his back and rolls silently with the heave of the water."[7]

While New York's bathhouses were intended as facilities for pleasure and cleanliness, they were sometimes the site of private tragedies. In 1832, the year William Drummond Stewart arrived in America, his friend the newspaper editor James Watson Webb published the following evocative vignette in the *Courier*:

> Suicide. — The body of Mr. Geo. T. Waldren, merchant of this city was found on Wednesday afternoon in the water, in a private apartment of the Salt Water Bath, at the Battery, where it is supposed to have remained ever since the evening previous. The deceased had evidently shot himself through the heart with a pistol which was found in the room, and which had been discharged. A gold watch, and a pocket book containing $125 was also found in the apartment. Mr. Waldon [*sic*] removed from Boston to this city about 18 months ago. He was modest and retiring in his manners, fond of solitude, and apt to indulge in melancholy, but a gentleman of amiable disposition, unexceptional character, and much esteemed by all his acquaintances.

Why the well-off but melancholy Mr. Waldren would shoot himself in the heart while naked in a public bathhouse can only be surmised.[8]

William Drummond Stewart arrived in New York City during a period of intense social upheaval. Londoners may have been scandalized by the goings-on in Hyde Park, but New Yorkers had their own reasons for concern. As already mentioned, one of the reasons why the flash newspapers railed against sodomites was the belief that they preyed upon the thousands of young men descending on New York City in the 1830s and 1840s. Suddenly outside the safe sphere of the family, living unsupervised in cheap rooming houses, these youths were perceived as prime targets for sexual predators.

The mass migration of young men from small farms to the hard streets of New York created a new cohort of American males. A generation earlier these youths could be quickly assimilated into the workforce through the system of apprenticeship, but by the 1840s their sheer numbers made such a smooth assimilation impossible. Traditional rural employments began to vanish just at a time when New York began to metastasize into a major urban center. Between 1810 and 1820 the city's population increased by an average of only 28 percent a year. For the next four decades the average was 60 percent. This explosion in growth happened at a time when the proportion of young people in the general population was greater than it had been since colonial times. While most young women stayed close to home, young men in overwhelming numbers descended on cities in order to find work — and adventure.[9]

New York City became the center of commerce for the country, and this mercantile revolution demanded an army of young male workers. By 1855 clerkships were the third most common occupation in New York City, providing more working-class jobs than the traditional male trades of carpenter, baker, mason, bricklayer, or coachman. At midcentury nearly fourteen thousand young men clerked in Manhattan's mercantile houses, banks, offices, and retail stores. Not surprisingly, some of these young unmarried men shared rooms — and sexual relations. Court reports for 1846 include a case in which "New York City police prosecuted two young wage earners who allegedly had engaged in carnal intercourse while living together in the same boardinghouse room."[10]

In what had once been a relatively homogeneous population these young men were viewed as a disruptive and alien element, exotic and beyond the control of "proper" society. The clerks in retail stores posed a particularly vexing social problem for New York City in the early nineteenth century. Part of the allure of these jobs was that they gave the illusion of social advancement to young men coming from small family farms or lower-class circumstances. Many of New York's mercantile emporia were decorated like shimmering palaces, and employees were required to wear suits and ties and conduct themselves with exaggeratedly fine manners. Yet wages were low and working hours were long. Employers were free to send employees home (and thereby reduce their pay) on any particular day if business was slow, and many stores laid off their clerks entirely for weeks at a time during exceptionally hot or exceptionally cold weather, when customers were scarce.

The endless procession of smiling, eager young men lining the counters of New York's department stores presented a growing social problem, especially in stores where the customers were primarily women. Merchants believed that a certain type of clerk — young, handsome, charming, and eager — was most effective in selling goods to women, yet critics felt that there was something distinctly unmanly in such work, something at odds with the traditional image of the rugged American male. These unctuously suave young salesmen were soon labeled with the pejorative term *counter-jumpers*. New York's *Vanity Fair* magazine lampooned them in an article titled "Genus, *Homo*: Species, *Counter-jumperii*":

> This truly singular and beautiful animal exists throughout the civilized world, but is only found in perfection in large cities. Its favorite haunts in this region are about the middle of the metropolis — in Broadway, Grand and Canal-streets, the Bowery, and vicinity. . . .
>
> In external appearance, this is one of the prettiest subjects of the Animal Kingdom. Its hair, which grows luxuriantly upon its head and face, is long, glossy, often curled gracefully, and of different colors in different individuals. Its eyes are rather small, but have a beautiful languishing expression. Its skin is exceedingly white, soft, and fine in texture, particularly upon its paws, or hands, of which it takes the most scrupulous care, as it also does of its hair and teeth. Indeed, its principal characteristic is an excessive neatness and love of personal adornment — a trait which places it considerably above the ape.
>
> A great peculiarity with the Counter-jumper, and one which it would be almost impossible to believe, were it not firmly established as a fact, is its total want of sex. It is neither male nor female, though its manners are more feminine than masculine, for which reason, probably, it is a much greater favorite with the ladies than with us. . . .
>
> Many of the handsomest specimens become quite intolerable on the least encouragement, and it is to be regretted that they are fre-

quently petted by inconsiderate ladies. The Counter-jumper, thus spoiled, changes from a harmless, pretty, and agreeable creature, to an insufferable, chattering, noisy nuisance; and goes strutting about, with airs of alternate self-admiration and contempt for others of its kind. The punishment for such cases is termed "snubbing," and it rarely fails to bring the animal to a properly crest-fallen appreciation of its absurd position.[11]

A second article in *Vanity Fair* goes beyond haughty sarcasm to open hostility and undisguised contempt: "These wretched effeminate, mostly uneducated, creatures, smirking and smiling all day long across a counter; these fellows whose highest ambition it is to be able to measure merino with a grace, and sell sarsenet with suavity; these muscle-less, slim-shouldered, flat-chested bipeds are at the bottom of one of the greatest social evils of the present time. A man, if he be a man, is always sure of an independence by labor. His resources are inexhaustable. But his place is out in the free fight of Life." The article is illustrated with an image of the interior of a typical New York dry goods store, with a clerk with muttonchop whiskers wearing a full-skirted dress.[12]

From this array of scandal-sheet exposés, magazine illustrations, travel guides, and ambiguous newspaper clippings we can assemble some tentative idea of what homosexuality entailed in the New York City that William Drummond Stewart encountered when he stepped ashore at Battery Park. If Stewart engaged in homosexual activities during his first visit to New York, he omits the encounters from his autobiographical novels — or he acknowledges them in ways that are so obscure that they cannot be identified with certainty. Still, there are tantalizing hints.

The opening pages of *Altowan*, for example, include a brief reference to a stranger loitering in Battery Park who may be surreptitiously cruising the men who gather there: "Two or three sailors seemed lounging in different directions; and stretched upon one of the stone seats, there lay a man who was, or seemed to be, weary of sleep. His repose, however, was now in some degree interrupted by the appearance of a person whose dress was that of a sailor." The supposedly drowsy observer follows the actions of the sailor with avid attention until the young mariner climbs into a gig and returns to his ship in the harbor. The "sleeper," whose survey reveals to him that all of the sailors have now gone, quickly leaves the park and heads up Broadway. It should be noted that during his 1832 visit Stewart stayed at America's first luxury hotel, the City Hotel, located between lower Broadway and Temple Street. The sleeper who heads up Broadway in the novel is never identified and plays no further role in the narrative, but he may serve as a stand-in for Stewart himself.[13]

Midway through the second volume of *Altowan*, when the setting switches from the Rockies back to New York City, the scene is once again the Battery and the discussion returns to the men who loiter there to observe the passersby.

> Emerging from Greenwich-street, and turning to the right, toward the water, where the wharves are at the garden gate, within which lie the boats of men-of-war, or the light craft that ply about under the name of wherries. The crowd from along the shore of the North River, press on here to pass through the garden; and those from the garden congregate here, to meet friends and to watch the ingress and egress of strangers; where, also, the usual loungers of the place have their stand when they leave the shade of the green trees to meet some person they wish to see, or to watch the movements of others.

Battery Park, with its population of eager young American men congregating to greet friends and meet strangers, made a strong first impression on Stewart and retained a persistent hold on his imagination.[14]

Of all the men William Drummond Stewart may have encountered during his first summer and autumn in New York, only one can be identified with certainty: James Watson Webb, the editor of the *New York Courier and Enquirer* newspaper. Webb was to become a longtime friend and would take upon himself the task of publishing Stewart's first novel, but how the two men met is a mystery. In Webb's introduction to *Altowan*, he gives this account: "In the summer of 1832, a British half-pay officer visited this city, and we were accidentally thrown much in each other's society. A similarity of tastes and pursuits, soon produced an intimacy, gradually ripening into a friendship, which I trust, is destined to continue through life." Why or how they were "accidentally" thrown together is unknown, but it can be presumed that Webb was not one of the people to whom Stewart had secured a letter of introduction before leaving Britain.[15]

Webb was handsome and physically imposing. He was known as the "Apollo of the press" and a rival once described him as "a frank, manly blackguard, a fine-looking, burly, honest kind of savage." With an enormous ego and a hair-trigger temper, he was frequently in conflict with his fellow editors and with the various public figures whose behavior he attacked in his newspaper. Webb wrote the introduction for *Altowan* which, in an act of astonishing egotism, he composed as a twenty-six-page autobiographical essay explaining why he was especially well qualified to recommend Stewart's novel. He included an extended footnote attacking James Fenimore Cooper for his inaccurate portrayal of Native Americans, and took it upon himself to dedicate Stewart's novel to Charles Fenno Hoffman (the eccentric New York writer who six years later would be declared insane and would spend the remaining thirty-five years of his life in an asylum). Webb even claimed primary credit for the existence of Stewart's novel: "When the author first visited the Great West, I urged him to keep a journal of his travels and adventures for publication; but to this he was greatly adverse. He made however, a half promise, that he would do something in the way of recording the incidents of his travels, and describing the countries of his wanderings; and the work I now take pleasure in dedicating to you [Hoffman], is the fulfillment of that promise. It was written solely for the eye of my family and for the amusement of my children." As has been noted, the rather salacious subject matter of the novel makes one wonder whether Webb fully understood what he was reading.[16]

Stewart had arrived in America with letters of introduction to members of the British-owned Hudson's Bay Company, but Webb was able to connect him with leaders of the American fur trade. With typical vanity, Webb takes full credit for the success of Stewart's adventure: "At that period, I was probably, of all others, the person in this city who could best further his views; and when the season for his departure arrived, he carried with him the necessary letters of introduction to my old fellow-soldiers in the West, and to such prominent gentlemen, not in the army, as could, by their position and advice, put him in the way of accomplishing the object of his visit to our shores. Among those to whom I gave him letters, were the late Governor Clarke of Missouri [William Clark, partner of Meriwether Lewis], and Generals [Henry] Atkinson and [William H.] Ashley."[17]

Stewart's travels during his first few months in America are impossible to trace with any exactness. In *Edward Warren* the protagonist leaves New York to escape an outbreak of cholera — and indeed a cholera outbreak struck the city in 1832, reaching its peak during the month of July, killing over 3,500 New Yorkers. Stewart wrote to Webb from Maryland at the beginning of October: "Why I am at Baltimore God knows. . . . I am much delighted with what I have seen of the country & am at a loss only to know how you are to manage it when peopled." He had visited Niagara Falls ("the greatest since that of our first parents") and had seen Washington Irving, who "neither said nor did anything remarkable." Though his travels had been "rather uncertain" for some time, he was now "fixed for the West" and asked the favor that Webb relates in the introduction to *Altowan*: "Will you give me a letter to Gl. Ashley there [St. Louis] or to any one in the west who may be of use in giving me good advice to spend the winter in shooting & how I may ascend the Missouri in Spring. I need not say how great a favour I shall esteem it."[18]

In *Edward Warren* Ned describes his first impressions of traveling the back roads of America alone, through a vast landscape so different from England. "I shall never forget the first storm, how the shadows of the lurid clouds came over the shade, and the great drops fell distinctly from leaf to leaf, and their coming was heard long before they reached the earth; and the lightning flashed more broadly in the dark vault, which gave a hundred echoes to the rolling thunder." He stopped at remote cabins, where he was welcomed by people who knew little of the world beyond their own hollow. "I told tales, of great cities I had seen, or sung, and the children used to hang upon my words, and stare with their great eyes; and their parents equally wondered, though they showed it less. . . . When the family was large, I partook of the children's bed, or shared it with another guest; when the family was small, I had, if there was one, a bed to myself on the floor."[19]

If Ned's travels in the autobiographical fiction mirror Stewart's own, he arrived in St. Louis by the middle of November 1832. He had a number of letters of introduction folded carefully in his pocket. One of those letters — to business partners and intimate friends William Sublette and Robert Campbell — proved to be particularly helpful. The men would play a critical role in Stewart's American adventure.

The relationship shared by fur traders Robert Campbell and William Sublette intrigues from a distance, but we will probably never know the full nature of their intimacy. Contemporary sources almost always refer to the two business partners as "fast friends," "companions," and both "partners and friends," a dual designation not used for any of the other business associates who took part in the fur trade. The clear implication is that Sublette and Campbell's relationship was exceptional in that it was as much personal as business, and certainly the documents they left behind indicate a long-lasting emotional closeness. They quickly supplanted James Watson Webb as Stewart's closest American friends — William Sublette in particular became a favorite comrade — and the couple were invaluable in providing Stewart with entree into the sometimes contentious world of the fur trade.[20]

Born in County Tyrone, Ireland, in 1804, Robert Campbell was the youngest of the eleven children of a Scots-Irish farmer of modest means and his second wife. At the age of six Robert lost his father, and since the eldest son, Andrew, was an alcoholic and ne'er-do-well, the next-oldest brother, Hugh (only sixteen years old himself), became the family's mainstay and Robert's father figure. The two would remain close throughout their lives.

In 1822 at the age of eighteen Robert sailed for America. Hugh had gone before him, settling in North Carolina, but Robert chose to live in Philadelphia. There, like so many ambitious young men of the age, he became a clerk in a store. His life took an unexpected turn when, within months of arriving in Philadelphia, he met businessman John O'Fallon, who had come east from St. Louis to sell his furs and buy supplies for the new trading season. O'Fallon had recently been appointed by his uncle, Indian Superintendent William Clark, as sutler at Council Bluffs; he would be leaving Philadelphia soon to take up his post. Impressed by what he saw in young Campbell, O'Fallon immediately offered him a job as an assistant clerk if Robert would return to Missouri with him. Campbell eagerly accepted the offer, and the two men rode off together.

Campbell arrived in St. Louis just as the fur trade was entering its golden age. Under such men as William Ashley and John Jacob Astor, fortunes were soon to be made feeding the fashion world's insatiable hunger for beaver pelts to make into top hats. Though life on the rugged frontier brought on a recurrence of Campbell's chronic respiratory problems, he struggled on, enthusiastic about his prospects and reveling in his new life.

Robert Campbell was recruited by the legendary Jedediah Smith, one of the original "Enterprising Young Men" who responded to an 1822 newspaper advertisement placed by William Ashley asking for men willing to "ascend the Missouri to it source, there to be employed for one, two or three years" in the fur trade. Smith, a seasoned veteran of the rough life of a mountain man, became Campbell's teacher and mentor. It was a rugged and lonely existence for the men who chose it, but beginning in 1825 and continuing for the next fifteen years it was punctuated each summer by one roaring, uninhibited debauch: the annual Rocky Mountain rendezvous. It was Ashley's idea to spare trappers the expense and inconvenience of hauling a season's worth of pelts eastward by designating a spot each year for a large social and commercial gathering. There all the trappers would meet to exchange their furs for money and supplies brought from St. Louis by the fur traders. Fueled by hard liquor and the presence of attractive Indian women, the rendezvous inevitably became a weeks-long bacchanal that left the men hung over and broke — and compelled to stay yet another season in the mountains.

Campbell could scarcely ignore the boisterous sexual exploits of his comrades, but he apparently did not take part in them himself. "While there are tantalizing hints in his letters that Campbell dallied with Indian women," his biographer notes, "none suggest that he ever 'packed a squaw.'" Rather than the presence of available women, it was the overflowing of food that captured the young immigrant's imagination. "The vivid memories that Campbell recorded about the rendezvous characteristically had more to do with sustenance than sex. . . . Certainly Robert enjoyed all the antics of the men, although he gives us no detail of his own indulgences." Campbell was in all things reticent. "He was rather above medium height," another historian writes, "fair haired, and though warm, friendly, and above all, loyal to his friends, he was considered by some rather reserved and difficult to approach."[21]

In 1826, when he was twenty-two years old, Campbell's quiet reserve was finally breached. At the rendezvous held that summer in Cache Valley, Mexico (now Utah), Campbell met William Sublette, the man who would become his most intimate lifelong friend. Sublette was nearly five years older than Campbell. Sublette's government-issued passport includes a detailed physical description: "Height six feet two inches; forehead straight and open; eyes blue, light; nose Roman; mouth and chin common; hair light or sandy; complexion fair; face long and expressive; scar on left side of chin." Born in 1799 in Kentucky, he was the eldest child of a farmer cum tavern owner who moved the family from small town to small town, eventually joining the great migration westward. William was eighteen when the family settled in Missouri.[22]

If Robert grew up in a conservative, strictly observant Calvinist household, William's youth was spent in quite a different atmosphere. His father's taverns were the resort of hard-drinking brawlers, men (and women) of questionable moral standing. In 1819 Phillip Sublette and his business partner were hauled into court charged with "keep[ing] and maintain[ing] a certain common misgoverned & disorderly house and [allowing] in their said house for their own [profit] & gain certain persons of evil name & fame, and of dishonest conversation, to frequent & come together there . . . at unlawful times, as well in the night as in the day . . . there to be & remain drinking, tippling, gambling & misbehaving themselves . . . to the evil example of others."[23]

William Sublette's father died in 1820, and his mother two years later. At the age of twenty-four he left St. Charles, Missouri, to join the rush to riches in the burgeoning fur trade. Sublette became one of "Ashley's Hundred" and he thrived in that atmosphere of danger and hardship. For the next three years Sublette learned the fur trade, and after a series of arduous trials and hair-raising adventures, he prospered enough that at the 1826 rendezvous he, Jedediah Smith, and David Jackson bought out Ashley's enterprise and went into business for themselves. Sublette's new friend Robert Campbell officially witnessed the contract of sale and was appointed clerk of the corporation of Smith, Jackson & Sublette.

For William Sublette and Robert Campbell the 1826 rendezvous was the beginning of a lifelong personal partnership. Sublette's biographer comments on the special bond that developed between the men: "Although Campbell was a 'genial hospitable gentleman . . . who was slow to admit strangers to intimacy,' over the years he and Sublette forged 'a community . . . [of] feelings, wishes, tastes and dangers' of brotherly proportions. They spent as much time together as possible, nursed each other in sickness, and planned for the future in harmony and accord." At the close of the rendezvous Campbell returned with Sublette to Sulphur Springs, Sublette's home near St. Louis, and the two men established a household.[24]

A year before William Drummond Stewart's arrival in the Rockies, Sublette and Campbell were involved in the legendary battle of Pierre's Hole, a bloody conflict that arose between the Gros Ventre Indians and a group of trappers (aided by allies among the Flatheads and the Nez Percés) after the 1832 rendezvous. Sublette and Campbell were still at the rendezvous site when word of the attack arrived, and they rushed off to aid their beleaguered colleagues — in the process pledging their support for one another at full gallop. "Mr. Sublette and I," Robert later wrote to his brother, "without being aware of the cause or nature of the approaching contest, felt convinced we were about entering on a perilous engagement in which one or both of us might fall. We therefore briefly directed each other as to the disposition of our property; or in other words, made our wills, appointing each other sole executor." In this letter to his brother, Campbell makes it clear that he and Sublette had by 1832 become constant companions. William Sublette is mentioned specifically and by name a total of nine times.[25]

As Robert entered his late twenties, and especially as he began to establish himself financially in America, his family looked for signs that he was making the expected move toward marriage. That he wrote constantly about William Sublette but not about anyone of the fair sex led to gentle ribbing. "How can you leave the charming ladies of St. Louis," wrote his sister-in-law, "particularly the interesting French dames or rather demoiselles for the fair or red set of the mountains?" His brother Hugh prodded him, "I should rejoice my dear Robert to hear that you had made [a] choice of a helpmate for life if it were a prudent one." Despite the existence of extensive Campbell family correspondence for the period, however, no reference to any such romances can be found.[26]

By the time of William Drummond Stewart's arrival in St. Louis in 1833, Sublette and Campbell were well-established and well-respected figures in the Rocky Mountain fur industry. They co-owned one of the most important trading businesses and were popular hosts, welcoming guests to their Sulphur Springs estate. Stewart knew little about the American fur enterprise before leaving Scotland, and had secured letters of introduction only to members of the British-owned Hudson's Bay Company. Those letters were now no longer needed. Sublette and Campbell would be his entrée into the world of the mountain men.

4

When William Drummond Stewart arrived in St. Louis, most likely during November 1832, he checked into the Mansion House, the finest hotel in town. He presented his letter of introduction to William Sublette and Robert Campbell, offering them $500 to allow him to accompany them on their journey to the 1833 rendezvous, to be held that year near Fort Bonneville in Wyoming. But first he was to spend the winter in rough-and-tumble St. Louis — a town that Stewart describes as unlighted and badly paved but full of raucous energy. "The reckless mountain boys, who had returned from their summer campaign, were the life and the terror of the place; and in the intervals of debauch, told the tales of the wilds with graphic and inspiring enthusiasm."[1]

Stewart spent the winter months attending dinner parties and "gumbo balls," and in the early spring headed off on an odd mission: on horseback in the middle of March to North Bend, Ohio, to try to convince Dr. Benjamin Harrison to join the expedition to the mountains. Historians have suggested that perhaps Harrison was a friend of Sublette and Campbell, and that they sent Stewart to him with an invitation to join their entourage. It is highly unlikely, however, that Sublette and Campbell would have sent a paying customer — and one unfamiliar with the territory at that — on such an errand. If their intent was to invite Dr. Harrison to join them, they had many associates and employees who were better qualified to serve as messenger. It is more likely that

Stewart and Harrison had met at some point during the former's travels around the country, and that it was Stewart's own suggestion that his new friend, a physician, would be a beneficial addition to the party.

Benjamin was the dissolute, ne'er-do-well son of William Henry Harrison, soon to become the ninth president of the United States. Twenty-six years old at the time he joined Stewart on his trip to the Rockies, Benjamin was "a fine looking man, fair hair and eyes, stood six foot high, fine form, very intelligent, and a perfect gentleman in manners and address," but he "suffered from alcoholism and family turmoil." He was not a promising addition to a traveling group that would (as Sublette and Campbell both knew from hard experience) face difficult challenges and dangers. Charles Larpenteur, one of the young clerks working for Sublette and Campbell at the time, later wrote that Harrison was brought along "with the view to break him of drinking whiskey," but his observation ignores an important point — it was not the Harrison family that sought a cure for Benjamin's disruptive conduct. Far from seeking a cure, William Henry Harrison was extremely reluctant to allow his son to go along on the journey, agreeing only on the condition that the company accept $1,000 (twice what Stewart was paying) to defray Benjamin's expenses. Evidently Harrison *père* had little confidence that his son would prove to be an asset to the party. The president later wrote of his "astonishment and regret" about the unprofitable outcome of his son's adventure. "In his trip he squandered a thousand dollars in a way wholly unaccountable."[2]

While in St. Louis waiting for the trip west to begin, William Drummond Stewart met Prince Maximilian zu Wied-Neuwied, who was traveling throughout the United States on an ethnographic and botanical tour. In his rather staid *Reise in das Innere Nord-America in den Jahren 1832 bis 1834* the prince explains that he and Stewart had very different goals in mind as they planned their respective trips to the Rocky Mountains that year:

Captain Stewart (of Grand Tully), an English traveller, with whom I had become acquainted at St. Louis, was on the point of setting out by land by the caravan; but after I had consulted many persons well acquainted with the country, the plan of following the course of the Missouri seemed to be the most suitable for my purposes; for, first, I should not be able to observe any Indians on the land journey; for if you happen to meet with them, you must fight them, and therefore, cannot become well acquainted with them; and, secondly, it is extremely difficult, nay impossible, to make considerable collections of natural history on such a journey.[3]

The prince was wise to decline an offer to accompany Stewart, as there was nothing in the least professorial about Stewart's aspirations for the journey. He was not a naturalist nor an ethnographer, and while he would in the future encourage scientists to travel with him on his journeys to the Rockies, he had little personal interest in anything he could not shoot or embrace (his passions were venereal, in both the obsolete and the more common meanings of that term). While Prince Maximilian boarded the steamboat *Yellowstone* for the slow journey upriver, Stewart set about equipping himself for the trail. The two English Manton rifles he had brought with him were the best available; in St. Louis he purchased a woolen capote (hooded cape) for $20, a pair of pantaloons, and two heavy shirts.

At the time Stewart prepared to head into the Rockies the fur trade was dominated by three main companies: the Hudson's Bay Company (headquartered in York Factory, Manitoba), the American Fur Company (founded by New York's John Jacob Astor), and the Rocky Mountain Fur Company (based in St. Louis). These companies expanded, contracted, and merged over the short boom period of the fur trade, and some companies, such as Sublette & Campbell, were established not to trap but to bring supplies to trappers in exchange for their season's worth of pelts.

Although the large companies hired men to trap exclusively for them, they also benefited from the services of so-called free trappers — men who were not affiliated with any one company but who were free to sell their pelts to the highest bidder. One-third of the trappers fell into this category, and they formed a colorful brotherhood. Free trappers were known for their "bold and adventurous spirit," and their eccentric and flamboyant modus vivendi quickly became the stuff of legend. In 1902 Hiram Chittenden wrote of them: "The leader could not always control them and they were prone to all sorts of excesses. Vain of their appearances, extravagantly fond of ornament for both themselves and their steeds, they rivaled the proud Indian himself in the profusion of gewgaws which decked out their attire." These sartorial displays were not intended to attract the Indian women whom the men occasionally encountered. As would be noted of the gold miners in the remote California camps of the 1850s, the free trappers "dressed up in order to look 'fascinating' for one another."[4]

Washington Irving details the unique appearance of the free trapper, who — despite a life of hardship and isolation — showed a degree of preoccupation with body presentation that is usually associated with the dandified city gentleman.

> His hair, suffered to attain to a great length, is carefully combed out, and either left to fall carelessly over his shoulders, or plaited neatly and tied up in otter skins, or parti-colored ribands. A hunting-shirt of ruffled calico of bright dyes, or of ornamented leather, falls to his knee below which, curiously fashioned leggins, ornamented with strings, fringes, and a profusion of hawks' bells, reach to a costly pair of moccasons of the finest Indian fabric, richly embroidered with beads. A blanket of scarlet, or some other bright color, hangs from his shoulders, and is girt round his waist with a red sash, in which he bestows his pistols, knife, and the stem of his Indian pipe; preparation either for peace or war. His gun is lavishly decorated with brass tacks and vermilion, and provided with a fringed cover, occasionally of buckskin, ornamented here and there with a feather.[5]

Hiram Chittenden is even more graphic in his description: "The headdress in summer usually consisted of a light handkerchief, adjusted in the style of a turban so as to be attractive in appearance while serving as a protection against heat and insects. The upper part of the body was clad in a light blue shirt of coarse cotton or other cloth, and in some cases breeches with long deerskin leggings were worn, leaving the thighs and hips bare. . . . All portions of this picturesque attire, whether for summer or winter use, were ornamented with gay embroidery, fringes, bead work, hair, feathers, and other gewgaws." It should be noted that the only other groups in the mountains who were noted for elaborate self-ornamentation with gewgaws were Indian women and male berdaches who adopted women's clothing.[6]

Philip L. Edwards, a lay minister traveling with Nathaniel Wyeth's party of 1834, was also impressed by the elaborate couture worn by the free trappers he encountered. Though he omitted references to naked thighs and hips, in a letter to a friend back east he wrote of the mountain dandies as frankly as he dared: "You will perhaps recollect to have seen in the 'far west' of our own United States, the buckskin hunting shirt and leggins gracefully hung with tasty fashion fringes carried to perfection. Here they are six or seven inches long, and hung densely on every seam, I believe, both of the hunting shirt and leggins. Indeed their weight is a great burden. But it is perhaps advisable, under existing circumstances, that I should leave your imagination to supply the picture."[7]

The free trappers' androgynous attire made a strong statement in early nineteenth-century America. "In no country has such constant care been taken as in America," wrote Alexis de Tocqueville in 1835, "to trace two clearly distinct lines of action for the two sexes, and to make them keep pace one with the other, but in two pathways which are always different." The golden age of the fur trade coincided with a period in American history when bifurcated gender roles were strongly enforced; anyone attempting to oppose — or even blur — gender expectations encountered hostility from his or her community. The trappers who chose to adopt flamboyant, gewgaw-adorned attire were not intending to dress as women (as a berdache might), but they were flirting with gender presentation in a way that would be unacceptable in most regions of early nineteenth-century America. Their direct descendants are the contemporary communities of gay or bisexual men known as bears — hirsute and heavy-set males whose denim and flannel may be set off with a single dangling earring.[8]

Trappers — and in particular free trappers — are an intriguing group to anyone investigating same-sex desire in the nineteenth century, since they were men who chose to remove themselves from traditional social structures for long periods. Any man who headed into the Rocky Mountains knew that he would have almost exclusively male companionship for months at a time. Indian women were sometimes available, particularly at the annual rendezvous, but these encounters tended to be fleeting. For the two or three weeks of the rendezvous females might be socially and sexually available, but for the remainder of the year many of the men traveled alone or with only a few companions — frequently with only one close "pardner." Following the beaver along remote, almost inaccessible tributaries proved impractical for large groups.

In the winter the trappers retreated to camps located in isolated spots known to provide some protection from the harshest weather. Camps were usually established around November and were maintained until around March. Sometimes the men built log cabins, but many soon discovered that the traditional Indian lodge or tepee provided greater comfort. Lodges typically held six or seven men, with their personal effects distributed around the perimeter and a fire in the center. The five months of enforced idleness were spent on a variety of tasks that included repairing clothes and equipment, and hunting for food to feed the camp. Given the variety of chores that needed to be undertaken in these small communities — some pleasurable, some onerous — one might expect that the tasks would be assigned to the men on a rotational basis. This was not the case. The men in the winter encampments divided into two groups — trappers and camp keepers — each with strongly gendered work assignments. The trappers were expected to hunt for food and take care of the horses, while the camp keepers cooked, cleaned, dressed beaver, made leather thongs, and guarded the camp in the absence of the hunters. Fur companies sometimes hired camp keepers, but for free trappers the work assignments were either voluntary or enforced (sometimes the older trappers compelled the younger to take on the traditionally female responsibilities). Having a younger man to provide creature comforts made winter encampment much more pleasant. "The frost," remembered trapper Joe Meek, "used to hang from the roofs of our lodges in the morning, on first waking, in skeins two feet long, and our blankets and whiskers were white with it. But we trappers laid still, and called the camp-keepers to make a fire, and in our close lodges it was soon warm enough."[9]

The question of what men did without women while in the wilderness intrigued British diplomat Augustus John Foster, and when he asked Secretary of the Treasury Albert Gallatin about the matter, he was told that "the Grecian Vice was common among the Indians as well as among the back Woodsmen." The liminal space of the American frontier remained for decades a place where many men accommodated themselves to having sex with other men. Some men remained celibate, of course, and some entered temporary or long-term unions (and sometimes traditional marriages) with Indian women, but for many "the Grecian Vice" was an alternative that was embraced — by some grudgingly, by others with more eagerness. The question of self-selection among participants in the fur trade — of whether men consciously chose a profession in which they knew sex with other men would be acceptable — is particularly intriguing where free trappers are concerned, since they alone do not seem to have entered the profession for the money.[10]

Most of the leaders of the fur trade — those who were not killed on the job — retired to the East or to the Pacific coast when they had made their fortune, or became more settled merchants on the frontier. A few became famous scouts when the fur trade collapsed and long wagon trains of migrants began rolling toward Oregon and California. Free trappers, on the other hand, did not seem to be working toward any conceivable picket-fenced future. They spent the entire year in the mountains, either alone or with a few companions. In the summer they would bring their pellews (beaver pelts) to the rendezvous, convert them to goods, food, or alcohol, spend the long, warm days roaring drunk and wildly gambling away all their resources, and then head back into the wilderness to do it all again. Eventually returning to the joys of "civilization" does not seem to have been part of their plan.

American Fur Company veteran Warren Ferris wrote about the free trappers he encountered in the Rockies: "They rove through this savage and desolate region free as the mountain air, leading a venturous and dangerous life, governed by no laws save their own wild impulses, and bounding their desires and wishes to what their own good rifles and traps may serve them to procure. Strange, that people can find so strong and fascinating a charm in this rude nomadic, and hazardous mode of life, as to estrange themselves from home, country, friends, and all the comforts, elegances, and privileges of civilization. . . . Yet so attached to it do they become, that few ever leave it." Ferris was no breathless city dude, daunted by the rigors and dangers of life in the mountains. For almost five years he traveled throughout the region, enduring unimaginable hardships and yet staying on. He felt himself fully capable of surmounting the challenges that came his way, and yet he still felt it was "strange" that any man would decide to embrace this life to such an extent that he would willingly separate himself from the bonds of home and family, with no plans ever to return.[11]

With the collapse of the fur trade in the 1840s, many trappers retreated to "residential communities" of like-minded individuals. Particularly popular were the settlements of Pueblo, Hardscrabble, and Greenhorn on the Arkansas River, which became the retreat of nearly one-quarter of the former fur trappers. Many trappers brought their Indian wives with them, but 17 percent of the men who retired to these communities in southern Colorado remained lifelong bachelors. Writing from Hardscrabble in 1845, Alexander Barclay explained to his brother back in London about the special quality of his new community: "Our wants are few, and as we witness no instance of ostentation and luxury in our neighbors, we have nothing to create envy. . . . Indeed, the men who have located here are all those whom the wreck of the mountain trade and hunting parties have left on the surface, unfitted to return to former haunts or avocations, with minds alienated by new connections from home and early friends." Profoundly changed by their years in the fur trade, unable to fit into settled society's expectations, these men found in communities like Hardscrabble a way to prolong the idyllic life they had come to know in the mountains.[12]

When the grasses had grown tall enough to support the horses and livestock, it was time at last for William Drummond Stewart to head for the mountains. For the 1833 journey Sublette and Campbell would split up, with Sublette taking a keelboat full of supplies up the river (with more in the steamboats *Yellowstone* and *Assiniboin*) and Campbell leading the party overland. The caravan set off on May 7, 1833, with around forty men, each with three mules. A flock of twenty sheep would assure them food until they could reach buffalo country. Once it entered the open prairie the party would travel from daybreak until late afternoon. Historian Bernard DeVoto evokes the setting: "This was prairie country, lush with grass that would be belly-high on your horse, or higher, by June. In May it was spongy from violent rains, in long stretches little better than a bog. The rains struck suddenly and disastrously, drowning you out of your blankets, interspersed with snow flurries or showers of hailstones as big as a fist, driven by gales that blew your possessions over the prairie and froze your bones. Continuous deafening thunder might last for hours at a time."[13]

Campbell divided the men up into messes of five or six men each, and every evening they would construct temporary scrub brush shelters that they called "bowers." The bowers were small, with room for either one or two men per shelter. Stewart at first slept alone, but after only a few days on the trail he acquired a companion. Traveling with the party was a young man from New York named George Holmes. Holmes's most notable feature was that he was astonishingly handsome; so remarkable were his good looks that the others nicknamed him Beauty. Stewart chatted him up as the party headed across the prairie, and soon the two men were making and sharing a bower for two each evening.

Stewart quickly adapted to the rigors of the trail, and his marksmanship won him the respect and admiration of the other members of the party. Though he was paying his way, he insisted on taking his turn at all chores, however arduous or menial, and he soon proved himself to be one of the more valuable hunters on the expedition, with the ability to drop a buffalo dead in its tracks while riding at a full gallop in the midst of a stampeding herd. He gained almost legendary status one day when the party crossed paths with a grizzly bear. The other men began chasing her, shooting wildly until, wounded and enraged, the bear turned on them, rearing on her hind legs and bellowing with a deafening roar, froth dripping from her menacing jaws. The startled men shot and shot and shot, but nothing seemed to faze the angry grizzly. They were running away in terror when Stewart galloped up and fired, seemingly without taking aim. With one shot he brought the beast crashing down. If there was any doubt that the aristocrat with the fastidious manners was a man's man, it was forever dispelled, and Captain Stewart's reputation with the mountain men was secured.

In George Ruxton's 1849 fictionalized history *Life in the Far West* William Drummond Stewart is remembered by an old mountain man named Killbuck:

The last as come out of Independence was that ar Englishman. He'd a nor-west capote on, and a two-shoot gun rifled. Well, them English are darned fools; they can't fix a rifle any ways; but that one did shoot "some;" leastwise *he* made it throw plum-center. He made the bufler "come," *he* did, and fout well at Pawnee Fork too. What was his name? All the boys called him Cap'en, and he got his fixings from old Choteau; but what he wanted out thar in the mountains, I never jest rightly know'd. He was no trader, nor a trapper, and flung about his dollars right smart. Thar was old grit in him, too, and a hair of the black b'ar at that.

Ruxton explains in a footnote that the expression meant that the man had a "spice of the devil." The rough trappers were not sure what to make of Stewart, could not quite figure out what he was doing there among them in the first place, but they strongly admired his courage and his hunting skill.[14]

Robert Campbell was impressed with Stewart's organizational abilities and with his quiet, commanding demeanor and soon designated him captain of the night guard, an appointment that precipitated a crisis when British military discipline clashed with American concepts of justice. One evening when making the rounds Stewart discovered a guard asleep on duty. He awoke the man and sent him to his tent, and then took the man's place himself as guard for the rest of the night. In the morning he called the miscreant to his tent and announced that for the infraction he would be fined $5 and given three "walks" — three days spent leading his horse rather than riding. In a rage, the man went straight to Campbell and complained of the punishment, insisting that he had no intention of allowing a greenhorn to tell him how to do his job. Campbell coolly replied that Captain Stewart was an officer who had fought at Waterloo, and his orders were to be obeyed without question. The man walked.

As the members of the caravan adjusted to life on the trail, personal hygiene began to slip. They all stopped shaving and let their hair grow long and wild — with one exception. Each morning Stewart would repair to the nearest clear-flowing creek, methodically lay out the various implements of his ivory-handled toilette set, work up a creamy lather and, peering into a small hand mirror, carefully shave all but his thick, dark moustache. He discovered that one of the men had some previous training as a barber and drafted him to make sure that his hair was clipped close to his collar. If the men thought Captain Stewart was a bit odd because of his meticulous grooming habits they kept it to themselves. Stewart's willingness to become one of the men — to share their hardships, to hunt for their food, and to join in their revelries — gained the respect of the crew and smoothed over any awkwardness that may have arisen because of his noble blood and his sometimes dandyish ways.

After two months on the trail, as the party approached the rendezvous site, Stewart surprised them all with one final flare of sartorial eccentricity. As the men jostled one another in front of the few available mirrors, shaving, trimming, and primping for their grand entrance at the trappers' gathering, Captain Stewart with great grace and dignity emerged from his improvised dressing room. He was wearing a chic white leather

English hunting jacket and a pair of tight trews made of the blue and green tartan plaid of the Stewart clan. Trews were form-fitting trousers made from fabric that had been cut on the bias, allowing the material to stretch and mold closely to the contours of a man's body, showing off his masculine assets. In fashionable London such tight pants were called "inexpressibles" because of their sexual daring; Count d'Orsay frequently caused a stir by wearing a pair that were flesh colored, making it appear at first blush that he was completely naked from waist to ankle. Tartan plaid was a bit less daring, to be sure, but nonetheless no one at the 1833 rendezvous would look quite like William Drummond Stewart.

Though no one could know it at the time, the rendezvous of 1833 was the last of the great trapper gatherings. There would be others, but each smaller and less successful than the previous year's. All of the rival American fur companies gathered on the Green River that year. Trapper Joe Meek remembered: "Here were the Rocky Mountain and American Companies; the St. Louis Company; under Capt. Wm. Sublette and his friend Campbell; the usual camp of Indian allies; and, a few miles distant, that of Captain Bonneville. In addition to all these, was a small company belonging to Capt. Stuart, an Englishman of noble family, who was traveling in the far west only to gratify his own love of wild adventure, and admiration of all that is grand and magnificent in nature."[15]

Washington Irving, in *The Adventures of Captain Bonneville, U.S.A., in the Rocky Mountains and the Far West* (1837), describes Stewart in much the same terms: "Captain Stewart, of the British army, [was] a gentleman of noble connections, who was amusing himself by a wandering tour in the Far West; in the course of which, he had lived in hunter's style; accompanying various bands of traders, trappers, and Indians; and manifesting that relish for the wilderness that belongs to men of game spirit." Irving based his book on maps and notes he had purchased directly from Benjamin Bonneville, and his narrative is filled with colorful observations and minute details. The leaders of the different companies, Irving wrote, mingled on terms of perfect good fellowship; interchanging visits, and regaling each other in the best style their respective camps afforded. But the rich treat for the worthy captain was to see the "chivalry" of the various encampments, engaged in contests of skill at running, jumping, wrestling, shooting with the rifle, and running horses. And then their rough hunters' feastings and carousals. They drank together, they sang, they laughed, they whooped; they tried to outbrag and outlie each other in stories of their adventures and achievements. Here the free trappers were in all their glory; they considered themselves the "cocks of the walk," and always carried the highest crests. Now and then familiarity was pushed too far, and would effervesce into a brawl, and a "rough and tumble" fight; but it all ended in cordial reconciliation and maudlin endearment.[16]

Irving confirms the reputation enjoyed by free trappers for eccentric personal ornamentation — the colorful turbans, naked thighs and hips, glittering gewgaws.

The free trappers, especially, were extravagant in their purchases. For a free mountaineer to pause at a paltry consideration of dollars and cents, in the attainment of any object that might strike his fancy, would stamp him with the mark of the beast in the estimation of his comrades. For a trader to refuse one of these free and flourishing blades a credit, whatever unpaid scores might stare him in the face, would be a flagrant affront scarcely to be forgiven. . . . Every freak of prodigality was indulged to its full extent and in a little while most of the trappers, having squandered away all their wages, and perhaps run knee-deep in debt, were ready for another hard campaign in the wilderness.[17]

The rendezvous of 1833 is remembered not only for its historic excesses but also for a horrific tragedy that befell the encampment. One of the victims was Stewart's new companion George Holmes, the young man nicknamed Beauty. Stewart is only one of several participants in the rendezvous who relate the story of Holmes's sad fate. In a long footnote in *Edward Warren*, Stewart describes the actual events behind what is only a brief reference in the novel:

> I was with Campbell's camp, we had moved to the spot but a day or two before, and George Holmes, a young mountaineer, had aided me in constructing a bower of birch and willow, over which to throw a blanket in case of rain, and in which to contain our couch; the leaves were fresh and fragrant, and the little abode had its open end upon the brink of the river, rushing past clear and swift over its pebbly bed. I had no news to read, and no letters; but the recollections of a former home were not obliterated, nor of country; and I loved to sit in the shade, and let my memory wander over bye-gone years, when tired of a visit to the Snake Camp, or the now frequent jollities of the wild free trappers, who came dropping in from distant and unknown haunts, where they had perilled their lives for the ephemeral joys and riot of the few days of jubilee. The best looking of the young squaws of the neighbouring camp, came over in groups to wonder at the riches of the white man, as well as to tempt him to dispense them, and many happy matrimonial connections were formed by means of a dower of glittering beads and scarlet cloth.
>
> On an evening of one of these days, I had for some cause, which appeared to me at the time sufficiently reasonable, begged of my friend Holmes to take his blanket, and make himself a welcome in some other hut, as I wished to have our shanty for the night at my own disposal; he consented, but as I afterwards found he had laid himself down on the ground to sleep by a brake of fragrant rose bushes close by, I thought, afterwards, there was some reluctance in his manner and that I could read some little expression of disappointment in his eye; his temperament was gay and reckless, or I might not have remarked this shade; but he removed his blanket and a small piece of skin, but left his saddle, the usual pillow of the wanderer.[18]

Disappointed and hurt at being asked to vacate their bower, Holmes still hoped to return before the end of the evening. His saddle would in a sense mark his rightful place at Stewart's side. "The night came," Stewart continues, and deepened on towards the middle watch, when I was roused by confused sounds, shouts, and the discharge of fire arms, as well as the deep roar of a bull, such as he emits in terror or in rage. There could be no Indian attack, and I still hesitated about getting up, when there came a sharp cry close to the bower and in a voice I well knew, and no longer hesitating, belted a blanket around me and rushed out. Poor Holmes was seated on the ground, the side of his head and his ear bleeding and torn; a mad wolf was ravaging the camp. We did not get her, she had other lives to sacrifice elsewhere.[19]

Charles Larpenteur, a clerk for Sublette & Campbell who was traveling with the party, describes the incident in this way: "After all hands had retired nothing was heard in the camp except, now and then, the cry of 'All's well,' and some loud snoring, till the sudden cry of, 'Oh, I'm bitten!' — then immediately another, and another. Three of our men were bitten that night, all of them in the face. One poor fellow, by the name of George Holmes, was badly bitten on the right ear and face. All hands got up with their guns in pursuit of the animal, but he made his escape."[20]

Warren Ferris, also an eyewitness, writing only a decade after the event, described a similar scene and added a few more details:

Whilst we were all asleep, one night, an animal, supposed to be a dog, passed through camp, bit several persons as they lay, and then disappeared. On the following morning considerable anxiety was manifested by those who were bitten, under the apprehension that the animal might have been afflicted with the hydrophobia, and several of them took their guns and went about camp, shooting all *suspicious looking* dogs; but were unable to determine that any one was positively mad. During the day information came from the R.[ocky] M.[ountain] F.[ur] Co., who were encamped a short distance below us on the same side of the river, that several men were likewise bitten in their camp during the night, and that a wolf supposed to be rabid, had been killed in the morning.[21]

After the attack, Stewart noticed a rapid change in the gregarious young man who had first attracted his attention. "Poor Holmes changed from that hour, instead of alertness and joy, melancholy and despondency grew upon him day by day. . . . I felt I was linked in a death struggle with one, who whatever he might do to help a friend, considered his own fate as sealed. That day at noon, he had quarrelled with the camp leader for calling him 'Beauty,' a nickname by which he was known, from his blithe and sunny smile. Next day the eye was wan, and the smile was gone."[22]

How much of the early change in Holmes's behavior was due to the effects of the attack, and how much to hurt and anger over Stewart's infidelity, is impossible to gauge. The expected early emotional symptoms of a rabies infection (crippling anxiety, melancholy, depression) usually do not begin to appear in humans until at least ten days after exposure, so almost certainly the virus coursing through his bloodstream was not the immediate cause of the young man's despondency.

The wolf attack happened in mid-July, and over the succeeding weeks Holmes grew more anxious, morose, hypersensitive, and disoriented. He suffered from hallucinations and seizures. "Two days before reaching the [Big] Horn," wrote Charles Larpenteur,

> one of our bulls commenced to show some symptoms of hydrophobia by bellowing at a great rate, and pawing the ground. This scared my poor friend Holmes, who was still in our party, but not destined to reach the Yellowstone. He was a young man from New York, well educated, and we became quite attached to each other on our long journey. The poor fellow now and then asked me if I thought he would go mad; although thinking within myself he would, being so badly bitten, I did all I could to make him believe other wise. When he said to me, "Larpenteur, don't you hear the bull—he is going mad—I am getting scared," I do believe I felt worse than he did, and scarcely knew how to answer him.[23]

Dr. Benjamin Harrison did what he could to help Holmes, but of course there was no cure for rabies. All that lay ahead for Holmes was agony, madness, and death. Stewart seems to have withdrawn himself from his friend's long struggle. He writes: "In November, a melancholy and wasted form set out with Dr. Harrison, the son of the General, and Major Harris, in search of the stone which is believed to be the talisman for the cure of hydrophobia." Larpenteur gives a fuller picture: "For some days he could not bear to cross the small streams which they struck from time to time, so that they had to cover him over with a blanket to get him across; and at last they had to leave him with two men until his fit should be over. But the men soon left him and came to camp. Mr. Fontenelle immediately sent back after him; but when they arrived at the place, they found only his clothes, which he had torn off his back. He had run away quite naked, and never was found."[24]

Trapper Joe Meek related that several of the men who were bitten by the rabid wolf eventually developed hydrophobia: "Two of these were seized with madness in camp, sometimes afterwards, and ran off into the mountains, where they perished. One [Holmes] was attacked by the paroxysm while on a hunt; when, throwing himself off his horse, he struggled and foamed at the mouth, gnashing his teeth, and barking like a wolf. Yet he retained consciousness enough to warn away his companions, who hastened in search of assistance; but when they returned he was nowhere to be found."[25]

The young man named Beauty died somewhere in the vast wilderness, alone, naked, panicked, and foaming at the mouth. Stewart felt deep sadness — and guilt — at the death of his companion. "His bones were left, we could never learn exactly where, on the branch of some stream, and the bough of some tree, where I would have willingly made a pilgrimage to render the last tribute of regret, and contrast the living memory with the dead remains. There never has quitted my breast a reproachful remorse for the part I played him on that sad night."[26]

But what exactly *was* the part that Stewart played Holmes on that sad night? What happened inside the bower after Stewart asked Holmes to absent himself? Stewart's account in the long footnote is crafted to suggest that his guest that night might have been an Indian woman, and historians have been quick to jump to that conclusion. But a closer reading of Stewart's actual words shows that he reveals nothing at all about the gender of his sexual partner. Given the homosexual activity that was an integral part of his life from this point on, it is probable that Stewart's companion that night was a man. The most likely candidate would be the hunter Antoine Clement, whom Stewart met at the 1833 rendezvous and who would become his long-time partner and the most enduring love of his life. Antoine Clement would prove to be alternately enticing and distant, diffident and demanding, fearless and infuriating. Perhaps the reason Stewart was so patient with him, and remained concerned about his welfare long after their sexual relationship had ended, is that the relationship was bought at such a dear price.

Alfred Jacob Miller, the artist who would accompany William Drummond Stewart and Antoine Clement on their 1837 journey to the Rockies, left behind a word picture of the couple that is even more evocative
than any of the several portraits he painted of the men. Miller, a timid
little man from Baltimore, lived in constant awe of his patron's noble
lineage and in abject terror of the Scotsman's explosive temper. He
was therefore completely incredulous when he witnessed an interplay
between Stewart and Clement during their fourth year together as a
couple.

The three men had ridden out of camp on a hunting expedition
when Stewart began to upbraid Clement for not obeying an order he
had given him earlier that day. Miller fully expected the hunter to
apologize profusely to the quick-tempered captain for his lapse but, the
artist soon learned, obsequiousness was not in Clement's character: "It
was a question of manhood, not social position." The situation quickly
escalated into a major confrontation, with Stewart and Clement curs-
ing at one another and hurling threats. "As they rode side by side, and
were not at all choice in their language, I expected every moment to
see them level their rifles at each other." The camp was a dozen miles
away and Miller was a poor navigator, so he wondered how he would
ever find his way back to the others if the confrontation turned deadly.
"While things were in this critical situation, but every minute growing

worse, as Providence would have it, a herd of Buffalo was discovered at a distance, this was too much! — the ruling passion overtopped everything, off went Antoine at a full gallop, under whip and spur, & in a moment our Captain followed suit. . . . The result in a short time was two noble animals biting the dust, each of the late belligerents in great good humor, and the subject of the quarrel entirely forgotten."[1]

If there is a common thread to the men to whom William Drummond Stewart was attracted, it is that they combined a wild temperament with an almost epicene beauty. Certainly Antoine Clement fit the bill. Clement appears as himself as a character in *Edward Warren* and is the basis for at least one other fictional character in the book. The character "Antoine Clement" makes his initial appearance in the novel with a strikingly dramatic entrance that is both mythic and erotic. The masculine counterpart of Venus rising from the sea, "Antoine" literally rises from the earth. "And a figure rose out of a little crevice, caused by the water in time of rain; it was but a crack in the earth, and tufts of grass grew on its lips like mustachios." The opening in the earth is both oral and genital, with the slender rising figure becoming either tongue or penis (or perhaps even clitoris). The regendered Aphroditean entrance is repeated with greater vigor later in the novel, as Ned describes "the sudden appearance of Antoine, who again stood before our leader, as if sprung out of the earth." (Stewart was perhaps familiar with the classical story of repression and liberation in which the god Uranus refuses to allow his children to emerge from the underground — until his youngest son, Cronos, emasculates him and throws his father's genitals into the sea, creating a white foam from which Aphrodite rises.)[2]

Clement was exotically handsome. "The figure which stood before us, was that of a youth under twenty," Stewart writes, "a half-breed, with light brown hair worn long, and the almond shaped hazel eyes of his mother's race — the fine formed limbs and small hands, with a slightly olive tinge of skin. His dress was almost Indian, consisting of a leather shirt and leggings, coming a little above the knee, almost to meet it, and tied up to the waist belt by a small strip of leather, on the outside of each thigh. The skirt of the shirt, though full, did not reach far down, thus forming a short Scotch kilt and coat all in one, which may probably be the original shape of that species of attire."[3]

Antoine Clement was the "son of a Canadian and half-bred Cree mother, born on the Siscatchnan [sic] of the north-west territory." Stewart describes Clement's long, tousled hair as "between a brown and auburn," showing his French Canadian father's Celtic heritage. In Miller's oil portrait of Antoine, now on display at the Walters Art Museum in Baltimore, Clement has blue-grey eyes, a long aquiline nose, and a cleft chin. The fingers of his right hand, draped over the muzzle of his rifle, are long, tapered, and almost delicate. Miller called Clement "that wild child of the Prairie," which perhaps best captures the untamed spirit that Stewart found so intoxicating.[4]

When William Drummond Stewart and Antoine Clement met at the 1833 rendezvous the course of both their lives radically changed. In a revealing passage unsurpassed in early nineteenth-century novels for its frank evocation of suppressed homosexual desire, Stewart in *Edward Warren* describes the main character's first encounter with a young Indian, an encounter that almost certainly draws upon the author's first meeting with Clement. In it Stewart reveals all the pent-up emotion of a man who has kept his homosexual impulses under control all of his life, but who finds his defenses crumbling as he looks deep into the eyes of a handsome man who acknowledges the naked flash of desire sparking between them. Ned is so "completely enthralled" by the man suddenly standing before him that he is rendered speechless, afraid to break the spell, uncertain at first if the stranger truly shares his sexual interest.

> I was so pleased at the survey, that I was in no hurry to break first the silence, and raised my eyes again to the countenance, to read if there was any sign to lead me on.
>
> However I may be alive to surprise or admiration, or to those mysterious sympathies which are electrically conveyed by the touch as well as by the sight, I have never been conscious of betraying it by outward emotion; but I must confess that now I had to controul

an exclamation as well as gesture of surprise, which I felt would be ill-bred. That countenance, on which I now gazed with fascination, was of the most faultless beauty; — the finely pencilled eyebrows, arched over those almond-shaped eyes, for a moment opened upon me with darkened fire from between the long lashes, which again reposed on the cheek, through whose tint the late exercise had brought a warmer hue.

I had never seen any thing to give me the idea of a perfectly noble head before, and I suppose my admiration also spoke through my eyes, for a smile, somewhat wanton and scornful, stole over the features and curled the lips of the Indian youth, — but he did not move.[5]

That the smile was both wanton and scornful suggests Clement was fully aware of Stewart's desire for him but was not at first receptive. Stewart — by nature forceful and assertive — was too unsure of himself to push forward in this instance, but the hunter in him could not drop out of the chase. In the novel Stewart's alter ego reports that he took leave of the young man reluctantly. "I was anxious to have made some propositions about meeting again, but there was something about my Indian friend that checked any advance; and I was both attracted by a hidden spell, and repelled by a half haughty smile." Ned takes leave of the stranger "with an imitation of his smile, at the same time making a silent vow that I would overcome his pride, and make him return the liking I had taken for him."[6]

Historians unaware of William Drummond Stewart's homosexuality (most recently, Monica Rico in 2007) have viewed the relationship between the two men as strictly that of employer and employee. Rico writes that Clement was "willing to ingratiate himself with Drummond Stewart, at least occasionally" but that the Scotsman's "patronage and friendship were but two of the many strands in a network of strategies that a man of little education and property could employ in order to survive." If, however, we add in the sexual dimension of the relationship, we uncover a much more complex portrait. In Stewart's autobiographical novels and in Alfred Jacob Miller's notes and correspondence, Antoine

Clement emerges as an impetuous, independent young man with an ambiguous sexual orientation. Clement was extremely proud of his renown as the most skilled hunter in the mountains, and far from striving to ingratiate himself with his employer, he was a constant source of anger and frustration because he refused to acknowledge that Stewart's patronage carried with it any obligations on his part. Clement had a wild, mischievous streak, an irreverence in the face of authority, and a pernicious addiction to alcohol.[7]

In *Edward Warren* Ned's frustration over the enticing but indifferent Indian leaves him in a state of prolonged emotional turmoil, wrestling with barely concealed sexual desire. In the young man's presence he is happier than he has ever been, and Ned is driven to force an intimacy on his reluctant partner, who yields and then withdraws again with maddening nonchalance, refusing even to tell Ned his name.

The fire burnt clear, and the stream run by in its rocky bed, sparkling and pure, retaining still the cold of the snows from which it came. I cannot tell how that evening passed, or how the next; all I can tell is, that I never tired, and that no period of my varied life calls up the memory of such perfect joy. There was one thing remarkable in my new friend, and that was the suddenness with which he would break off our gambols without any apparent cause; on one occasion, I had caught him in my arms, and rolled down a bank with him to the edge of a pool of water; it was at the noon halt, he contrived to stop, notwithstanding my efforts, just as I hope to have soused him. I could not understand his dread of wetting his clothes. I knew he must have been an excellent swimmer, from his having crossed the river; and I said our clothes would have easily dried in half an hour in the sun, while we might run about in the heat without them; but he took a decorous air, and I perceived these little familiarities, if carried beyond a certain point, brought a shade upon his brow, and I had to sing him into good humour again; he was completely spoiled, and to win that smile which came so stealthily from the dark eyes, flashing below the long lashes, I would have joyfully perilled my life.

"But will you never tell me your name," I said one evening, after he had come back from a temporary absence, during which I had in vain searched for him. "I could not call you had their [sic] been anything amiss, and besides, it is so stupid not to have a name."

"I never tell my name, but you may give me one, and I will answer to it as faithfully as a dog, will that please you?" he said, as he run his fingers through my entangled locks, and looked down on my face, which lay in his lap. "Call me Sancho, that's not long, and I am your squire." . . .

We went on so well together and that little reserve of his left always something to be desired, and some further intimacy to be longed for; I knew not very well what, but there was an enchantment over me, one of those mysterious sympathies of romantic affection, as well as the most rational and practical intercourse.[8]

"That little reserve of his" never quite left Antoine Clement, and it suggests that he was not completely committed to the relationship. He was, perhaps, not so far to the "homosexual" end of the Kinsey scale as was Stewart, and it is likely that the material benefits that he gained from being Stewart's partner were as much an incentive as his sexual attraction to the man. Still, the sexual attraction *does* appear to have been real, however ambivalent Clement was about expressing it. If he truly objected to Stewart's sexual overtures, he could easily have found another employer, since his skills as a hunter were completely portable and in great demand. Yet he stayed. On Stewart's part Clement's refusal to commit only served to whet his appetite. Because of his noble blood and his military rank, Stewart was used to a certain level of deference from the people he met, but Clement was extraordinarily unimpressed by either. Clement's willingness to stand up to Stewart, the very real possibility that at any moment Clement might mount his horse and simply ride away from the relationship, made him completely irresistible. Stewart writes that he was equally attracted by "his waywardness and his beauty."[9]

On Clement's side it was not only the material benefits that held him. Stewart played almost a Scheherazade role, being an emissary from a magical world that was beyond Clement's ken. In *Altowan* the relationship between Clement and Stewart is mirrored in that between Joe Henry, a young Missourian with little knowledge of the wide world, and Roallan, the son of a British peer. Stewart offers a touching portrait of the two friends as they make their way across the prairie.

> Henry had taken an interest in Roallan, and felt an affection for him, which the superior knowledge and acquirements of the one were likely to inspire in the breast of a backwoodsman, who derives instruction when he can give an equivalent in another way. The nights when Roallan and he lay together on the buffalo robes of their lodge, if it afforded the one an opportunity of giving an account of things of which the other had only gleaned a faint idea from books of history and travels, the advantage was counterbalanced by the wandering of the succeeding day, when, though with a head as high as that of the proud young lord by whose side he rode, there was not the slightest sign on the wild prairie that the woodsman did not note.

Stewart was an excellent horseman and a crack shot, but he was profoundly ignorant of the American landscape. Clement knew nothing of New York, London, or Constantinople, but he was completely at home in the Rockies. Tutor and pupil switched roles with a frequency and ease that quickly created a lasting bond.[10]

At the close of the 1833 rendezvous Campbell and Sublette headed back to St. Louis, but William Drummond Stewart, after savoring the freedom of the frontier, was not prepared to return to civilization quite yet. He had paid $500 for a round trip from St. Louis to the rendezvous and back, but he decided to forfeit the return portion. A company headed by Jim Bridger and Tom Fitzpatrick had engaged Antoine Clement as their chief hunter. Throwing his plans to the winds, Stewart packed his horse and followed his new friend. Washington Irving records the dissolution of the rendezvous: "The moment Mr. Campbell and his men embarked with the peltries, Fitzpatrick took charge of all the horses, amounting to above a hundred, and struck off to the east, to trap upon Littlehorn, Powder, and Tongue Rivers. He was accompanied by Captain Stewart, who was desirous of having a range about the Crow country." No longer merely a gentleman tourist and paying guest, Stewart was about to embark on a path that would lead him very far from the aristocratic ways of his youth.[11]

As William Drummond Stewart rode off toward Crow country, William Sublette and Robert Campbell split the remaining party between them. Campbell, Nathaniel Wyeth, and Sublette's brother Milton floated the year's accumulation of furs down the Big Horn River on bull boats (improvised rafts made of buffalo hides stretched over a frame of willow branches). From the Big Horn they traveled down the Yellowstone and on to the Missouri. There they waited to reconnect with William Sublette, who had gone overland with the livestock.

The firm of Sublette & Campbell remained in operation for one more year, and then at the 1834 rendezvous the partners sold their assets to Thomas Fitzpatrick, Jim Bridger, and Milton Sublette. With the profits of the sale of their enterprise, Sublette set about improving the rough accommodations of his farm at Sulphur Springs. He contracted for the construction of six log cabins on the property and for an elegant house that he could share with Robert Campbell.

In 1835 Sublette sent Hugh Campbell a sample of the water that bubbled up from the sulphur springs that lent its name to the property. Hugh had the sample analyzed in Philadelphia and excitedly reported that it contained the same mineral content as White Sulphur Springs, the noted resort in Virginia. Sublette erected guesthouses and organized the St. Louis Jockey Club, with a horse racetrack and ninepins alley. "Sulphur Springs became a lively, idyllic retreat from the congested, polluted, expanding nearby city," Campbell's biographer records. "While health seekers bathed in the mineral waters, Sublette, with Campbell often at his side, entertained a mingled parade of mountain men, merchants, politicians, industrialists, lawyers, bankers, farmers, relatives, professors from nearby Kemper College, artists such as Alfred Jacob Miller, dilettantes such as Sir William Drummond Stewart, and various supplicants. One can imagine Campbell and Sublette, drinks in hand, discussing business strategies in the parlor, or hosting friends or investors with cards, dinner, or songs around the piano, and plying them with whiskey and cigars."[12]

The original three-year business contract for the firm of Sublette & Campbell was due to expire on January 1, 1836, so during the Christmas season of 1835 Sublette drafted a new partnership agreement, also for a period of three years, in which the couple agreed to operate a mercantile business together. Each partner was to contribute $9,700 in capital and to share equally in all profits and losses. But it was not until September of the following year that they were able to locate a suitable building, an imposing brick structure at No. 7 Main (First) Street, opposite what had been the St. Louis branch of the United States Bank. The new company of Sublette & Campbell would offer for sale "an entire new stock of goods consisting of domestic and foreign dry goods, shoes, hats, &c., which they will sell on accomodating [sic] terms, by wholesale or retail."[13]

With the opening of the Sublette & Campbell dry goods store the partners became part of the early nineteenth-century merchant/clerk culture that was described in an earlier chapter. The question necessarily arises whether St. Louis experienced the New York phenomenon of "counter-jumpers" — eager young clerks of ambiguous sexual orientation. Certainly the mercantile community of St. Louis never reached the numbers associated with that of New York City, but there is some evidence that — at least where Sublette and Campbell were concerned — employers could be unusually indulgent with clerks who were young, handsome, and single.

Charles Larpenteur, one of the partners' earliest clerks, wrote a memoir rich in appreciation of Robert Campbell. Larpenteur as a young man was determined to enter the fur trade and obtained a letter of recommendation from Maj. Benjamin O'Fallon. This he first presented to Jean Baptiste Sarpy of the American Fur Company. "As I was a young, well dressed, and not a bad-looking lad, but did not seem to be very robust, he remarked that he did not think I would answer for his purposes." Undeterred, Larpenteur next went to see Robert Campbell, who also thought him too delicate for the rugged life of the mountains but who was a bit more welcoming to the not bad-looking lad. "Being very much of a gentleman, he had the politeness to invite me to his office, and there did all he could to make me abandon the idea of taking such a trip, giving me a full description of what I should be likely to undergo. But nothing could deter me; go I must, and under the promise that he should never hear me grumble, I signed an article of agreement for 18 months." Campbell, however, was reluctant to let the young man leave St. Louis. "Now I was thus enlisted, ready for service," wrote Lapenteur, "but Mr. Campbell was kind to me and always did his best to make my situation pleasant. So he employed me in St. Louis to assist in packing goods for the upper country, and in equipping the men who were getting ready to leave with the mules for Lexington, Mo. . . . I was kept in the store until all the outfits had left St. Louis."[14]

Sublette and Campbell began their business partnership during a period when the character of the workplace in America was undergoing a radical shift, from a familial structure with the employer playing a paternalistic role, responsible for the physical and moral welfare of his employees, to a more modern corporate structure, with workplace relations based strictly on concern for the company's bottom line. As we have seen in the case of clerks in New York City, employees were expected to work at the whim of the employer and could have their hours extended or curtailed with little regard for their personal needs. In this respect Sublette and Campbell's very intimate concern for the welfare of their young male employees may have been atypical of the time — but that of course in no way confirms that there was a sexual element to their interest or that the clerks were sexually active among themselves. Scattered references to the social life of St. Louis clerks *do*, however, suggest that something similar to the scene in New York City was being reenacted on the banks of the Mississippi.[15]

In a letter to historian Hubert Howe Bancroft written in 1878, Jesse A. Applegate recalled the very personal attention he received from a representative of the American Fur Company.

Just 50 years ago I was junior clerk in the Surveyor's Office at St. Louis.... As it was my business to attend to the mails I soon became acquainted with Wilson P. Hunt P.M. at St. Louis and such intimacy as may exist between an old bachelor of 50 and an inquisitive boy of 17 soon existed between us. I boarded at the Old Green Tree Tavern and spent my evenings there or my master's study as I chose.... The Old Green Tree Tavern was the meeting place each winter of Wm L. Sublette with his partners Smith and Jackson of the American Fur Company to settle the affairs of the past year, and make their arrangements for the coming one. I was then handy with the pen and handier still with figures and <u>volunteered</u> my services as clerk to these mountaineers my sole reward being to hear them recount their adventures. They took me to places in the city after the work of the evening was done, where no youth ought to go and where I never would have ventured except under their powerful protection, and would have taken me to the Rocky Mountains if my kind master Col. McKee had not forbade it.[16]

In 1837 young Englishman Alexander Barclay, employed in St. Louis as an entry-level bookkeeper, found it expensive to maintain the proper level of sartorial display. To his sister in London he wrote that "every mechanic goes as well dressed in America as some of your more able owners of large mercantile and business houses in England, so that a clerk to keep his bearing has to keep himself at all points faultless in appearance as regards dress." He was censorious of the extent to which many of his fellow clerks took their pursuit of fashion, assuring his sister that while he was attentive to his personal appearance, he was not excessively clothes conscious. "Do not imagine I mean foppish, though a great many fall into that error." Barclay was repelled by what he saw of the licentious lifestyle of St. Louis clerks. As he contemplated abandoning his American adventure to return to England, he wrote, "I shall at least have the satisfaction to console me, that when I had a life of dissipation and reveling in reach of my unbiassed will, I chose a state where if I did no good, at least I was guilty of no crime or ill to check the conscious memory of the past."[17]

A much more explicit suggestion that homosexuality played a role in the life of the clerks of the Sublette & Campbell firm is raised by an exchange of correspondence between William Sublette and William Drummond Stewart. In 1838 Sublette wrote Stewart a letter (which, unfortunately, has not survived) that evidently detailed his complaints against a clerk named Silas who had proved to be less compliant than Sublette wished. Writing from New Orleans, Stewart expressed his sympathy: "I hope you are getting on better with your other boy than Silas who is not a Fairy." In the 1940s when historian Bernard DeVoto was researching *Across the Wide Missouri*, he encountered Stewart's letter in Sublette's papers at the Missouri Historical Society. He was taken aback by the comment, unsure what to make of it. He finally decided to include a reference to it in his book but merely commented that it was "a sentence one could wish expanded."[18]

As William Sublette and Robert Campbell struggled to make a go of their new business enterprise, their personal relationship encountered a crisis that forever changed the way the two men related to one another. In 1835 the couple made their last trip to the Rockies together. Campbell became seriously ill during the return journey and was scarcely recovered by November when he decided to visit his brother and his family. By the time he reached Philadelphia Robert was weak and exhausted, and he was immediately put to bed, cared for by his sister-in-law. Hugh Campbell, who was about to leave for a visit to Ireland, wrote to Sublette:

> Mary is a pretty good nurse — but after all I fear he will never believe he can have any nurse to be compared with you . . . if you will only contrive to come on & take lodgings with him, I think you can contrive to make the time pass agreeably until my return. . . . He is constantly talking of you and of your noble & disinterested conduct during his late dreadful illness. I know not when I was more amused than to hear of the partnership he wished to establish while suffering under the attack. He firmly believed you have divided the pain and thought

it queer that you should be moving about while he was laying prostrate. Perhaps there are few whims more rational — for your feelings, wishes, tastes, and dangers have been so much in common of late years, that a community in suffering might readily be considered as a natural consequence.[19]

With their business in St. Louis at a critical juncture, Sublette was unable to come to Philadelphia to take care of his partner, but Campbell soon found another nurse: Mary's cousin Virginia Kyle, who was visiting the family. Weak and bedridden, Robert was smitten by the young girl's inexhaustible vivacity. Hugh at first did not take the infatuation seriously. Virginia was only fourteen years old, and she exhibited no romantic feelings at all toward the thirty-one-year-old patient. That his brother, who had never shown any sexual interest in women before, should be seriously attracted to this young girl was simply beyond belief.

Hugh wrote disapprovingly to Sublette that Virginia was

tall for her years & good looking; — without having any pretensions to being a beauty. Her manners are like those of all school girls, when they get clear of the restraint of their teachers — affable and lively. I have not discovered anything like talent or genius in her conversation but she seems to have a better capacity for learning than her sister. It has been the misfortune of both sisters to have had too much latitude allowed them in their intercourse with society; — and of course to be allowed to think themselves young ladies when they were only girls. The elder sister (Ellen) has been four times regularly courted and twice engaged. Virg. has also been courted two or three times. The consequence is that both of these young ladies are more of coquettes than is agreeable to me. They talk of beaux until I am sick of the subject; — or rather untill I put a decided stop to the subject.

There was no immediate crisis to deal with, since Virginia's mother absolutely forbade her to marry before the age of eighteen. Much was likely to happen in the next four years. Hugh assured Sublette that distance would soon cool his brother's ardor.[20]

Campbell returned to Sublette in December and told him all about young Virginia Kyle. Sublette gave the romance his cautious support. As was the case with Clement and Stewart, it is likely that Campbell was closer to the heterosexual end of the Kinsey scale than was Sublette, and — perhaps of greater consequence — his Calvinist upbringing made him yearn for a more conventional, more acceptable home life. Sublette was wise enough in the ways of the world to realize that the duration of his and Robert's intimate relationship was curtailed due to the expectations of society. Now that they had left the mountains to settle in St. Louis, each would be expected to marry, and as a prospective wife this young girl appeared to offer the least possible threat to their continued intimacy. Campbell said as much, reassuring Sublette that they would continue to be close, whatever the outcome of his extended courtship: "But to tell the truth my happiness would be incomplete if I did not share it with you my dear Sublette."[21]

Over the next two years William and Hugh continued to correspond — in a sense behind Robert's back — as each tried to help the other come to terms with the unwelcome romance that showed no sign of fading quietly away. "And now William," Hugh wrote, "having scribbled nearly all my paper — let me again thank you for a letter which proves you to be no common friend to Robert. It is a pity that either, would ever get married — for you get along wonderfully." Sublette replied that he could not believe that his partner "could be over come by and blinded by love at his age as I have no doubt but he was. . . . But I am not capable of judging for I must candidly confess which you may think strange for a man of my age to say I was never seriously in Love in my life nor would I permit myself to be so for I never was in a situation to get married as that which I could wish." Sublette acknowledged the monetary benefits possible through marriage. "It's a pitty we both could not get married to wives of fifty thousand each as I have more need of her money than love or services at present and in faith I think Robert would have no objection to the cash, if so, he could keep the wife & give me the cash. We are getting on as well as could be expected but I think a wife would be of no incumbrance to one or both with a fieu shillings, if there is one of that kind please send her to me by Robert."[22]

For his part, Robert Campbell continued his courtship of Virginia Kyle with unflagging devotion, and as the girl approached closer to her eighteenth birthday her mother began to warm to the idea of the union. But then Virginia herself began to have second thoughts. Lucy Kyle advised her daughter to "never marry a man if you do not respect or esteem him more highly than any other nor if you have a secret reason (provided it is a good one) for not marrying him, which must be the case with yourself, or you never would have acted so strangely, you know you never communicated with me on the subject." Campbell's biographer wonders, "What rumors or innuendos were whispered about Robert Campbell that may have caused Virginia to doubt her commitment to him? Just how did Virginia act 'strangely'? Apparently, Virginia never revealed just what was troubling her."[23]

In July 1839 Virginia wrote to break off the engagement. Robert replied that she had "blighted the happiness through life of a Heart that Loved only you." His distress was real. No one reading Robert's letters to Virginia can doubt that his devotion to her was unfeigned; there is nothing forced or artificial about them. He was doggedly determined to get married. Virginia's eighteenth birthday came and passed, and still there was no wedding. The engagement was on, and then off, and then on again — Virginia apparently the one unable to take the solemn step.[24]

Finally, on February 25, 1841, Robert Campbell and Virginia Kyle were at last married. He was thirty-seven, and she was only nineteen. They honeymooned at Hugh Campbell's house in Philadelphia and then settled in St. Louis. Sulphur Springs was large enough to accommodate them all — especially since it had been expanded to serve as a health spa — but Campbell perhaps realized the awkwardness of that living arrangement. He and his new wife moved into a suite in the Planter's House, a hotel on Fourth Street not far from the partners' store.

Sublette wrote to William Drummond Stewart: "We are doing Business in the same places and much after the Same Old Style Only we have one more in the firm as a Silent partner as Mr. R. Campbell took it on him self whilst in Philadelphia Last February to take to him self a _____ Wife a Miss Kyle of North Carolina." The meaning of the underlined blank is unclear. Sublette had difficulty picturing his partner fulfilling the requirements of a husband. As the new couple's first anniversary approached he advised Stewart, "Sublette & Campbell still moves on much after the Same Old Style with the exception of Mr. Campbell who moves home every evening &c &c he has not made any Babeys as yet and what the Prospects is I cant say."[25]

Sublette continued to live alone in the rambling house at Sulphur Springs. Despite the constant stream of visitors, it was a lonely life without Campbell, a life that became more isolated as one after another his acquaintances wed. After writing to Stewart about Campbell's marriage, Sublette observed that "Mr. John Kerr has Been guilty of the same act Brought on a Kentucky girl about two months since So goes the World. I remain here much after the same sort George Clark turned a fool and got married & so did Mitchel to Miss Berry Coxe's Wife['s] Sister &c &c." A little over a year after his partner's marriage he wrote again to Stewart, "We are all well and I spend most of my time in the country — and I wish to God you was with me as I am still a bachelor our Friend R C I presume will be called Father Before Long. Please write me frequently."[26]

The marriage affected more than their living arrangements. In January of 1842 Sublette and Campbell agreed to dissolve their business relationship. Campbell bought out Sublette's share for $6,656.82 but continued to operate the business under the old name for the next two years. He explained the dissolution to Stewart: "Our business has been profitable and satisfactory to both Mr. Sublette and myself, and he was disposed to continue with me but now that I have become a Benedict it does not suit me to be so much absent from St. Louis and Mr. Sublette has done nothing in the business except when it was necessary to collect — We part very good friends." Campbell insisted that it was an amicable separation, but his oblique criticism of the amount of time Sublette was devoting to the business suggests dissatisfaction on his part.

Sublette — and indeed Stewart — may have placed the blame for the dissolution squarely on the marriage itself, with Virginia Campbell's intrusion into what had been a happy partnership.[27]

As Sublette explained to Hugh Campbell, he had no interest in taking a wife, except one who could bring with her a dowry of much-needed cash. He remained a bachelor — but not for want of interested partners. In his papers at the Missouri Historical Society are two letters from Mary A. Town, the daughter of the architect Sublette hired to build the resort at Sulphur Springs. When her father moved away she was forced to live with relatives in Kentucky or Ohio, but she evidently carried a torch for Sublette. Before leaving St. Louis she wrote him a plaintive note. "My Dear William," the letter began. "This is my second attempt I have made in writing a few lines to you . . . you are well aware of the love and esteem I have for you, there is know [sic] other person has a place in this heart . . . little did you think how many tears it made me shed to see that you would not confide in me so much as to let me have the scrapes of a pen from your hand. . . . My Dear do let me hear from you or I shall go crazy. . . . [C]ommit this to the flames as soon as read."[28]

Five months later she wrote again, this time from Kentucky, making it clear that she was having a difficult time accepting his silence as a rejection of her offer of love. "William if you do not answer this letter you shall despair of ever having another from me answer it on the receipt of this I shall be looking anxious every day for it. . . . If you do not intend to answer this enclose the same in a piece of paper and direct it to me — for I should dislike you to keep it to make a laugh of at my expense." It is interesting to note that Sublette neither burned the first letter nor returned the second, as she requested. We can only speculate on the reason he saved them — perhaps because he wanted to reserve the possibility of eventually taking on the role of a husband, or perhaps as proof (to others, and even to himself) that he was capable of inciting ardor in the heart of a woman.[29]

Sublette's friends worried that his reputation was being irreparably harmed by his continued involvement with the all-male community headed by William Drummond Stewart, and they urged him to follow his partner's example and get married. All of his friends were making the expected transition to becoming a husband and a father, and as the altars and baptismal fonts were increasingly frequented, Sublette's persistent bachelor status was beginning to raise eyebrows. Albert Boone, the grandson of Daniel Boone, wrote Sublette suggesting that he marry a woman named Theresa Cook. Boone conceded that Sublette had perhaps never considered such a union, but assured him that "was I placed as you are with good landed property so near the noble city that I would prefer marrying her and enjoying her society to that of all the <u>Sir Wm Stewarts</u> and <u>Mountaineers</u> and <u>Buffalows</u> that the world ever produced, for one is all fleeting show and soon vanishes, the other is real, and lasting — it certainly makes a man more happy, and much more respectable in society."[30]

William Sublette *would* eventually marry, but only at the very end of his life and only in the wake of a scandal that drove William Drummond Stewart away from America forever.

William Drummond Stewart and Antoine Clement left the rendezvous of 1833 in a party of about thirty men headed by Tom Fitzpatrick. There were at first a number of different companies that rode together or only a day or so apart, one headed by Robert Campbell, one by Benjamin Bonneville, one by Nathaniel Wyeth, one by Henry Fraeb. They traveled eastward, through the South Pass, then turned north toward the Big Horn, the Yellowstone, the Powder River, and the Three Forks. Fitzpatrick helped Campbell load his furs safely onto bull boats heading down the Big Horn on their way to St. Louis and then pointed his horses toward Crow country, accompanied by Nathaniel Wyeth, Dr. Benjamin Harrison, William Drummond Stewart, and Antoine Clement. (That Harrison continued to accompany Stewart rather than return with Sublette and Campbell further supports the suggestion that it was Stewart who invited him on the journey.)

The country of the Crows, or the Absaroka, was a large area on the Wyoming and Montana border. Until the early nineteenth century the Crows had been a loosely affiliated group of independent villages, but with the arrival of the fur trade they began to consolidate. "The fur trade offered the possibility of great wealth," explains Frederick E. Hoxie, "as well as access to the power represented by steel knives, hatchets, pack horses and rifles. In the orbit of the trade, bands could kill more game, transport more possessions over a larger area, build larger lodges and devote more energy to military competition." Though it offered the possibility of great wealth for the Indians, the fur trade also had a dark side. As Ned Blackhawk writes, "In the Great Basin, trappers vied with one another in scorched-earth trapping practices, emptying fragile watersheds of small game, while traders ferried resources into and out of the region, enmeshing Native communities in webs of economic dependence." Spurred on by the desire for the manufactured goods offered by the fur traders, the Crows expanded the territory over which they ranged and soon came in conflict with the Blackfeet, Lakotas, Cheyennes, and Shoshones. At the time that William Drummond Stewart first encountered the Crows they were going through a period of rapid social and economic change that resulted in a fundamental restructuring of their tribal institutions.[1]

The Crows had a reputation among the trappers for possessing insatiable sexual appetites, a reputation that was as unquestioningly accepted as it was unfounded. Yet in the same way that it was somehow fitting that Stewart first set foot on American soil in the sexually charged environs of New York City's Battery Park, it is particularly appropriate that his first close encounter with Native Americans was with the Crows, as they promised to fulfill all of his armchair fantasies about the virile warriors of the American Plains. As early as 1742 the French Canadian explorers Louis-Joseph and François Vérendrye dubbed the Crows the *Beaux Hommes* (beautiful men), but their tribute is merely one of the earliest in what would become a long paean to the physical attractiveness of Native American men. Rare is the early nineteenth-century writer who upon first encountering a seminaked Plains Indian does not compare him to Adonis or to the Apollo Belvedere.[2]

The physiques of the men of the Crow tribe were singled out for particular praise. "The male grown portion of the Crows are decidedly prepossessing in their appearance," wrote Edwin Thompson Denig. "The warrior class is perhaps the handsomest body of Indians in North America. They are all tall, straight, well formed, with bold, fierce eyes, and as usual good teeth. These also dress elegantly and expensively. A single dress often brings the value of two, three, or four horses. The men of this age are neat and clean in their persons, fond of dress and decoration, wear a profusion of ornaments, and have different dresses suitable for different occasions."[3]

While there are also occasional complementary mentions of Indian women's attractiveness, it was not unusual for early nineteenth-century writers to sing the praises of the men they encountered while denigrating the women. Denig himself goes perhaps further than anyone else in this regard, barely able to control his feelings of disgust.

> Of all the horrid looking objects in the shape of human beings these [Crow] women are the most so. Bad features and worse shapes, filthy habits, dresses and persons smeared with dirt and grease, hair cut short and full of vermin, faces daubed over with their own blood in mourning for dead relations, and fingers cut off so that scarcely a whole hand is to be found among them, are the principal things that attract the attention of the observer. The young women are hard, course-featured, sneaky looking, with sharp, small noses, thick lips, red eyelids caused by the venereal diseases, and bare arms clothed with a coat of black dirt so ground in as to form a portion of the skin. The old hags can be compared to nothing but witches and demons.

Self-mutilation as a sign of mourning was commonly practiced by both men and women, and any venereal disease that plagued the tribe would obviously affect both sexes, so observations by Denig and many like him are almost certainly projections, perhaps revealing more about the psychology of the writers themselves than about the Native Americans they are attempting to describe. That visitors to the American West (whatever their sexual orientation) found Native American men to be extraordinarily handsome is, nonetheless, well documented.[4]

Bernard DeVoto writes that the Crows "had a Plains reputation for pederasty but this appears to have been a libel. There were a good many 'berdashes' [sic] among them, homosexuals who dressed and lived as squaws (though many were warriors) and who had full dignity in public estimation since they were supposed to be obeying instructions given them in a vision by their medicines. But there were berdashes in all tribes." The existence of berdaches in North, Central, and South America has been documented by writers since the sixteenth century, but it was not until the 1955 article "A Note on Berdache" by Henry Angelino and Charles L. Shedd that an attempt was made to summarize and synthesize what was known about this cultural phenomenon. Angelino and Shedd noted that the term was probably derived from the Arabic *bardaj* — a kept boy, a male prostitute or catamite. It apparently entered the vernacular of the fur traders through the French *bardashe*.[5]

But when Angelino and Shedd attempted to describe the characteristics of a typical berdache, they encountered a bewildering mixture of contradictory traits, all of them at some time appearing in the writings of western observers. While in most accounts the men were described as cross-dressing male homosexuals, there were also homosexuals who did not cross-dress, transvestites who did not engage in homosexual activity, men who adopted the habits and duties of women but not their clothing, berdaches who were revered and berdaches who were scorned, individuals who were physiologically hermaphrodites, and women who cross-dressed as men — in short, over the centuries the term *berdache* had been applied to a wide range of gender-variant behaviors that had little commonality other than that they were non-normative. Angelino and Shedd proposed a definition that was inclusive enough to cover some variations but that excluded others. "In view of the data we propose that berdache be characterized as an individual of a definite physiological sex (male or female) who assumes the role and status of the opposite sex, and who is viewed by the community as being of one sex physiologically but as having assumed the role and status of the opposite sex."[6]

In general, this definition has been accepted, though a more nuanced understanding of these cultural practices indicates that when an individual adopts the role of a berdache, he or she does not become gendered as the opposite sex but instead occupies an interstitial position — a third gender. There is, however, much dissatisfaction with the term itself, with some writers arguing that the linguistic association of "berdache" with Arab boy prostitutes is inaccurate and offensive, and that "to use this term is to participate in and perpetuate colonial discourse, labeling Native American people by a term that has its origins in Western thought and languages." An alternative has been suggested with the newly coined "two-spirit," a term that has been adopted by many contemporary Native Americans (though it is not universally popular). Others reject this effort at relabeling: "Some politically correct, confessional, writers have worked in vain to introduce the term 'two-spirit' for berdache because a few present-day native gays are offended by it."[7]

As a historian of sexuality, the current author would argue that the term *two-spirit* privileges the spiritual aspects of the tradition (two-spirit rather than two-sex) to the almost explicit exclusion of the earthier, more corporeal aspects that were also a significant feature of these lives. Certainly the exchanging of a term from one colonial language for a term from another colonial language does not significantly advance the cause of cultural sensitivity. The ideal solution would be to adopt the term that these people use(d) for themselves, but such a course is not possible since each tribe had its own designation: *ake·śkassi* (Blackfeet), *heemanah* (Cheyenne), *aayahkwew* (Cree), *boté* (Crow), *ma'kali* (Flathead), *miati* (Hidatsa), *twĺinna'ek* (Klamath), *kupałke·tek* (Kootenai), *winkte* (Lakota), *alyha* (Mojave), *tai'up* (Mono), *nádleeh* (Navajo), *agokwa* (Ojibwa), *mixu'ga* (Osage), *wi-kovat* (Pima), *tïwaša* (Shoshone), *tuva'a* (Northern Paiute), *kwidó* (Tewa), *la'mana* (Zuni), to name only some. Nor would it be wise to appropriate the term *two-spirit* but translate it into one of the many Native American languages. In Shoshone a literal translation would indicate that the individual was not a real person but a ghost.[8]

In the absence of a universally accepted alternative, the present work will continue to employ the term *berdache*, though with the recognition that some may find it unsatisfactory. Despite the unpleasantness at the deep reaches of its linguistic roots, the term currently has no such connotations for most English speakers, who come to the word unaware of its Arabic origins. Sabine Lang is correct when she asserts that for scholarly purposes "replacing 'berdache' with 'two-spirit' would blur differences as well as changes that have occurred in the course of time

. . . that cannot be ignored." Lang provides an excellent overview of the genesis and diffusion of the term *two-spirit*, noting the wide range of social and political connotations it has now taken on (though her ultimate decision to use the cumbersome and linguistically imprecise "man-woman" *and* "woman-man" in its place is less than ideal).[9]

Perhaps the strongest argument for using the term *berdache* in this work of history is that it is the word recognized and employed by William Drummond Stewart and his associates. Judging from the number of corruptions of the word that appear in the literature of the period — Stewart uses the term *broadashe* — the writers were adopting a new word, rendered as they thought they heard it, for a phenomenon they had never before encountered, a term many of them did not view as a slander or slur. In Stewart's novel *Altowan*, Watoe the "broadashe" is a much-beloved figure who falls in battle while fighting valiantly to defend his non-Indian friends.

Because it is such a complex topic, with many differing manifestations and a long history of competing theories about its ontogeny and cultural significance, a detailed survey of the scholarship concerning the berdaches is beyond the scope of the current volume. (I would refer readers to the Callender and Kochems article "The North American Berdache" and to Sabine Lang's *Men as Women, Women as Men: Changing Gender in Native American Cultures*.) The present book will focus instead on the berdache tradition among the tribes that William Drummond Stewart encountered during his years in America. The goal will be to illuminate what Stewart might have experienced and to try to reconstruct the ways that those manifestations of same-sex desire among Native Americans that Stewart and his colleagues observed — or, more accurately, that they *perceived* — molded their view of the Rocky Mountains as a haven for men who were sexually attracted to other men.[10]

The Crows are a tribe for whom the tradition of the berdache was documented well into the twentieth century. In a 1919 interview with a Crow berdache named Woman Jim, Maj. Hugh L. Scott asked why he dressed in women's clothing. Woman Jim answered, "That is my road." Scott asked if a medicine man had instructed him to become a berdache, or if he had received a dream or vision concerning it. Woman Jim answered each question with a simple "No." Scott pressed the issue again by asking if a spirit had ever told him to become a berdache. "No!" Woman Jim answered in exasperation. "Didn't I tell you — that is my road? I have done it ever since I can remember because I wanted to do it. My Father and Mother did not like it. They used to whip me, take away my girl's clothes and put boy's clothes on me but I threw them away — and got girl's clothes and dolls to play with."[11]

A similar event was reported after a 1900 visit to the Crows in which an anthropologist learned that there were three berdaches among the tribe, each living in a different district. "I was told that, when very young, these persons manifested a decided preference for things pertaining to female duties, yet were compelled by their parents to wear boys' attire; as soon as they passed out of the jurisdiction of their parents, however, they invariably donned women's clothes." Such persistence in the face of parental (and, one may assume, tribal) opposition suggests that these individuals may have been transgendered, and that they were experiencing the phenomenon of having the wrong body for their own gender identity.[12]

The earliest mentions of berdaches occur in the writings of travelers who reached the Americas in the sixteenth century, and sporadic references can be found throughout the seventeenth, eighteenth, and nineteenth centuries. When in 1833 Prince Maximilian zu Wied-Neuwied parted from William Drummond Stewart in St. Louis, the prince headed north for the purpose of studying the Indian tribes along the Upper Missouri. Of the Crows he wrote, "They have many bardaches [sic] or mannish women [Mannweiber] among them, and are more so than other nations masters of unnatural practices." Maximilian's use of the term Mannweib is intriguing, as it is usually translated as "virago" or "amazon" and would suggest that he perceived the berdaches to be biologically female, though it probably reflects only the poverty of his language in explaining the gender status of the people he encountered. Certainly the phrase "masters of unnatural practices" suggests that he perceived these berdaches as men playing the role, particularly the *sexual* role, of women.[13]

Prince Maximilian ascended the Missouri River in the steamboat *Yellowstone*. Traveling at the same time in its sister ship *Assiniboin* was Edward Thompson Denig, a newly appointed clerk for the American Fur Company, whose admiration for Crow men and abhorrence of Crow women was mentioned earlier. Denig would spend the next twenty-three years among the tribes of the Upper Missouri. He, too, mentions the berdaches of the Crows, whom he labels "hermaphrodites." In this case the term *hermaphrodite* also is ambiguous, as in the mid-nineteenth century it was a commonly used term for an effeminate homosexual and did not necessarily refer to someone with both male and female genitalia. Though he wrote with unalloyed disgust about Crow women, Denig described the berdaches he encountered in terms that were surprisingly enlightened for the period. "Most civilized communities recognize but two genders, the masculine and feminine. But strange to say, these people have a neuter." Denig's impression was that berdaches were self-selected — men who from the time they were boys preferred to assume a female role. "The disposition appears to be natural and cannot be controlled," despite the disapproval of the parents. Denig says nothing about visions or religious experiences and records that the berdache is "seldom much respected by either sex."[14]

That the berdaches were not always respected from one tribe to another is indicated in a report for the winter of 1848–49 by army surgeon William Henry Corbusier. Referring to American Horse (also called Iron Plume), a minor Lakota chief, he wrote, "American Horse's father captured a Crow who was dressed as a woman, but who was found to be a hermaphrodite and was killed."[15]

Anthropologist Robert H. Lowie first visited the Crow Agency in 1907, and over the next five years he made repeated visits. In his reports on his field research he makes several references to berdaches among the Crows, indicating that the tradition had survived into the twentieth century. Lowie encountered a berdache in the Bighorn District, a man over fifty years of age who dressed as a woman. Over the years U.S.

agents had repeatedly attempted to force the *boté* (the Crow term) to wear male clothing, but they finally relented when other Indians insisted that it was "against his nature" to dress as a male. Lowie was told that the man had once fought valiantly against the Sioux, and that he was very accomplished in feminine crafts.[16]

Lowie recorded the Crow explanation for the existence of *bāté*. According to Crow tradition, the wife of Old Man Coyote (the creator spirit) and Red-Woman (a malevolent spirit) established the proper procedures for how the Crows should live — how skins should be tanned, fires started, grease extracted from buffaloes, and so on. Then:

> Old-Man-Coyote's Wife said, "I have forgotten something."
>
> Red-Woman said, "You have not forgotten anything." Red-Woman wanted all men and women to be all of the same size and to run all the same way and be the same way.
>
> "That way you'll have trouble. We'll give women a dress and leggings to be tied about the knee so they can't run, and they shall not be so strong as men."
>
> This is why men are stronger than women. They made a mistake with some, who became half-men and since then we have had *bāté*.

Lowie was not able to determine whether the idea of *bāté* as a mistake was a part of the original Crow creation myth or whether it was a twentieth-century accretion.[17]

This is the chief dilemma facing anyone attempting to understand the institution of the berdache as it was practiced and conceptualized during William Drummond Stewart's years in the West. By the time anthropologists and ethnographers arrived, the institution of the berdache was in its waning years. Informants were usually elderly and were speaking about events that had, in most cases, happened decades before, and they were speaking to outsiders who were perceived to hold very negative views of male-male sexuality (a perception that was almost universally true). Anthropologist Alfred Kroeber was aware of the limitations on his own research, writing, "While the [berdache] institution was in full bloom, the Caucasian attitude was one of repugnance and condemnation. This attitude quickly became communicated to the Indians, and made subsequent personality inquiry difficult, the later berdaches leading repressed or disguised lives."[18]

In the early years of the gay liberation movement, some historians embraced the berdaches as representatives of a halcyon era in America's past when homosexuals were honored members of their communities. Anthropologist Robert Lowie's early twentieth-century research on the Sun Dance was cited to suggest that, among the Crows at least, berdaches played an honored role in an important tribal ceremony. A close analysis of Lowie's writings, however, suggests that these historians were perhaps too sanguine in their assertions. According to Lowie, the berdache played a clearly defined — but marginal — role in the Sun Dance ceremony. A berdache was required to cut down the first tree in preparation for the erection of the sun lodge, but that tree was not subsequently used in the construction of the lodge. Lowie reports that the berdache was uncomfortable with his brief role in the spotlight. He would be forcibly brought forward "amidst the laughter of the crowd. Being ashamed, he would cover his face." Having performed his one function, he disappeared. "After felling the tree, the berdache hid in the crowd, being ashamed." These are, of course, Lowie's interpretations of how the berdache felt.[19]

By the 1930s, when Demitri Shimkin began his doctoral research on the Wind River Shoshones (partially under the direction of Lowie), he reported that the berdaches in former times were not merely nonparticipants in the traditional Sun Dance, they were actively excluded. "The old Shoshone Sun Dance," Shimkin writes in his dissertation, "allowed freely a wide range of participation to men. Many aptitudes: shamans, warriors, dancers, wise old men, industrious lodge-builders, and singers — were given opportunities for public recognition in the rite. Only fops and berdaches, for whom the Shoshone had little sympathy, played no definite part."[20]

If we assume that the berdaches once *did* play some important role in the Northern Plains Indian cultures — and most evidence suggests that they probably did — what are we able to reconstruct of their participation during William Drummond Stewart's time? Unfortunately very little with any degree of certainty. By the time anthropologists began studying the Northern Plains Indians, only among the Crows was there a remaining role designated for berdaches in such ceremonies as the Sun Dance, and that role was so attenuated as to be almost negligible. Perhaps it is necessary to look not at the few functions that managed somehow to survive into the twentieth century but instead at those that may have been transformed when outsider antipathy led to the suppression of the berdaches. Here we may have a case where the pentimento reveals more than the painting.

One aspect of the Sun Dance in particular may represent a vestige of an earlier participation by the berdaches. When George A. Dorsey observed the Arapahos in 1901 and 1902 he noted a very unusual ritual. Among the Arapahos the three most important participants in the Sun Dance were the Lodge-Maker (who was the man undergoing the painful rigors of the ceremony), the Lodge-Maker's wife, and the Transferrer, an elder member of the tribe who had himself once performed the Sun Dance. On one evening of the ceremony the elder Transferrer and the Lodge-Maker's wife went off together to a secret place and engaged in real or simulated sexual intercourse, during which the Transferrer placed a piece of root in the mouth of the wife. This she carried to her husband, kissed him, and in the process transferred the root to his mouth. The Lodge-Maker then also received a piece of root directly from the mouth of the Transferrer. Clark Wissler noted a similar procedure among the Blackfeet, adding a vivid description of the older man (referred to as the "father" in Wissler's description), who would crook his finger into the shape of a horn and bellow like a bull buffalo before having intercourse with the young wife. "As he does so," writes Wissler, "the father spits into the woman's mouth with the piece of turnip in his own."[21]

The phallic connotation of the piece of root or turnip — transferred per os among the participants — is unmistakable. The oral-genital simulation may perhaps be a vestige of a ceremony in which the berdache performed fellatio on the two most important participants in the Sun Dance, acting as mediator to transfer power from one to the other. Ceremonial sexual intercourse (usually male-female) played a documented role in Northern Plains Indian culture. Male-male oral-genital contact may have once played a similar ritual function. The sources are unclear about whether the root was whole when it was deposited in the mouth or was a masticated mush, but whether the root represented the phallus or the semen, the act retains its symbolic weight.[22]

The likelihood that this type of exchange of power via fellatio was part of the original ceremony is strengthened if A. B. Holder is correct in his 1889 essay on the Crow *boté*. Holder's professional demeanor as an anthropologist slipped when he was faced with a sexual practice far beyond his experience or understanding; he writes: "The practice of the bote among civilized races is not unknown to specialists, but no name suited to ears polite, even though professional, has been given to it. The practice is to produce the sexual orgasm by taking the male organ of the active party in the lips of the bote, the bote probably experiencing the orgasm at the same time. Of the latter supposition I have not been able to satisfy myself, but I can in no other way account for the infatuation of the act." Later Holder adds, "Pederasty is by no means unknown among the tribes of Indians where the bote is found, but the bote is less than any other a pederast. With him it is the oral and not the rectal cavity into which he admits the male organ."[23]

Ritual sexual intercourse between a man and a woman was almost always vaginal, but perhaps in the post-contact era, with the decline or disappearance of the berdache, a woman was chosen to perform the symbolic act linking two men. It should be noted how closely the idea of using a woman — or, for that matter, a berdache — as the intermediary in the ceremony matches Eve Kosofsky Sedgwick's idea of "erotic triangles" in literature, in which two males who are unable to consummate their desire for one another connect instead through having sex with the same woman. For the Plains Indians, the transfer of power that could have been done in a direct way might have been instead achieved through an intermediary, allowing both men to maintain their masculine status.[24]

While berdaches were overwhelmingly men who adopted the gender role of women, the reverse was also witnessed in a number of tribes.

One cross-dressing woman who was credited with supernatural powers was a member of the Kootenai of Montana, eastern Idaho, and British Columbia. Known by several names during her lifetime, she is called Qánqon by anthropologist Claude E. Schaeffer, though he admits that it is "a derisive term taken from her self-conferred name" (Sitting-in-the-Water-Grizzly). It is very likely that her story was known by William Drummond Stewart, as Stewart met missionary William Gray at the 1837 rendezvous only a few weeks after Gray had had an encounter with Qánqon. Gray was returning to the East Coast after helping Marcus and Narcissa Whitman establish their mission in Oregon when he and Francis Ermatinger of the Hudson's Bay Company found themselves near mutually hostile encampments of Flathead and Blackfeet Indians. The woman, whom Gray refers to as Bowdash (yet another corruption of berdache), was serving as a peace envoy, going between the two camps, dressed as a man.[25]

On June 13 Gray recorded in his diary, "We have been told that the Black Feet have killed the Kootenie woman, or Bowdash, as she is called. She has hitherto been permitted to go from all the camps, without molestation, to carry any message given her to either camp. She was with the Blackfeet that came to our camp on the third." It was reported that it took several shots to fell her, and that when Blackfeet warriors slashed at her chest and abdomen with their knives, the wounds healed themselves. Her companions, who fled, could hear her crying out with her distinctive whoop. Finally a warrior sliced open her chest and cut out a portion of her heart. After her death no wild animals disturbed her body, which gradually decayed on the spot where she was struck down.[26]

Gray would almost certainly have shared this story with his companions at the rendezvous only a few weeks later. William Drummond Stewart perhaps appropriated some of Qánqon's traits for the valiant Indian maiden Rose in his novel *Edward Warren*. In the novel Stewart gives evidence of his appreciation of strong, self-reliant women by expressing Ned's admiration for Rose's fortitude as she meets every challenge they face together. "There was a singular firmness and decision in this wild girl," the narrator records, "and I felt a delicious pleasure in making her show off in all her courage and independence." There is another possible connection between Qánqon and Rose. As described earlier, Rose first appears in the novel so convincingly cross-dressed that Ned is unable to detect that she is in actuality a woman.[27]

It was not only the phenomenon of the berdache that would catch the attention of white men who traveled to the American West in hopes of finding a safe space for their homoerotic attractions. When Francis Parkman visited the Lakota in 1846 he noted intense friendships between young male members of the tribe. "Neither should the Hail-Storm's friend the Rabbit, be passed by without notice. The Hail-Storm and he were inseparable; they ate, slept, and hunted together, and shared with one another almost all that they possessed. If there be anything that deserves to be called romantic in the Indian character, it is to be sought for in friendships such as this, which are common among many of the prairie tribes." Victor Tixier in his travels among the Osages in 1839–40 noted the same type of special male-male friendships. Tixier was present at what observers called a *danse du charbon*, a ritual celebration in preparation for a war sortie, and he described the actions of Ishta-Ska. "Married and already a father, he wanted a friend, a brother in arms: he set his choice during the dances on a young warrior of the same age as he. According to the established custom, the two young men slept for two nights in the same lodge, covered with the same bison-skin; then they exchanged ornaments and arrows and called each other brother."[28]

Among the Skidi Pawnees, according to George A. Dorsey and James R. Murie, an "unusual form of friendly attachment" was common, "which often bound two young men . . . together for life. In this formally recognized type of friendship each shared the other's joys and griefs." Among the Yumas also a special relationship could unite two men. Though there was no official ceremony creating the union, the bond between the two men was referred to as *mataxcuva'k*, a variation on the word for "married," and the two men referred to each other as *mataxavi'k*, similar to the word for "co-wife." Among the Hopis the two men would be called *na·'mi'ɩni*, or "partners," though again there was no official ceremony for declaring the special status taken on by the men. A partnership that is reminiscent of ancient Sparta was common among the Plains Cree. "When two such friends grew up and went on the warpath," writes David G. Mandelbaum, "they shared all dangers. If one were killed, the other was also usually killed. The relationship term they used was . . . *niwɩtcewahakan.*"[29]

Lowie noted a type of ritualized male-male friendship among the Crows that he dubbed "comrades," an intense relationship that could be of many years' standing. "If two boys became very intimate with each other, continuing their friendly relations even after marriage, joining in war parties, and so forth, they were regarded as comrades" and "exchange[d] gifts in the manner customary among relatives, giving each other elk-tooth dresses and other articles of value." The term *ī'rapàtse* was used among the Crows for this particular relationship, the equivalent of the especially close friendship customarily referred to as a "pardner" in cowboy slang. Lowie noted that this institution of male-male friendship was "very highly developed" also among the Dakotas, the Blackfeet, and the Cheyennes.[30]

What would have been striking to Euro-American visitors about these relationships was the fact that they were *ritualized*. The Native American men were participating in a recognized social contract; there was even a word in their language to explain the special nature of this male bonding. For visitors with even a smattering of a classical education (and many were well educated), the echoes of a Greco-Roman prototype would have been inescapable. Those who as young boys had pored over their Homer and Cicero and longed for an earlier time when male-male ardor was praiseworthy were quick to seize on the Native American model as proof that these sorts of unions were still possible. Still, it should be noted that there is no confirmed evidence that homosexual behavior was an aspect of these Native American friendship pairs. Sexual contact was almost certainly *assumed* on the part of non-Indian observers of the pairings, but it may not have actually occurred.

It is against the background of these two manifestations of male-male intimacy — the overt sexuality of the berdaches (perceived as homosexuality by outsiders who did not comprehend the berdache's interstitial gender status) and the unabashed emotional bonding of pairs of Native American comrades — that we should read William Drummond Stewart's novels. In *Altowan* the berdache Watoe is deeply enamored with the title character (Stewart's alter ego), and while Altowan does not return Watoe's sexual interest, he does feel profound affection for him — he is nearly undone by grief when Watoe is killed in an enemy raid. In his first novel Stewart was still coming to terms with his own homosexuality, and as a result he includes a wooden, perfunctory romance with the beautiful Idalie, a romance that is as unconvincing as it is abortive. With no supporting plot development Altowan suddenly decides that he must be in love with the woman — and just as quickly (within a few pages) changes his mind when he discovers she is in reality his half sister.

By the time Stewart came to write *Edward Warren*, he was more comfortable with his sexuality, and while the homosexual themes of the novel are still to some extent masked, they are covered over by only the thinnest skip coat of conventionality. Ned Warren's undisguised sexual attraction to the Indian or Métis men who capture his attention (various manifestations of the real-life Antoine Clement) reveals a longing for the type of special friendship Stewart noted among the Native Americans. As has been discussed in chapter 2, it is the intriguing sight of pairs of Indian men heading for the privacy of the tall rushes screening the river that draws Ned irresistibly toward the water, hoping to encounter his new special friend — "one of those mystic instincts which communicate between certain persons, told me plainly through every fibre in my frame, that the Indian I sought was before me" — and he reaches out to embrace the stranger in a way he would have never dared to do in Scotland.

So it was into the country of the Crows — the men reputed to be the most strikingly handsome of the Plains Indians, the tribe with berdaches who had a documented proclivity for fellatio and a social role so strongly established that its rudiments survived into the twentieth century — it was into this apotheosis of all the fantasies spun by James Fenimore Cooper novels that William Drummond Stewart now rode for the first time.

When on the fifth of September Fitzpatrick's party first made contact with the Crows, he discovered that they were not in a welcoming mood, blaming him for the murder of one of the American Fur Company factors the previous fall. As has been noted, the Crows were experiencing a period of rapid and unsettling tribal change, and since they had allied themselves closely with the American Fur Company, the murder of one of their allies by a member of a rival fur company was a matter of grave concern. Fitzpatrick had his men pitch camp and then rode off to make a ceremonial call on the village chief in hopes of smoothing over the difficulties. In his absence he left William Drummond Stewart in charge, which may be read as proof of the change in Stewart's status: already he was no longer the greenhorn on his first western tour but a trusted member of Fitzpatrick's team. Fitzpatrick warned him to be wary of any Crows who visited the camp while he was gone; in their current mood they could be easily provoked. Stewart was to be firm but not aggressive toward them until Fitzpatrick returned with a better idea of which way the wind was likely to blow. For Stewart it was a test of how skillfully he could handle himself in this unfamiliar world.

No sooner had Fitzpatrick ridden off than a party of around one hundred Crows descended on the camp. They immediately began to make themselves at home, flinging their blankets around the shoulders of the trappers in a gesture of welcome, slapping them on the back, laughing heartily. Then they began to pilfer small items. When the trappers reached for their weapons in protest, the Crows reacted in shocked offense, and Stewart gave the order for the men to stand down. Pilfering escalated to outright appropriation — blankets, traps, trading goods. Antoine Clement could understand enough of the Crow language to translate, and he explained to Stewart that the tribe's medicine man had told them that the Indians would prevail if any violence occurred — but only if the white men struck the first blow. The Crows outnumbered the trappers four to one, and any conflict would end in complete slaughter. Gritting his teeth, Stewart ordered the men not to resist. The Crows taunted and jeered, they brandished their tomahawks and hurled insults, but they could not provoke the trappers to violence. When the looting was done, the Indians rode off with all the horses, all the powder, all the guns. Even Stewart's pocket watch was taken. (Artist Alfred Jacob Miller, though not present at the event, later created a large oil painting of the scene based on his patron's description of the encounter.)[31]

When Fitzpatrick returned he found the camp completely stripped. He did not blame Stewart, agreeing that nonresistance was the only course of action to avert a massacre, but he was furious. He tore back to the Crow camp and loudly protested. "What eloquence and management Fitzpatrick made use of we do not know," writes Washington Irving (taking his account from an interview with Robert Campbell, who provided secondhand information), "but he succeeded in prevailing upon the Crow chieftain to return him his horses and many of his traps; together with his rifles and a few rounds of ammunition for each man." Fitzpatrick, according to Irving, gathered together his men and left the Crow territory as quickly as possible, catching up with Jim Bridger to rearm and reequip the party.[32]

In 1856 trader James Beckwourth published a memoir of his years in the Rockies ("written from his own dictation by T. D. Bonner"). The memoir gives a very different version of the Crow encounter. Beckwourth was a quadroon from Virginia who was employed by the American Fur Company, but he had lived with the Crows for many years, even marrying the daughter of a Crow chief. His memoir has been widely disparaged and discounted as unreliable, but much of the criticism leveled against him by historians is so tinged with overt racism that it is difficult to weigh the extent to which his account should be mistrusted. In Beckwourth's version, Fitzpatrick is being hosted in the Crow village when Beckwourth learns that some of the young men are attacking the trappers' camp. He rallies his relatives and they ride off to protect the white men, arriving only to find the camp already stripped.

I then requested each man to mount behind my relatives, and return with us to the village. All did so except Stuart. I requested him also to mount. "No," said he, "I will get on behind no d — d rascal; and any man that will live with such wretches is a d — d rascal."

"I thank you for your compliment," I returned; "but I have no time to attend to it here."

"Captain Stuart," said Charles A. Wharfield, afterward colonel in the United States army, "that's very unbecoming language to use at such a time."

"Come, come, boys," interposed Dr. Harrison, "let us not be bandying words here. We will return with them, whether for better or for worse."[33]

Beckwourth says that he conducted the party to safety in the Crow village, but he adds that Stewart almost precipitated a massacre.

I was informed subsequently that the Englishman, as soon as he approached me, cocked his gun, intending to shoot me. It was well for him, as well as his party, that he altered his mind; for, if he had harmed me, there would not have been a piece of him left the size of a five-penny bit. I was doing all that lay in my power to save the lives of the party from a parcel of ferocious and exasperated savages; his life depended by the slightest thread over the yawning abyss of death; the slightest misadventure would have proved fatal. At that moment he insulted me in the grossest manner.[34]

Beckwourth is able to use his influence with the tribe to recover and return all of the property stolen from Fitzpatrick's party — all except Stewart's horse, Otholoho.

Accordingly, he visited me, and said, "*Mr.* Beckwourth" (he mistered me that time), "can you get my horse for me?"

I replied, "Captain Stuart, I am a poor man in the service of the American Fur Company, to sell their goods and receive the peltry of these Indians. The Indian who has your horse is my best customer; he has a great many relatives, and a host of friends, whose trade I shall surely lose if I attempt to take the horse from him. Should the agent hear of it, I should be discharged at once, and, of course, lose my salary."

"Well," said he, "if the company discharge you for that, I pledge you my word that I will give you six thousand dollars a year for ten years."

"Captain Stuart is a man of his word, and able to perform all he promises," said Fitzpatrick.

"Well," replied I, "I will see what I can do."[35]

Beckwourth says he was able to recover Stewart's horse, and the party rode out of Crow country. The account may be completely fictitious, but it has in parts the ring of truth and is at base more believable than the accepted story that Fitzpatrick himself was able to use mere "eloquence and management" to talk the Crow chief into returning the confiscated goods. Indisputably, Beckwourth held a position in the tribe of sufficient authority to intervene in the way his narrative describes.

Missing from the narrative is, of course, the point of view of the "ferocious and exasperated savages" who viewed these new traders as enemies of the American Fur Company, with which (through Beckwourth) they had developed a degree of loyalty and dependence. No doubt their interpretation of the contretemps, had it survived, would vary substantially from the two recorded accounts. Stewart, however, was able to exact a type of literary retribution on the Crows who humiliated him in this, his first foray into a leadership role with the fur traders. Altowan is a member of the Blackfeet tribe — the fiercest enemy of the Crows.

There is no reliable record of where William Drummond Stewart spent the winter of 1833–34, but it is likely that he was in Taos and/or Santa Fe, as he writes that in the spring he was with Jim Bridger "in a range of mountains whose western slopes give birth to the waters of California, and near the city of Taos." (He and Antoine Clement appear to have separated, as Clement is not mentioned in any of the narratives.) In a note in *Edward Warren* Stewart relates an incident that occurred during this period, an event substantiated by a number of contemporary accounts. Not for the first nor the last time, it involves his partiality for a handsome but troubled young man. "This youth," writes Stewart, "whose name was Marshall, had become so lazy and disobedient, that Bridger and Fitzpatrick had discharged him, and he was (without an animal) obliged to follow the camp on foot. I took compassion on him and hired him, giving him traps and a mule to ride, but having found that he was perfectly unwilling to do any thing, had recourse to frequent lectures, and at last threatened to turn him adrift also."[36]

Tired of receiving lectures from Stewart about his laziness and realizing that he had already worn out his welcome with all the other men in the camp, Marshall absconded during the night with two horses (one of them Otholoho) and with Stewart's favorite Manton rifle. Stewart could hardly contain his anger after all the extra care he had lavished on the young man, "scarcely believing in such ingratitude." He was particularly humiliated because the other men chided him for being taken in by the youth, and his humiliation led him to make a rash pronouncement. "I exclaimed in my wrath, for they laughed a little at my having thought to get any good out of such a scamp, 'I'd give five hundred dollars for his scalp.'"[37]

Stewart organized a search party to go after Marshall but another member of the camp, Mark Head, found him first. In the novel Stewart describes the character "Mark Head" as "a mild looking, handsome youth, with yellow hair hanging over his shoulders," but Head was anything but mild when he tracked Marshall down: he shot him dead and took his scalp. "In the evening, between us and the sun, the loiterers of the camp saw two men leading two horses making their way towards camp, and on a rifle was displayed the scalp of the horse-thief. This was a little more than I looked for, and I tore the bloody trophy from the gun and flung it away. The horse returned to my hands, but I never afterwards crossed his back." Once again Stewart's improvident conduct toward one of the young men who had caught his fancy had resulted ultimately in the young man's death, and he made an extravagant gesture of atonement: never again riding Otholoho.[38]

It was probably during this winter and spring near Taos that Stewart first met Kit Carson, who appears under his own name as a character in *Edward Warren*. Carson makes a dramatic entrance in the novel in a scene of encoded sexual violence that casts Ned Warren (Stewart's alter ego) as a damsel in distress. Ned is attacked by a brawny, half-naked mountain man named Shunar, but he eludes the blow and is about to return it when a handsome young man riding bareback pushes his way between the combatants. "Easy, easy, Shunar," the stranger murmurs, and then adds (in a line that could have been lifted whole from a bodice-ripper romance), "that stranger belongs to me for this night; you shall have your will with him to-morrow." The narrator notes that there was "a pistol in the hand of him who thus claimed me," and when the stranger in a low voice orders Ned to jump up behind him on his horse, he quickly complies and they gallop off together. That night the claimer and the claimed share a tent — and a bed.[39]

> The light of a fire now showed me the face of my new friend, who I could perceive as he sat before me was of much shorter and slighter stature than myself; his head, without other covering than waving locks of light brown hair, was occasionally turned to me as he carolled some stanzas of the air of Bruce's march, then much the fashion among the American boys, and showed a pleasant and open countenance, with blue eyes. . . .
>
> Kit and I lay down together to be lulled by a slight murmur of the stream at a casual obstruction of rocks close to our simple bed. . . . However I had arranged to meditate in the deep stillness of the night; scarcely had the muscles of the limbs been relaxed, and the head searched out on its hard pillow the easiest spot to rest, when a gentle oblivion stole over the senses, and care was suspended until it could thrust itself among the pursuits and occupations of the coming morn.[40]

Whether or not Stewart was conscious of the degree to which he was encoding a sexual encounter with Kit Carson, his choice of words in a single sentence — muscles, deep, limbs, hard, senses, thrust, coming, oblivion — leave little doubt of what was in his imagination.

7

Stewart spent the spring and summer of 1834 hunting in the Rockies and attended that year's rendezvous, held on Ham's Fork in Wyoming. In a diary entry for June 24, 1834, William Marshall Anderson (traveling with William Sublette) writes, "Mr Stewart an Englishman & I am told a gentleman and a scholar, has just arrived from Mr Bridgers party." Sublette was carrying letters for Stewart from Scotland, including one from his younger brother George filling him in on the latest news of Murthly Castle, the first he had received in nearly two years. To his disgust he learned that the construction of the new Murthly Castle, a project launched by his brother John shortly after inheriting the estate and title, had become something of a money pit. Architect James Gillespie Graham's creation, a glorious confection of faux medieval towers and turrets (with a few Dutch guildhall elements thrown in), was rising on a large flat field adjacent to the old house. Sir John's hope was to outshine his neighbor, Lord Breadalbane, whose newly expanded Taymouth Castle was one of the opulent wonders of the Scottish countryside. For William, who was chronically short of cash, the idea of John's architectural extravagance was galling.[1]

Stewart's mood was improved somewhat by the appearance of a mysterious and handsome stranger, "a young man named Ashworth, an Englishman, blond, with tattered clothing and elegant, supercilious manners." Charles Howard Ashworth was the fifth son of Richard

Ashworth, a barrister of Pendleton, Lancashire. He is mentioned only in the journal of John Townsend, a naturalist traveling with Nathaniel Wyeth's party, which describes his unkempt appearance as he stumbled into camp hungry, bedraggled, and vague. Little would be known of his life were it not for a short article that was published in the *Manchester Herald* on September 12, 1835.

The article describes how Ashworth, though the son of a barrister and himself well educated, was in the habit whenever he had a little pocket money of traveling on foot to odd places where he would seek out the seediest part of town and remain until his funds were exhausted. Members of his family could not understand his attraction to low life, but they had come to accept his secretive comings and goings. They were therefore concerned but not surprised when, at the age of seventeen, he dropped completely from sight and they heard nothing from him for many months. He was last known to be in Liverpool, which was at that time experiencing an outbreak of cholera, and the family feared that he had succumbed to the disease. Then to everyone's relief they received a letter from him written in the Sandwich Islands, letting them know that he was alive and well, though penniless. The newspaper article reprinting his letter carried the ironically understated title "Extraordinary Instance of Youthful Enterprize."[2]

"He has since," the article read, "without the means being afforded his family of sending him any supplies, from the utter uncertainty of his position at any given time, travelled, chiefly on foot, up as far as Fort St. Louis, Upper Mississippi — visited Lake Michigan — joined a company of fur traders — passed over the continent of North America — gone down the coast, in company with a Captain Stewart, for 200 miles — and embarked from the mouth of the Columbia, whence he reached Onolula, one of the Sandwich Islands in the Pacific, and was heard from through the brig *Eagle*, lately arrived from that quarter."[3]

Ashworth wrote to his family of his deep gratitude to the American Indians he had encountered, whose kindness and hospitality to strangers were at odds with the stereotype he had been led to expect. "He says, in the last letter, received by his eldest brother, the Rev. T. A. Ashworth, that what are called the *savage and blood-thirsty* children of the desert have ever been most kind to him, and in their wigwams he has chiefly slept, at their simple board most commonly eaten, and been welcome without money and without price; but that frequently also he had the wilderness for his couch, and the desert air for his supper."[4]

The Manchester newspaper article was picked up and reprinted by the *Army and Navy Chronicle* of November 19, 1835, where it caught the eye of a reader who responded with his own view of the young traveler. "In perusing the account of this youthful adventurer," the reader wrote to the editor of the *Chronicle,*

> his destitute situation, his sufferings and travels with the Indians, and visit to Lake Michigan, I was forcibly reminded of a young man who, in the fall of 1833, passed a day or two in the house of the Agent of the American Fur Company at this place; and finally made his appearance at my quarters, inside the fort. His appearance was most forlorn; his principal raiment consisted of a buckskin hunting shirt; he was starved, pale, and sick with the ague and fever. He enquired for employment as a clerk; after some talk, I told him the impossibility of getting employment among strangers with appearances so much against him. Becoming interested for him, and truly commiserating his situation, I advised him to apply to the recruiting officer and enlist — if, upon inquiry in town, he should be able to do no better. After a day or two he was enlisted, taken into the hospital, cured, well clothed, and fed. Immediately after having possessed himself of all these necessaries and comforts, he deserted the service, which had taken him from the most abject want, and which he had sworn, faithfully, to maintain and perform. He appeared to have been well educated, both morally and literally.

The reader included a detailed description of the deserter: "Charles H. Ashworth, 19 years old, 5 feet 11½ inches high, light complexion, blue eyes, light hair; born in the County of Lancaster, England. Enlisted on the 22d day of October, 1833, at Fort Dearborn, by Lieut. Thompson, for three years. Deserted 23d Jan., 1834, from Fort Dearborn." Ashworth wandered westward for the next six months, and entered the trappers' camp once again tattered and hungry.[5]

He did not need to subsist on the desert air for his supper once he stumbled across the fur traders' rendezvous, for he was soon taken under Stewart's wing. There was probably not a sexual connection, as well-educated supercilious blonds were not Stewart's preferred type, but Ashworth was able to take advantage of Stewart's penchant for attractive waifs and wastrels. Stewart provided the young man with a horse, a gun, and a blanket, and welcomed him into his own mess. Botanist John Townsend, a member of the party, records in his journal several incidents involving Ashworth but includes no information about his background — not even his given names. Townsend had a scientist's eye for detail and an encyclopedic memory about his experiences on the trail, and so the total absence of any biographical information about Ashworth strongly suggests that the young man did not provide any.

It may seem strange that Ashworth was able to insinuate himself so quickly into the group while being reticent to share information about himself, but he was probably accepted without much fuss on the mistaken assumption that he represented a familiar type in the American West: the remittance man. For most of the nineteenth century, English families sent their black sheep abroad with the understanding that, in exchange for a steady allowance, or remittance, they would conduct their dissolute lifestyles in distant lands, keeping the shadow of scandal from the family hearth. Since quite a few men in the western wilderness had biographical details they would just as soon not share with others, an etiquette developed under which everyone agreed not to pry. As a result, the historical record contains many brief sketches of mysterious men who to the modern reader are maddeningly elusive.

Visitors to the American Fur Company's Fort Union would, for example, encounter James Archdale Hamilton Palmer, who served as adjutant to Kenneth McKenzie, "the King of the Missouri." The two men reigned in regal splendor over the American Fur Company's holdings. Charles Larpenteur, who was for many years the chief clerk at Fort Union, recalled his eccentric employer:

As I have had frequent occasion to mention Mr. "Hamilton," I will introduce him to the reader. His real name was Archibald Palmer. He was an English nobleman who had been obliged to leave England and come to America, apparently without any means. How Mr. McKenzie became acquainted with him I am not able to say. Mr. Hamilton was a man of uncommon education, conversant with many subjects, and quite capable of keeping books. As Mr. McKenzie required a bookkeeper at Fort Union, he made arrangements with Mr. Hamilton to come here. What salary he received I never learned. Mr. Hamilton — as I shall continue to call him, for his real name was not known until after he left Fort Union and his English difficulties were over, when he resumed his proper name — was a man of fifty, who had habitually lived high, in consequence of which he had the gout. This brought him to the two extremes of being either very pleasant or very crabbed, but, upon the whole, kept him crabbed; so he was not liked, though much respected.[6]

Hamilton was "an object of wonder and gossip" in the region. He insisted on bathing and putting on a new clean shirt every day. He had intense contempt for the Native Americans who came to trade at Fort Union, and once threw a beautiful silk handkerchief into the fire because an Indian had picked it up to examine it. "Hamilton wore only the finest clothes and always dressed in the latest London fashions," one historian writes. "Every year boxes were sent from London to St. Louis and then forwarded to him at the mouth of the Yellowstone. The trader wore ruffled shirt fronts, a great gold chain about his neck, and was always polished, well-scented, and oiled."[7]

McKenzie and Hamilton furnished their rooms at Fort Union with art prints and luxury goods as fine as they could procure, and were gracious hosts to the wide variety of Americans, Canadians, and Europeans who visited Fort Union. "They were worldly gentlemen," writes Bernard DeVoto, "good talkers, of quick minds and a rich past. . . . They ran a good drawing room in the Assiniboin country." While expansive in their hospitality to visitors, McKenzie and Hamilton held themselves aloof from the rough employees within the enclosed world of Fort Union. It may be inferred from Larpenteur's reminiscences of his years with McKenzie and Hamilton that the managers maintained a social distance even from their own clerks. Larpenteur was able to learn little about what brought the two men together.[8]

William Drummond Stewart and Kenneth McKenzie met probably in the spring of 1833, and Stewart felt comfortable enough in the relationship later to write a letter of protest to McKenzie after Fitzpatrick's outfit was stripped of its belongings by the Crow Indians. The Crows, as has been noted, had allied themselves with McKenzie's American Fur Company. After the incident, in a letter to Hudson's Bay Company's governor David Mitchell, McKenzie mentions "my friend Captain Stewart," so while the relationship was perhaps at times strained, there seems to have been a mutual regard.[9]

The rendezvous of 1834 was attended by a wide variety of traders, trappers, and fellow travelers. Besides William Sublette, and in competition with him, was Nathaniel Wyeth. Wyeth had contracted the previous year with Milton Sublette, William's younger brother, to supply the Rocky Mountain Fur Company trappers in 1834, but when Wyeth appeared with his trade goods the company repudiated the contract and paid him a $500 forfeiture, taking their business to William Sublette instead. Wyeth found himself in the Rockies with a full complement of goods and almost no one willing to buy them from him. The reasons why Milton would agree in the first place to do business with a supplier other than his own brother are complex, probably involving a large dose of sibling rivalry. Milton suffered from a "fungus" caused by an old leg wound (probably osteomyelitis); in February 1835 he would have his leg amputated, and in April 1837 he died at his brother's estate at Sulphur Springs at the age of thirty-six.[10]

Traveling with Wyeth were mineralogist Thomas Nuttall, botanist John Townsend, and Capt. Joseph Thing, a navigator intent on measuring the route to the Pacific by observing the stars. Also in the entourage were two Methodist ministers, Jason Lee and his nephew Daniel Lee, together with three lay missionaries, hoping to establish a mission to the Flatheads and Nez Percés.

Writing in his diary one Sunday while on the trail, Rev. Jason Lee expressed his conviction that his fellow travelers were firmly on the road to perdition.

> This seems more like Sabbath than any we have passed since we left the settlements. The rain prevents the men from being out hallooing cursing and shooting. . . . I have no doubt that many are complete Infidels who have taken but very little thought of the subject. They know that if future rewards and punishments await mankind that the scenes which await them as individuals unless their characters are changed (of which they see little prospect) are appalling indeed and[,] ardently and vehemently desiring that it may not be so[,] they by the assistance of Satan easily persuade themselves that a compassionate God will make some more merciful disposition of man than to punish him forever though he may have done wrong and they soon persuade themselves that Christianity can not be true[,] according to that system apparently few will be saved.[11]

Rev. Lee discovered that the men with whom he was traveling were not hostile to religion so much as indifferent to it — a stance he in his burning religious fervor found completely incomprehensible. Their hope of a "merciful disposition," their belief that a just God would look at the circumstances of their rough life, understand the exigencies behind their inevitable transgressions, and give them a free pass to heaven, did not fit easily into the minister's conservative Methodism.

But when the party reached the rendezvous site, Rev. Lee came to believe that even agnostic indifference might be preferable to what he encountered there. In the camp were men who had spent the year enduring the hardships of a trapper's life, and for the next few weeks they fully intended to drink, dance, gamble, fight, and fornicate, and they did not welcome any greenhorn preacher's concern for the fate of their immortal souls. "They threatened that when we came they would give them Missionaries 'hell,'" Lee wrote, "and Capt. W. informed us and advised us to be on our guard and give them no offense and if molested to show no symptoms of fear and if difficulty did arise we might depend upon his aid for he never forsook any one who had put himself under his protection."[12]

Rev. Lee did not shrink from the threat. When he arrived at the rendezvous he went directly to William Sublette's tent and introduced himself. He was welcomed warmly, and in turn he was presented to many of the men who had expressed objections to his presence at the rendezvous. He and Sublette "spent some time in conversation with them on the difficulties of the route, changes of habit and various topics," and the men found enough common ground to call a truce. "How easy for the Lord," wrote Rev. Lee, "to disconcert the most malicious and deep laid plans of the devil."[13]

Soon another party arrived, this one headed by Edward Christy, and the rendezvous swelled into full celebration. William Anderson recorded in his diary: "Yells, songs and oaths are heard all day and all night long. Like flies on a sugar barrel, or niggers at a corn shucking, the red-skins are flocking to the trading tents. We have now perhaps not less than fifteen hundred around us." Anderson also records the unsettling presence of Baptiste Charbonneau, son of the legendary Sacagawea. The melancholy young man came to the 1834 rendezvous with a compelling history.[14]

Jean-Baptiste Charbonneau was born in the course of the Lewis and Clark expedition and was later informally adopted by William Clark, who offered a home for him in St. Louis and oversaw his education. In 1823, when the twenty-five-year-old Duke Paul Wilhelm of Württemberg first visited St. Louis, he was drawn to the young man. "Here I found a youth of sixteen," the duke later wrote, "whose mother was of the tribe of Sho-sho-ne, or Snake Indians, and who had accompanied the Messrs. Lewis and Clark to the Pacific ocean in the years 1804 to 1806 [as] an interpretress. This Indian woman was married to the French interpreter of the expedition, Toussaint Charbonneau by name. Charbonneau rendered me service also, some time later in the same capacity, and Baptiste, his son (the youth of sixteen) of whom I made mention above, joined me on my return and followed me to Europe, and has remained with me ever since."[15]

Baptiste was eighteen, not sixteen, at the time but appeared younger. Sacagawea had died (reportedly of "putrid fever"), but both Toussaint Charbonneau and William Clark realized the great opportunity Duke Paul Wilhelm was presenting by offering to take the youth under his wing, and with their blessing Baptiste sailed for Europe with his new patron, eventually settling in the duke's eleventh-century castle on the outskirts of Stuttgart. The two traveled extensively, and Baptiste became fluent in Spanish and German (he was already fluent in French and English, and perhaps a least one Indian language). He received a classical education and developed an appreciation for European art and music. Sacagawea's son was only the first of many protégés gathered by the German nobleman on his journeys. "Over the years, Duke Paul brought back several foreign boys from his various travels, including a mixed blood Mexican, two Africans, and a 'small Indian' named Antonio."[16]

Regardless of his private interests Paul Wilhelm was expected to take a wife, and in 1827 he performed his duty, wedding Princess Sophie Dorothea Caroline of Thurn und Taxis. The marriage lasted less than a year but did produce the required heir. At the time of her lying-in Princess Sophie had already separated from her husband and returned to her family, leaving the duke free to pursue his friendship with Baptiste and other exotic lads. Recent scholarship suggests that Baptiste fathered an illegitimate child while in Germany, but that the infant died at only three months old. If the record is indeed accurate, this would appear to be a case of youthful heterosexual experimentation. Baptiste never acknowledged the woman or her child, and he remained a lifelong bachelor.[17]

In 1829, after nearly six years abroad, Duke Paul Wilhelm and Baptiste Charbonneau returned to America for the first time, arriving in St. Louis at the beginning of December. The couple traveled up the Missouri as far as Fort Union but there they separated, with Charbonneau heading out into the wilderness on his own. Perhaps with his return to America, Baptiste began to feel uncomfortable with the relationship.

Perhaps at twenty-four he had grown too old to continue to engage the duke's interest. The details of the rupture have never been revealed.

In the mid-1950s historian Clyde Porter (husband of Mae Reed Porter) began to explore the life of Baptiste Charbonneau. He learned that an elderly Jesuit then teaching at St. Louis University had as a young man begun a biography of Baptiste, and Porter was intrigued that the research had been started during a period when it was still possible to locate individuals who had known Sacagawea's son personally. Porter wrote to the Jesuit in St. Louis, asking if there was anything remaining of his research materials that Porter might consult for his planned biography. The priest replied that he had dropped the project long ago after he had been told a "loathsome" story about Baptiste. Porter himself never completed his planned biography.[18]

At the 1834 rendezvous Baptiste Charbonneau appeared sullen and volatile, at turns manically active and darkly withdrawn. Anderson recorded that "there is something whispered which makes him an object of much interest to me." After years of living abroad Charbonneau was unsure of where he fit in. He was not European nor French Canadian, not Anglo nor Shoshone. In their respective diaries both William Anderson and Jason Lee describe a dramatic scene that unfolded one night around the campfire. A few drunken trappers began stomping and whooping and whirling, pretending to perform an Indian war dance. When they had had their fun and collapsed in exhausted laughter, several young Indians and two or three Métis, led by Baptiste Charbonneau as the "principal actor in this scenic representation," took their places around the fire and with great dignity and respect performed the traditional dance properly, chanting the ancient chants around the flickering flames as the white men looked on in hushed awe.[19]

Finding himself unable to sell his goods at the rendezvous, Nathaniel Wyeth decided to construct a trading post on the Lewis River (the post was called Fort Hull, after the chief partner in his enterprise) where he hoped he could drum up sufficient business to salvage the trip from complete economic disaster. His plan was then to proceed to the mouth of the Columbia to meet his ship the *Mary Dacre*, which had sailed from Boston around the Horn. William Drummond Stewart decided to ride with Wyatt's party. On July 2 John Townsend recorded in his diary: "We were joined at the rendezvous by a Captain Stewart, an English gentleman of noble family, who is travelling for amusement, and in search of adventure. He has already been a year in the mountains, and is now desirous of visiting the lower country [i.e., west of the Rocky Mountains], from which he may probably take passage to England by sea. Another Englishman, a young man, named Ashworth, also attached himself to our party, for the same purpose."[20]

The first day the party traveled as far as Muddy Creek on the Bear River and camped for the night. It was the Fourth of July. "This being a memorable day," Townsend wrote, "the liquor kegs were opened, and the men allowed an abundance. We, therefore, soon had a renewal of the coarse and brutal scenes of the rendezvous. Some of the bacchanals called for a volley in honor of the day, and in obedience to the order, some twenty or thirty 'happy' ones reeled into line with their muzzles directed to every point of the compass, and when the word 'fire' was given, we who were not 'happy' had to lie flat upon the ground to avoid the bullets which were careering through the camp." Captain Wyeth himself took part in the festivities. Normally rather taciturn and sober in his entries, he recorded in his diary for the Fourth of July, "I gave the men too much alcohol for peace took a pretty hearty spree myself."[21]

About a week later Wyeth's party encountered another large group of travelers, this one led by Capt. Benjamin Bonneville. While the party itself continued on its way, Wyeth and Stewart rode off to pay a social call on Captain Bonneville, one that the captain perhaps came to regret. Townsend records the story Wyeth told upon rejoining his men.

He and Captain Stewart were received very kindly by the veteran, and every delicacy that the lodge afforded was brought forth to do them honor. Among the rest, was some *metheglen* or diluted alcohol sweetened with honey, which the good host had concocted; this dainty beverage was set before them, and the thirsty guests were not slow in taking advantage of the invitation so obligingly given.

Draught after draught of the precious liquor disappeared down the throats of the visitors, until the anxious, but still compliant captain, began to grow uneasy.

"I beg you will help yourselves, gentlemen," said the host, with a smile which he intended to express the utmost urbanity, but which, in spite of himself, had a certain ghastliness about it.

"Thank you, sir, we will do so freely," replied the two worthies, and away went the metheglen as before.

Cup after cup was drained, until the hollow sound of the keg indicated that its contents were nearly exhausted, when the company rose, and thanking the kind host for his noble entertainment, were bowed out of the tent with all the polite formality which the accomplished captain knows so well how to assume.[22]

On July 14 the party halted "upon the banks of the noble Shoshoné or Snake river," and construction began on Fort Hall, the trading post that Wyeth hoped would provide him a base for commerce in the region. While most of the men set to work felling trees and digging post holes, twelve set out on a hunting expedition to supply the camp. Townsend, who rode with the hunters, does not mention if Stewart was one of the twelve but it is likely that he was, as he was one of the best shots and was carrying the finest rifle. "Mr. Ashworth has also consented to join us," Townsend records. The young Englishman had decided to stick close to his noble protector, or perhaps he merely wanted to avoid the arduous labor involved with the construction of the fort. "There will be but little hard work to perform [on the hunt]," the naturalist notes in his journal, "our men are mostly of the best, and no rum or cards are allowed."[23]

The next two weeks would be the epitome of what Stewart had come to America seeking. The men hunted buffalo, prepared the meat, watched for Indians, slept under the stars. Even for Townsend, who was an academic and no sportsman, the expedition took on something of the aspect of a dreamlike idyll.

It is true we have nothing but meat and good cold water, but this is all we desire: we have excellent appetites, no dyspepsia, clear heads, sharp eyes, and high spirits, and what more does a man require to make him happy?

We rise in the morning with the sun, stir up our fires, and <u>roast</u> our breakfast, eating usually from one to two pounds of meat at a morning meal. At ten o'clock we lunch, dine at two, sup at five, and lunch at eight, and during the night-watch commonly provide ourselves with two or three "hump-ribs" and a marrow bone, to furnish employment and keep the drowsy god at a distance.

Our present camp is a beautiful one. A rich and open plain of luxuriant grass, dotted with buffalo in all directions, a high picturesque hill in front, and a lovely stream of cold mountain water flowing at our feet. On the borders of this stream, as usual, is a dense belt of willows, and under the shade of these we sit and work by day, and sleep soundly at night.[24]

The men slept soundly — except when grizzly bears visited the camp under the cover of darkness, drawn by the smell of blood and drying meat. The men could hear the huge bears grunting and snorting in the bushes, scraping and tramping, their large paws shaking the ground and their snouts emitting loud snuffling wheezes as they followed the scent of blood. The hunters would lie quietly in their bedrolls, tense with suspense to see if the bears would come any closer, but any sharp noise from the camp would send "old Ephraim" lumbering away.

Townsend had a closer encounter with a grizzly one day while hunting by himself. Sauntering near a copse of willow and current bushes, he heard an angry growl and grunt "and instantly after, saw a grizzly bear of the largest kind erect himself upon his hind feet within a dozen yards of me, his savage eyes glaring with horrible malignity, his mouth wide open, and his tremendous paws raised as though ready to descend upon me." The naturalist, at first frightened witless, gathered his courage, raised his rifle, and prepared to empty both barrels into the snarling monster. For a moment they stood staring at one another, then Townsend began to retreat slowly, step by step, creeping backward. When he felt there was enough space between him and the bear, he turned and ran with all the speed he could muster all the way back to the camp.[25]

To his astonishment, when he told his fellows about the close encounter, Charles Ashworth announced that he wanted to go kill the bear and asked to borrow Townsend's double-barreled gun. Townsend at first refused, and all of the men tried to talk the young Englishman out of doing something so foolish, but when it became clear he was determined to go after the grizzly, even if it meant arming himself with only a light rifle, Townsend relented. The men watched Ashworth head toward the copse where the grizzly was last seen, "then, with a sigh that one so young and talented should be lost from amongst us, and a regret that we did not forcibly prevent his going, I sat myself down, distressed and melancholy." The camp held its collective breath, listening anxiously for the double report of the rifle — or for snarls and a death scream. After an agonizing few minutes of suspense, Ashworth slowly sauntered back, appearing angry and disappointed. He had found many tracks, but no bear.[26]

One day a Nez Percé Indian visited the hunters' camp and Townsend, like so many other travelers of the period, was fascinated by the athletic beauty of the man's near-naked body. "But his person was a perfect wonder," Townsend recorded,

and would have served admirably for the study of a sculptor. The form was perfection itself. The lower limbs were entirely naked, and the upper part of the person was only covered by a short checked shirt. His blanket lay by his side as he sat with us, and was used only while moving. I could not but admire the ease with which the man squatted on his haunches immediately as he alighted, and the position both of body and limbs was one that, probably, no white man unaccustomed to it, could have endured for many minutes together. The attitude, and indeed the whole figure was graceful and easy in the extreme; and on criticising his person, one was forcibly reminded of the Apollo Belvidere [i.e., Perseus] of Canova.[27]

The hunters encountered a group of trappers headed by Thomas McKay, the stepson of the chief factor of the Hudson Bay Company at Fort Vancouver, and McKay traveled with the hunters back to the construction site of Fort Hall. The party had been gone for two weeks and when its members returned, laden down with buffalo meat, they discovered that the rest of the men had been subsisting on a starvation diet. Townsend was shocked when he saw his fellow scientist Thomas Nuttall.

> My companion, Mr. N., had become so exceedingly thin that I should scarcely have known him; and upon expressing surprise at the great change in his appearance, he heaved a sigh of inanity, and remarked that I "would have been as thin as he if I had lived on old Ephraim for two weeks, and short allowance of that." I found, in truth, that the whole camp had been subsisting, during our absence, on little else than two or three grizzly bears which had been killed in the neighborhood; and with a complacent glance at my own rotund and cow-fed person, I wished my poor friend better luck in the future.[28]

It was the end of July and McKay was eager to get on his way to return to the Hudson's Bay headquarters. Both William Drummond Stewart and Jason Lee (together with his missionary party) decided to join McKay for the rest of the journey to the Pacific. There was still much construction work to do on Fort Hall before Wyeth could depart, and the missionaries hoped that by getting a head start they and their slow-moving herd of farm cattle would no longer impede the party's progress. Stewart had evidently grown tired of Ashworth, or felt the younger man no longer needed a protector, for the Englishman stayed at Fort Hall. The two parties agreed to rendezvous at Fort Walla Walla and then descend the Columbia River together.

The McKay party traveled northwesterly through the mountains. Here the terrain was steep and perilous but breathtakingly beautiful. Rev. Lee recorded in his diary:

> Started out hunting in company with Capt. Stewart and one other. We ascended a very high mountain in search of sheep. We were obliged to climb it in a zigzag direction and I think we ascended 3000 ft. above the level of the prairie on which it is based and still there were

others whose summits were above us. We commenced descending on the opposite side and [I am] persuaded we passed places with our mules that it would be utterly impossible to pass with a horse. The rocks were what they call cut rocks composed of quartz and we passed over some piles of them where the mules were forced to leap from one rock to another and there were so many creveses and the rocks were so sharp that I would scarcely [have] thought it possible for them to pass without breaking their legs. . . . While looking about the base of the mountain for game I heard stone ratling down the side of it and concluded that they started themselves as it appeared impossible for any animal to climb a mountain which appeared almost perpendicular but on more minute observation I discovered sheep nearly to the top but the distance was such that I could but just discern them[,] but by help of a small telescope I saw probibly a hundred and they looked very beautiful but we could not get at them.[29]

Rev. Lee also records in his diary that along the way he read a copy of Lord Byron's drama *Sardanapalus*, which almost certainly was lent to him by Stewart. The play tells the story of the king of Nineveh and Assyria, who first appears onstage "effeminately dressed, his Head crowned with Flowers, and his Robe negligently flowing." When his kingdom is threatened, Sardanapalus puts aside his female drag, robes himself like a warrior king, and with manly courage defends his throne. It is not clear why this particular (and very minor) work of Byron resonated so deeply with Stewart, but perhaps in recommending the play he sought to convey something significant about his own behavior. Whatever his reasons, the play is an odd choice to recommend to a Methodist minister. Rev. Lee was not impressed with what he read, noting in his diary, "I do not think that sort of writing will tend to better the heart or mend the life though it may inform the head."[30]

Meanwhile, back at Fort Hall construction had progressed to the point where Captain Wyeth felt he could continue on his journey, leaving only a few men to finish and staff the trading post. As usual, a celebration was in order, and as usual, the men got roaring drunk. "All in camp were then allowed the free and uncontrolled use of liquor," recorded John Townsend, "and, as usual, the consequence was a scene of rioting, noise, and fighting, during the whole day; some became so drunk that their senses fled them entirely, and they were therefore harmless; but by far the greater number were just sufficiently under the influence of the vile trash, to render them in their conduct disgusting and tiger-like. We had 'gouging' [of eyeballs], biting, fisticuffing, and 'stamping' [of testicles] in the most 'scientific' perfection. . . . Such scenes I hope never to witness again; they are absolutely sickening, and cause us to look upon our species with adhorrence and loathing."[31]

Two days later, leaving a dozen men behind to complete the trading post, Wyeth set off for the Pacific. He was joined by Paul Richardson, a seasoned hunter who reminded Townsend of James Fenimore Cooper's character Hawkeye. Following a different course than that chosen by McKay and Stewart, the party soon found itself in a barren desert. Wyeth records laconically in his diary that "the day was hot and we suffered some for water and found but a small supply on the N. side of the Bute a miserable chance for our horses and not a good one for ourselves." With the greater scientific precision of a naturalist, Townsend described the same scene:

> We saw not a drop of water during the day, and our only food was the dried meat before spoken of, which we carried, and chewed like biscuits as we travelled. There are two reasons by which the extreme thirst which the way-farer suffers in these regions, may be accounted for; first, the intense heat of the sun upon the open and exposed plains; and secondly, the desiccation to which every thing here is subject. The air feels like the breath of a sirocco, the tongue becomes parched and horny, and the mouth, nose, and eyes are incessantly assailed by the fine pulverized lava, which rises from the ground with the least breath of air.[32]

The men sucked on bullets, pebbles of chalcedony, and smooth pieces of obsidian to try to slake their thirst. They shot a stray buffalo and were able to make several meals from his meat, but their supplies soon grew slim again. On the twelfth of August they began to climb into the mountains but discovered there was no pass and were forced to backtrack. It was another week before they succeeded in finding a passable trail and began their ascent. Here they encountered a band of Snake Indians and were able to barter for a supply of dried and fresh salmon sufficient to get them to Fort Walla Walla, where they hoped to rendezvous with McKay, Stewart, and Rev. Lee.

One day while Wyeth was busy trading with the Indians, Townsend looked up and saw "Hawkeye" Richardson and Charles Ashworth riding into the camp. Ashworth, he could see, was angry and upset.

> I felt very certain that no ordinary matter would be capable of ruffling this calm, intrepid, and almost fool-hardy young man. He said that while riding about five miles behind the party, (not being able to keep up with it on account of his having a worn out horse,) he was attacked by about fifty of the Indians whom we passed earlier in the day, dragged forcibly from his horse and thrown upon the ground. Here, some held their knives to his throat to prevent his rising, and others robbed him of his saddle bags, and all that they contained. While he was yet in this unpleasant situation, Richardson came suddenly upon them, and the cowardly Indians released their captive instantly, throwing the saddle bags and every thing else upon the ground and flying like frightened antelopes over the plain. The only real damage that Mr. Ashworth sustained, was the total loss of his saddle bags, which were cut to pieces by the knives of the Indians, in order to abstract the contents. These, however, we think he deserves to lose, inasmuch, as with all our persuasion, we have never been able to induce him to carry a gun since we left the country infested by the Blackfeet; and to-day, the very show of such a weapon would undoubtedly have prevented the attack of which he complains.[33]

When Richardson rode up to rescue him, Ashworth was on his back on the ground, wielding his only weapon: a buffalo hide whip. This he "applied with great energy to the naked backs and shoulders of the Indians," but he was unable to stop the theft of his property. The situation was dramatic and desperate, with the solitary and terrified young man being robbed by a band of knife-wielding attackers, but Richardson — and later Townsend — saw only humor in the scene. "Richardson gives an amusing account of the deportment of our young English friend while he was lying under the knives of his captors. . . . Richardson, says, that until he approached closely, the blows were descending in rapid succession, and our hunter was in some danger of losing his characteristic dignity in his efforts to repress a loud and hearty laugh at the extreme ludicrousness of the whole scene."[34]

It had been nearly two months since the young Englishman with the elegant manners first drifted into camp, tattered, hungry, and weaponless. In the interim he had traveled with the others, hunted with them, starved with them, and shared the hardships of heat and cold — but still at base he was viewed as an object of humor. Captain Wyeth records in his journal that some Indians tried to steal some of their horses that evening and also that he found a scorpion in his blanket, but he does not make even a passing mention of the violent attack on a member of his party. Though one might expect some level of empathy from the Philadelphia naturalist Townsend or the Harvard botanist Nuttall, Ashworth remained for them to the very end a faintly ridiculous figure.

On August 24 Wyeth wrote, "This day at noon parted from Richardson and 8 men to go up Malheur and other creeks to trap there is something melancholy in parting with men with whom one has travelled so far in this uncertain country. Our party is now 17 boys Indians literati and all." A week later the party encountered two of the men from the McKay party, who informed them that Captain Stewart and Rev. Lee had passed that point only two days previously.[35]

Stewart and Lee reached the Hudson's Bay Company post at Walla Walla on September 2 (McKay himself had chosen to remain in the mountains). They were exhausted and unwell. Though they hoped to find a wider variety of food at the settlement, they encountered only "corn and flour, salt, a little fat, and [a] few fish from the Indians." They had been living largely on salmon for over three weeks, and Stewart had become dangerously ill. "Capt. Stewart killed a horse for meat," recorded Rev. Lee, "being the only kind he could get here, as he could not eat fish." Back on the trail, Townsend and his party were experiencing the same problem. "The sudden and entire change from flesh exclusively, to fish, ditto, has affected us all more or less, with diarrhœa and pain in the abdomen; several of the men have been so extremely sick, as scarcely to be able to travel; we shall, however, no doubt, become accustomed to it in a few days."[36]

Townsend did eventually adjust to the change in diet, and as they approached Fort Walla Walla and the relative refinement represented by the Hudson's Bay Company outpost there, the men began to concern themselves with their personal appearance.

> As we were approaching so near the abode of those in whose eyes we wished to appear like fellow Christians, we concluded that there would be a propriety in attempting to remove at least one of the heathenish badges which we had worn throughout the journey; so Mr. N.'s razor was fished out from its hiding place in the bottom of his trunk, and in a few minutes our encumbered chins lost their long-cherished ornaments; we performed our ablutions in the river, arrayed ourselves in clean linen, trimmed our long hair, and then arranged our toilet before a mirror, with great self-complacence and satisfaction. I admired my own appearance considerably, (and this is, probably, an acknowledgement that few would make,) but I could not refrain from laughing at the strange, party-colored appearance of my physiognomy, the lower portion being fair, like a woman's, and the upper, brown and swarthy as an Indian.[37]

At Fort Walla Walla Stewart engaged a large barge to take a portion of the party down the river as far as The Dalles. Townsend and Nuttall, by now thoroughly tired of riding on horseback, looked forward to an easy passage on the barge but were told that, unfortunately, there was no room for them. Besides Stewart, Wyeth, Lee, and the other missionaries, a place onboard had been found for Charles Ashworth. Stewart had evidently softened his feelings toward the Englishman, or perhaps he had yielded to the young man's pleas to be able to continue the journey with people who did not treat him as a laughable fool.

Townsend and Nuttall continued on horseback as far as The Dalles, where they transferred to canoes for the treacherous descent of the Columbia. For the next four days they battled rapids and rainstorms. Their canoes overturned and their collections of preserved plants and animals were soaked. They were hungry, cold, and drenched to the skin. At times the rapids became so wild they were impossible to navigate, and the men were forced to portage along the steep and rocky cliffs. After one particularly arduous portage they were climbing down to the river's edge when they noticed a group of white men struggling to force a large barge through the cataract. "Upon approaching them more closely, we recognized, to our astonishment, our old friend Captain Stewart, with the good missionaries, and all the rest who left us at Walla-walla on the 4th. Poor fellows! Every man of them had been over breast deep in water, and the rain, which was still falling in torrents, was more than sufficient to drench what the waves did not cover, so that they were most abundantly soaked and bedraggled. I felt sadly inclined to laugh heartily at them, but a single glance at the sorry appearance of myself and my companion was sufficient to check the feeling."[38]

On September 16 they finally reached Fort Vancouver, the main headquarters for the Hudson's Bay Company on the Pacific coast. Here they were greeted by the chief factor, John McLoughlin, the Canadian gentleman who ruled as lord over the region. For the men who had been so long on the trail and had endured so many hardships and privations, it was like walking into paradise. "Arrived at Fort Vancouver at 3 o'clock," wrote Rev. Lee,

found the governor and other gentleman connected with the fort on shore awaiting our arrival, and conducted us to the fort and gave us food, which was very acceptable, as we had eaten our last for breakfast. We received every attention from these gentlemen. Our baggage was brought and put into a spacious room without consulting us and the room assigned for our use, and we had the pleasure of sleeping again within the walls of a house after a long and fatiguing journey, replete with mercies, deprivations, toil and prosperity. I have been much delighted today in viewing the improvements of the farm, etc. The dinner was as good and served in as good style as in any gentleman's house in the east. Fine muskmelons and water melons and apples were set before us which were, indeed, a luxury, after the dry living we have had for some time. After dinner took a turn in the garden and was astonished to find it in such a high state of cultivation. The orchard is young, but the quantity of fruit is so great that many of the branches [would] break if they were not prevented by props.[39]

Visitors to Fort Vancouver were always enchanted by what they encountered and impressed by the hospitality that McLoughlin showered on his guests, even those who, like Wyeth, had arrived with the intention of going into competition with the Hudson's Bay Company. McLoughlin felt as much loyalty to the territory as to the company, and welcomed anyone who sought to secure a fragile hold on the wilderness. To that end he had constructed a compound that could not help but dazzle weary travelers who had spent months sleeping on hard, damp ground or entombed belowdecks in storm-tossed ships. Frederick Holman describes the layout of Fort Vancouver: "The interior of the fort was divided into two courts, having about forty buildings, all of wood except the powder magazine, which was constructed of brick and stone. In the center, facing the main entrance, stood the Hall in which were the dining-room, smoking-room, and public sitting-room, or bachelor's hall. Single men, clerks, strangers, and others made the bachelor's hall their place of resort. To these rooms artisans and servants were not admitted."[40]

The denizens of bachelor's hall lived in a relaxed comradery in which the absence of women was barely noticed. Social contact with the neighboring Indian tribes was curtailed, and there were few white women, but the men developed an all-male environment that appears to have provided them with all they desired. A historian of the Hudson's Bay Company has noted, "The homosocial culture was not necessarily a poor imitation of allegedly real, natural, or legitimate gender organization. While men's desire for white women was often assumed, the lives of many backwoods British Columbian men — lived in lifelong bachelorhood, with no apparent quest for formal marriage — suggests that same-race, heterosexual desires were not universal."[41]

To his compound John McLoughlin welcomed Wyeth, Stewart, and the missionaries — but not Charles Ashworth. Sensing something odd about the young man's presence, McLoughlin inquired after him. He was not pleased by what he learned. In his regular report to the Hudson's Bay Company headquarters he explained his actions.

> With the party came a person who calls himself Ashworth and gives out that he is the son of Sir Richard Ashworth a Lawyer on the Northern Circuit, but all that Captain Stewart and the rest of the party know of him is from his own story and that they found him in the Rocky Mountains among the American trappers without being employed by any one and going for his food from one party to another which to say the least of is discreditable.
>
> When I found this out and that he had introduced himself into the Room I had given the missionaries and taken his lodging with them (which I did not know till the evening when I sent for the missionaries for supper) and had followed them into our house I allowed him [to] take his supper at our table on account of the missionaries with whom he had obtruded himself but as he was withdrawing and seeing that he was inclined to make himself at home I told him the house was not an Hotel [and] desired the servant to open the doors of the Fort and let this Gentleman go out.
>
> As we could not allow him [to] starve alongside of the Fort I have given him the same rations as to our own men[:] salmon and biscuit or potatoes and salmon as it occurred.[42]

There was, McLoughlin realized, the outside possibility that Ashworth really *was* the son of a peer. There were certainly queerer fish floating around the western territories, remittance men who were embarrassments to their families but who were nevertheless perfectly capable of writing letters of complaint to Papa that could lead to awkward questions in Parliament and unpleasant letters to the *Times*. "I do not know what he intends to do," concluded McLoughlin in his report, "but I am told he is desirous of going to Woahoo [Oahu] and to get rid of him I will give him a passage to that place — and which I mention that incase he is what he states, and complains of not being better treated your honors may know what I have done." Ashworth sailed to the Sandwich Islands on the brig *Eagle*, which on its return voyage to England carried his letter to his family with the story of his adventures that eventually made its way into the Manchester newspaper.[43]

McLoughlin was perhaps so severe with Ashworth because at the time he was troubled by his own black sheep problem: his son, heir, and namesake, John. Young John's story reveals how sadly twisted homosexual desire could become among men isolated by the fur trade. In 1811 while stationed at Kaministikwia, the elder McLoughlin met Marguerite Wadin McKay, the daughter of an Indian woman and a Swiss fur trader. Marguerite at the time was married to Alexander McKay, one of the men on the Astor expedition, but he had abandoned her and their small children. McLoughlin began a relationship with the woman, and on August 12, 1812, she bore him his first child, John. The couple eventually had four children together — John, Elisabeth, Eloisa, and David.

The two eldest children were sent to Montreal for their education, under the supervision of McLoughlin's uncle, Simon Fraser. Elisabeth was placed in the Ursuline convent in Quebec, where her delicate health was a source of continual concern. John was enrolled in a school run by the Reverend Mr. Glen, but he hated it and adopted a rather strange mode of acting out: he would intentionally soil himself and then walk around for days in that condition in order to provide the greatest olfactory offense to his teachers and classmates. "I blamed your mother for this filthy habit," his great-uncle Simon later wrote to him in disgust, "I am now convinced I was wrong the blame lay solely on your innate perversity." Finally, at the age of sixteen, John was expelled from Rev. Glen's school, charged with corrupting the morals of the other boys.[44]

John wrote plaintive letters to his father, begging to be allowed to join the rest of the family at Fort Vancouver, but McLoughlin patiently stressed to his son the importance of getting a good education and of making influential friends. Great-uncle Simon Fraser in the meantime was deeply regretting having agreed to assume in loco parentis responsibilities. "You went on from bad to worse," he scolded his nephew's son, until "finally I could find no body to take you for any consideration . . . your reputation was such that I could find no situation for you in Canada. I applied in vain to Mr. Moffat, Mr. Leslie &c, &c, &c in Montreal and to Mr. J. M. Fraser in Quebec your reputation always prevented every application."[45]

As a last resort the troublesome young man was sent to Paris to live with his uncle David McLoughlin, who was a physician in practice there. John began to study medicine under his uncle and was reportedly making great progress when Dr. McLoughlin abruptly and with a minimum of recorded explanation sent his nephew packing. The doctor had written a letter to his brother at Fort Vancouver criticizing something about John's behavior in Paris, taking the extra step of showing the complaint to his nephew before mailing it off. The letter precipitated some act on young John's part that was so egregious that the doctor refused to describe it in any detail. The elder John McLoughlin wrote to his uncle Simon: "I did not Expect when I learned that my Brother had handed his letter to me of March 1834 to John to Read, that he would have shown such Want of respect to me and Ingratitude to my Brother for pardoning the trouble he had given him as only Four Days after this to commit an act (my Brother does not write me what it is and he ought to have done so) Which obliged my Brother to send him away."[46]

Arriving back in Montreal and again at loose ends, John began to live what was euphemistically termed "a gay life," sponging off relatives and running up debts. Simon Fraser simply washed his hands of the young man.

You know better than I do what character you brought from France you have been kept at school for a number of years in fact till and after you were 21 years of age you must know that you are illiterate to the degree that if by any favor you should pass an examination for a Physician you would infallibly disgrace the Profession You really possess considerable abilities your invincible indolence and perverse disposition have marred your good qualities I write these lines more in sorrow than anger. I have against my will been driven to the conclusion that you are incorrigible. . . . I am wrong to pity you. You are well bodied can work as a common labourer and support yourself by doing so your relatives would have no cause to blush for you since your head thru want of education is so lamentably deficient you have nothing left besides being a day labourer in civilized society or an hunter among savages.[47]

Uncle Simon and John appear to have exchanged words regarding the religious offense that John was committing by following his current path. Fraser's letter ends with a parting shot in the form of a postscript sermon. "Recollect that there is no real atheist than vicious persons who assent that there is no God [but] do not themselves believe what they affirm. [T]he truth is that they dare not reflect[.] Knowing their innate depravity they wish . . . for no after state."[48]

Finally giving into the family's pleas that he remove from its elderly members the burden of dealing with the incorrigible young man, McLoughlin gave his son permission to come west, and John arrived at Fort Vancouver in August 1837. Here John settled down, and for the next few years seemed to be making a life for himself. In 1840 he was chosen to aid his brother-in-law, William Glen Rae, in the development of a trading post within the Russian territory at Fort Stikine, and when Rae was transferred to San Francisco, John was left in charge of the fort. On the evening of April 20/21, 1842, John was murdered by one of his own men.

The circumstances of the murder are confused, rendered especially so by a hasty investigation by Governor George Simpson during his tour of the Northwest coast. The men at the fort told Simpson that young John McLoughlin was subject to drunken bouts during which he would wield his whip and flog them mercilessly. On the night of the murder he had issued the men a ration of liquor and had allowed them to have a dance. Two of the assistants, however, stole additional liquor and distributed it to the party, after which the men grew dangerously drunk. One of the men became particularly abusive, and John ordered that he be bound and prepared for a flogging. The man hurled an insult that hit home, and John struck him. When the man ran away, John reached for his rifle and went after him, but the man quickly armed himself and when John approached, shot him point-blank in the chest. When he collapsed to the floor, writhing and gasping in agony, the man put his foot on John's neck and beat his head in with the butt of his rifle.

Governor Simpson attempted to put a swift end to the affair by declaring that the man had acted in self-defense as John, in one of his habitual drunken rages, had threatened his life. Family members disagreed with the verdict, insisting that John was no longer a drunkard, pointing out that the supply of wine they had sent him was nearly untouched and that the fort's books had been kept with meticulous (and presumably sober) care; Simpson himself had praised John's administration only a few months earlier. There were twenty-two men at the fort, and John was without a trustworthy assistant. The men could have easily mutinied and overpowered him if they felt the floggings were unjust. Something about that night, they were certain, was being covered up. "There is a mystery in this affair," his younger brother, David, wrote, "and I am afraid there will be some difficulty to find the truth of this atrocious Murder."[49]

The elder John McLoughlin became obsessed with overturning the verdict in his son's murder, inundating Governor Simpson and the committee of the Hudson's Bay Company with so many fact-filled letters that in the end the committee agreed that Simpson had been overly hasty in trying to dispose of the unpleasant matter. James Douglas was sent to reinterview the men who had been at the fort the night of John's death, but the stories the men related proved even more bizarre. On the evening of the murder the men were forced to take part in a strange drinking ritual with a dark undercurrent of dominance and submission.

John told them to sit in a ring on the floor and ordered them to consume alcohol until they were drunk. "On entering the room," one man reported, "Mr. John told Peter to sit down with the other people, and ordered his servant, Fleury, to give him a good dram, which he did, in a tin pan. Peter could not drink the whole, and was threatened by Mr John with violence if he did not finish it. He succeeded in emptying the pan, by allowing the liquor to run into the bosom of his shirt." John himself was not drinking, but he eagerly watched as his men become inebriated while he looked on "in a half-playful mood," and he appeared "flushed and excited" by what he observed.[50]

Douglas was told that all of the men at the fort hated young John McLoughlin for his arbitrary cruelty, and they had all signed a document agreeing to murder him at the first opportunity in order to end their oppression. "Peter also says that one principal cause of their dislike to John, and their plots against his life, was the strictness with which he prevented their sallying from the fort in quest of women; that he flogged Martineau for having given his blanket to a [Indian] woman with whom he maintained illicit commerce, and he also flogged Lamb and Kakepe for giving away their clothes in the same manner."[51]

Douglas's report reinforced the idea of a conspiracy to murder young McLoughlin and verified the existence of premeditation, but Douglas was unable to fix the identity of the murderer or even verify the sequence of events that led to the killing. The elder McLoughlin seized upon the report as proof that the verdict of justifiable homicide was incorrect, but he was unable to get the Hudson's Bay Company directors to take the next step of clearing his son's name. He could not let the matter rest, and in the process he lost all sense of proportion. His intemperate letters escalated into attacks, and the attacks became so vituperative that the committee decided in the end that he had to go. In 1846 John McLoughlin was forced to resign his position with the Hudson's Bay Company.

Young John's murder was only the first of a series of emotional blows to hit the great man. Three months after the murder McLoughlin's mother died. In 1844 his favorite uncle, the patient and long-suffering

Simon Fraser, also died. His son-in-law, William Glen Rae, committed suicide in San Francisco where he was in charge of the Hudson's Bay Company store. His favorite sister, Marie Louise (Sister St. Henry) died in the Ursuline convent in Quebec. His younger son, David, resigned and left his post in Oregon City.

John McLoughlin, who for twenty years ruled with grace and probity a region larger than the country of France, spent the few remaining years of his life scraping out a living as just another merchant on the Pacific coast, selling goods and farm tools to the immigrants who began to flood into the region. Little was left of the stately, urbane life of the gracious sovereign who had greeted Nathaniel Wyeth, Jason Lee, and William Drummond Stewart that day on the beach in the autumn of 1834.

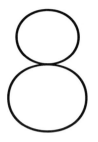

William Drummond Stewart spent the winter of 1834–35 at Fort Vancouver living in baronial splendor with his generous host, and then in February joined a supply party led by Francis Ermatinger, a Hudson's Bay Company man. Nathaniel Wyeth recorded in his journal, "Went to the Cascades and there found Mr. Ermatinger with a brigade of 3 boats taking up the outfits for the upper forts also Capt. Stewart Mr. Ray [William Glen Rae, who would later commit suicide in San Francisco] and one more gentleman." Stewart would stay at Fort Walla Walla until the mountain passes opened, and then the party would push on. At the beginning of the summer trapper Osborne Russell recorded in his journal at Fort Hall: "On the 10th of June a small party belonging to the Hudson Bay Company arrived from Fort Vancouver on the Columbia River, under the direction of Mr. F. Ermatinger, accompanied by Capt. Wm. Stewart, an English half-pay officer who had passed the winter at Vancouver and was on a tour of pleasure in the Rocky Mountains. On the 12th they left Fort Hall and started for the grand rendezvous on Green River."[1]

The rendezvous of 1835 did not get under way until late in the summer. The trappers gathered and the revelries began as best they could in the absence of sufficient alcohol, but it was not until August 12 that the supply caravan of the partnership Fitzpatrick, Sublette & Bridger arrived at the Green River. The caravan, under the direction of Lucien

Fontenelle, had gotten a late start and had then been delayed by an outbreak of cholera. Traveling with the party were two missionaries on their way to minister to the Flathead Indians: Rev. Samuel Parker and his young assistant, Dr. Marcus Whitman.

Parker and Whitman had been sent by the New England–based American Board of Commissioners for Foreign Missions, a joint Congregational-Presbyterian enterprise. Whitman was a trained physician, so when en route the fur traders began to experience violent diarrhea and projectile vomiting, and their skin began to wrinkle and turn blue, Fontenelle turned to the missionary doctor for help. The epidemic of cholera sweeping across America that summer had unfortunately reached the Fontenelle party. "For twelve days," writes Bernard DeVoto, "they had a vicious battle with the plague, new cases every day, one of them Fontenelle himself, and at least three deaths. Whitman saved the caravan. . . . He warmed them, fed them, comforted them, saw them through, got the camp moved to higher ground and cleaner surroundings — and suddenly they were all convalescing, the attack was over."[2]

Fontenelle took the caravan as far as Fort William, where he met up with Tom Fitzpatrick and turned the command over to him. Fontenelle, still weak from his bout of cholera, convalesced at the fort for the rest of the summer and then resumed command of the party on its return trip to St. Louis. By the time Fitzpatrick's party reached the rendezvous, Dr. Whitman had taken on a somewhat legendary status and the story of his skill as a physician quickly spread throughout the encampment. Men who had been without professional medical care for years began to line up to be treated. One of them was Jim Bridger, who had been carrying an arrowhead in his back since the battle of Pierre's Hole in the summer of 1832.

When Dr. Whitman made an exploratory incision he discovered that the three-inch, barbed-iron arrowhead "was hooked at the point striking a large bone and a cartilaginous substance had grown round it." In an open-air operating theater, with trappers and Indians shouting encouragement and helpful instructions, Whitman dug deep and at last extracted the arrowhead. When Whitman marveled that Bridger had been able to function with a piece of barbed iron festering in his back, the mountain man answered with a laconic, "In the mountains, Doctor, meat don't spoil."[3]

Jim Bridger handed the extracted arrowhead to William Drummond Stewart, who slipped it into his pocket. Stewart would one day repay the gift by bringing Bridger the oddest object ever to be carried to the annual rendezvous.

Rev. Parker and Dr. Whitman were delighted to learn that Stewart was thoroughly familiar with Rev. Jason Lee, whom the missionary society had sent out before them. Stewart gave them a detailed update on Lee's settlement on the Willamette, adding informed suggestions about where they might want to set up their new mission. This was an advantage Parker and Whitman had not anticipated. Their plan had been to reach Oregon, reconnoiter the situation, and then one (or both) would return to Boston to gather supplies and recruit assistants. The missionaries now felt secure enough in Stewart's information to make a major alteration to their plans: Rev. Parker would proceed to Oregon, but Dr. Whitman would return to Boston immediately to begin the task of assembling the needed personnel and supplies.

Before the two missionaries parted an incident occurred that revealed the character of both men, and that gave some indication of the relative level of success they were destined to experience in their proselytizing. As trapper Joe Meek remembered it:

> The Rev. Samuel Parker preached, and the men were as politely attentive as it was in their reckless natures to be, until, in the midst of the discourse, a band of buffalo appeared in the valley, when the congregation incontinently broke up, without staying for a benediction, and every man made haste after his horse, gun, and rope, leaving Mr. Parker to discourse to vacant ground.
>
> The run was both exciting and successful. About twenty fine buffaloes were killed, and the choice pieces brought to camp, cooked and eaten, amidst the merriment, mixed with something coarser, of the hunters. On this noisy rejoicing Mr. Parker looked with a sober

aspect: and following the dictates of his religious feeling, he rebuked the sabbath breakers quite severely. Better for his influence among the men, if he had not done so, or had not eaten so heartily of the tender-loin afterwards, a circumstance which his irreverent critics did not fail to remark, to his prejudice; and upon the principle that the "partaker is as bad as the thief," they set down his lecture on sabbath-breaking as nothing better than pious humbug.

Dr. Marcus Whitman was another style of man. Whatever he thought of the wild ways of the mountain-men he discreetly kept to himself, preferring to teach by example rather than precept.[4]

Antoine Clement also appeared at the rendezvous, and he and Stewart resumed their relationship. This time when the rendezvous came to an end and the tents were packed up and the horses loaded, they would not go their separate ways. The couple joined Fitzpatrick (and Dr. Whitman) on the return trip to St. Louis, where Antoine Clement's family welcomed home their wandering son.

For Stewart this was his first reengagement with "civilization" in two and half years. Life at Fort Vancouver had been graced with comforts and small luxuries, but it was only a simulacrum of the life of an established Anglo culture. St. Louis, on the other hand, though it still retained some of its frontier rambunctiousness, was beginning to assume the trappings of true bourgeois respectability. Stewart would for the first time be emerging from the laissez-faire ethos of the fur trade, with its pragmatic acceptance of sexual relations. As the long line of horses and mules in Fitzpatrick's party left the open prairie and drew ever closer to boardwalks and brick houses, Stewart began to feel anxious and disoriented, like a diver surfacing too rapidly after an extended stay in the ocean's depths. "I was leaving the vagueness of the West," Stewart writes in his second novel, "for a country through which (whatever its own charms) every step I took led nearer the spinning jenny and the exchange."[5]

Reaching St. Louis, Stewart wrote his first letter in many months — a letter not to his family but to James Watson Webb, the newspaper editor who had eased his entrance into the world of the mountain men. "The life I have led since my Indian pilgrimage commenced, in April 1833," Stewart marveled,

has been one of very varied but never failing interest. Sleeping under the canopy [of] the night was the only moment of inactivity & often danger & pleasure divided its watches, in an almost dreamy confusion — Of the day, the living day, of those high climes it is almost impossible to write, the memory of them may be internally accused of lying, & the [*illegible*] the poet & the painter, have never in the wildest flights of their imaginations soared to the ordinary pitch where the free Mountaineer hunts his daily prey. . . . The Rocky mountains are capable of producing but few pleasures I have not tasted & few dangers I have not tried — such has been my tour across to the west sea & back I could willingly devote any little power of writing that remains unforgotten to a description of some of these scenes which I know must interest you but it is really a matter of such difficulty to write & even spell to one so long dead to such things that you must allow me to defer it until I am somewhat familiarized with literature & orthography.[6]

The dreamlike idyll of his first years in the mountains made adjustment to life in St. Louis almost physically painful for him. Letters from home did not help. A missive awaited him from his younger brother George, again effusive in its description of the progress on the new Murthly Castle — but it all seemed like an echo from a long-lost world. Stewart had experienced his western journey as a rebirth, and all that had come before he felt was now dead and buried. In the opening chapter of *Edward Warren* he would describe how "the startling cry of the grey dawn came upon men who leaped from the earth as if into a new life, to whom all previous existence had been a blank." Mountain men were the new Adams, fashioned from the very earth itself, raw and joyful with primordial freedom. He saw himself as one of those men now, and felt that everything that had come before — his privileged childhood in Perthshire, his venturous adolescence in the Fifteenth King's Hussars, his debauched manhood in smoky London gaming rooms — all that had died in the Rockies, and he had built a brand-new life for himself upon the burial mound. Now, in the fall of 1835, in the noisy bustle and bruising commerce of St. Louis, that long-dead world slowly stirred to life again in all its disorienting and discomfiting reality.[7]

As Stewart was journeying eastward to St. Louis in 1835, one of his cousins was setting out on his own prairie adventure. Charles Augustus Murray was the second son of the fifth Earl of Dunmore, and like many second sons he was high on enthusiasm but short on funds. He left for America two years after William Drummond Stewart, his imagination brimming with romantic ideas about Indian life that he had gleaned from the novels of James Fenimore Cooper. He had cut a dashing figure in London and it was reported by a society publication that the ladies "sigh and soften their voices" whenever his name was mentioned, though to their mothers, who were aware of his wild, unconventional temperament, he was considered "the most dangerous of all detrimentals." Upon his return from America, Murray published the requisite two-volume travelogue, *Travels in North America during the Years 1834, 1835, & 1836*, which he dedicated to the young Queen Victoria.[8]

Like his cousin before him, Murray landed first in New York City. From there he traveled up the Hudson River, visited Niagara Falls, Toronto, Montreal, and New England, and then returned to New York. For his next tour he visited Philadelphia, Washington DC, Maryland, and Virginia. Feeling himself by then an old hand at traveling the back roads of America, Murray decided to head west to fulfill a long-held desire to live among the Pawnees.

In Louisville he was invited to dine at the home of Senator Henry Clay, and there he met a young German who was to become his traveling companion for the next few months. In his reminiscences of America Murray identifies the man only as V——, but he is almost certainly Adolph Sillem, the twenty-four-year-old son of Jerôme Sillem, a Hamburg banker. Jerôme Sillem was a successful international financier — banker to the tsar of all the Russias — and he had sent his son to the New World on family business, first to the Netherlands Antilles and then to Mexico. Adolph, having toiled successfully for three years in the intolerable climate of the tropics, felt he deserved a holiday in America, so he pursued his passion for hunting by heading into the Rockies (dabbling as he did so in some fur trade speculation).[9]

Murray and Sillem spent the evening together after their dinner with Henry Clay, and Murray excitedly described his scheme to live like a Red Indian among the wild Pawnee. Always up for an adventure, Sillem quickly agreed to join him. The Scotsman and the German eventually did manage to take up residence with a village of Pawnee Indians — where they discovered that what had seemed thrilling and romantic while sitting in an armchair in London or Hamburg reading Cooper novels could be somewhat less so when transferred to a cold morning in a tepee on the windswept American prairie. Murray found his inborn fastidiousness challenged on a daily basis.

"Not being yet thoroughly drilled to a prairie life," he wrote in his travel memoirs,

> I had not learned to consider cleanliness as a useless and supererogatory luxury; and, accordingly, after sleeping in my clothes, in the midst of a scene too dirty to depict, where we were as closely packed as the horses in a stage-coach stable, I was weak enough to imagine that it was desirable to wash my hands and face, and change my linen. . . . Accordingly, I armed myself with a towel, some soap, a tooth-brush, and a clean shirt, and sallied forth in search of the creek, the banks of which were to be my dressing-room on the occasion.
>
> I found it to be a muddy streamlet, from four to eight inches deep, having neither brushwood nor timber to mark its course. It was completely alive with animal industry, which seemed all exercised in endeavouring to make it more and more turbid and muddy. Women washing their children, and their blankets; boys and girls splashing; dogs swimming, and horses tramping in every direction.
>
> As this did not seem a favourable spot for the bath and toilet of one who can boast of having, in his day, made a respectable appearance

in Bond Street, I walked above a mile up the little stream, in hopes of finding a place less pre-occupied by my biped and quadruped competitors in ablution. Finding this attempt fruitless, and seeing that the "ladies" were not at all afraid of me, I determined not to evince less courage; and putting my watch, my knife, my *mauvaise honte* [bashfulness], and other trifles in my pocket, I proceeded quietly to undress; and having bathed for a few minutes, proceeded with my toilet. I ought to mention that I effected this bath lying down and rolling where the water was about nine inches deep.[10]

Murray and Sillem lived with the Pawnees for a month, during which time all of the romance was drained from the idea and they decided it was time to take to the trail again. Just as they were getting under way, Sillem's vanity intervened to create a potential problem: he decided to trade his horse ("a quiet and safe grey pony") for an unbroken Indian mount. When the time came to leave, Sillem's horse was so unruly that he could not ride it, so Murray exchanged with him, and with ample applications of a cudgel was able to subdue the horse enough to allow them to leave the Pawnee camp. After a few days the horse seemed sufficiently broken to allow Sillem to ride, but when the German made an attempt, the horse bucked him off and trampled him so badly that he temporarily lost the use of one arm.

After many weeks of arduous traveling, the men finally reached St. Louis, where to his surprise and delight, Murray encountered his cousin William Drummond Stewart, about to board a steamer for a trip down the Mississippi. They decided to travel south together for the winter, first to New Orleans, and then on to Cuba. "I was fortunate enough to be able to collect a very pleasant little party," Murray later wrote, "and we agreed to embark and keep together; it consisted of Captain S ——, a cousin and old acquaintance of mine in Scotland, who had been above two years among the Indians, in and beyond the rocky mountains; my friend V ——, and a Dr. W ——, also from Scotland, a lively and well-informed companion."[11]

The identity of Doctor W —— has not been established, but Sillem himself appears briefly as a character in Stewart's novel *Edward War-*

ren, once again under the pseudonym V —— (suggesting perhaps that Sillem had added the aristocratic "von" to his name, though it was not used by his family). The novel's narrator describes the young man from Hamburg as being "a beautiful singer" but "the most unlucky man I ever met."[12]

On November 29, 1835, the party set off from St. Louis on the steamboat *The Far West*, but the captain encountered so much ice on the river he was forced to turn back. His insurance carrier refused to cover him if he set out again, and the party seriously feared being iced in at St. Louis for the winter, but in a few days the weather warmed and the group was able to set off once more. The boat was not out of danger, however. For the next two weeks it repeatedly ran aground on sandbars and needed to be towed off, at great expense; so frequent were the accidents that Murray suspected that the pilot was completely unfamiliar with the river.

As they approached New Orleans the travelers were pleasantly surprised when the boat was suddenly invaded by a large cadre of darkly handsome youths. "Our boat had received a great addition in mirth," wrote Murray, "in the shape of eighty or a hundred boys returning from Jefferson College, which is about a hundred miles above New Orleans, to spend the Christmas holidays in or near that city. They were most of them Creoles, and it did me good to hear their light and joyous laughter, after our dull and tedious voyage."[13]

Sometime in the course of the voyage down the Mississippi, Sillem, who Murray had up to this point consistently referred to as "my companion" or "my friend," began to transfer his interest to Stewart. When the party arrived at New Orleans, Murray secured a room in the same boardinghouse as the British consul, "where I got a clean bed, an airy room (to myself), a good table, and a very pleasant society, consisting of three or four Germans, one or two Creoles, and several English or Americans." He does not indicate where Stewart and Sillem found lodging. In all the many stops along the Mississippi, Murray specifies that Sillem (and not Stewart) was his partner in exploration, but when he describes strolling around New Orleans, he speaks of seeing the city entirely on his own.[14]

For William Drummond Stewart, New Orleans was the first international port he had visited since the autumn of 1832, his first opportunity
to read the latest newspapers from Scotland. When traveler James Stuart
had visited New Orleans only a few years earlier, he was pleased to
notice an advertisement in a local newspaper, placed by a Miss Carrol,
announcing a newly opened reading room where gentleman could retire
to peruse the latest periodicals from America and Europe. Miss Carrol
could afford to provide only one British newspaper — as yet she had only
fifty subscribers to her establishment — but to James Stuart's delight
he discovered that that one newspaper was the *Scotsman*, published
in Edinburgh.[15]

If William Drummond Stewart, newly arrived in New Orleans and
hungry for news of his native country, had happened to stop into Miss
Carrol's reading room and pick up a recent issue of the *Scotsman*, he
would have been able to read news only a few weeks old. Among the
information he would have gleaned: the steamship *Perth* would be sailing from Dundee, destination London, on December 9 at three in the
afternoon, but "to prevent disappointment, passengers are requested
to be in attendance at least half an hour before the time advertised
for sailing." He would have noted that Robert Gibbons, at No. 30 St.
Andrew Square in Edinburgh, was offering "Small VEAL and MUTTON
PIES, which he has constantly ready during the Winter, and which he
prepares with utmost care, according to the most approved receipts in
the modern systems of cookery." He would have been concerned to
read that a hurricane had recently struck near Aberdeen, and "when
at sea, betwixt 11 a.m. and 2 p.m. ten of the fishing boats belonging to St
Comb's Cairness, were drifted on the rocks and sands of Rattrayhead,
when melancholy to relate, two of the boats swamped, when all on
board perished!"[16]

If, turning from news of mutton pies and hurricanes, he had paused
to read the column headed in bold type "High Court of Justiciary," he
would have been informed: "The first case brought before the Court on
Monday was that of John Pottinger, charged with an unnatural crime.
The panel [i.e., defendant], an old man upwards of 50 years of age,

pleaded guilty, and was sentenced to 14 years' transportation." Though Stewart had reveled for three seasons amid the easy sexuality of the backwoodsmen, he would have been reminded that the same conduct at home could land him on a convict ship on its way to Australia.[17]

Stewart was busy during his brief stay in New Orleans. In the months since he had left the mountains, his tastes had undergone a gradual but significant transformation. In his first letter from St. Louis he had written to James Watson Webb about his sense of disorientation upon returning to civilization, and while the change in scenery was almost painful to encounter, the pleasures of the city quickly superimposed themselves on his memories of the prairies. He had in a very real sense achieved his goal in coming to America. He had formed male friendships of unimagined intimacy. He had hunted buffalo on horseback, shooting at a gallop and bringing down a bull with a single shot. He had faced down hostile Indians and enraged grizzly bears, and he had crossed the Great Divide to stroll along the sands of the Pacific Ocean. He had roasted buffalo tongue on a stake over a campfire and eaten dog when the occasion required it. At night he had slept under the stars and awakened as the sun rose golden over the vast prairie. Once he returned to St. Louis, however, he became reacquainted with the joys of clean linen sheets, hot baths, and *filet de boeuf en croûte.*

Stewart had given James Fenimore Cooper a try and had found his romanticized view of the West almost laughably inaccurate, and yet the reality had proved to be even more seductive than the myth. But now Lord Byron began to reassert himself. In *Don Juan* Byron had praised the "art of living in all climes with ease" and in St. Louis, Stewart came to believe that Byron perhaps had the right idea. Unfortunately, living in all climes with ease required money, and Stewart had very little of that. The letter waiting for him from his brother's solicitor included a draft for only part of the remittance owed to him from his trust fund, and that small infusion of hard cash would quickly evanesce in cigar smoke and champagne. Adolph Sillem, Stewart soon realized, was not Antoine Clement. Clement could be made happy with a bottle of whiskey and a new rifle; Sillem had a taste for finer things. Stewart needed money — a lot of it — and he needed it fast.

Once they arrived in New Orleans, Stewart began speculating in cotton futures by entering into a partnership with a young businessman from Texas named Ebenezer B. Nichols. Stewart and Nichols began as business partners, but in time Stewart would become close friends with Nichols, his wife, and his three sons — a friendship that would bring Stewart both pleasure and tribulation, and eventually have devastating consequences for Murthly Castle.

New Orleans at that time had just entered a period of explosive economic growth, the fruits of wise investments in the local commercial infrastructure. New canals had been dug, swamps drained, levies widened, obstructions on the Mississippi River cleared. By 1834 New Orleans had outstripped New York as the major export city of the United States. For a few men that meant great wealth. Demand for cotton was high, and 80 percent of the business was controlled by only seven factoring houses.[18]

The cotton factor served as banker for the planter, lending him money for the next season's crop and charging him a 2½ percent commission on his total profits for the year. Four-fifths of the American cotton crop was exported, primarily to Great Britain, whose mills were hungry for the raw material. In only one year — from October 1835 (when William Drummond Stewart arrived in New Orleans) until September 1836 — over two hundred thousand bales of cotton were shipped to Great Britain. Stewart knew nothing of the trade and had only a modest amount to invest, but perhaps his most valuable asset was his social position. Distant though he was from the mill owners of Great Britain, he was still brother to the sixth Baronet of Murthly, and noble titles carried their own type of currency. Because communication was slow and uncertain, and market fluctuations were rapid and unpredictable, cotton factor operations depended on a network of social and family ties that allowed for decisions to be made quickly with a high degree of trust. Stewart's family connections inspired confidence, even though he himself was completely ignorant of the cotton business.[19]

Stewart could not possibly have picked a better time to enter the cotton market. From 1832 to 1834 Great Britain experienced three consecutive years of plentiful harvests, which drove down the cost of food. With less being spent on food, the average family had more to spend on manufactured goods, and the demand for cotton articles soared — and along with it the price paid per bale of cotton. For a modest dabbling in the market, Stewart was able to clear a substantial sum of cash. With it he was able to begin to reestablish himself (and Adolph Sillem) in a life made pleasant by luxury items unknown to the mountain men.

When the men left New Orleans for Havana on December 29 in the brig *Rolla*, the traveling party had increased. "Having had the good fortune to collect a party of acquaintances, consisting of six persons," writes Murray, "we took the whole cabin to ourselves, and had before us every prospect of a speedy and pleasant voyage." Murray never identifies his cabin mates, but they almost certainly included Stewart and Sillem, who are known to have spent the winter of 1835–36 in Cuba. Once they reached Havana, Murray gives short shrift to the breakup of the traveling party, saying only, "Being anxious to acquire the language, I left my companions, and took up my lodgings in a sort of Spanish boarding-house, kept by one Don Juan Gonzalez." Murray proceeds to give an extremely detailed discussion of the inner workings of the Cuban sugarcane industry, but says nothing at all about his cousin and his new friend.[20]

After spending a leisurely winter in Cuba, William Drummond Stewart and Adolph Sillem arrived in Charleston, South Carolina, in February of 1836. Stewart wrote to William Sublette, "I have just arrived here from the island of Cuba on my way to St. Louis by Washington Philadelphia &c." After nearly four years, travel in America had for him become almost a predictable routine.

I hope this finds you well and planning a western trip. I am not sure how I shall go but still intend proceeding to the West in April. I shall learn at Washington if there is to be a party sent by the U.S. to make a survey of the country and shall let you know as soon as I hear. I write this to let you know that there are two gun cases that I have directed to be sent from New Orleans to your care. I must also remind you of your promise of a black horse. I beg you to get me one other as fast as you can secure and two hardy, quiet mules. Mr. Sillem a German gentleman who accompanies me begs you will be good enough to procure him three good horses & four mules saddle — packsaddles &c.&c. I am answerable for all this.[21]

Clearly, Stewart was planning on entering into some of the high-stakes horse races that were a feature of most trapper gatherings and was requesting a mount fast enough to give him good odds. That he designated himself as the one who would be paying for Sillem's procurements suggests that once again he had associated himself with a young man who was more than willing to be showered with presents from a gentleman who was slightly older and significantly more wealthy.

By the time they arrived in St. Louis, Stewart and Sillem had accumulated a cache of luxury goods to assure themselves a pleasant journey to the Rockies: sardines, ham, and plum pudding (preserved by the new method of tin canning), dried fruits, sugar, coffee, tobacco, imported cheeses, as well as an impressive array of brandies, whiskey, and vintage wines — enough provisions to require two supply wagons. They would also be bringing with them three servants and two dogs. To assure themselves sufficient comfort and privacy, the two men procured a heavy canvas tent; no longer would Stewart and a companion share a rough bower of scavenged brush and bushes.

The supply party traveling to the Rockies that year was under the command of Stewart's friend Tom Fitzpatrick, assisted by Moses "Black" Harris. They were supposed to be accompanied by a party of missionaries sent by the American Board of Commissioners for Foreign Missions to proselytize among the Nez Percé Indians, but the day of departure arrived with no missionaries in sight. The American Fur Company was in dire financial straits and could not afford to arrive at the rendezvous late so, missionaries or no missionaries, Fitzpatrick gave the order and the large entourage set out on the trail.

Capt. William Drummond Stewart in the uniform of the Fifteenth King's
Light Dragoons (Hussars) at the time of the Napoleonic Wars. Courtesy of
the Murthly Castle Collection.

Courtyard of Murthly Castle, Perthshire, Scotland, undated but perhaps late
nineteenth century. Collection of the author.

Sir George Stewart, seventeenth Lord of Grandtully, fifth Baronet of Murthly.
Courtesy of the Murthly Castle Collection.

Lady Catherine Drummond Stewart. Courtesy of the Murthly Castle Collection.

Sir John Archibald Drummond Stewart, eighteenth Lord of Grandtully, sixth
Baronet of Murthly. Courtesy of the Murthly Castle Collection.

George Drummond Stewart. Courtesy of the Murthly Castle Collection.

Portrait of Thomas Drummond Stewart by Count Alfred d'Orsay. Courtesy of the Murthly Castle Collection.

THE TRAPPER AND THE INDIANS

The Trapper and the Indians, from *Ballou's Pictorial Drawing-room Companion,* shows a naked (and improbably buff) John Colter facing his Indian attackers. Such homoerotic images drew many young men to the American West. Denver Public Library, Western History Collection, z-3570.

A wherry carries passengers to Battery Park in New York City, with Castle
Clinton in the distance. Battery Park was the primary homosexual gathering
place in New York in the 1830s and 1840s. Collection of the author.

SHAKSPEARE FOR THE COUNTER-JUMPERS.
You should be women,
And yet your beards forbid me to interpret
That you are so.—MACBETH, *Act 1, Scene 3.*

Effeminate store clerks, known as "counter-jumpers," were lampooned in *Vanity
Fair.* Many young men were drawn to New York City to take jobs in elegant
clothing and dry goods stores.

(*Above*) Fur trader Robert Campbell (and his intimate friend William Sublette) provided Stewart with an introduction to life in the Rocky Mountains. *History of Saint Louis City and County* by J. Thomas Scharf (1883).

(*Right*) A free trapper in a fringed capote fashioned of plaid calico. Free trappers were known for their flamboyant attire and their unconventional behavior. Courtesy of The Bancroft Library, University of California, Berkeley.

Trapper Joe Meek sports a highly embroidered parfleche and a jaunty sash.
The River of the West by Frances Fuller Victor (1870).

Antoine Clement. The "wild child of the prairie" was Stewart's first and most enduring love interest. *Portrait of Antoine*, Alfred Jacob Miller, American, ca. 1840, oil on canvas. Photo © The Walters Art Museum, Baltimore.

The Crow men were considered to be the most handsome of all the Indian tribes; they were particularly noted for their physiques, which reminded observers of Greek and Roman statues. Yale Collection of Western Americana, Beinecke Rare Book and Manuscript Library.

(*Above*) Miller painted *An Attack by Crows on the Whites on the Big Horn River East of the Rocky Mountains* from details provided by his patron. In this copy of the painting, Stewart calmly rebuffs the provocations of a band of Crow Indians while Clement translates for him. Courtesy of the Murthly Castle Collection.

(*Right*) A heroic image of Kit Carson, with his rifle suggestively placed, inspired young men with romantic visions of the American West. Stewart wrote of a memorable night with Carson. Courtesy of The Bancroft Library, University of California, Berkeley.

BEADLE'S
Dime
New York Library

COPYRIGHTED IN 1878, BY BEADLE & ADAMS.

Vol. I.   Complete In One Number.   *Beadle & Adams, Publishers,* No. 98 WILLIAM STREET, NEW YORK.   Price, Ten Cents.   No. 3.

Kit Carson, Jr., the Crack Shot of the West.

A WILD LIFE ROMANCE, BY "BUCKSKIN SAM."

KIT CARSON, JR.

(*Above*) A vintage photograph shows the old Murthly (*left*) and the new Murthly (*right*). The new Murthly Castle, begun by William Drummond Stewart's brother, was never completed, and the entire structure was demolished in 1950. Courtesy of the Murthly Castle Collection.

(*Right*) Alfred Jacob Miller. After studying in Europe, Miller reached his greatest fame with images of the American West commissioned by Stewart. *Self-Portrait*, Alfred Jacob Miller, American, ca. 1850, oil on canvas. Photo © The Walters Art Museum, Baltimore.

Interior of an Indian Lodge

(*Above*) Alfred Jacob Miller frequently depicted Antoine Clement gazing rapturously at William Drummond Stewart. The paintings provide an unprecedented view of a male couple in early nineteenth-century America. Alfred Jacob Miller, American, 1810–1874, *Interior of an Indian Lodge*, sepia ink and pencil on paper, 7 x 6¾ in., Joslyn Art Museum, Omaha, Nebraska. Museum Purchase, 1988.10.13.

(*Top right*) Stewart and Clement lived in Dalpowie Lodge on the Scottish estate, where they could enjoy greater privacy than was possible in Murthly Castle. Courtesy of the Murthly Castle Collection.

(*Bottom right*) Stewart had himself painted in an Albanian national costume in imitation of his hero, Lord Byron. Courtesy of the Murthly Castle Collection.

(*Top left*) Murthly Castle in 2007. Collection of the author.

(*Bottom left*) The formal gardens at Murthly Castle in 2011. Courtesy of the Murthly Castle Collection.

(*Above*) Grandtully Castle, one of the Stewart family properties, was the home of Lady Stewart in the later years of her life. She and her son are buried in the chapel there. Collection of the author.

(*Top left*) *Hunting buffalo near Scott's Bluff. Route from Liverpool to Great Salt Valley* by Frederick Piercy (1855).

(*Bottom left*) *Devil's Gate gorge on the Sweetwater River. Route from Liverpool to Great Salt Valley* by Frederick Piercy (1855).

(*Above*) Sir Archibald Douglas Drummond Stewart, twentieth Lord of Grandtully, eighth Baronet of Murthly. Courtesy of the Murthly Castle Collection.

Murthly Chapel, burial place of Sir William Drummond Stewart, with the "Dead Walk" to the right of the path. Courtesy of the Murthly Castle Collection.

There were over seventy men and four hundred horses and mules strung out in a line that extended nearly a mile. Fitzpatrick rode at the head of the party, ramrod straight, his eyes on the horizon. "Beside him on a superb black horse rides his hawk-nosed, mustached friend of three years' standing now, Captain William Drummond Stewart," writes Bernard DeVoto, and riding next to Stewart was "the unexplained Sillem." As with other historians who were unaware of Stewart's sexual orientation, DeVoto is unable to account for Adolph Sillem's unscripted role in the story. Stewart, in the words of Marshall Sprague, "always had males in tow," but Sprague also, convinced of the Scotsman's heterosexuality, could find no explanation for these extraneous men.[22]

The entourage this year was comprised of nineteen carts and three wagons, including one carrying Milton Sublette, whose diseased leg had finally needed to be amputated in an attempt to save his life. His brother William had supplied him with a prosthesis made of rubber, and Milton was now determined to attend one more rendezvous. The party traveled for four days with nothing unusual to record — but on the fifth day the wheels on the wagons and the carts began to squeak, and then to screech, and then finally to shriek as though they were in extremis, a noise that drove off game as effectively as it announced their presence to potentially hostile Indians. To the men the sound was like fingernails on a chalkboard. In the rush to leave Bellevue on schedule no one had remembered to bring any axle grease, and now that small oversight threatened to abort the entire operation.

Without grease to use as a lubricant they would need to improvise with tallow and ashes, but to produce ashes they would need to burn wood, and unfortunately the surrounding prairie was barren of timber. A small reconnoitering party was sent out to look for trees; meanwhile two of the oxen were slaughtered and the men began the slow processing of rendering the fat over a pathetically small fire fed by handfuls of dried sunflower stalks. After four days the search party returned with a meager supply of wood, and as darkness began to fall a lumpy mixture of tallow and ashes was smeared on the offending axles. Fitzpatrick set the night watch and announced that the journey would resume at dawn.

Around midnight the sound of wagons and pack animals was heard in the distance, and half of the abandoned missionary party straggled out of the prairie darkness toward the dying glow of the fur traders' campfire. At five o'clock the next morning the rest of the missionaries arrived, driving before them the slow-moving livestock. The missionaries had been delayed by a miscommunication with the steamboat captain engaged to carry them to Bellevue, and they had spent the previous days in a desperate, frustratingly slow attempt to catch up with the American Fur Company. Their only hope of reaching the Rockies safely was to journey with the fur traders as far as the rendezvous, where they were scheduled to meet with Rev. Samuel Parker and return with him to the struggling mission in Oregon. Only the providential delay over the squeaking axles had spared them the disappointment of canceling that year's effort to preach to the Nez Percés. Stewart was immensely pleased to greet his old friend Marcus Whitman, and he was amazed when Whitman introduced his new bride, Narcissa.

When Whitman left Samuel Parker at the rendezvous of 1835 and returned to the East, he did so with the hope of securing funds and recruits for the Oregon Mission — and of marrying the beautiful, vivacious Narcissa Prentiss. At twenty-seven, Narcissa was fast approaching spinsterhood, a strange fate for a woman who combined an impeccable reputation for great piety with a physical beauty that some men found disturbing in its barely repressed sensuality. Tall and zaftig, with a mass of red-gold hair and an irrepressible congeniality, she was the type of woman who lit up rooms when she entered, and half the young men in the local Presbyterian church desired her. But at sixteen she had had a deeply moving religious experience that left her with an intense longing to become a bride of Jesus.

Marcus Whitman was not Jesus, but he was strong, handsome, kind, and pious, and he burned with an undeniable vocation to bring Christianity to the Indians. The American Board did not want its missionaries to marry until just before leaving on their assignments, for fear that pregnancy or an infant might delay a deployment. It was therefore not until the eve of their departure that Marcus and Narcissa married. For her wedding the bride wore black and stood alone before the congregation singing in her pure soprano voice:

In the deserts let me labor
On the mountains let me tell,
How he died — the blessed Saviour —
To redeem a world from hell!
Let me hasten,
Far in heathen lands to dwell.

At dawn after their wedding night the couple left to begin the journey westward. Narcissa commented on the hurried nuptials, "We had to make love somewhat abruptly, and must do our courtship now that we are married."[23]

Joining the Whitmans on the combination honeymoon and missionary assignment was another couple, Henry and Eliza Spalding. The Spaldings had been married for nearly three years, and at the time they set out for the Oregon Mission Eliza was still recovering from the birth of a stillborn daughter. Weak and frail for most of her life, Eliza was ill prepared for the rigors of the journey and would suffer greatly, but she was sustained by her deep and abiding religious faith. She and Narcissa were complete opposites. While Narcissa's religious fervor gave her wings to soar above her worldly troubles, Eliza's faith was a strong and trusted staff that supported her on her journey through a vale of woe and tears. Despite their differences — or perhaps because of them — they became fast friends on the journey westward.[24]

Not so their husbands. William Drummond Stewart had developed a deep respect for Marcus Whitman during their first trip together to the Rockies, and he continued to admire him throughout his life, writing of him in a footnote in *Edward Warren* that he was "a most excellent man, a curious divine . . . a most bold operator." In contrast, few of his contemporaries wrote of Henry Spalding with any degree of sympathy. He is described as brooding, ill tempered, sarcastic, and intolerant. He and Marcus Whitman were a bad fit, would quarrel repeatedly on the journey westward, and would go their separate ways as soon as they reached Oregon.[25]

Bernard DeVoto suggests that there was something more than a difference in temperament that kept the two men at odds: "Moreover, during [Spalding's] early student days he had lived in the home town of Narcissa Prentiss and worshiped in the same church. The beautiful soprano, in whose eyes was peace and in whose body was disturbance, affected the insecure aspirant to the ministry as she affected many men. Spalding fell in love with her and she rejected him. Now, married in a true union of souls to the twice-born, guilt-ridden Eliza Hart, he was going to help establish the Oregon Mission as a subordinate to Marcus Whitman, who has succeeded where he had failed. And he was privileged to travel west with the lost Narcissa on her honeymoon." Spalding biographer Clifford Merrill Drury discounts the stories of a Henry-Narcissa-Marcus love triangle, however, saying that writers who suggest such a connection are "more concerned with romance than with history."[26]

Spalding was not the only member of the missionary group whose sour disposition would make the trek a trial for everyone involved. The American Board sent William Gray to accompany the Whitmans and the Spaldings in a role variously described as "lay assistant" or "mechanic" or (Gray's preferred title) "secular agent," but he functioned as a type of majordomo, overseeing operations and dealing with problems as they arose. Gray was a man of strong opinions frequently voiced, and he seems to have approved of no one on the journey except for the frail and pious Eliza Spalding.

When he met William Drummond Stewart and Adolph Sillem he took an instant dislike to the men: "The caravan altogether consisted of nineteen carts," Gray writes,

[including] two mules and two wagons belonging to an English nobleman, his titles all on, Sir William Drummond, K.B., who had come to the United States to allow his fortunes to recuperate during his absence. He had been spending his winters in New Orleans with the Southern bloods, and his bankers in England complained that his income was not sufficient to meet his large expenditures; he was advised to take a trip to the Rocky Mountains, which would occupy him during the summer and sickly season, during which time he could only spend what he had with him, and could have a fine hunting excursion. This English nobleman with his party consisted of himself and a young English blood. . . . Sir William D., K.B., messed and slept in the same tent with this traveling companion of his, who between them, had three servants, two dogs, and four extra fine horses, to run and hunt the buffalo.[27]

Gray provides a rather jaundiced physical description of Stewart:

He was about five feet nine inches high. His face had become thin from the free use of New Orleans brandy, rendering his nose rather prominent, showing indications of internal heat in bright red spots, and inclining a little to the rum blossom, that would make its appearance from the sting of mosquito or sand-fly, which to his lordship was quite annoying. Though his lordship was somewhat advanced in years [Stewart was forty to Gray's twenty-six], and, according to his own account, had traveled extensively in the oriental countries, he did not show in his conversation extensive mental improvement; his general conversation and appearance was that of a man with strong prejudices, and equally strong appetites, which he had freely indulged, with only pecuniary restraint.

If the Whitmans and the Spaldings were able to overlook the significance of Stewart and Sillem's relationship — or perhaps miss it entirely — Gray was not, and he was unsparing in his snide and pointed comments.[28]

Shortly after joining with the American Fur Company party, Narcissa Whitman wrote a letter home to her brother and sister describing a typical day along the trail. "We all cover quite a space. The pack mules always string along one after the other just like Indians. There are several gentlemen in the Com. who are going over the Mountains for pleasure. Capt. Stewart, Mr. Lee speaks of him in his journal — he went over when he [Rev. Jason Lee] did and returned. He is [with] an Englishman, — Mr. Chelam. We had a few of them to tea with us last Monday eve — Capts. Fitzpatrick, Stuart, Maj. Harris and Chelam."[29]

It is curious that both William Gray and Narcissa Whitman refer to Adolph Sillem as an Englishman, suggesting either that he spoke particularly unaccented English (unlikely given how little opportunity he had had to learn it) or that he spoke little around them — or perhaps that they spent a minimum of time in his presence. The latter is probably the case, as neither managed to get his name correct despite traveling with him for many weeks.

Narcissa Whitman's tea party on the prairie is a small but important social event in American history, a landmark in the "civilizing" effect of the movement westward of white women, and it is wonderfully typical of her. Even Gray, who had little else nice to say about Narcissa, referred to her as "a lady." When encountering a nobleman of William Drummond Stewart's station she, like most Americans, must have felt compelled to demonstrate her civility. There was little she could offer in the way of sophisticated hospitality, but she carried it off with pluck and humor. "Our table is the ground," she explained in a letter to her family,

> our table-cloth is an Indian rubber cloth used when it rains as a cloak; our dishes are made of tin — basins for tea cups, iron spoons and plates, each of us, and several pans for milk and to put our meat in when we wish to set it upon the table — each one carries his own knife in his scabbard and it is always ready for use. When the table things [are] spread, after making our forks of sticks and helping ourselves to chairs, we gather around the table. . . . We take a blanket and lay down by the table and those whose joints will let them follow the fashion. . . . For my part I fix myself as comfortably as I can, sometimes on a blanket, sometimes on a box, just as it is convenient. Let me assure you of this, we relish our food none the less for sitting on the ground with eating.[30]

It should be noted that while Narcissa Whitman mentions Stewart and Sillem both in her letters and her diary entries, Eliza Spalding does not. Despite sharing the trail with them all the way to the rendezvous, Eliza chose not to include the men in her personal narrative.

When they reached Fort William (astonishing the white men there, who had not seen white women for many years, and the Indians, who had never seen a white woman at all), the party took a long rest. Here Stewart and Sillem established another first in the history of American hospitality by hosting their own luncheon party. Thanks to the amenities that were available at the fort, the couple were able to serve their guests with a little more comfort and style than Narcissa Whitman was able to muster on the trail: a sturdy table and chairs with buffalo-hide bottoms instead of a rubber mat on the ground, china plates and saucers instead of tin basins for tea. Stewart and Sillem selected their menu from their extensive supply of imported foods, dazzling their guests with an exotic spread that included fine wine, potted meats, pungent aged cheeses, Seville marmalade the color of rich amber, and spicy green mango chethumaangakari, presumably the first time the chutney-like condiment had ever been served west of the Mississippi.

At Fort William, Stewart and Sillem encountered a kindred spirit in a fur trader named Joshua Pilcher. Pilcher was born in Culpepper County, Virginia, in 1790, the eighth child of a dirt-poor farmer who barely scraped a living from the fields he rented. When Joshua was three years old his family made that most American of migrations, through the Cumberland Gap and into the promised land of Kentucky. There his sister married a man in the hatter's trade, and when Joshua was old enough he was apprenticed to his brother-in-law, learning how to turn beaver plews into felt hats for fashionable gentlemen. As he grew into manhood Pilcher's profession changed through a natural progression: from store clerk to owner of a millinery store to commercial banker to entrepreneur in the burgeoning Rocky Mountain fur trade.

Pilcher was handsome and well respected, ambitious and hard working, and although his financial situation fluctuated wildly he always had good prospects, so his status as a lifelong bachelor was a puzzlement that some felt needed an explanation. His family provided it by spinning a very typical story. His biographer explains:

Pilcher family tradition holds that Joshua, during his fur-trading career, was engaged to a girl in Lexington. According to the story, passed along from generation to generation by Joshua's cousins, Hiram Shaw, Joshua's nephew, was escorting the girl to St. Louis to meet Joshua when his wagon overturned while fording a stream or crossing a marsh. The young lady was drenched, developed pneumonia, and died before she and Joshua could be married. If there is any truth to the story, Joshua may have become engaged to the girl during his visit to Lexington during the winter of 1823–24, or, at least, may have met her at that time. . . . The tale is poignant, and if not apocryphal, may account for Joshua's failure to marry — at least with license or benefit of clergy.

Shortly before meeting Stewart and Sillem, Pilcher did take a Native American woman *à la façon du pays*, and she bore him a child, but she died soon after in the cholera pandemic that swept across the plains in 1835. Pilcher showed little interest in his son, and the boy was taken away and reared by Big Elk, an Omaha chief.[31]

Though he spent many years in the Rockies, Joshua Pilcher never forgot his youthful experience in men's haberdashery. He was an elegant dandy to the extent that his residency in the wilds permitted, and perhaps inevitably he drew sarcastic scorn from the pen of the missionary agent William Gray: "With the company was a gentleman from St. Louis, a Major Pilcher. He usually rode a fine white mule, and was dressed in the top of hunting or mountain style, such as a fine buckskin coat trimmed with red cloth and porcupine quills, fine red shirt, nice buckskin pants, and moccasins tinged and nicely trimmed; he was, in fact, very much of a gentleman in all his conversation and deportment. The major was also considerable of a gallant (as I believe most titled gentlemen are)." Pilcher, the son of a failed sharecropper, was about as far from being a titled gentleman as white America was capable of producing, but he carried himself with an elegant insouciance that concealed his humble background.[32]

Gray was always on the lookout for the sin of worldly vanity and never ceased to rejoice when it received its just punishment. He could therefore barely contain his glee when in giving a tour of the trading post's salt pits to Narcissa Whitman and Eliza Spalding, Pilcher suffered a humiliating accident. "He was proceeding around one of those clay salts pits, and explaining to the ladies their nature and danger, when suddenly mule, major and all dropped out of sight, except the mule's ears and the fringe on the major's coat. Instantly several men were on hand with ropes, and assisted the major and mule out of the pit. *Such a sight!* you may imagine what you please, I will not attempt to describe it. However, no particular harm was done, only the thorough saturation of his fine suit of buckskin, and mule, with the indescribably adhesive mud." Pilcher soon joined Stewart and Sillem in their enclosed social group, and the three men rode together to the rendezvous.[33]

The annual gathering for 1836 was being held once again on the Green River, near the fork of Horse Creek. Fitzpatrick's company was only two days' journey from the gathering, just approaching the Continental Divide, when an event occurred that made several members of the party wonder if they would arrive at the rendezvous with their scalps intact. On July 3, as they made camp on the Sweetwater, over the brow of the hill rode around twenty horsemen, galloping in a mad charge, whooping and shrieking bloodcurdling yells, waving their rifles over their heads as they urged their horses onward. The camp hurriedly assumed a defensive formation; Narcissa Whitman and Eliza Spalding retreated to the shelter of the wagon. The party braced itself and waited tensely — until someone pointed out that at least some of the riders were white men, and that they had tied a white rag to one of the rifles and were waving it in greeting. Word had reached the rendezvous that Fitzpatrick was approaching and that he was bringing with him — mirabile dictu — white women.

Joe Meek, the organizer of this mountain-style welcoming party, later described it to an interviewer:

On they came, riding faster and faster, yelling louder and louder, and gesticulating more and more madly, until, as they met and passed the caravan, they discharged their guns in one volley over the heads of the company, as a last finishing *feu de joie*; and suddenly wheeling rode back to the front as wildly as they had come. Nor could this first brief display content the crazy cavalcade. After reaching the front, they rode back and forth, and around and around the caravan, which had returned their salute, showing off their feats of horsemanship, and the knowing tricks of their horses together; hardly stopping to exchange questions and answers, but seeming really intoxicated with delight at the meeting.[34]

When Fitzpatrick's caravan reached the Green River the rendezvous was already well under way. Nearly fifteen hundred whites and Indians (Snakes and Bannocks, Flatheads and Nez Percés) were camped in scattered groups that extended for three miles along Horse Creek. The missionaries camped at a discreet distance from the bacchanal, but the rumor that there were white women in the tents quickly spread up and down the creek. Mountain men wandered over for a furtive peek, while the Indians for their part were determined to welcome these strange and honored guests with a formal grand promenade.

"The procession commenced at the east or lower end of the plain in the vicinity of the Snake and Bannock camps," William Gray remembered.

The Nez Percés and Flatheads, passing from their camps down the Horse Creek, joined the Snake and Bannock warriors, all dressed and painted in their gayest uniforms, each having a company of warriors in war garb, that is, naked, except a single cloth, and painted, carrying their war weapons, bearing their war emblems and Indian implements of music, such as skins drawn over hoops with rattles and trinkets to make noise. . . . When the cavalcade, amounting to full five (some said six) hundred Indian warriors (though I noticed quite a number of native belles covered with beads), commenced coming up through the plain in sight of our camps, those of us who were not informed as to the object or design of this demonstration began to look at our weapons and calculate on a desperate fight. Captain Stewart, our

English nobleman, and Major Pilcher waited on the mission ladies and politely informed them of the object of the display; they assured them there would be no danger or harm, and remained at their tents while the cavalcade passed.[35]

Rev. Henry Spalding wrote from the rendezvous including his only reference to his unusual traveling companions. "At this camp we found about 300 men, and three times the number of animals, employed by the Fur Company in taking furs, and about 2000 Indians, Snakes, Bonnaks, Flatheads, and Nez Perces. Captain Steward, an English gentleman of great fortune, and Mr. Seileim, a German, traveled with us for discovery and pleasure."[36]

Eliza Spalding, though still weak from the rigors of the journey and needing to spend much time in her tent, became a great favorite of the Indian women, especially after she began a serious effort to learn the Nez Percé language. Though all of the missionaries recognized that the language barrier would present a significant obstacle to their proselytizing, Eliza alone embraced the hard work of meeting the Indians halfway.

Narcissa, to her evident delight, became the belle of the rendezvous, and the trappers would invent excuses to linger near the missionary camp hoping to catch a glimpse of her but becoming flustered to the point of being tongue-tied if she spoke to them. Gray could not resist comparing the conduct of the two women.

Mrs. Spalding's rest from the fatigues of the journey soon enabled her to commence a vocabulary of the Indian language. Mrs. Whitman also commenced one with her, but she was often interrupted by the attentions thought necessary to be paid to gentleman callers. Excuse me, whoever believes that thirty-three years since there were no gentlemen on top of the Rocky Mountains. I can assure you that there were, and that all the refined education and manners of the daughter of Judge Prentiss, of Prattsburg, Steuben County, N.Y., found abundant opportunity to exhibit the cardinal ornaments of a religious and civilized country. No one, except an eye-witness, can appreciate or fully understand the charm there was in those early days in the sight of the form and white features of his mother. The rough veteran mountain hunter would touch his hat in a manner absolutely ridiculous, and often fail to express a designed compliment, which the mischief or good-humor of Mrs. Whitman sometimes enjoyed as a good joke.[37]

Joe Meek was less censorious of Narcissa's conduct and praised her ability to resurrect the dormant civility of his fellow trappers, noting that "the leaders of the American Fur Company, Captain Wyeth and Captain Stuart, paid Mrs. Whitman the most marked and courteous attentions. She shone the bright particular star of that Rocky Mountain encampment, softening the hearts and the manners of all who came within her womanly influence."[38]

The missionaries were distressed to discover that Rev. Samuel Parker, who was supposed to meet them at the rendezvous and lead them on to Oregon, had decided not to come. From Thomas McKay and John McLeod of the Hudson's Bay Company they learned that Rev. Parker had in fact abandoned the Oregon Mission entirely, sailing to Oahu and then home to Ithaca, New York. McKay and McLeod volunteered to guide the Whitmans and the Spaldings on the final leg of their journey. Stewart, Sillem, and Pilcher parted with the missionaries in the final days of the rendezvous, wishing them well as the small band headed west into the rugged Rockies.

When the Whitmans and the Spaldings reached the Pacific coast they paused to recuperate at Fort Vancouver, then went their separate ways. By then it was clear to all parties that Marcus Whitman and Henry Spalding would never be able to cooperate with one another. Marcus and Narcissa Whitman settled at Waiilatpu, in the Walla Walla Valley, and opened a mission to the Cayuse Indians. Henry and Eliza Spalding traveled on to Lapwai, near present-day Lewiston, Idaho, to preach to the Nez Percés.

Twelve years later, after his return to Britain, William Drummond Stewart would open his copy of the *Times* of London to read a shocking headline: "The Massacre of the American Mission in Oregon." The newspaper reprinted a letter from the governor and committee of the Hudson's Bay Company announcing, "Our lamented friend Dr. Whitman, his amiable and accomplished lady, with nine other persons, have fallen victims to the fury of these remorseless savages." The Cayuse Indians, ravaged by dysentery and measles, suspected that Dr. Whitman, who claimed to be dispensing medicine in an attempt to relieve their suffering, had actually poisoned them and brought about the deaths of their tribesmen.[39]

Stewart's movements in the weeks immediately after the rendezvous are undocumented. It is likely that he and Adolph Sillem rode off for an extended hunting excursion into the Wind River Range. An encounter with them may have been recorded in George Frederick Ruxton's *Life in the Far West*. Ruxton was an Englishman who traveled throughout the West in 1846 and 1847, returning home to write an account of his adventures that was serialized in *Blackwood's Edinburgh Magazine*. His dramatic narrative interweaves Ruxton's personal experiences with those of others told to him along the trail. Though he could not himself have met William Drummond Stewart (who had returned to Scotland before Ruxton's visit to the Rockies), his secondhand account of a wilderness encounter is clearly a description of the Scotsman and a friend:

> The two strangers approached. One, a man of some fifty years of age, of middle height and stoutly built, was clad in a white shooting-jacket, of cut unknown in mountain tailoring, and a pair of trousers of the well-known material called "shepherd's plaid;" a broad-brimmed Panama shaded his face, which was ruddy with health and exercise; a belt round the waist supported a handsome bowie-knife, and a double-barrelled fowling-piece was *slung* across his shoulder.
>
> His companion was likewise dressed in a light shooting-jacket, of many pockets and dandy cut, rode on an English saddle and in *boots*, and was armed with a superb double rifle, glossy from the case, and bearing few marks of use or service. He was a tall, fine-looking fellow of thirty, with light hair and complexion; a scrupulous beard and mustache; a wide-awake hat, with a short pipe stuck in the band,

but not very black with smoke; an elaborate powder-horn over his shoulder, with a Cairngorm in the butt as large as a plate; a blue handkerchief tied round his throat in a sailor's knot, and the collar of his shirt turned carefully over it. He had, moreover, a tolerable idea of his very correct appearance, and wore Woodstock gloves.[40]

Both men remain unnamed in Ruxton's narrative, and while the young companion might be the dandyish Joshua Pilcher, the newness of the man's equipment makes an identification as Adolph Sillem much more likely. (Also, Pilcher was forty-six while Sillem was twenty-five — closer to the "fine-looking fellow of thirty" described in the encounter.) The strangers share their supplies with two starving mountain men, and with the enumeration of the victuals there is no mistaking the identity of the host: "Hams, tongues, tins of preserved meats, bottles of pickles, of porter, brandy, coffee, sugar, flour, were tumbled promiscuously on the prairie; whilst pots and pans, knives, forks, spoons, plates, &c. &c. displayed their unfamiliar faces to the mountaineers."[41]

At some point in their wanderings Stewart and Sillem met up with Jim Bridger, who was trapping in the mountains, and they traveled together as far as Fort William, where they joined Thomas Fitzpatrick. Stewart and Sillem made the long trek back to St. Louis with Fitzpatrick and his party.

Adolph Sillem appears to have ended his American adventure during the early autumn of 1836. He eventually returned home to Hamburg, where he formed a trading company with his older brother Carl under the name C & A Sillem; among other business ventures he owned a cookie factory and a slaughterhouse that provided salted meat to the British navy. He became an avid collector of fine art, eventually donating his private collection of Spanish Masters and other paintings to the Hamburg Kunsthalle. At the age of forty-eight he married a woman named Johanne Bornemann; the couple had no children of their own but adopted a daughter, who died young. Adolph Sillem himself died in 1884 at the age of seventy-three, never having returned to America.

When he arrived in St. Louis at the close of the summer of 1836, William Drummond Stewart found several letters waiting for him. Archibald, his youngest brother, wrote welcoming him home from the wilds. George, the fourth of the Stewart sons (a lifelong bachelor who was then living with his two spinster aunts on one of the family estates, Logiealmond) enthused about progress on the new Murthly Castle. One of the Logiealmond aunts, Frances Marie Drummond (Aunt Fanny), worried that poor William was being forced to endure a prolonged stay in America because he had no money to purchase a return ticket. She offered to send him £100. She also wrote that his brother Thomas was visiting on leave from the seminary, but that he would soon be returning to Rome.

At this time, in a letter that has not survived, William learned that his elder brother, John, was seriously — perhaps fatally — ill. Given the unresolved rancor concerning their father's estate, the information perhaps triggered a storm of conflicting emotions. If John were not to recover from his illness, William's life would necessarily undergo profound changes. In 1832 John had married the former Lady Jane Steuart, but they were as yet childless. Were John to die without a son, William would inherit the title, the lands, and the bulk of the family fortune. Notably missing from the stack of letters that awaited him in St. Louis was any envelope with the stationery mark of his brother's

Edinburgh solicitor forwarding the much-needed remittance checks, so — family affection aside — the question of money loomed large.

William wrote to John pointing out that the trust had failed to send him his annuity and requesting once again that he receive the entire £3,000 as a lump sum. John eventually replied that due to the enormous amounts being expended on the construction of the new castle, there was simply no money available to send to him. It is perhaps an indication of the emotional distance between the brothers that John's letter is dated December 26, 1836, but makes no mention of the fact that it was written on William's birthday.

Now that Stewart was once again back in St. Louis, and with the departure of Adolph Sillem for Hamburg, Antoine Clement resumed his former prominence in Stewart's life. Their on-again, off-again relationship had continued since their first acquaintance at the 1833 rendezvous, but it is difficult to trace the course of their romance since, unlike some of the other men traveling to and from the Rockies, Clement often passed without comment in the letters, journals, and memoirs that are the chief sources of information about the events of those years. If he is noted at all, it is a brief reference to his hunting skills. As a Métis he blended into the background, little more than one of "the boys" — local color for the American or European travelers who eagerly devoured the buffalo ribs his hunting skills procured while never considering it necessary to learn his name. Hence we know much more about the actions of less important figures such as Charles Ashworth and Adolph Sillem. If Clement is mentioned at all in the contemporary sources, he is usually referred to as "Antoine the Hunter" — with no last name.

By the autumn of 1836, as Stewart and Clement boarded a steamboat heading for New Orleans, the Scotsman had probably been sexually active in America for over four years, and while all of his possible partners have not been identified, a pattern does begin to emerge. Stewart was attracted to somewhat younger men. Adolph Sillem was only twenty-five. In *Altowan* the young English nobleman Roallan is nineteen at the beginning of the novel, and the title character in *Edward Warren* is "not [yet] nineteen." The mysterious and alluring Lord Fernwold is "about twenty." When "Antoine Clement" first appears in *Edward Warren* he is "under twenty." Stewart seems to have considered that an ideal age. Most of his partners fall into an age group of eighteen to twenty-five — young men who have reached physical maturity but who retain an adolescent boisterousness, reckless in their profligacy, insatiable in their appetites, effusive in their gratitude, mercurial in their affections, by turns playful and petulant, neglectful and demanding, intellectually curious but with a frustratingly short attention span. In other words, young men who might be labeled "high maintenance."

Antoine Clement fits the profile to perfection, with the added fillip that he seems to have displayed only a sardonic acquiescence to Stewart's sexual overtures. As has been noted, he was also not the slightest bit impressed by Stewart's noble blood. Judging himself by the criteria that were of importance in the mountains, he considered himself Stewart's equal — if not his better. Clement held a place in Stewart's affections for many years, and though he remains a somewhat shadowy figure in the historical record, it is easy to understand why at that first rendezvous in 1833 George "Beauty" Holmes, with his quiet puppy-dog loyalty, was relegated to sleeping by the campfire while the untamed Antoine Clement perhaps shared Stewart's improvised bower.

In New Orleans Stewart received a letter from his friend and Scottish neighbor at Taymouth Castle, Lord Breadalbane. The laird made an odd request. Evidently unaware of the difficulties involved in the endeavor, he casually asked Stewart to send him several buffaloes "or any other animal of the west that is good to eat." These would be the first of many animals and plants that would make their way from the prairies of America to the banks of the River Tay.[1]

Early one April morning Stewart left his New Orleans hotel, walked one block down Canal Street, and turned onto Chartres. There above the dry goods store of L. Chittenden at number 26 he entered the studio of a young artist named Alfred Jacob Miller. Miller later recalled the visit in some detail — how a well-dressed gentleman entered the studio and began examining the paintings on the walls. The man was wearing a grey suit with a black stripe along the seams of his trousers, and he held himself with a stiff military air. Finally the stranger pointed to a landscape painting of the city of Baltimore. "I like the management of that picture and the view," he said, and left without further comment.[2]

Miller was a Baltimore native who had shown much artistic promise as a youth. In 1833 he studied painting in Europe for a year, spending time in France and Italy, living in a deeply homosocial milieu that included sculptors Bertel Thorvaldsen, John Gibson, and Horatio Greenough — artists who were drawn to a classical style that provided plentiful opportunities to render muscular male nudes. "On Sundays in Florence," writes art historian William Johnston, "Miller joined Greenough in watching the traditional, local ball game, pallone, held in an amphitheater in the suburbs. This sport, in which the participants were flimsily dressed, provided the sculptor with 'invaluable hints' in the study of movement and muscular development." (Greenough's seminude statue of George Washington, commissioned by Congress for the Capitol Rotunda, proved so controversial that it was moved to the east lawn of the Capitol, then to the Smithsonian, and is now in the National Museum of American History.)[3]

Miller traveled from Rome to Florence in the company of the flamboyant American aesthete Nathaniel Parker Willis. Willis, a poet and a journalist, was one of the first Americans to become famous merely for being famous. Oliver Wendell Holmes described him as "something between a remembrance of the Count D'Orsay and an anticipation of Oscar Wilde," and Edgar Allan Poe satirized him as "The Duc De L'Omlette." Willis was effusive, theatrical, and campy, and the shy Miller was completely charmed. "I could not have been more fortunate in my travelling companion," he later noted of his European sojourn. "He had a fine person, handsome face; courteous manners & although young had already acquired an enviable reputation as a poet." It was a reputation of a different sort, however, that unsettled sculptor Horatio Greenough when Miller and Willis came to stay with him in Florence. Willis's fey posturing and ribald pronouncements were embarrassingly indiscreet. Greenough wrote to S. F. B. Morse that Willis was "too much dressings and stuffing — *altogether* too much red pepper by the by for our moral latitude." After the visitor's departure Greenough again wrote Morse, "W. is not a man after my heart; he is corrupt, depend on it; I have been obliged to haul off, for he assumed intimacy of the closest kind."[4]

Upon returning home to Baltimore, Miller opened a small studio and experienced some local success selling landscapes, portraits, and copies of Old Masters. To an exhibition held at the Boston Athenaeum he submitted a painting intriguingly titled *The Destruction of Sodom* and the following year *The Capture of Andre*, illustrating one of the most romantic episodes of the Revolutionary War. Maj. John Andre was a British officer captured and sentenced to hang for spying. Before his execution he managed so completely to charm his captors with his bravery, gracious manners, and dashing good looks that he became the epitome of correct behavior for an American gentleman.[5]

Miller's father and his mother died in quick succession, and when their estate was probated there was very little money left to support the nine surviving siblings. Alfred was also entangled in some other, unspecified troubles, and that situation — whatever it was — became so serious he felt he had no choice but to leave his family and his beloved Baltimore. "A young man left his home to seek a fortune in New Orleans," Miller later wrote. "Trouble of all kinds had accumulated and in order not to be burdensome, engaged passage on a merchant ship and in a week reached his destination with $30 in his pocket."[6]

Miller had just begun to establish his reputation in New Orleans when William Drummond Stewart entered his studio, returning a few days later to offer him the commission of a lifetime: a trip to the Rocky Mountains during which Miller was to produce watercolor sketches, later to be worked into a series of large canvases. It is unknown how Stewart came to be familiar with Miller's work. Stewart offered as a reference the British consul in New Orleans, John Crawford (who was also a business partner with Stewart in the cotton trade). In the exhibition catalogue for a recent major exhibition of Miller's work, Lisa Strong points out that Crawford had been consul in Baltimore from at least 1829 to 1833. While this was before Miller's European studies, he had already established by that time a local reputation as a talented artist.

It is not unlikely that a Baltimore acquaintance wrote to Crawford informing him of Miller's presence in New Orleans, and that when Stewart asked his business partner about an artist who might be willing to travel to the Rockies with him, Crawford suggested Miller's name.[7]

In desiring an artist to accompany him and record the trip, Stewart was following in the footsteps of Prince Maximilian zu Wied-Neuwied, who had brought the painter Karl Bodmer with him on his journey to the American West in 1833. It is probable that Stewart, anticipating his brother's death and his own ascendance to the baronetcy, assumed that this would be his last visit to the Rocky Mountains and he wished to have a permanent record of this important phase of his life. For Miller it was a chance to move beyond the piecework of portrait commissions and to take on a new and exotic subject matter, one that might make his reputation as a painter.

Miller was also fascinated by what he saw of Stewart and Clement. Their personal relationship was ambiguous, but clearly not what one might expect between two men of such different social standings. "He had Antoine with him," Miller later wrote, " — a famous Western hunter & on visiting Capt. S. at his residence of an evening — have seen him play cards with Antoine in order to amuse that wild child of the Prairie who was like a fish out of water in New Orleans — I learned afterwards that he was instrumental in saving Capt. S's life on one or two occasions in the mountains." Miller had mingled with a highly bohemian crowd in Europe and was to remain a lifelong bachelor, with no recorded romances with women. If he was not actively homosexual at the time he met Stewart, he almost certainly sensed that there was something of that nature associated with his new patron.[8]

If Miller was romantically drawn to any man at this point in his life, it was probably his longtime Baltimore friend Brantz Mayer. His letters to Mayer are flippant and flirtatious, providing an interesting contrast to the more sober letters he wrote to his brothers and sisters. Describing the adventure upon which he was about to embark, Miller assured Mayer that there were no *personal* entanglements involved with his decision to accept the offer from such a wealthy patron. "I have much gratification in informing you, that I am at present under engagement to proceed with Capt. W. Stewart, (an affluent gentleman,) on an expedition to the Rocky Mountains, (professionally) the tour to accompany six months, — and I speak candidly & truthistically when I say, that I wish you were with us — it's a new and wider field both for the poet & painter — for if you can weave such beautiful garlands with the simplest flowers of Nature — what a subject her wild sons of the West present."[9]

Once Stewart, Clement, and Miller arrived in St. Louis, Stewart began to assemble his personal entourage. It was to include the experienced mountain man François Lajeunesse, a cook, three *engagés* (young men, usually French Canadians, who were hired to perform general tasks), and two packers. Stewart purchased two wagons, eight mules, and a wide variety of hams, dried fruits, marmalades, and other luxury edibles. He also took possession of a heavy box that had come addressed to him from London. The box became an object of great mystery; he would reveal to no one what it contained.

The men made the expected courtesy call on Governor William Clark, who welcomed his visitors seated in an enormous armchair covered by a large grizzly bear robe. The famous explorer was in the twilight of his life (he would die the following year). They found him surrounded by a personal museum of Indian arrowheads, bows, war clubs, peace pipes, parfleches, beaded moccasins, buckskin shirts, blankets, spears, shields — artifacts he had gathered for decades beginning with his historic journey with his companion Meriwether Lewis, who had committed suicide shortly after the two men returned to St. Louis. Miller was impressed by the great man's "fine head (surrounded with a mass of hair falling over his shoulders)" and with his "quick vigorous eyes & expressive features. It seemed to delight him to recount to us some of the perils of his Early journey, — its hardships, privations, & dangers; — regretted that from old age & infirmaties he could not go with us."[10]

Stewart left Miller in St. Louis and continued on "above fort Independence" to see to the final arrangements for the trip. From the finest hotel in St. Louis, Miller wrote Brantz Mayer a letter that was coquettish in tone and almost giddy with excitement. "I shall not tell *you* why I have penned this 'first impression' — because, it's best, never to be too explicit — *truly* remarked — it is not — (I have found in painting that whenever I left any thing for the imagination to fill up, that it invariably did me more than justice) — but, if any one else should ask me confidentially — and I felt at the moment disposed to enlighten them — I would answer — because I highly esteem you, & value your friendship."[11]

In April 1837 Stewart and his men joined the party of Pratte, Chouteau and Company making the annual trek to the Rockies with trading supplies for the rendezvous, again led by Stewart's old friend Tom Fitzpatrick. David L. Brown, a young man traveling west to recover his health, signed on to accompany the caravan, and he recorded that "there were some sixty or seventy daring and hirsute men, whose special business it was to protect this property in its tedious and somewhat dangerous transit across the almost interminable prairies." Brown writes that the party included "Captain Stewart, of the British army, Mr. Miller, (an artist) and a Mr. Phillipson, both of whom were in the Captain's suite, as likewise an Indian half-breed, who was to act as hunter and purveyor to the party." Again, Antoine Clement is referred to only obliquely, through his race and function rather than as a full-fledged member of the group.[12]

"Mr. Phillipson" was Louis Phillipson, the son of a St. Louis merchant. Stewart uses Louis's older brother Philippe as a character in *Edward Warren*, describing him as "a young fair haired Jew . . . the most beautiful boy I ever saw." In the novel Philippe dies near Lexington, Missouri, after eating too many ripe peaches. "Phillipson of the year before, so young and full of life, had fallen a victim to his love of those luxuries of which he had been so long deprived, inducing a cholera which proved fatal, and his remains lie there under the shade of the forest; a lesson how little is respected by our common enemy, beauty or youth, with its seemingly unquenchable fire." In a footnote added to the novel Stewart describes the Phillipson patriarch as "a Polish Jew, an agreeable old man," whose "family consisted of Philippe, the belle of the mountains, the darker and more serious, but no less handsome Louis[,] and Miranda; the two last, the most extraordinary pianists I ever heard. . . . Louis accompanied the author to the rendezvous of 1836, and was drowned in Lewis's Fork." (Note Stewart's focus on the brothers' good looks — especially his reference to Philippe as a belle rather than a beau — and his rather slighting reference to their sister.)[13]

Two days out of Westport Fitzpatrick appointed Stewart as second in command of the entire enterprise. Despite his penchant for French wines and Valencia marmalades and his unapologetic status as a gentleman on a "pleasure trip," Stewart was already recognized by his peers as a strong leader and an experienced hand in the fur trade.

How strong that hand could be was driven home to Miller early in the journey, when he learned that his position as official artist did not exempt him from his share of camp chores. (Miller later described Stewart on the trail as a "military martinet" and a "capricious tyrant.") When he complained to his patron that he could not possibly chase horses, gather firewood, keep the night watch, *and* paint masterpieces, Stewart agreed to let him hire other men to set up his tent and take his place as night guard — *if* Miller paid for it out of his own pocket.[14]

Stewart's meticulous attention to detail extended even to — perhaps especially to — the artistic work he had commissioned from Miller. One day as he was delivering a laundry list of subjects he felt the artist should not fail to paint, Miller finally snapped.

"Well!" he exploded in exasperation, "if I had half a dozen pair of hands, it should have been done!"

Stewart, realizing he had pushed the normally mild-mannered artist to his limit, flashed a disarming smile, and murmured soothingly, "That would be a *great* misfortune."

"Why?"

"It would be *very* expensive in the matter of kid gloves."[15]

Miller was entranced by what he saw and quickly covered his pages with rough watercolor sketches of mountain men and Indians, of horses and buffalo and grizzly bears. He would later copy and recopy the watercolors, and he added descriptions of many of the events that the

paintings recorded. As a result we have meticulously detailed information of daily life along the route.

Miller's fascination with the strange landscape that surrounded him
was so enthralling that it could have led to his demise. "Selecting the
best site & setting to work being completely absorbed, about half an
hour transpired when suddenly I found my head violently forced down
& held in such a manner that it was impossible to turn right or left. An
impression ran immediately through my mind that this was an Indian
& that I was lost. In five minutes, however, the hands were removed. It
was our Commander. He said, 'Let this be a warning to you or else on
some fine day you will be among the missing. You must have your eyes
and wits about you.'"[16]

Life on the trail quickly settled into a routine. The day began just
before sunrise, with the rousing cry of "Levez! Levez!" Members of the
mess gathered for coffee and leftovers from the previous night's meal,
served on tin plates and speared with a single utensil. "With a 'Bowie'
you separate a large rib from the mass before you," Miller explained,
"hold firmly to the smaller end, and your outrageous appetite teaches
all the rest." By the time the sun rose above the horizon, the caravan was
on the move, not stopping until midday, for a two-hour break called a
nooning. After a meal and a rest, the party got under way once more.[17]

As the end of each day's travel approached, scouts were sent out to
find a likely campsite, a large flat area with sufficient grass and water.
When the caravan had wended its way to the selected spot, the wagons
and horses would swing in a wide arc, eventually closing into a circle
around five hundred to six hundred feet in diameter. While campfires
were lit and tents were erected, the horses were released to graze until,
near sunset, the call would be issued, "Attrapez des chevaux!" The men
would run out, capture the horses, and lead them into the encircled
encampment, where they were tethered for the night.

Supper would be eaten around the campfire, with the men of each
separate mess sharing a meal and entertaining one another with songs
and lies. Stewart, who had traveled to lands more exotic than many
of the others could ever imagine, held them all rapt with his tales of the

Egyptian pyramids and Turkish bazaars. "Our Leader," Miller wrote, "would entertain them with his adventures in foreign lands, the curious cities, and monuments of antiquity he had visited; it was edifying to see the patience with which he answered their simple questions, as if they were matters of course, and full of importance. . . . It is not to be wondered at that he became immensely popular amongst them." As darkness settled in, Stewart would retire to his private tent, and Miller to his. Other men slept under wagons or, on particularly cold nights, wrapped themselves in horse blankets and slept with their feet toward a roaring fire, spread out like spokes on a wheel with a warm glowing hub.[18]

Stewart possessed the shrewd ability to manage the disputatious and unruly spirits under his command, playing in turn the implacable martinet and the wise father. One day two men who had for days been spoiling for a fight at last came to blows. Someone ran to get the captain, but he calmly replied that they should be left alone to slug it out until one had been soundly beaten. Afterward he sent for the man who had been defeated.

"You have been fighting and you are whipped."

"Oui, mon Capitan."

"By Jove! I am heartily glad to hear it. I am certain you have nothing to boast of. Go."

Then he sent for the man who had won the contest, who swaggered over with a cocky and impudent grin.

"You have whipped Louis?" Stewart asked.

"C'est vrai."

Stewart then told him in no uncertain terms that if he ever heard him boasting of his victory in any manner whatsoever, he would confiscate his horse and make him walk for a week. "No more fighting took place in the camp," Miller reported.[19]

The captain was quick to share his exotic provisions with the men, though the strangeness of the food led to some awkward social situations. One morning Stewart decided to treat the men in his mess to a traditional British breakfast. Lacking kippers, he opened one of his precious cans of tinned sardines. He handed the opened tin to the first man, who exclaimed, "Fish!" and dumped the entire contents onto his plate. Rather than embarrass the man, Stewart retrieved his entire supply of sardines and gave a tin to everyone around that morning's campfire.[20]

Miller had known Stewart only as a cultivated, gentlemanly patron of the arts and a connoisseur of fine dining. On the trail he soon discovered that his patron had morphed into another persona. Once Stewart was placed in a command position, he became "the Captain" — a strict disciplinarian, laying down the rules and seeing to their swift enforcement. He pushed his men — and he pushed himself — whatever the trail conditions. When it rained for two or three days in a row, soaking the men's clothing as well as their bedrolls so that it was impossible ever to be completely dry, Miller fell into a deep depression. "What is the matter with you?" Stewart asked. Miller grumbled that the constant damp was wearing him down and would no doubt bring on a bout of rheumatism. Stewart only laughed. "Your early training . . . has been faulty; — on such days I am more exhilarated, if possible, than if the day is clear. There is something to contend against."[21]

For one agonizing day the something to contend against was overpowering thirst. As the party approached the Continental Divide the men knew that there would be no water until the end of the day's journey, when they would at last reach the rivers that flowed in the opposite direction, toward the Pacific. The logical response would have been to carry extra water to see them through this stretch of the trail, but among the mountain men this expedient was considered "effeminate." Tradition dictated that a man test his mettle by going without. The day was long, hot, and dusty, the sun a disk of molten iron in a burning sky. Just before sunset, when tongues had begun to swell, throats were parched, and thirst had become almost unbearably excruciating, water was at last spotted on the horizon. The sight set off what Miller described as "a general stampede among the horsemen." Stewart dismounted and walked the remaining distance at a slow, dignified pace, proving his mettle — to his men, to Miller and, perhaps, to himself.[22]

Stewart at times insisted that others test themselves just as severely.

One day Miller was sketching a foaming, booming mountain stream when he noticed the Captain surveying the cataract, apparently searching for a good crossing place — a pointless risk to take as he would only have to cross it again to get back to the camp. Incredulous, Miller asked him if that was his intention, and Stewart answered with a curt "Yes." Soon a mountaineer called out, "Allons nous en — mes amis! J'ai la trouvé la place." Miller really did not care whether or not the man had found a likely fording place and was appalled when he realized that the Captain not only intended to attempt the dangerous crossing but also insisted that Miller accompany him. Stewart advised him to keep his horse's nose out of the water but otherwise to allow the horse to have his own way. The animals stumbled and swam through the rushing current, at one point in danger of drifting up against a perpendicular bank, an event that would almost certainly have caused both horse and rider to drown. Miller reached the other side cold, wet, and unnerved by how close he had come to being swept downstream to certain death. Stewart merely shook himself like a playful drenched dog.

"You swim, don't you!" he asked the artist.

"No!"

"Well, neither do I, it will teach you self reliance, you know not what you can do until you have tried."[23]

The long cavalcade as a whole traveled at such a steady but measured pace that Miller was able to stop briefly along the way to sketch and paint without fear of being left behind. At times Antoine Clement would accompany him, and his skill as a hunter proved beneficial to the artist. Clement knew how to graze a bullet off a buffalo's skull in such a way as to stun the animal without harming it. Dazed by the impact, the beast would stand still for several minutes, allowing Miller to approach and make quick but detailed sketches. On one occasion Clement, in a typical burst of bravado and devilment, ran up behind a groggy buffalo, grabbed the tail, and wrapped it firmly around his wrist. When the animal recovered its senses, it "turned first one way & then another, swinging A. round about as if he was a feather, and lifting him completely off the ground."[24]

Mindful of the request of his friend Lord Breadalbane, one morning Stewart took Clement with him and rode out to capture some buffalo to send back to Scotland. They returned with seven specimens (male and female) that were then dispatched overland to Bellevue, by steamer to St. Louis, and then down the Mississippi to New Orleans and a ship voyage to Europe. "Afterwards," wrote Miller, "while sojourning in Scotland, we paid a visit to these animals, — they were enclosed in a paddock, with a circumference of 5 or 6 miles, but had become completely tame; — they were however healthy and with an addition of 2 calves." The buffalo would delight a young Queen Victoria during her visit to the wilds of Scotland.[25]

Miller was particularly awed by the Indians he encountered, and he sketched many scenes and individual portraits. There was an innate nobility in their carriage and a powerful beauty in their nearly naked bodies that the artist found irresistible. "American sculptors travel thousands of miles to study Greek statues in the Vatican at Rome, seemingly unaware that in their own country there exists a race of men equal in form and grace (if not superior) to the finest beau ideal ever dreamed of by the Greeks."[26]

Not surprisingly, Stewart himself is the primary subject of most of the twenty-eight oil paintings and eighty-seven watercolors and sketches that Miller produced for his noble patron between 1837 and 1842. With his white buckskin jacket, wide-brimmed hat, and prominent aquiline nose, Stewart is unmistakable. Unmistakable also is the presence of Antoine Clement. "Antoine was Stewart's constant companion during the American sojourn," writes art historian Lisa Strong. "His distinctive facial features, belted jacket, and loose-brimmed hat are recognizable in over a third of Miller's sketches."[27]

Miller's images document this intensely close period of the relationship that developed between Stewart and Clement, though at the distance of 150 years we cannot be certain how to read the paintings. At the very least they suggest that the men were, as Strong observes, constant companions — though with Clement's status as premier hunter on the trip this might be expected. Still, in painting after painting Clement is seen in a similar pose: his head raised, his long dark bangs falling over one eye as he gazes up at Stewart in rapt attention. Clement's focus is not on the Indians nor on the prey nor on the stunning landscape, but directly and intensely on one man. In these images Miller may have been recording what he actually saw or, in an effort to please his patron (and frequently at his patron's expressed directive), he may have been merely painting what Stewart *wanted* to see and to remember of this trip. But whether they represent an actual or a psychological record of the events, the images provide an unprecedented and unsurpassed series of views of an intense male-male relationship in America during the early nineteenth century.

About five weeks into their journey the party reached Fort William, the large stockaded trading post belonging to the American Fur Company. Here Stewart was reunited with a superb white stallion he had left behind the year before with orders that no one was ever to ride him. The Captain sent Auguste, one of the engagés, ahead to retrieve the horse, and as the party approached the fort the great wooden gates slowly swung open and the French Canadian galloped out on the white stallion, hollering an Indian war whoop. Unused to being ridden and spooked by the noise and confusion, the horse shied and threw his rider head over heels onto the hard ground. Miller made a quick sketch of the incident showing Auguste pitching forward over the horse's head and Stewart and Clement looking on. In 1841 Fort William was torn down and replaced by the adobe-walled Fort John, so Miller's paintings are the only record of the original structure. In 1849 the federal government purchased Fort John and changed its name to reflect its more popular designation: Fort Laramie.

The caravan traveled on to Independence Rock, where a number of the men could not resist the temptation to add their names to the graffiti covering the huge granite extrusion. David L. Brown, who had described the "daring and hirsute men" of the party, joined a group determined to climb to the very top of the rock. He was stunned by what he saw from that vantage point. "As far as the eye could reach, with an uninterrupted horizon on every side, the field of vision was literally covered and blackened over with multitudinous herds of buffaloes." Buffalo meant fresh meat, and a shout went out for hunters. "Determined to let no feature of prairie life escape my experience," Brown later wrote, "and having as fleet an animal as any in camp, with the exception, perhaps of a powerful grey horse that Captain Stewart rode, I was amongst the first to leap into the saddle. We proceeded leisurely towards the countless herds in compact order, led on by Capt. Stewart and Antoine Clement, his half-breed hunter, with a few men bringing up the rear, with led mules having empty pack-saddles on their backs, in order to take into camp the anticipated spoils of the hunt."[28]

At a signal from Stewart, the men put spurs to their horses and raced into the thundering herd of bison. Brown's account of the hunt is especially vivid:

> I found myself in the centre of a living cataract, almost blinded by the stream of sand and gravel thrown in my face from the hoofs of the terrified mass in their desperate and headlong flight. A cataract, it might well be called, for we were descending into an immense hollow or ravine, which had been hidden from our eyes by the apparent levelness of the whole surface of the prairie. . . . The gigantic animals, snorting with terror and foaming with fatigue, were literally pressing against my horse on every side. Their bloodshot eyes, gleaming fitfully from under the pent-house of their bushy eye-brows, and their shaggy manes, streaming meteor-like on the swift and cleaving air, was a sight at once sublime, fearful, and menacing. To have checked my horse at this time would have been in all probability to incur instant death, as the masses behind would certainly have trodden me, horse and all, into a jelly.[29]

Brown shot and killed a bull buffalo, but when the immediate excitement of the hunt had abated he looked around to discover he had ridden far away from his companions. His concern turned to abject terror when he heard gunshots in the distance and saw Stewart and Clement apparently in hot pursuit of what he assumed must be Indians. Tearing across the prairie to join them, he found that the prey was an immense grizzly bear, rearing on his hind legs and roaring with anger, his snout dripping blood. "The *coup-de-grace* was given to this fierce monster by Capt. Stewart, from the muzzle of a holster pistol, which pierced the brain of this ferocious sultan of the western deserts, and laid him life-less on the prairie-sward. He was quickly denuded of his skin, by the half-breed, Clemment, which, along with some portions of fat, was transferred to the back of a pack-mule."[30]

That night around the campfire Brown enjoyed an experience of warm fellowship that was unparalleled. "Having eaten a hearty supper of roasted buffalo meat, basted and seasoned with the fat of the bear, many a thrilling story of 'perilous adventure' and 'hair-breadth escape' having been told in the intervals, worn out and jaded with fatigue and excitement of the day, I retired to rest, with my saddle for a pillow, the green sward for a bed, the star-lit and eternal vault for a canopy, and for a lullaby the melancholy howlings of innumerable wolves, which, however, neither retarded nor broke the serenity of my slumbers."[31]

After weeks of travel the men finally reached the rendezvous, which in 1837 was once again held on the Green River, between New Fork and Horse Creek. Here Stewart met up with old friends Andrew Drips, Kit Carson, and Joe Walker. In a profession in which danger was ever present and death all too common, seeing an old companion stride forward with a grin on his face and his arms outstretched for a bear hug was a welcome sight. Stewart was especially pleased and relieved to see Jim Bridger, with whom he had trapped and traveled every year since his first rendezvous in 1833. Stewart retained the arrowhead Dr. Whitman had removed from Bridger's back, and this summer he had a special present to give Bridger in return.

The mysterious wooden box with the London shipping label was brought forward and placed on the ground before the puzzled mountain man. When its lid was pried off everyone's eyes grew wide with amazement and delight. Inside were the casque (helmet), cuirass, and greaves of a member of the Queen's Life Guard (Victoria had ascended the throne only the previous month). The cuirass was gleaming plated steel with brass mounts, and the casque sported a flowing white horsehair plume. Bridger quickly donned the armor, and for the remaining days of the rendezvous could be seen parading around the camp, gloriously pleased with his present. It was an odd gift and one Stewart had gone to a great deal of trouble to acquire; clearly it was the result of some private understanding between Stewart and Bridger — a story told, a boyhood wish revealed — but if either man ever explained the meaning behind the present, it has not been recorded. Though Miller made several watercolor sketches featuring Bridger in his gleaming armor, splendidly incongruous among the Indians and the trappers, his notes reveal nothing at all about the significance of the gift.

The sight of Bridger in his armor promenading through the tents and horses, the rendezvous ablaze with color and raucous with the laughter of a midsummer's market faire, may have planted the seed that in 1843 would blossom as the theme of Stewart's last great men's party in the Rockies. David L. Brown was himself struck by the Arthurian pageantry the scene suggested:

> As I gazed in wrapt admiration upon this, to me, dream-like exhibition, my mind instantly reverted to the storied wonders of my childhood and early youth, and I almost expected every moment to see issuing from the bosom of this Indian cantonment, in martial pomp and pride, the mailed and steel-clad forms of the old feudal times, so striking was its resemblance to the pictures already enshrined in my imagination from pouring over the delightful pages of Scott and Froissart, whose inimitable descriptions floated before my mental eye. . . . The tents were identical in shape with those we see represented in old English engravings as belonging to knights, and warriors; and between and around their dazzling white and symmetrical outlines, were grouped in exquisite tableaux the dusky and Apollo-shaped forms of the flower of Indian chivalry.[32]

The dusky Apollos were at first Crows, but the day after the Fitzpatrick-Stewart party arrived at the rendezvous a large contingent of Snake Indians made a grand entrance. Bernard DeVoto describes the scene: "About two hundred and fifty braves on their best horses . . .

rode in full dress ahead of the village. Stately chiefs, caracoling horses, medicine men juggling as they rode, deep-voiced chants, warwhoops, muskets firing, arrows skittering across the plain. Sometimes a squad of young braves break into a gallop, angling away from the column in pursuit of an imaginary Sioux, hanging by their heels on the far side of their horses, shooting arrows under their necks. . . . Others leap to the ground and take imaginary scalps, then ride on singing the scalp song."[33]

With the arrival of the Snakes the rendezvous was officially launched, and that evening Stewart hosted a private party for the most important participants. "The entertainment alluded to," Brown recorded, "was given by the English Captain in a large tent, which he had occasionally used in his journey up from the 'States,' and which resembled very much in size and general construction, those now [1845] used in the U.S. Army by general and field officers on a campaign, and was capable of containing, with perfect comfort to themselves, some twenty-five or thirty persons. On the present occasion it contained some thirty men in all." The menu included buffalo ribs accompanied by the many imported delicacies Stewart had brought along for just this occasion. There was also a wide array of fine liquors, and "if the quantity swallowed be any criterion by which to judge the quality of any given drinkables, then were the Captain's superlative indeed."[34]

In the place of honor at Stewart's right "sat, or rather squatted in oriental fashion" Jim Bridger, his armor set aside for the moment. Brown was impressed by the shear physicality of the man. "Tall — six feet at least — muscular, without an ounce of superfluous flesh to impede its force or exhaust its elasticity, he might have served as a model for a sculptor or painter, by which to express the perfection of graceful strength and easy activity." Also at the dinner party were mountain men Bill Williams and Joe Meek, and — reclining on the ground at the far side of the tent like a coiled snake — Mark Head, the sociopath who three years earlier had taken literally Stewart's call for young Marshall's scalp. Brown was obviously fascinated and repelled: "It would take a stronger pencil than the author of these sketches is capable of wielding, to embody the dark depths and shadows that alone could make up a true picture of this ruthless and remorseless original."[35]

Also present at the rendezvous was William Gray, the dyspeptic missionary agent. This year he was on his way back east in hopes of convincing the American Board to grant him funds to open his own mission. Gray once again looked out over the joyous carnival and saw only godless depravity. "No Sabbaths dawn here to give rest to the body and food to the mind; desolation and profanity is inscribed on all that pertains to man, as if all who had reached these heights had already attained the final consummation of every Earthly object, and once here, they have no fears in relation to this world or the next. They seem to have cast off all fears of both God and man."[36]

Albeit in his sour waspish way, Gray here captured the essence of what life in the Rockies meant to the men who sought refuge there. They existed for however brief a time in a state of perfect solipsism. If the men turned a deaf ear to the preacher's stern warning of inescapable damnation, it was only because his sermonizing did not "speak to their condition." All around them they saw manifest the splendor of creation, in the majesty of the mountains and rivers and in the dignity and grace of the indigenous population, and they could not help but feel themselves a part of something that was exactly as it was supposed to be. In the mountains they had indeed "attained the final consummation of every Earthly object" and any suggestion that they should change their wicked ways was met with angry (or amused) repudiation. This deep affinity for place is why so many men stuck to the fur trade long after there was any hope of profit, and why so many later became trail guides or trading post factors — or simply vanished into the mountains and were never heard from again.

For all its pageantry, the rendezvous of 1837 was not well attended in comparison to earlier gatherings, and it was not a commercial success. Clearly the glory days of the fur trade were over. In London and New York fashionable men were wearing silk top hats instead of felt hats made from beaver pelts; in a few short years the market had completely collapsed. The Panic of 1837, a banking crisis precipitated by

President Jackson's refusal to renew the charter of the Second Bank of the United States, also contributed to the demise of the fur trade, and it was followed by five years of economic depression in America. For old friends gathering on the Green River that year, the frenetic revelry was tinged with both grim foreboding and wistful nostalgia.

His responsibilities as an official leader of the commercial expedition fulfilled with the arrival at the rendezvous, Stewart was determined not to forget that he was on a "pleasure tour" and set off with a small party for some exploration and amusement. He loaded a mule with two ankers of brandy and port wine and headed out into the surrounding mountains. When the members of his party reached a beautiful and secluded lake they decided to camp for the evening and broke open the wine casks. "We are compelled to draw a slight veil over the proceedings," Miller later wrote of that evening's revelries. "Suffice it to say, it was a time (as the Trappers style it) of 'High Jinks.' . . . On retiring that night they went to bed without candles, it was found advisable to let them lie under the first bush they happened to fall, invoking for them Sterne's charitable sentiment that 'the recording angel in writing down the account, would drop a tear and blot them out forever.'" An anker was a measure roughly equivalent to ten American gallons. Only seven men appear in the sketch Miller made of the lakeside camp, and if the artist holding the paintbrush is counted as the eighth (and if no one is hidden in the tents or bushes depicted in the watercolor), each man would have had two and a half gallons of brandy and/or wine to imbibe before the casks were drained to the dregs. It was a memorable evening, and perhaps not unique.[37]

Stewart's wanderings after the rendezvous are unknown and can be speculated on only in reference to the drawings that Miller produced of the sites they visited. It appears they traveled to the Big Horn and then on to the Yellowstone and Cross Creek, eventually arriving at the Grand Tetons. Before the middle of October they had returned to St. Louis. Miller proceeded down the Mississippi to New Orleans, where he began the project of transforming his watercolor sketches into oils on canvas.

In St. Louis Stewart received a letter from his brother George informing him that Lady Harriet Drummond, one of the maiden aunts with whom George lived on the family estate of Logiealmond, had passed away, leaving William a legacy of £10,000. Unfortunately, since at the time of her death the traveler's whereabouts were unknown, she had left the money in the control of his elder brother, John. Not only had John not forwarded the money to William's account, he had failed again to supply the annuity payments owing to William from their father's estate. It was time to take legal action.

"Know all men by these presents," Stewart wrote through his solicitor, "that I, William Stewart, late of Grandtully in Scotland, now at St. Louis, Missouri, have appointed John Stewart, of Marshall Place, Perth, Scotland, my lawful attorney, to ask and demand, sue and receive, all such sums of money, debts and demands which shall be due, owing, and payable to me, especially all rights from the estate of the late Lady Harriet Drummond, deceased, of Logiealmond, and also, for me, to demand annuities coming from Sir John Drummond Stewart, Baronet of Grandtully, of Scotland."[38]

Having attended to the things of this world, Stewart turned his attention to those of the next. On November 25, 1837, in the Cathedral of St. Louis, King of France, the newly constructed edifice on the banks of the Mississippi, William Drummond Stewart was received into the Catholic Church. The reasons for his conversion are unknown. He makes no reference to his faith life in his correspondence, and there is no incident in either of his autobiographical novels that might shed light on his religious beliefs. A Stewart family tradition suggests that while traveling in the Rockies his life was spared by the intercession of a Jesuit priest, who either nursed him to health after he contracted a life-threatening disease or rescued him from drowning after he fell into a raging river (or perhaps nursed him back to health after he fell into a raging river). In gratitude for his recovery, or in fulfillment of a vow taken at the time, Stewart converted to Catholicism. A 1906 article in *Chambers's Journal* credits the conversion to "the kind nursing by the Spanish monks after some border raid."[39]

There are several problems with the various versions of the story. Such a dramatic and picturesque event is unlikely to have been excluded from his autobiographical novels, particularly in the writings of a convert who remained an active and proud member of Scotland's small Catholic community. It is telling that no one in any of the contemporary documentation mentions this illness or accident. Porter and Davenport suggest that the crucial event was an illness that occurred during the 1837 trip to the Rockies, and that Stewart "swore Miller to secrecy" about the Jesuit's ministrations, thus providing an explanation for Miller's complete silence on the subject in his otherwise meticulous notes about daily happenings. Of course, there would be no reason for Stewart to hide the circumstances of his conversion, no reason for Miller to remain silent.[40]

What is more likely is that the formal baptism in St. Louis was the culmination of a personal faith journey that had begun long before Stewart reached America. He was reared in a region of Scotland deeply devoted to Presbyterianism; his home county of Perthshire was a vibrant center of the Scottish Reformation of the sixteenth century, though Murthly itself for many years remained a small island of Catholicism amid an overwhelming Presbyterian hegemony. If Stewart was reared in any religious tradition it was probably Presbyterian, since under Roman Catholic canon law he could not have received the sacrament of baptism a *second* time in St. Louis. The Stewart household was by all evidence divided in its religious affiliations. His father and his brothers John and Archibald were Protestant (Archibald militantly so). His brother George was a member of the Scottish Episcopal Church but was sympathetic to the Free Church of Scotland, a Reformed Presbyterian denomination established in 1843. In 1845 George donated land and building materials for the construction of a church for the Free Church congregation of Ardoch. His brother Thomas converted to Catholicism in 1829 and was later ordained a Catholic priest. Christie was herself a Catholic, and she raised their son, Will, as a member of the Roman Catholic Church. Stewart's movement toward Catholicism probably had its origins in this home atmosphere of mixed religious loyalties.

Many of Stewart's companions in America (in particular Antoine Clement) were French Catholics, and he came to know a number of Jesuit missionaries during his travels, including the legendary Father Pierre-Jean De Smet, the Belgian priest who spent many years among the Flathead and Nez Percé Indians. Jesuits were among the parties traveling with the fur traders on several of Stewart's trips to and from the Rockies, and he came to know them and to admire many of them for their good (if at times misguided) intentions toward the Indians they had come to serve. His experiences with Protestant missionaries were mixed. He had profound respect and admiration for both Jason Lee and Marcus Whitman, but on the whole he found the others with whom he traveled insular, ignorant, and argumentative. His cousin and traveling companion, Charles Augustus Murray (through whom he was introduced to Adolph Sillem), was himself a Catholic. Murray had come under the influence of the renowned John Henry Newman while a student at Oxford.

Much of Stewart's time in America was spent in St. Louis or New Orleans, two cities with a strong French Catholic presence, so what had begun as a leaning toward Catholicism while in Scotland was no doubt reinforced when it became an enveloping part of his environment in the United States. Perhaps because his conversion was slow and incremental it was also undramatic, and he felt no inclination to discuss it in his novels or in his correspondence.

Because Stewart made no explicit reference in his correspondence or his novels to either his Catholicism or his overt homosexual activity, it is impossible to know how one might have influenced the other. It is likely that Stewart, like many contemporary Catholics, simply accepted that the two were irreconcilable on any official level. During his years among the followers of the fur trade, Stewart interacted daily with faithful Catholic men who might spend the night in drunken debauchery but then with perfect piety attend a missionary priest's Mass the next morning, and the ease with which these men integrated the spiritual and the sensual no doubt had a profound effect on his own perceptions. When he returned to Scotland, Stewart assumed a leadership position among Catholics in Perthshire — accounts of his patronage appeared in the local newspapers — and yet he does not seem to have burned with the usual convert's need to witness and proselytize. His was a quiet, undemonstrative, and unassuming faith.

Whatever his reasons, he completed his journey toward membership in the Catholic Church during the winter of 1837 at the cathedral in St. Louis. There the baptismal record for "Wm Stewart of Grandtully" reads: "On the twentyeth day of November eighteen hundred and thirty seven We undersigned Bishop of St Louis have baptised William Stewart of Grandtully in Scotland second son of Sir George Stewart and Lady Catherine Drummond Stewart forty years old, who has returned to the faith of his illustrious ancestors. The Godfather has been the Right Revd. Dr. Simon Bruté Bishop of Vincennes." (Stewart was, in fact, older: in a month he would be forty-three.)[41]

The document is signed by Bishop Joseph Rosati, the first bishop of the Diocese of St. Louis, and Bishop Simon Bruté of nearby Vincennes, Indiana. That Bishop Bruté is listed as Stewart's godfather is of particular interest, as the bishop was also the spiritual advisor of Mother Elizabeth Ann Seton, the first American-born Catholic saint (canonized in 1975). Unfortunately, there is no evidence that Seton and Stewart ever met — or, for that matter, that Bishop Bruté and Stewart had any contact other than the 1837 ceremony. An examination of the letters written by Bishop Bruté to Bishop Rosati during the period from Stewart's first arrival in New York City to his baptism in St. Louis reveals no mention of Stewart's name, and mapping their respective travels gives no indication that Bruté and Stewart were ever in the same place at the same time except for the baptismal service. It is likely that the bishop's role as godfather was purely ceremonial, a nod to Stewart's noble birth rather than any indication of spiritual mentorship.[42]

10

William Drummond Stewart spent the winter of 1837–38 in New Orleans, and by the spring he and Antoine Clement were in St. Louis once again, planning for the annual trek to the Rockies. The announcement had been made that the rendezvous would be held in the usual location on the Green River, but Pratte, Chouteau and Company were having second thoughts. The weakened state of the fur trade had everyone nervous. Moving the rendezvous to the spot where the Popo Agie and the Wind rivers joined to become the Big Horn would eliminate over one hundred miles of slow, expensive mountain travel. The fur trading party this year would be led by Andrew Drips.

For his 1838 journey Stewart would bring only a small contingent with him: one wagon pulled by four mules. Antoine Clement was his sole companion. The absence of an entourage was probably the result of Stewart's straitened economic circumstances. Nothing had come of his demand for the £10,000 he had inherited from Lady Harriet, and even his annuity had been withheld. Adding to his financial woes, the cotton market had taken a dip and as a result his investments were less lucrative than he had hoped.

From an Indian village on the Kansas River, Stewart wrote to Bishop Rosati back in St. Louis, "We are fairly launch'd, a weeks journey on the Prairie, & I commit this to a boat that decends this river which we have just cross'd. We are accompanied by a half dozen of reverend Parsons male & female who go out to convert the Indians & breed cattle. [T]hey are of a curious eastern breed with large hands & feet, who do not know the vulgate from an act of the first congress & sing strange hymns out of tune."[1]

Among that curious eastern breed of hymn singers was the ever-irascible William Gray. In the months since the two men had last encountered each other at the rendezvous, Gray had made his plea to the American Board of Commissioners for Foreign Missions to grant him funds to set up a mission of his own. The board was open to the suggestion in principle but unwilling to compromise on its established policy that only married men could become missionaries. While a guest in the home of Rev. Samuel Parker (who had returned to Ithaca from his own sojourn on the West Coast and in Hawaii), Gray mentioned his need for a wife. It was Parker who had suggested Narcissa Prentiss to Marcus Whitman, and he did not hesitate to suggest that a woman named Mary Augusta Dix might be a suitable helpmeet for Gray. William and Mary were promptly introduced at a church social, and before the evening was over he proposed to her, following up the proposal with a letter the next day in which he repeated his offer and spoke bluntly about the life she would lead as his wife: "Many things you may expect to meet and see that will appear revolting, yet you will remember that it is to reform and render more happy the beings for who[se] good you may be permitted to devote your life." What the letter lacked in romance it made up for in religious zeal, and Mary accepted. The couple were married on February 25, 1838, and the next day headed west.[2]

Accompanying the Grays were three other newly married missionary couples: Elkanah and Mary Richardson Walker, Cushing and Myra Fairbanks Eells, and Asa and Sarah White Smith. Their courtships and weddings had followed much the same pattern as that of William and Mary Gray. William Drummond Stewart, the forty-three-year-old bachelor, had reason to take a sardonic view of the young newlyweds. From the beginning the couples experienced strains in their relationships (both between spouses and among members of the group), spats and bickering that were recorded in woeful detail by Myra Eells and Mary Walker, who both kept diaries during the long and tedious journey.

The missionaries began the journey one day behind the main party, as they at first refused to travel on the Sabbath. It was April 28 before they caught up and were first able to make the acquaintance of the leaders of the cavalcade. "Almost as soon as our tents were pitched," Myra Eells wrote in her diary,

> Captain Drips and Stuart called on us, had a social talk, gave them some biscuit and cheese. They appeared pleasant, though they said we had better travel by ourselves, either before or behind camp, as they should have their animals guarded nights and it might not be convenient for our men to stand guard. Mr. Gray told them his men expected to stand their proportion of the guard. They seemed to think each company had better take care of their own horses. This gives us to understand they did not want us to travel with them. However, Mr. Gray did not mean to take the hint, as he knew it would not be safe for us to travel alone, and insisted on a due proportion of the guards being given to us.

William Gray was being more than just abundantly cautious. They believed that three of their best horses had already been taken by Indians during the night, and they could not afford to lose others.[3]

Along the way the party encountered the Swiss immigrant John Augustus Sutter, whose mill on the American River would in 1848 yield the nuggets that started the California gold rush. "Fell in company with a gentleman from New Orleans who has traveled in Europe, Africa, &c.," noted Mary Eells, "who has entertained us with descriptions of Switzerland, Italy, etc. Gave an account of Swiss dogs digging men out who are buried in the snow." Sutter was not the only guest entertained by the missionaries. The diaries mention Andrew Drips, Lucien Fontenelle, Moses "Black" Harris, J. Andrew Chute, William Preston Clark (son of explorer William Clark), Joe Walker, Jim Robinson, Philip Edwards, F. Y. Ewing, and others. William Drummond Stewart, however, appears not to have shared their hospitality except for the initial offering of biscuit and cheese. He and Clement kept their distance, perhaps sensing that William Gray's tales about Stewart and Sillem had almost certainly poisoned any possibility of a pleasant encounter with the devout missionaries, or perhaps simply deciding that as they had nothing in common, it was not worth pursuing the acquaintance. The party was large enough that if they chose to remain aloof, their paths would cross only briefly and at a distance.[4]

On May 21 Stewart's mules were spooked and in the ensuing melee his wagon was overturned and his provisions scattered. The next day the party had a late start, as it had to wait for repairs to Stewart's wagon. Progress, though slow, was steady, proceeding at the rate of a brisk walk. The party reached Fort Laramie on May 30 and while its members paused to wash, bake bread, and stretch from the rigors of the trail, Black Harris rode off to the site on the Green River where the rendezvous had been held the previous year, and where many of the trappers still assumed it would be held in 1838. To notify them of the change of plans he nailed on a tumbled-down cabin a handwritten sign that read, "Come on to the Popoasie. Plenty of whiskey and white women." The notice promised more than it could deliver, but it was sure to bring the trappers to the right location.

The rendezvous was (as it had always been) a wild carnival of excess. The missionaries were (as they were expected to be) appalled, and when Rev. Elkanah Walker preached his first sermon to the trappers and traders the text was well chosen: 2 Peter 3:7. "But the heavens and the earth . . . are kept in store, reserved unto fire against the day of judgment and perdition of ungodly men." To the immense satisfaction of everyone involved, Rev. Walker and his associates were not required to linger long among ungodly men. On July 8 a party arrived from the Pacific coast led by Francis Ermantinger of the Hudson's Bay Company. Traveling with him were F. Y. Ewing, Philip Edwards, and Jason Lee from the Methodist mission on the Willamette. (For Lee and Stewart, it was their first reunion since the minister borrowed the captain's copy of *Sardanapalus* and came to the conclusion that Byron's tale of the cross-dressing king would not "tend to better the heart or mend the life.") Lee was heading east to ask the mission board for more personnel and more supplies for Oregon, but he carried encouraging news about the efforts of the Whitmans and the Spaldings. When Francis Ermantinger at last led the Grays, the Walkers, the Eells, and the Smiths out of the valley of iniquity, their hearts were uplifted with great hope for the future.[5]

At the close of the annual rendezvous, Stewart and Clement headed off for an extended hunting trip. Their route and their traveling companions are unknown, but by August they had returned to St. Louis. There Stewart found letters waiting informing him that his elder brother, John, had died on May 20 in Paris. One letter was from his friend Lord Breadalbane, addressed to Sublette and Campbell, requesting that they find a way somehow to notify Stewart of his brother's death. Another was from his brother George, assuring him that he had overseen the sealing of the papers and rooms at Murthly Castle, and that they would be secure until William's return, which he presumed would be by the very next available ship. George's letter gave no hint of the melodrama surrounding Sir John's death and the settlement of his estate, or of the scandal that had come so close to engulfing the Stewart family in an inheritance dispute worthy of the pen of Charles Dickens.

When Sir John became ill with the unnamed life-threatening disease, he and Lady Jane traveled to Paris, where it was believed he would get better medical care. There the eighteenth Lord of Grandtully, sixth Baronet of Murthly became a virtual prisoner of the sickbed, while his wife Lady Jane indulged in all the civilized delights that life in sunny France had to offer a nineteenth-century woman of means. Perhaps inevitably she began to dread the day when her husband would be once again well and she would be expected to return with him to Scotland: to damp woolens, reeking bogs, poor drains, and haggis. Though there is no hard evidence with which to convict her, it appears that when Lady Jane weighed the delights of France against the return of her husband's health, France won.

To his family's surprise, one cold December day in 1837 Sir John appeared alone and unannounced at the gates of Murthly Castle, ill and distraught. When he had recovered sufficiently from the exertions of his journey he explained that in France while he was heavily sedated his wife had coerced him into signing a document that he feared was a revised will, leaving to her all of his estate not covered by the entail. This was not his intention, and he was not entirely sure that this was in fact what he had done, but when he later demanded that she show him the document he had signed, she refused. Sir John felt certain that Lady Jane was in league with his doctor, and that the two of them were trying to gain control of as much of the Stewart family property as the law would allow. Sir John's solicitor, James Condie, was quickly summoned from Perth and a new will was drawn up, signed, and witnessed. Sir John returned to France, where Lady Jane either discovered or suspected the reason for his quick visit home. She forced him while under medication to sign yet another will, once again making her the primary beneficiary.[6]

After Sir John's death and burial, the trustees of the estate gathered for the legal formalities. Brother George was the family's representative on the trust, and when Lady Jane's solicitor brandished the second French will and began to explain that his client was the sole heir to all and sundry movables, household furniture, plate, books, pictures, jewels, bed and table linens, horses, cattle, sheep — George cut him off. James Gillespie Graham later wrote to Stewart, "George literally took the <u>Bull by the Horns</u> & — promptly set about and employed the most energetic measures and by his perserverance, & determination, he not only broke down all Lady Janes Barriers, but eventually forced her to abandon the horrid Parisian deed, & every claim she had set up, & fall back on the deed executed by Sir John last year, in short she does not get <u>a pins worth</u> which belonged to the Family, & on your return you will find every thing in the house as you left it."[7]

Condie had left Lady Jane's solicitor very little room to maneuver, as the will that Sir John signed while he was at Murthly began with a bold accusation:

Know all men by these presents that I Sir John Archibald Drummond Stewart of Grandtully Baronet considering that when in France in the year eighteen hundred and thirty six I was attacked with violent indisposition which reduced me to a state of excessive bodily and occasionally mental weakness that while in a state of great suffering and while I was unable to peruse its contents with attention or accuracy a deed was laid before me for execution which I signed in ignorance so far of what it contained that I have not been able since to obtain a perusal of the said deed but have reason to believe that it was a deed conveying to my spouse Lady Jane Stewart the whole furniture and effects belonging to me in the house of Murthly and nominating her my Executrix . . .[8]

Sir John made it clear that this was not his intention, and that with this new will he was revoking any agreement he may have made in France while under medication. Under the terms of the new document Lady Jane would receive a legacy of £2,000 — but only on the condition that she not challenge the will. If she challenged the will, her legacy would be immediately revoked, and she would receive only the amount entitled to her under their marriage contract. Unexpressed but palpable was the threat that if she did not immediately concede, the family was prepared to make public Sir John's accusation against her and to bring legal action against Lady Jane, the doctor — and perhaps even the solicitor himself. Little wonder then that she "broke down." Lady Jane retreated with her £2,000 and the remnants of her dignity, and on August 25, 1838, only three months after her first husband's death, she married Dr. Jeremiah Lonsdale Pounden.

Gillespie Graham in the same letter informed Stewart that George had consolidated the family's control by "kicking over board" his late brother's trustees, forming a new board with George at the head. The stranglehold on the siblings' finances was at last broken. With evident glee Gillespie Graham assured William that at the time of his brother's death Lady Jane was "not with Child" — adding a cryptic and suggestive observation: "You had no reason from the beginning to apprehend such an event." William Drummond Stewart was now officially and indisputably Sir William, nineteenth Lord of Grandtully, seventh Baronet of Murthly.[9]

When Sir William received the news of his brother's death and wrote to his trusted friend the architect James Gillespie Graham for details, he included in this very first letter an indication of how seriously he took his recent conversion to Catholicism. On the Murthly estate was already a sixteenth-century family chapel; Sir William instructed Gillespie Graham to draw up plans to restore it and reconsecrate it to the Roman Church, assuring that it was in compliance with all canon laws by consulting with the local bishop.

There was also the question of Christie and their young son, Will. This, too, he committed to Gillespie Graham's very capable and discreet care. The architect reported:

> I brought Christie & William here [Edinburgh] some months ago & placed him at a School in the Royal Circus, where Gentlemen send boys of his age to prepare them for the High School. [H]e is a stout healthy little fellow & applys well to his Education & you may rely on my attending to all your wishes regarding him till your return. I procured a cheap & very nice small flatt of a house for them near Inverleith, which situation may be said to be both in Town & Country. [I]t contains a very small parlour a Bed room, & a Bed Closet. [T]his small but comfortable abode is really comfortably furnished, chiefly with the furniture which Christie brought from Perth. [W]ith regard to her, it is my duty to say, that since you left your Native land, she had not only conducted herself with the greatest propriety but ever evinced the greatest degree of contentment. I never heard her utter a complaint, & never said she wanted any thing beyond your allowance. You may keep your mind easy on their acct.

As laird of Murthly Castle, Stewart would be assuming a more prominent role in county society. Christie was in a position to cause him much trouble, so her willingness to remain quietly in the background was a great relief.[10]

Sir William left Antoine Clement in St. Louis and traveled on to New Orleans by himself, taking residence at 46 Bourbon Street in the French Quarter. Alfred Jacob Miller had reoccupied the studio on

Chartres where he and Stewart had first met, and in the year since his return from the Rockies had made progress in converting his watercolor sketches to large canvases meant to grace the walls of Murthly Castle.

In mid-September Sir William wrote to William Sublette asking him to instruct Antoine Clement to procure some gourds "of the best form for dippers," as well as some red birds, and to be ready to travel by March. (That he did not write directly to Clement suggests that his friend was most probably illiterate.) The letter indicates that already in the fall of 1838 Stewart was planning that Clement would accompany him when he returned to Scotland the following year. Stewart wrote to his New York friend James Watson Webb, asking the newspaper editor to procure a stateroom for them on the *Liverpool*, the new and fashionable side-paddle steamer sailing from Manhattan at the end of May or the beginning of June. With feigned insouciance he explained why he had been remiss in his social correspondence since returning from the Rockies: "I have been living the usual lazy life of a traveller & write about three letters a year, but from the death of my elder brother have been obliged to make these of the disagreeable nature of business letters this last autumn." The passing reference to his elder brother's death was a tactful way of announcing that he had succeeded to the title and estate, in case Webb had not yet heard.[11]

Meanwhile Alfred Jacob Miller received an invitation from the Apollo Gallery in New York City requesting to display his oil paintings of the West for two weeks in June. With his patron's permission, Miller packed up eighteen canvases and shipped them to the gallery, where they were displayed to great acclaim. The paintings included Indians, trappers, prairie landscapes, hunting scenes, and mountain vistas, and though New Yorkers had two years earlier seen George Catlin's paintings of the Indians of the upper Missouri, these were the first representations of the Rocky Mountains they had ever viewed. The art critic for the *New York Morning Herald* enthused that the "principal merit of these works is their originality — boldness and accuracy of drawing and per-spective," though he noted a "slight rawness in the coloring." The New York art critics were not completely bowled over by the paintings, but

New Yorkers were. Augustus Greele, the chairman of the executive committee of the Apollo Gallery, wrote to Stewart to assure him "that the paintings . . . have so far attracted the attention and favor of the public and the public press, that the receipts of the exhibition had more than doubled the amount of any former week since the formation of the Association, and that the attraction continues to increase." Greele sought and received Stewart's permission to extend the exhibition through the end of July to accommodate the crowds.[12]

Greele had to request the extension in writing because Stewart had already returned to Scotland; he did not stay on to attend even the opening of Miller's New York exhibition. His decision to leave the city early perhaps reveals something about his attitude toward the paintings. He was not acquiring them as status possessions, as objects to advertise his wealth or his taste. He had no desire to swan his way around the Apollo Gallery, playing the part of the wealthy art patron. The paintings, like the gourds and the red birds, the Indian artifacts and the buffalo skin rugs, were all destined to become part of a diorama, a stage setting to surround himself with a facsimile of the American West that was far removed in time and place from the glens of Perthshire. He was returning to Scotland as his new position required, but it would be Scotland on his own terms.

On May 25, 1839, William Drummond Stewart sailed out of New York harbor. Seven years earlier he had first set foot on American soil at New York City's premier location for homosexual cruising, Battery Park. Now as "Sir William" he stood on the deck watching the leafy walkways of that park recede in the distance. His male lover stood at his side.

James Watson Webb managed to secure the stateroom on the *Liverpool* that Sir William had requested, though with some difficulty. The newly launched luxury ship was completely booked weeks in advance of sailing. "She brought 86 cabin passengers," reported the *Times* when the ship finally docked in England, "the whole number for which she has accommodation, having refused many who offered." One American not refused passage on the fashionable steamer was Senator Daniel Webster of Massachusetts, who was traveling to Europe with his wife and daughter. If Sir William had sailed with them we might have learned much about him from Mrs. Webster's gossipy and perceptive diary of the trip, later published under the title *Mr. W. & I.* Unfortunately for posterity, when Stewart became aware of the hoopla surrounding the luxury steamer's voyage he switched his ticket to the less frenetic and intrusive atmosphere of a packet leaving New York at about the same time.[13]

Stewart crossed the Atlantic on the equally comfortable *Sheridan*, one of the vessels in E. K. Collins's evocatively named Dramatic Line, whose ships were named after figures of the English stage: *Shakespeare, Garrick, Siddons*, and the like. The *Sheridan* sailed from New York on May 25 with no great fanfare and only forty cabin passengers. Sir William had a private carriage waiting for him when the ship docked in Liverpool, and from the port he began the long journey home to Perthshire, nearly three hundred miles over country roads. (A railroad between Glasgow and Edinburgh was under construction but was not completed until the early 1840s.) He was returning to his homeland a very different man from the one who had left in 1832. He was now forty-three years old, titled, landed, and wealthy. As a young man in London he had lived the sybaritic life of a second son with noble connections and few responsibilities, but he had now demonstrated that he could not only survive but actually thrive in conditions that were harsh and dangerous, coping with challenges that taxed his physical and mental resources to their limit. When financial support from home lagged, he had supported himself in comfort — even, to a limited extent, in luxury — through his own investments in the cotton market. He had also spent nearly seven years traveling discreetly yet unashamedly with men who were his sexual partners.[14]

Stewart was now bringing one of the those partners, Antoine Clement, with him on his journey home, but as their carriage passed through village after village — Preston, Lancaster, Carlisle, Lockerbie — his resolve perhaps began to waver. This was not the Wind River nor the

Big Horn, this was not even boisterous St. Louis nor decadent New Orleans. This was settled, conservative, profoundly Presbyterian Scotland, and it appears that the bravado that had been so easy on the banks of the Mississippi slowly ebbed as they approached the River Tay. By the time he and Clement reached Murthly and their carriage turned off the public road and clattered down the long, straight, tree-lined drive, he had decided on a compromise: he would occupy the castle, run the estate from his study there, entertain in the ballroom and music room — but in the evenings he and Clement would retire to the nearby Dalpowie Lodge, a spacious and well-appointed retreat on the estate where they could enjoy a high degree of privacy. In public they would maintain a fiction that would allow them to live in intimate contact without necessarily making a challenging statement: Antoine Clement would be explained as Sir William's valet.

That the new laird would inherit Murthly Castle and yet live in a lodge was a puzzlement in the village and one that needed an explanation, and since Stewart had no intention of illuminating the situation, perhaps inevitably a story arose to explain this odd turn of events. A legend began to circulate suggesting that when Sir John and William clashed over their father's estate, William stomped out of Murthly Castle in high dudgeon, vowing he would never again for as long as he lived spend a single night under its roof. Now that he had returned to Murthly — even though as its laird — he felt compelled to uphold his honor through a very literal interpretation of this angry vow. The laird would therefore retire at night to the lodge. It was a harmless fiction, easily believed by those familiar with his volcanic temper, and a convenient explanation for the odd sleeping arrangements. He made no effort to correct it.

There was no need to clarify further Antoine Clement's position in the new laird's life: a gentleman obviously required a valet. Yet a lord also required a lady, and Stewart's prolonged bachelorhood was an anomaly less easily explained. The duty to produce an heir had now moved front and center. His sister Catherine wrote from France, urging him to marry, "a measure I would strongly recommend as conducive to your comfort & I can speak from experience, and highly necessary in the present state of the family — who seem in a fair way to follow the example of its connexions the Douglasses of whom there were once five sons eligible for matrimony, & there are only two now, & those more fit for bachelors than to become votaries of the little blind god." The Douglases did manage to reproduce sufficiently in the years to come, eventually giving birth to Lord Alfred Douglas, the infamous "Bosie" who would precipitate the downfall of the man who loved him, Oscar Wilde.[15]

Catherine also cautioned her brother about making too many changes to the old estate. "You will surely leave untouched the dolphin & his Cupid, with the pond, where, at the expense of a dipping, you first put your power of navigation to the trial, if I have not forgotten, in a washtub. Without doubt the bowling green will remain in its present form, were it only to serve as a dancing room for the tenentry on the event of your marriage."[16]

The largest change to the estate, of course, was the new castle. From the exterior the castle looked complete, with picturesque towers and romantic turrets, but it was a mere shell of a palace, resplendent on the outside but hollow and unfinished in its interior. All construction had ceased with Sir John's death, and Sir William was unsure whether he wanted to proceed with the architectural confection. In the meantime he went forward with plans to refurbish the chapels at both Grandtully and Murthly, making them floridly, defiantly Catholic in the grandest Gothic Revival style.

He also saw to the planting of the trees, the propagation of the animals, and the careful cultivation of the seeds that began to arrive in shipping crates from America. The hills of the estate, long ago denuded of Shakespeare's Birnam Wood, became the new home of Douglas firs, oaks, and ashes carefully wrapped and carried on horseback from the Rockies. When Alfred Jacob Miller visited Murthly he described a favorite stroll over the grounds: "From the end of the Terrace a walk still continues through some wooded ground to a Steep hill, — surmounting this, you are brought into a valley called the American Garden, — of Artificial

Lakes & Islands that have the appearance of a little fairy abode, — some trees peculiar to America grow along the borders which give a character to this charming resort."[17]

In Dalpowie Lodge on the estate, Stewart created a refuge for himself and Antoine Clement, one that consciously excluded the outside world by creating a space that was rich and exotic and removed from its context, a fantasy setting of American Indian and Middle Eastern travel souvenirs. The walls were covered with crimson cloth and the floors with Persian carpets. All along one wall ran a raised divan about three feet wide, covered with damask silk and buffalo rugs. This served as a bed. On a small table lay the tomahawk he had worn in the mountains, and in another corner were arrayed numerous painted and carved Indian peace pipes and a Turkish chibouk with a clay bowl and a stem nearly five feet long. The windows were completely obscured with silk shades that assured privacy for the couple and at the same time filtered the sunlight, turning the hunting lodge into a hazy, tobacco-scented masculine sanctuary. The whole effect was rather like a tepee cum seraglio.

It was perhaps this improvised Indian lodge that Stewart evokes when in *Altowan* he describes the Rocky Mountain tent occupied by Roallan, the son of an English lord, that is the setting for his sexual excesses:

> Dissipation of every sort, left but a sadder vacuum between the acts; and he felt it necessary to give way to unceasing debauchery, to defend himself from that terrible feeling of melancholy, which, like jealousy, creates its own nourishment. . . . His tent was a harem; and when he left the soft skins and the scarlet drapery, which shed a rosy glow over the luxurious revelry within, it was to seek in male companionship and the bowl, a stimulant to flagging spirits, and a change from satiated joys. In the song, the dance, sometimes the footrace, at the target, or wrestling ring, his performance brought forth shouts of applauding wonder; and the brimming cup, formed of the deep horn of the bull, was passed from lip to lip to crown the orgie.[18]

It is interesting to note that in the paragraph immediately following this passage, Roallan (as described in an earlier chapter) seeks out the male companionship of his new friend Joe Henry in the shady spot along the river where he knows the young Kentuckian goes to bathe. Roallan's fevered body and troubled soul are cleansed and refreshed by an intimate Arcadian encounter with the handsome American.

Art historian Lisa Strong makes a cogent observation about Stewart's carefully assembled retreat in Dalpowie Lodge. While he surrounded himself with physical objects that reminded him of his American journey, the objects he chose were representative of *Indian* culture, not the white culture of the trappers among whom he had lived and traveled. The choice of objects had little to do with empathy or identification with Native Americans. Stewart in no sense "went native" during his sojourn; on the contrary, he identified most closely with the rugged fur traders who were his companions, while he never strayed far from his aristocratic roots. He adopted the mountain attire of a buckskin jacket with Indian fringes, but he insisted on having it tailored to be nipped tightly at the waist and form-fitted in the chest. With his Jermyn Street–styled jacket and wide-brimmed hat he is instantly recognizable in all of Miller's paintings. Yet it was the representations of Indian culture with which he chose to surround himself in Scotland. There were bows and arrows — but no beaver traps. Perhaps one should be careful not to read too much into these choices. A nineteenth-century beaver trap was, after all, a common utilitarian object in Perthshire; a painted Indian parfleche was not. Stewart might be expected to collect the exotic and unusual as his souvenirs on his journeys, not objects available from the local ironmonger. Still, it is significant that in re-creating the American West on the banks of the River Tay, it was a decidedly *Indian* environment he chose to replicate.[19]

Eventually he would install brass rods along the ceiling of the lodge from which were suspended several of Alfred Jacob Miller's oil paintings: *The Death of the Panther, Return from Hunting, Indian Belle Reclining, Auguste, Roasting the Hump Rib, Porte d'Enfer,* and others. They completed the stage setting in which he could recline and imagine himself far away, a player in a different, more romantic drama. Yet when he opened the front door of Dalpowie Lodge he most definitely stepped into Scotland, and though the estate was breathtakingly beautiful, with its ancient walls, carefully groomed lawns, and colorful parterres, he began to feel confined and restless. Only four months after returning home he left once more, taking Antoine to see the sights of London. When life in the family's London townhouse became too constricting, the two men took off for an extended trip to the Adriatic, Constantinople, and Egypt, a trip projected to last seven months. It was perhaps during this trip that Stewart acquired an Albanian folk costume, later having his portrait painted in imitation of the famous National Portrait Gallery painting of his hero, Lord Byron.

Before he sailed for the Levant, Sir William received a reminder that there were young men he had left behind in America who were in a position to importune him. A letter arrived from St. Louis written by Rudolph Ulrich, one of his barely literate youthful companions. "Yesterday I met your yellow boy who accompanied you to New York," the young man wrote, "he told me that you had taken passagge in the Steam vessal, but she being so crowded, you preferred to take a Packet. I expect that you are so much pleased with the old country that you will hardly return again to America, you told me before you left that you was uncertain whether to remain in England or to travel on the Continent. I often times feel very lonesome, and dont know what to do with myself in the evenings." Ulrich added a postscript: "As this is letter is written in a great hurry, and being the only one I wrote since the one which you received in New Orleans, there will be a good many faults in it which you must excuse."[20]

The fact that Stewart carefully preserved the letter in his private papers raises questions that are now unanswerable. Did he feel some affection for this young man? Was he preserving evidence in case of attempted blackmail? Similar letters would play a central role in the trial of many a Victorian gentleman. Sir William was not completely averse to hearing from Ulrich, for in a letter to William Sublette sent four months later he asked to be remembered to him. Ulrich's would be the first of several letters from young American men, grammatically challenged missives that would find their way to Scotland and be opened with perhaps a mix of feelings.

By the autumn of 1840 Stewart had returned from his voyage to the Middle East and was back at Murthly Castle, facing the unpleasant reality that he was not quite so wealthy as he had once imagined. His brother John's pursuit of grandeur in the guise of a new castle had left the estate deeply in debt. New revenues were needed, and Stewart decided that there was money to be made in providing hunting facilities for wealthy gentleman. (He could not know that the marriage of Queen Victoria to Prince Albert the previous February, and the deep affection the couple would feel for Scotland after their first visit in 1842, would soon have half the fashionable gentleman of England sporting tartan kilts for shooting parties in the Highlands.) He built an elegant hunting lodge that he named Rohallion, after a castle that once stood on the property, with the intention of renting it out during hunting season.

In August Alfred Jacob Miller arrived, followed in a few weeks by crates of completed oil paintings and the precious Rocky Mountain watercolor sketches that would be the basis for large oil canvases for Murthly Castle. He also carried a variety of Indian props — pipes, powder horns, and at least one complete outfit of buckskin leggings and a feathered headdress. These would make their appearance in many of his paintings. For the next year and a half Miller would reside at Murthly, and his letters to his brothers and sisters in Baltimore provide a detailed record of the daily life of the castle. He was overwhelmed by the beauty of the estate and quickly seduced by the elegance of life among the aristocracy. "I shall not say anything about the manner in which I travel here," he wrote to his family, "or you will begin to think that my republicanism is fast oozing away." To his intimate friend Brantz Mayer he described the studio Sir William had prepared for him: "I have a delicious little painting room which looks out upon the garden & when I raise the window in the morning — the birds pour in a perfect flood of song."[21]

Reunited with Antoine Clement, Miller experienced some uneasiness in expressing to his family exactly what function Clement was playing there. To his brother Decatur in Baltimore he wrote, "I believe I have not mentioned to you that Sir William Stewart brought to Scotland 'Antoine', his famous Indian hunter. He has been metamorphosed into a Scotch valet and waits on the table in a full suit of black, and this is every thing that he does. I am told that while in the mountains he was twice instrumental in saving his master's life, and for this reason I have no doubt he indulges him. He presented him the other day a full Highland suit which cost fifty pounds — that he may attend the balls the peasantry hold in the neighborhood." Here a large section of the original letter has been cut away, perhaps by the recipient, and the letter continues in mid-sentence on a more neutral note, with nothing further about Antoine. The question of what Decatur Miller might have excised is, of course, intriguing.[22]

Antoine Clement makes several appearances in Miller's letters, usually as a mischievous figure capering before the amazed Scots, pushing the limits of his ambiguous status in the castle. "Murthly is full of company just now," Miller writes, "and yesterday Antoine put on my Indian chief's dress and made his appearance in the drawing room, to the astonishment and delight of the company, for the dress became him admirably. Afterwards he made his debut in the servant's hall to the great wonderment of the butlers and valets and to the horror of the ladies' maids." One unconfirmed story says that Clement became very drunk one night, hitched two buffaloes to a boat on wheels, and careened through the streets of nearby Dunkeld, piercing the night with savage war cries. The scenario has its unlikely elements, but at base it reveals what was probably true about the "wild child of the Prairie" — Clement was bored and chafing at the restrictions of the charade that Stewart was asking him to play. Regardless of what transpired between the two men at night in the privacy of Dalpowie Lodge, Clement was expected during the day to make an effort to appear a properly obsequious servant. If he trespassed into the drawing room it was only to shock and amuse the aristocratic guests, after which he was quickly banished to the servants' quarters. Yet to the servants, with a sensitivity to precedence and proper conduct more rigid even than that of their employers, it was abundantly evident that Clement had never been in service.[23]

Miller writes to his brother that Clement had been "metamorphosed into a Scotch valet," but he subsequently says that the only duties Clement performed were to serve at table. Sir William's first plan, it would seem, was to have his companion appear to fill the role of valet or body servant, an assignment that would provide the two men with many opportunities to share moments of private intimacy. Perhaps later the laird felt that it was necessary to make a more public declaration of Clement's status as merely a servant, and he gave him the duties of a footman instead, waiting on table. Neither assignment would have been convincing, since it was entirely unnecessary for the laird to import either a valet or a footman from America — and in any case, Clement displayed no particular talent for either role. A more persuasive case might have been made if Stewart had hired the hunter as his gamekeeper, or ghillie. Other ghillies in the neighborhood would have grumbled about the interloper on the estate, but an argument could have been made that the buffalo required a knowledgeable American hand. At least Clement would have been employed at a task somewhat consistent with his experience and interests. But employment as a ghillie by the very nature of the job would have kept Clement primarily outside the castle and away from the lodge, providing few opportunities for intimate encounters — and so the best hunter in the Rockies was reduced to serving soup. Antoine Clement in truth did not belong upstairs *or* downstairs. No wonder then that he and Stewart spent so much time in London or traveling abroad.

When at Murthly Castle, Sir William followed a set routine. "His habits are regular & very simple," Miller wrote to his brother Decatur. "He rises about 7 in the morning, breakfasts at half past, on steaks and cutlets, eggs under done & a bottle of claret, never touching either tea or coffee, cream or butter, although these articles are here in perfection, walking out to see improvements and returns at 1 to lunch, and to see letters by post, reads papers, etc., walks out again & does not return until the dinner bell at half past six, dines heartily on the richest dishes, but takes little wine, converses or reads until 9 or 10, smokes his merschaum & then to sleep."[24]

Stewart also kept a close eye on the works Miller was completing in the special studio created for him in the castle. The patron "visits the painting room almost every day after luncheon to examine and perhaps to offer a criticism on any point wherein he thinks I may be wrong and woe to the Indian who has not sufficient dignity in expression and carriage, for *out* he must come." Miller was artist in residence at Murthly Castle until November 1841, when with Stewart's blessing he transferred to a studio to London. There he began to work on two religious paintings for the chapel at Murthly.[25]

George Catlin was in London at the same time as Miller, and the two American painters socialized on several occasions. Catlin was in some sense Miller's rival as both men had achieved renown for their evocative paintings of American Indians, though Catlin's fame (then as now) was greater than Miller's. Miller was not impressed by Catlin's work. "There is in truth however a great deal of humbug about Mr. George Catlin," wrote Miller to his brother. "He has published a book containing some extraordinary stories and luckily for him there are but few persons who have travelled over the same ground." From London Miller returned to Baltimore, where he continued to paint for Sir William and for a growing clientele who commissioned their own copies of the western paintings.[26]

In the summer of 1841 William Drummond Stewart began to receive letters from a J. E. Handie, one of the young American lads who had attached themselves to the older gentleman while he was in New York. Handie had fallen on hard times, and he wanted money. His first letters to Sir William were ignored, but by October he was becoming increasingly insistent, and though he tried his best to assume a playful, cajoling tone, there was an undercurrent of menace.

And now I will state to you a circumstance which has only come to my knowledge a few weeks since — It has been <u>generally</u> believed <u>here</u>, & been circulated as fact by many persons, that the reason of my leaving you, was that you had <u>turned</u> me <u>away</u> for <u>misbehaving</u>.

Now really my dear Sir William, could you imagine that anyone would circulate such an untruth; I never believed that any person could have such an enmity towards me — It appears that it has been generally believed to be true, & has done me considerable injury, for I am believed to be a very hard case; exceedingly dissipated &c — now you well know the contrary of that, & certainly.[27]

When this letter too failed to elicit any response, Handie became more desperate and demanding in his next.

Steamer after Steamer has arrived & I have in vain been looking for a letter from you — I hope to God, the next one will bring me some news of you for really I am desirous of knowing what answer you will make to the letter I wrote you. — Oh my dear friend if you knew what I have suffered mentally lately, I am sure you would sympathize with me — It is impossible for me to remain in New York; I cannot, I will not; go where I may, I must leave this place — my reasons for wishing to do so are what really make me unhappy. One of the reasons I will clearly state to you, the other I cannot at present, but when I tell you I am not happy I suppose you can guess it. — I know that you are my friend, & for that I do not hesitate to communicate to you that which I would wish no one else to know.[28]

Handie explained that a Mr. Delaforest had insinuated himself into Handie's immediate family and had turned them all against him. He pleaded with Stewart to be his "protector" and to allow him to join Stewart in Scotland.

Oh! Sir William Do have pity upon me I beg you, let me return to you again, & if you do not wish me to be with you, I can remain in Scotland, until I find an opportunity of doing something. Here besides I can never get along well, for it is cruelly believed, as I told you in my last letter, that you have withdrawn your protection from me on account of my bad behavior — that is really too hard. If I had deserved it, I would bear up with it; but it is so unjust. I am sure you yourself will feel indignant at it — But my dear friend I am afraid I tire your patience. I have written you this long letter for I have no one in whom I can confide my trouble — it seems as if all had abandoned me; do not I entreat you join with the rest & leave me friendless, for I should then be really miserable — I do not know what I would not do. I am desperate. . . . I care not where I go, but I know no where, where I can find a friend like you. Dear Sir William, I beg you, send me a favorable answer to this letter.

Whether Stewart responded to the pleas is unknown; J. E. Handie slips from the record at this point.[29]

Other letters from America were more pleasantly received. William Sublette wrote to tell him of Robert Campbell's marriage and that their business continued much as before. "I see Antuoins Mother frequently and she Enquires after him but I have no[t] heard from him in any of your Letters." Robert Campbell in turn wrote that he had been offering $200 a head for any buffalo that could be captured and sent east for transport to Scotland, but the shaggy creatures were proving to be uncooperative.[30]

Stewart received a letter from his sister in France attempting to dissuade him from another long sojourn in America and once again urging him to marry and carry on the family line. "Who knows what may happen in the space of three, perhaps four years," Catherine wrote, "time gets on meanwhile — neither you nor George think of grafting young shoots on the almost whithered family tree of the antient house of Grandtully, which must necessarily become extinct — it may be remarked 'in passing' that all the great and petty lairds in Perthshire, excepting our family, & not omitting the 'Dull gooses' [Douglases] have done their possible to perpetuate their names; some like the above named, have been blessed with too many of the frail sex, unluckily, perhaps they are not to blame, one does not know who is at fault in these matters."[31]

Sir William's major concern at this time was the estate's finances, which were perilous. His brother had left him deeply in debt over the construction costs of the new Murthly Castle and efforts to raise revenue had been largely unsuccessful. One solution had occurred to him: he might sell Logiealmond, one of the three Stewart family estates. The sale would allow him to pay off all of the construction debts and with one dramatic sacrifice bring the family to financial solvency. He resisted the idea for a time because the estate was the home of Elizabeth and Frances Drummond (his two elderly aunts) and his brother George, but as the interest on the debts mounted it became clear that selling Logiealmond would be inevitable. He offered the estate to his friend William David Murray, fourth Earl of Mansfield, and the earl promptly agreed.

George and the elderly aunts were devastated by the news of the sale and their impending eviction, but in the summer of 1841, before she was forced to leave her home, Elizabeth Drummond died. When George began to settle her estate he discovered that his parsimonious aunt had been wealthy beyond anyone's wildest imaginings. Most of the estate was left to her sister, Frances Marie (known as Fanny). "Mines of Wealth seem opening up every hour for her & for us after her death," George wrote to William. "More than £1000 which Fanny knew nothing of has been found — and claims to the extent of perhaps £30-000 may be made good for her & for the heirs of dearest Bess. Last night alone we found property in money — bonds, & personal effects to the amount of many thousands of pounds — and it will take a month to make the necessary investigations." Still, George resented the loss of Logiealmond. Not only was it his home at the moment, but also it was he who had fought Lady Jane so skillfully to keep all of the family's property intact. Now his wandering brother, with seemingly cavalier disregard for this hard-won patrimony, was disposing of a third of it. George wrote with a mixture of sorrow and bitterness, warning his brother that "to have done this will be no comfort to poor Sir William on his Deathbed."[32]

There was one problem that needed to be addressed before the transfer of Logiealmond could be completed. In 1767 Sir William's grandfather, Sir John Drummond, had secured an entail on the property. He had no sons, and he feared that if Logiealmond were to be inherited by one of his daughters the property might pass out of control of the Drummond family. The entail he therefore established delineated a strict line of inheritance that would eventually deliver the property to a male heir. Sir John reserved to himself the right to change the terms of the entail during his own lifetime — an escape clause that proved to be a fortunate addition, since subsequent to the establishment of the entail his wife was delivered of two sons, first William and then Thomas. Having been provided with the requisite heir and spare, and cognizant that his mounting personal debts would pass along a significant burden to his son, Sir John exercised his right to retract the entail, thereby freeing his heirs to sell the property if circumstances made a sale necessary. Unfortunately, this document was never officially registered.

Sir John died, and the property passed to his elder son, William, who subsequently died without issue. Logiealmond then passed to the younger brother, Thomas, who also died without issue, and so the estate passed to their eldest sister, Catherine — William Drummond Stewart's mother. Though this was technically in violation of the entail (if the entail was still in force), no one at the time objected. When Lady Catherine Stewart died her son John inherited, and when John died William became the new owner of Logiealmond. Now that Sir William wanted to sell the property to Lord Mansfield, it was necessary to clarify whether or not conveyance of the estate was controlled by the entail and to remove this cloud on the title. Fortunately Scottish law (unlike English law at the time) allowed for a proceeding called a declaratory action, in which an issue of potential litigation could be resolved in a court of law before it became an actual dispute, and so Lord Mansfield sought a judgment on whether he was the legal owner of the property he had just purchased. A second case was brought by William's brother George who, at the time he joined in the legal proceedings, was next in line to inherit Logiealmond if the entail was upheld. Despite his personal objections to the sale, George cooperated with the declaratory action and, representing all the potential heirs, agreed to break the entail. The two lawsuits were combined into one by the court, and during the subsequent four years the case wended its way to the House of Lords. There on June 19, 1846, the case was presented, and on July 3 the judgment was issued: Logiealmond was not entailed and Sir William Drummond Stewart was free to dispose of it as he wished.[33]

The published decision of the House of Lords is of great interest because of one brief passage. In discussing the issue of potential heirs being represented by brother George, the decision mentions that "one of the substitutes of entail, who was an illegitimate son of the respondent, legitimated by the marriage of his parents subsequent to the taking of the appeal, was allowed to compear upon it for his interest." Despite unofficial records that maintain that William Drummond Stewart had married Christian Battersby nine months before their son Will's birth, the decision in the House of Lords reveals that the two did not marry until sometime between 1842 and 1846. The reasons for the marriage centered on legitimizing Will for inheritance purposes — allowing him in his role as the next heir to agree to break the entail (if the House of Lords were to uphold it). The marriage and legitimization also secured Will's rights to Grandtully, Murthly, and the baronet title. After officially becoming Lady Stewart, Christie moved to Grandtully Castle, where she remained until the time of her death. The marriage, however, was one on paper only. Her husband remained at Murthly Castle.[34]

In 1842 with the sale of Logiealmond, Sir William overruled the objections of his family and did what he felt he needed to do to clear the family estate from the debts that his brother John had accumulated during the construction of the new Murthly Castle. The debts were paid in full. His bank account was now flush. His bachelor brother and the remaining aunt were settled comfortably in nearby Braco Castle. And so his thoughts turned once again to the Rocky Mountains. He wanted to return to America, and this time he would have the money to return in style. He was going to host a traveling pleasure party like none the Rockies had ever seen or would ever see again.

Shortly after dawn on September 7, 1842, servants on the Murthly estate raised a Union Jack at the crest of the highest hill in Birnam Wood. As the flag snapped and billowed in the morning breeze it created a "wild yet fine effect" and could be seen for miles around. The nearby village of Dunkeld was decorated with two large triumphal arches composed of intertwined evergreens and heather, and the buildings along the high street were festooned with greenery. On the lawn of the old cathedral had been erected a marquee, sixty-four by twenty feet, composed of alternating stripes of scarlet and white cloth; its floor was covered with crimson. At artistic intervals were placed carefully pruned orange trees bearing real fruit, and down the center of the marquee a table had been laid for thirty-four guests, its crisp white linen agleam with ornate ormolu centerpieces of silver and gold.

Amid the splendor of the celebration it was not the flowers nor the swags of heather nor the gleaming silver plate that held the eye of the correspondent for the *Evening Courant*. Perhaps accustomed to the diminutive, epicene specimens of mankind found in the metropolis, he was completely entranced by the hardy male pulchritude of Perthshire. "The Atholl men composed a body of 160 individuals," he wrote,

> and of these a body of 60 men, remarkable for their manly proportions, were armed with Lochaber axes. . . . Next to the interest excited by

the appearance of these stalwart hillmen, was the Duke of Leeds, who appeared with a following of Highlanders from Dumblane (his Grace being Viscount Dumblane in the Scottish Peerage). This body, though small in number, were splendidly equipped, and with their noble chief, formed a body of picked men equal in muscular strength to any others that appeared on the ground. . . . There were a hundred hillman in kilt and hose, and a hundred of the Lowlanders on horse-back. When this fine body of men were marshalled in line on the beautiful lawn in front of the old Cathedral, the scene was eminently imposing. . . . To aid in the spell, the strange sounds of [a] language, totally dissimilar from that spoken in other parts of the island, was heard on every side — uttered, not by vulgar looking persons, as is sometimes heard in our streets, but by manly handsome men.

At one o'clock the bells of the cathedral began to peel — a sound unheard in the village for a dozen years — and a carriage rounded the corner of the high street bearing Her Majesty Victoria the Queen and Albert, the Prince Consort. As the royal couple descended from their carriage and approached the marquee, "21 guns upon Stanley-mount opened their iron throats, and the roar was reverberated from hill to hill, prolonging the sound for some minutes, giving to the whole a singular effect."[1]

This was Victoria's first visit to Scotland, and she was overwhelmed by her reception and by the wild natural beauty surrounding her. Later the queen made a long entry in her journal describing the festive day. "To the left; but more immediately before us, we saw where once stood *Birnam Wood*, so renowned in *Macbeth*. We passed a pretty shooting place of Sir W. Stewart's, called *Rohallion*, nearly at the foot of *Birnam*. To the right we saw the Stormont and Strathlay. Albert said, as we came along between the mountains, that to the right, where they were wooded, it was very like Thuringer, and on the left more like Switzer-land. Murthly, to the right, which belongs to Sir W. Stewart, is in a fine situation, with the Tay winding under the hill. This lovely scenery continues all along to Dunkeld." From Dunkeld they proceeded to the estate of Stewart's friend Lord Breadalbane. "We saw part of *Loch Tay*, and drove along the banks of the *Tay* under fine trees, and saw Lord Breadalbane's American buffaloes."[2]

Missing from the day's celebration was the laird of Murthly Castle. The very day that the queen of England was admiring the buffaloes he had sent from America, William Drummond Stewart was disembarking once again onto the leafy paths of Battery Park in New York City. With him he had Antoine Clement and two servants: Corbie (his actual valet) and a young boy named Tom Craig. Included in his baggage were crates containing a very unusual cargo: Elizabethan finery (doublets and jerkins, gauntlets and plumed hats). The plush velvet and gold lace were for the young men he intended to invite to a Renaissance costume party in the remote wilds of the Rocky Mountains.

Sir William spent some time in New York City with his friend James Watson Webb and then boarded a ship to Baltimore, where he inspected Alfred Jacob Miller's latest paintings and commissioned two more for the chapel at Murthly. By November he was once again in New Orleans. There he reconnected with Ebenezer B. Nichols, one of his early business partners who was now living in Texas. Nichols had married the former Margaret Clayton Stone and the couple was honeymooning in the Crescent City. Nichols had a new focus for his entrepreneurial enthusiasms. Since his first business trip to Texas in 1838, Nichols had become convinced that the republic was the best place for a speculating man to make money. He had entered into a partnership with William M. Rice, and their dry goods business had prospered so rapidly that they were able to provide substantial financial support for the building of a plank road from Brazos to Houston. Now he was enthusing about the bright future of Texan railroads. Nichols had recently built a fine home on a plantation near Dickinson Bayou, about twenty miles north of Galveston, and he was bringing his bride home to the plantation he had named Nicholstone (a combination of his and his wife's names). He invited Sir William to join them. Stewart wished to spend the winter in a climate more hospitable than that of St. Louis, and a side trip to the rough and raw Republic of Texas promised to be an interesting diversion.

That winter as he relaxed at Nicholstone and made plans for his pleasure trip, Sir William was much in the thoughts of a least one Rocky Mountain entrepreneur. Transplanted Londoner Alexander Barclay had entered into a partnership with his brother back in England, a scheme to collect buffaloes and ship them to English estates. The business was floundering when Alexander wrote from Fort Saint Vrain about a prospective customer that he hoped his brother could track down. "There is a Baron Stewart, fell heir to the title some two years since, somewhere in England and Scotland, formerly Captain, who would very likely purchase. He has been two trips to the Mountains here and appears somehow to have a predilection for Mountain Men, matters and customs." Barclay's tip was vague (and inaccurate) as to Stewart's biography and current whereabouts but well informed about his predilections.[3]

Sir William's visit with the Nichols family proved to be a pleasant interlude, and he was intrigued enough with Texas to consider investing in one of the many financial schemes being proposed by Nichols. He returned to Louisiana by the early spring and began final preparations for the journey, doing whatever he could from New Orleans and depending on William Sublette to complete the arrangements in St. Louis. The two men had been corresponding since Stewart's departure from America in 1839, and in the salutations Sublette wrote on his letters may be noted the increased intimacy between the two men: "Dear Sir," "Dear Sir William," "Ever Dear Sir," and finally "Ever Dear Friend." Sublette's health had declined significantly by 1843 as consumption began to sap his strength, but his love of the Rocky Mountains and his deep affection for Sir William overcame any concerns about the rigors of the journey. Sublette was to be the co-captain of the entourage, but it was Stewart who would be underwriting all of the costs, and so the trader was punctilious about recording his reimbursable expenses. He purchased a new journal and as he traveled around the St. Louis area he entered meticulous notes: "Breakfast . . . 62½" or "had Sir D. W. [sic] Stewart mule shoes remove in front as he took lame . . . 25." Sublette's account books also show that he purchased wine, champagne, gin, brandy, and rum. Because of restrictions against bringing alcohol into the Indian territories, it was necessary for Stewart to obtain a special permit to "take with him as much spiritous liquors as he may deem necessary for the use of himself and his party."[4]

Stewart and his guests were not the only party hoping to head west as soon as the prairie grass would support the horses and livestock. Lt. John C. Frémont was planning another exploratory expedition to the Rockies. Santa Fe traders with an escort of dragoons also waited to head toward the southwest. A group of four Jesuit missionaries was on its way to the Flathead country. Largest of all was an emigrant party of nearly one thousand men, women, and children, the Burnett-Applegate expedition, whose 111 wagons were gathered at Round Grove, Missouri, ready to start out for the Oregon Territory.

On March 25 Stewart at last boarded the luxury steamboat *J. M. White* in New Orleans and started the long journey up the Mississippi. The paddle wheeler was only a year old, and its eight double flue boilers made it one of the fastest passenger steamboats on the river. Unfortunately, only three days into the excursion, about thirty-five miles above the mouth of the Ohio River, the boat collided with a submerged ledge of rocks known as the Grand Chain, ripping a long gouge in its wooden hull. The *St. Louis Evening Gazette* reported that the *J. M. White* sank to the roof of its hurricane deck in only three minutes. Holes were chopped in the deck through which passengers scrambled to safety as the water quickly filled the lower chambers. Most of the baggage was saved, as at the time of the accident the steamboat had been towing a large barge alongside; the passengers' bags and some of the cargo were quickly transferred to safety. Despite the speed with which the boat sank, only one life was lost — that of a young woman of color. Shaken but undaunted, Stewart transferred to the *Julia Chouteau* and finally arrived in St. Louis a few days later.

William Sublette had agreed to lead the cavalcade to the mountains in tandem with Stewart himself, but it was necessary to engage a significant number of experienced hands to make the trip a success. Though the threat of Indian attack had significantly lessened since Sir William's first trip west, the party needed to be large enough to discourage depredations — a few men traveling alone could easily be overwhelmed and stripped of their belongings. Stewart and Sublette would be traveling independently this year, not as part of a commercial venture under the direction of one of the trading companies. (The fur trade was by 1843 far past its golden age; there had been no rendezvous since 1840.) Even more challenging than rounding up the necessary trail hands was the selection of a guest list for his party. Though Stewart's selection process is of critical importance to a full understanding of the 1843 trip, there is no definitive evidence of how and why he made his choices.

"[Stewart] would take with him, with a few notable exceptions, only young men with no experience in the wonderful world to which he intended to introduce them," Porter and Davenport explain, "or in any world that had been hard, difficult or really dangerous. Furthermore, he would exert over these young men a discipline as unyielding as might have been imposed by the Iron Duke, his military hero under which he had served in his youth. . . . He determined to combine on this trip the three seemingly incompatible ways of life toward which his diverse character strongly attracted him — the world of adventure, the world of military discipline, and the world of luxury."[5]

In his journal William Sublette recorded that the company consisted of "Individual gentleman, Some of the armey, Some professional Gentleman, Come on the trip for pleasure, Some for Health, etc. etc. So we had doctors, Lawyers, botanists, Bugg Ketchers, Hunters and men of nearly all professions, etc. etc. One half or rather more was hired men Belonging to Sir William, which he had employed on the trip." The *Missouri Republican* announced the gathering in St. Louis of "a large party of amateur hunters" being hosted by Sir William Stewart. "The party embraces every variety of character. . . . How the stalwart mountaineer will be amused to see the London cockney shivering in the blasts of the Rocky Mountains, or satisfying the cravings of his delicate stomach on a half cooked round of a starved dog. Among the company, however, are men who are enured to the toils, labors and privations of the chase; others who have the minds and indomitable spirits requisite for the hunter, and take it all in all." By the time the party set off for the mountains, Stewart had gathered a decidedly odd and colorful entourage, a mismatched mélange of characters for a costume drama that almost inevitably promised to end in disaster.[6]

Stewart had become fully convinced of the benefits of bringing a talented artist along to document his journeys, and though a severe and chronic case of rheumatism would keep Alfred Jacob Miller from once again serving in that capacity, in New York Stewart had learned that John James Audubon was planning a trip up the Missouri to gather specimens and sketches for a volume tentatively titled *Viviparous Quadrupeds of North America*. Stewart personally made the trek up into the rural region of Manhattan to Audubon's secluded retreat, Minnie's Land, only to discover that the artist was in Boston, attempting to drum up subscriptions for his latest work. Stewart left an invitation, suggesting that they rendezvous in St. Louis.

"It is now determined," Audubon later wrote to his young friend Spencer Baird, "that I shall go towards the Rocky Mountains at least to the Yellowstone River, and up the latter Stream four hundred miles, and *perhaps* go across the Rocky Mountains. I have it in my power to proceed to the Yellowstone by Steamer from St. Louis on the 1st day of April next; or to go to the '*Mountains of the Wind*' in the very heart and bosom of the Rocky Mountains in the company of Sir William Drommond Stewart, Baronet, who will leave on the 1st of May next also from St. Louis." From Baltimore Stewart wrote once again, reiterating his invitation and offering to provide transportation for Audubon's baggage and specimens "in consideration of the pleasure of having you with me & the honor you will do us in associating our voyage with the usefulness & Fame attending your pursuits."[7]

Audubon had his doubts about the wisdom of joining Sir William's pleasure party, reservations that were confirmed when the two finally met in Stewart's hotel room in St. Louis. The laird had spread out some of the elaborate costumes he had brought for his young companions, the velvet and lace having gotten damp with the sinking of the J. M.

White. "[Edward] Harris and I called on Sir W^am last evening and spent about one hour with him," Audubon wrote. "He was engaged in Drying his effects by the fire. — he is a rather tall, very slender person and talks with the lisping humbug of some of the English nobles. . . . He had the most superb Uniforms for Cavaliers that I have seen since We left England. Scarlet Blue &c covered with *Gold lace* and truly Splendid. — These he probably takes to the Great Chiefs he may have to encounter." Stewart renewed his invitation, but Audubon declined. In a curious twist of miscommunication Audubon assumed that Stewart was less interested in his services as an expedition artist and more anxious to procure the extra rifles of Audubon and his companions as added protection against Indian attack. It did not seem to occur to Audubon that the services of a nearly sixty-year-old painter (accompanied by an ornithologist, a taxidermist, a botanist, and a personal secretary) would be of questionable help in protecting a large party headed by two experienced mountain men.[8]

Sir William's entourage began to gather in St. Louis, and to the startled inhabitants it was clear that this party was something quite different from anything that had yet set out for the Rocky Mountains. The men for the most part were citified and delicate, appearing unprepared for — and even unaware of — the rigors of the trek ahead of them. "Sir W^am Stewart goes off in about a week to Independence with his 70 followers of all Sorts," Audubon wrote to his wife. "How many of the *Young Gents* will return before they have a sight of the Mountain is more than I can say?" To his friends Audubon wrote, "He is most anxious that we should join his party and offered us every kind of promises &c but it wont do for us. [H]e has just[?] too many people of too many sorts." As the month of April wore on, spring showed no sign of arriving. The river failed to clear of ice, and the prairie grass had barely begun to grow. Audubon was forced to mingle with Stewart in increasingly awkward social encounters. "No one *here* can understand that man, and I must say that in my opinion he is a very curious character."[9]

One of the Heermann brothers from New Orleans, either Adolphus or Theodore, appeared in St. Louis, hoping that Audubon would introduce him to Sir William. "Young Heermann, to Whose Mother I gave formerly Drawing lessons for about 6 months, brought me several letters of introduction, thinking I was going to join Sir W^{am}'s Expedition. He is sadly disappointed at my not going <u>that Way</u>." Audubon's comment is of course curious. The final sentence, if written without emphasis, would be a commonplace with no special meaning. The deliberate underscoring in the letter, however, raises the possibility that Audubon is using "<u>that Way</u>" to refer not solely to a geographical orientation.[10]

Once we obtain the key to understanding William Drummond Stewart's story — his sexual orientation — questions inevitably arise concerning the "casting" of his pleasure trip. How overtly homosexual did he intend the party to be? The costumes, the lavish tents, the liquor, the imported delicacies, the all-male company — together they suggest that Sir William envisioned a truly memorable months-long traveling theme party of like-minded individuals. As documented in numerous contemporary sources, he assembled a group of young men who were completely unsuited for the rigors of mountain life, men who accepted his invitation solely because it sounded like a great lark to journey into the wilds in the company of an elegant Scottish lord.

At the same time, however, he invited seasoned veterans who were familiar with the territory — both literally and figuratively. Certainly no one who had ever attended a rendezvous would be shocked by anything that might go on in the tents along the trail. He invited the young sons of prominent figures in the St. Louis community, receiving the blessing of parents who were perhaps only dimly aware of what Stewart had in mind. In a nod to his new faith (and as a personal favor to Father Pierre-Jean De Smet), he invited the four Jesuits to travel with him for part of the way, until they needed to branch off northward for Flathead territory. He invited five scientists — three botanists, a mineralogist, and an astronomer — who were intent on conducting serious scientific investigations, presumably unimpaired by champagne. He invited two army officers (each accompanied by a military servant) who were ostensibly conducting an officially sanctioned military reconnoiter, but who as the journey unfolded made only a token attempt to add to the government's store of knowledge about the Far West. Dilettantes and scientists, priests and army officers. Clearly there were, as Audubon observed, too many men of too many sorts.

What *was* Sir William thinking? It is likely that the traveling costume party started with a vision: Jim Bridger in his cuirass and helmet striding among the colorful tents at the 1837 rendezvous. Once Stewart had the financial resources to make that vision a reality, he lavished his money on costumes, tents, and exotic provisions, then sailed for America determined to host the most fabulous party the Rockies had ever seen. But when he got to St. Louis he knocked up against the hard reality of life on the trail. He would need a large company to move in safety, staffed with experienced hunters and trail hands. At least some of those locals would want to bring their Indian wives. Almost immediately the character of the pleasure faire changed as the attractive young revelers in velvet jerkins were far outnumbered by grizzled hunters and rugged horse wranglers. Stewart, who should have known better in the first place, came to realize long before the ice broke up on the Missouri that the Rockies were not yet ready for a fashionable party comprised solely of elegant young gentlemen, and so — ever the pragmatist — he compromised on his vision.

Tales of the men-only pleasure party spread along the banks of the Mississippi, attracting a ragtag assortment of drunks and grifters. One dubious character who called himself Doctor Matthew was expelled before the journey even started. (His nickname was perhaps an ironic reference to the Irish temperance leader Father Mathew.) "[He] pours whiskey into his throat through a funnel," wrote one of the participants. "This lout waltzes drunkenly about in the wilds around Westport and the only thing he seems to have the energy to do is to spread corruption." Another man hoping to join the party was arrested by the sheriff of Independence, charged with embezzling $40,000 in Treasury notes from the post office in New Orleans. William Drummond Stewart's colorful Shakespearean pageant proved to have its share of rogues and arrant knaves.[11]

In St. Louis Sir William's role as autocratic impresario — the wealthy host dispensing elegant favors to his grateful guests — became increasingly unsustainable as he was forced to employ more hired hands for hard cash. The costume party gradually morphed into an enterprise that was less a lavish entertainment and more a serious professional undertaking; in the process Stewart's entourage became more fractiously heterogeneous. In one area alone was he able to continue to work his Svengali-like magic: in his ability to recruit as guests for his mountain idyll handsome young men with romantic notions.

We have an intimate view of one such episode of recruitment thanks to the memoirs of Clark Kennerly. Kennerly was the nephew of William Clark, and he and the explorer's son Jefferson Clark were "more like twin brothers than cousins." In his old age Kennerly reminisced about a dinner party at which William Drummond Stewart was the guest of honor, a guest who over the port and cigars played Othello to a pair of breathless young Desdemonas. "Jeff and I listened with bated breath to tales of wonderful adventure in the far-away Rockies and to plans for another trip across the wide prairies. Sir William probably noticed our intense interest in the subject, particularly in his plans for the near future. Anyway, he invited us to accompany him, and, both being ready to go anywhere at any moment, we accepted with alacrity. My mother's consent was with some difficulty gained later."[12]

Though Stewart had no way of knowing it at the time, one man who joined the party in St. Louis would almost single-handedly immortalize the adventure: a journalist and sometime actor named Matthew C. Field. Matt Field wrote for the *New Orleans Daily Picayune* under the pen name Phazma, and he sensed that Sir William's "hunting frolic" (as Field called it) would provide a wealth of subject matter for many issues of the newspaper and assure a steady readership for months to come. In over forty columns published first in the *Daily Picayune* and then picked up and republished by other newspapers in the country, and in a diary that was published after his death, he recorded the daily events of the colorful cavalcade. It is because of his prolific, satiric pen that we know so much about what happened during those four eventful months.

Though as an actor Field had performed in New Orleans, Mobile, and St. Louis (at one point renting a garret room whose window opened directly across from the spire of St. Louis Cathedral, where Stewart was baptized in the sanctuary far below), it is most likely that the two men first met in New Orleans, probably after Field became "Phazma" and had gained a local reputation for his clever and observant writing. Stewart, determined to succeed with Field where he had failed with Audubon, offered to cover all of the writer's expenses and even to provide for his family during the months that he would be on the trail. "I want for nothing," Field wrote to reassure his wife, "and shall want for nothing . . . for Sir William will do anything & everything for me."[13]

Stewart's party left St. Louis on board the steamboat *Weston* on the second of May. Only a few days into the journey upstream, the steamboat made a short stop along the banks, probably to take on more wood for fuel. Stewart and his entourage got off the boat to take a much-needed stroll, and when they returned they discovered that the *Weston* had caught fire and burned to the water line. Most of their belongings had already been sent overland, so the only loss was the items they had brought with them for the short trip. First the *J. M. White* and now the *Weston*. If Sir William had been a man troubled by omens, he might have felt uneasy. They boarded the next available steamboat and reached Chouteau's Landing on May 6 or 7. From there they crossed into Shawnee Country and set up a camp that Field dubbed "Camp William."

A member of the party published an anonymous letter in a Savannah newspaper (later reprinted in the *Daily Picayune*) describing the temporary settlement:

> My tent is pitched in the centre of a grove of crab apple trees, which are now in full blossom and fill the air with a most delicious perfume. These, with wild cherry trees and various shrubs, form a kind of connecting link between the woods on the Missouri and the great prairie, as it were, a gradual transition from the trees of the forest into the grass of the prairie. . . . Our camp presents generally a very

animated scene. It is composed of ten tents, of different shapes and colors. Sir William's is very elegant, and large enough to contain a dozen people. They are scattered without order among the shrubs, in such manner, however, that they may be all seen from some points. Generally, during the day, the spaces between the tents are filled with men on horse-back and on foot, visiting our Tartar village on business, but at night the scene becomes picturesque, when the fires are gaily burning in front of the tents, and throwing their moving light on the groups which have formed around them.

The tents were not the only colorful objects that Sir William had provided to assure a festive mise-en-scène. Each company of six men was allotted a two-wheeled cart called a charette that was pulled by two mules and was covered with a canopy painted a brilliant scarlet.[14]

In his first column to the *Picayune* Field gave a brief description of his traveling companions, summarizing them thus: "They are all men cast in that fascinating mould of character which tunes down the loftiest sublimity of soul to harmonize with the gentlest associations of our kindest nature — men to sigh over a love song and meet the red savage knife to knife." He singled out two of the young gentleman for particular attention. "We are likewise accompanied from St. Louis by Jefferson Clark, the younger son of the famous 'Clark' whose mountain travels with 'Lewis' are well known. Jefferson Clark is a noble youth of about seventeen, full of Western enthusiasm and love of adventure. A friend of about the same age is with him, young Kennerly, of St. Louis." Clark Kennerly's memoirs, as told to his daughter in his old age and later published under the title *Persimmon Hill*, provide a fascinating counterpoint to Field's contemporary columns for the *Picayune*.[15]

One member of the company was even more famous than the host, but he kept a low profile and appears little in the writings of the period. Baptiste Charbonneau, son of Sacagawea, was hired as a trail hand. The little boy born during the Lewis and Clark expedition was now thirty-eight years old. Since his separation from Duke Paul Wilhelm of Württemberg in 1829 he had worked as a trapper for the American

Fur Company, gaining a reputation as someone who was hard working but unsociable; few people knew him well. Clark Kennerly was frequently asked if Charbonneau spoke fondly of his legendary mother, and Kennerly always replied, "I regret to say that he spoke more often of the mules he was driving and might have been heard early and late expatiating in not too complimentary a manner on their stubbornness."[16]

While William Sublette continued to make preparations in Westport, Stewart bided his time and played the gracious laird, striding through the camp loudly greeting newcomers or hosting dinners in his lavish tent. "Sir William Stewart," wrote Field, "is in fine health and spirits, and makes himself beloved by all around him. He is not exactly the 'fine old English gentleman,' as described in Russell's famous melody, for we find him leaving the halls and parks of 'Muthly,' (the name of his hereditary mansion on the Tay) to seek the exciting sport of the chase on our wild prairies and mountains, but that he is at once the nobleman and the gentleman all who know him cheerfully proclaim."[17]

Before he began his journey, Stewart had learned that the U.S. government was sending John C. Frémont on another exploratory mission, one that would be heading west at about the same time as Stewart's own party. He tried without success to get Frémont to agree to travel with him at least for the first part of the expedition. One member of Frémont's party was a young man from Kentucky named Theodore Talbot. Talbot and another young man, Frederick Dwight from Massachusetts, held an ambiguous status in Frémont's enterprise, as neither man had enlisted in the army and there is no record of their being officially employed as civilians to accompany the expedition. Their presence remains unexplained.

Shortly after joining Frémont, Talbot suffered a massive nasal hemorrhage and he was bedridden when Stewart came to call on his captain. "I am of course unable to rise," wrote Talbot in his journal,

> but I still had the pleasure of listening to the conversation of Sir Wm. Drummond Stewart the distinguished rover of the western prairies, and other gentlemen of his party. Sir Wm. is again going to make a

248

pleasure tour, accompanied by several gentlemen anxious to share the toils and enjoyments of this untrammeled life. It is his intention to proceed to Little Lake on Green river near the Rocky Mts. to spend there some weeks devoted to the pleasures of the chase, fishing &c as each ones taste may dictate, then to return slowly homeward — In this manner they will get rid of 5 or six months very pleasantly and those who are in delicate health very profitably.

Sir William took an interest in Talbot's nasal problem, sending over his party's official physician, Stedman Tilghman, to examine the young patient. Dr. Tilghman advised Frémont against allowing the young man to travel. Talbot, however, was adamant, despite the doctor's recommendation: "But Mr. F. has left that to myself and *live* or *die*, of course I go."[18]

The temporary camp in Shawnee Country proved more permanent than intended, as the ice on the river held well into May that year. The eventual thaw was followed by days of rain that fell with such ferocity that the men needed to get up in the middle of the night to dig trenches around their tents in an attempt to keep them from flooding. The rain, in any event, promised a quick growth for the prairie grass, so it was endured with patience and even some humor.

Still, the men became restive as boredom set in. A field trip was organized to visit a nearby Shawnee village to witness the traditional Bread Dance, and one evening Matt Field helped to organize a variety show in which he drew on his experience as a Shakespearean actor. "We are to have a grand dramatic performance in camp tomorrow night," he wrote to his father-in-law, " — Katherine & Petrucio [*The Taming of the Shrew*] — Petrucio, Don Mateo del Campo ['Sir Matthew Field' in Spanish] — Katherine, *Miss Power* — after which, Song, 'Little Pigs,' Mr. Dr. Tilghman — Grand Shawnee Bread dance, by the whole company — to conclude with Romeo & Juliet — the balcony scene — Romeo, Don Mateo, Juliet, *Miss* Power." The actors appeared in full costume, so it is likely that Stewart broke open the trunks containing the velvet doublets. For the scene from *Romeo and Juliet* one of the wagons was converted to a Capulet balcony, and a tin stable lantern stood in for the inconstant moon. The fair Juliet in drag appeared on the Conestoga wagon crowned with a wreath of prairie wildflowers. The man whom Field refers to as *"Miss* Power" remains unidentified, but if he was a professional actor (as he almost certainly must have been to essay the roles of Katherine and Juliet on such short notice and without a script), he was perhaps a member of the multigenerational Irish and American acting dynasty whose most famous member was the film star Tyrone Power.[19]

On May 22 the river had cleared sufficiently and the grass had grown high enough that the party at long last set out. The group reached the Kansas River in five days. Here the men halted near Soldier Creek (also known as Black Warrior Creek) until May 30, when William Sublette and his portion of the party caught up with them. Sublette had been delayed in part because of bad roads, which he recorded as being "much Cut up by Waggons." Wagon trains of pioneer families were beginning to arrive in large numbers, tearing deep ruts in the prairie where once only men on horseback had ventured, leaving behind a litter of discarded household items. All around was inescapable evidence that the days of Eden were drawing to a rapid close.[20]

The party branched off to a less traveled route, and the emptiness of the prairie spread around the men in splendid isolation. With over ninety men, together with their carts, wagons, and animals, the entourage moved slowly. Each day an advance party would set out to reconnoiter the best route ahead and then return to lead the group forward. After a few days of uneventful travel, the riders encountered a war party of about seventy Osages resting after an attack on their sworn enemies, the Pawnees. Several of the Osages were standing next to blood-spattered poles from which fluttered newly taken scalps. The advance horsemen halted to watch the Indians cautiously, waiting until the slower wagons had a chance to catch up.

The reunited party then began moving warily past the Osage camp and would have continued unmolested except that the Indians spied three stray Pawnees who had been following Stewart's wagons, hoping to use the white men for protection. Realizing that they had been spotted, the Pawnees sought refuge in the wagon belonging to the Jesuit priests. The Osages swiftly dragged them out, stripped them of their belongings, and tied their hands behind their backs before anyone could move to stop them. Father Peter De Vos and Father Adrian Hoecken finally intervened, demanding in sign language the release of the prisoners. When the Osages refused, the other members of the party physically wrested the Pawnees free and pushed them toward the safety of the priests' wagon. Furious, the Osages mounted their horses and began riding in large threatening circles, weaving in and out among the company.

After a few tense moments an Osage approached the priests' wagon and extended his hand in a sign of friendship to one of the Pawnees, who cautiously responded to the gesture. Instantly the Osage grabbed the Pawnee's arm and tried to jerk him up onto his horse. With great effort the man was able to pull himself free. All three Pawnees were transferred to a larger, more secure wagon, which was then surrounded by horsemen who made clear their resolve to provide sanctuary. The Osages continued to follow the entourage until evening, at which point they silently disappeared into the prairie.

In the official report that the army officers, Lieutenants Graham and Smith, filed after their return, they perhaps misremembered the events of that morning, as they labeled the Pawnees as the aggressors rather than the Osages. They assured the government that there was "no danger whatever to be apprehended from the Pawnees by the whites travelling in this country in any force, but should two or three white men alone on the prairies be so unfortunate as to meet with the Pawnees, they are certain of being stripped of their horses and guns."[21]

Stewart had taken along only sixteen days' provisions, assuming from his previous experience that those would easily last until they reached buffalo country, but the buffalo proved elusive and food began to run short. Rations were restricted, and the men did the best they could to supplement their meals with whatever they could scavenge along the way. Field reported that they feasted on fresh turtle soup, which provided a certain gastronomic elegance even when slurped from tin platters while squatting in the grass. There were no trees from which to gather firewood, so the men used buffalo chips. The presence of the dung at least promised that buffalo were nearby.

Twenty days soon passed and still no buffalo appeared. The mood of the party darkened. "Some had let their good spirits forsake them a week after leaving Westport, some kept up brave faces for a fortnight longer, but about this time nearly everybody looked serious." Field recorded "every man in a moody state of let-me-alone-ativeness; and *noli me tangere* seemed to be the selfish and solitary order of the day. . . . Nothing could have exceeded the heaviness and hopeless lassitude that oppressed us all."[22]

Then two dark spots were seen on the horizon, and twenty riders tore off in pursuit of the buffalo. Unfortunately the two spots turned out to be two other members of the party, themselves out hunting. When those two men in turn saw "spots" approaching them, they likewise thought they had discovered buffalo and took off toward the spots at a gallop — until they got close enough to see that the "buffalo" were horseman, at which point they concluded they must be Indians and veered around to ride as fast as they could in the opposite direction. The men from the camp, seeing the "spots" turn and run, became even more convinced they had at last found buffalo and set off after them at a mad dash — strengthening their comrades' belief that they were being pursued by Indians. The mistaken chase continued until night began to fall, at which point the larger hunting party pulled up and returned to camp. There they discovered that Antoine Clement had killed an antelope, and at last there was meat to eat. "Over a supper of antelope, with a fair prospect of finding buffalo the next day, we laughed and sung and fell back again into our old fancies about the delights of wild life. But what enlivened us all into even a merrier mood was the coming back into camp of our two hunted companions, declaring that they had been chased for ten hours by the whole Pawnee nation! We at once saw through the whole mistake, and roars of laughter, repeated again and again, were heard around the camp fires until we all sank into our buffalo robes to rest."[23]

In his accounts published in the *Picayune* Matt Field assigned nicknames to most of the members of the party, allowing him a greater level of frankness — and perhaps of creativity — in telling their stories. One of the most amusing characters is William C. Kennett of St. Louis, whom Field nicknames "Crockett" (perhaps an ironic reference to Kennett's droll refusal to embrace the inevitable discomforts of the wild frontier). "Crockett had been the pet of a sumptuous home, and was particularly fond of personal comfort, so that in our rough travel he met of course with perpetual annoyance, all of which he encountered, however, with the same quiet and admirable humor." Kennett adopted the persona of the exasperated dandy, meant for the finer things in life but doomed to eternal frustration in dealing with a world that was constantly assaulting his sensitivities and wearing on his aesthetic nerves.[24]

Their first night on the Platte, with rain pouring down in buckets swamping the tents, Kennett looked around with exaggerated disbelief, as though he had just learned that his reservation at Delmonico's had been inexplicably cancelled. "Why, for heaven's sake, shall we have no supper?" It was pointed out that there was no firewood within a hundred miles. "But the *bois de vache*," he offered. It was explained that the buffalo chips were too wet to burn. "And, good lord! how are we to sleep in this water?" It was suggested that no one would be sleeping much that night.

> "And this is what you call a *pleasure excursion*, is it!" said Crockett. "What imaginative minds you must have! How lucky it is for people to have the faculty to fancy that misery is mirth, downright hardship nothing but fun, bitter privation lively amusement, and wild-goose wandering a pleasure excursion!"
>
> "Mr. Crockett, you are on first guard, sir," said a messenger from Col. Sublette, our camp-leader.
>
> "On guard? [T]*o-night!*" exclaimed poor Crockett, in a tone of desperation and despair.
>
> "On first guard, sir — you and your mess. — Wake up the 'Widow' at one o'clock."

The Widow was a wise-headed, old-womanish young gentleman, who may be introduced hereafter.

"Will anyone have the goodness now to lend me a little imagination?" said Col. David Crockett. "I should be happy to fancy that walking about for three hours in the dark, over a wild prairie, and under a visitation of cats and dogs from the sky, is a pleasant and gentlemanly recreation! I have no doubt this is all very fine sport, but, unfortunately, I find the prejudice of education strong upon me, and I can't get over the mental hallucination that it is excessively disagreeable."

That evening the party sat down glumly to a meal of crackers and whiskey.[25]

Twenty-seven days passed with no sight of buffalo. The food situation was becoming critical. Father De Vos offered Sunday Mass with a special prayer for the arrival of sufficient game to feed the men, and the old hunter Joe Poirier, kneeling beside the priest, uttered a sincere invocation: "Forgive us some sin, O *mon Dieu* — let us see some fat cow this to-day — we have not no bacon more — and even old bull was better than no meat at all — thank Heaven for all everything — Amen!" Others echoed the invocation with varying levels of belief in its efficacy — and at ten o'clock Antoine Clement, who had gone out to reconnoiter the countryside, tore into camp with the news that there were indeed buffalo just over the horizon. Fourteen hunters were soon mounted and following Clement, and an equal number of young gentlemen hurried after, eager to observe the spectacle. They had almost begun to believe that the buffalo had become extinct. Now suddenly the camp exploded into action with the excitement of a hunt.[26]

The young gentlemen soon learned that a buffalo hunt was no place for weak nerves or amateur horsemanship. Clement rode at breakneck speed over the roughest terrain. "Those whose attention was not entirely absorbed by the buffalo, might have seen some pale faces among the novices at this time. Antoine paused for no impediment." Before long two dead buffaloes were stretched out on the prairie and Clement and

Poirier ("our two professors in the art of buffalo butchering") were hard at work. By the afternoon other buffalo were spotted, a much larger herd, and even the young gentlemen who at first had been content with being observers joined in the excitement this time, leading to some inevitable confusion about who had shot what and when.[27]

"That's my cow!" called out a little sharp-nosed, pale-faced, thin-whiskered Englishman [A. M. Storer], riding up to where Joe Pourier was sharpening his knife upon the horn of a fallen animal.

"How is you lef you mozer?" said Joe, making a desperate attempt to say, "How did you leave your mother!"

"That's my cow!" called the Englishman again, in a shrill treble, amounting almost to a shriek. The little fellow had really popped a ball through a cow's lungs, but at the shot his horse made a sudden circumbendibus, and he just saw the game fall as he was carried over a hill and out of view of everybody. Coming back, he concluded the first cow he saw was his, and once again he more vehemently reiterated in feminine falsetto, "That's my cow!"

Joe by this time was stripping the skin from the animal, and slashing away with his butcher knife, he replied — "How you say? — wat make him you cow? [G]uess no cow much wait for you 'bout here!"[28]

That evening the party experienced one of the most frightening events of the entire journey. Clark Kennerly (whom Field describes as "a lively and interesting youth of sixteen or eighteen") was removing the saddle from his horse when he happened to touch a sore spot on the horse's back, causing the animal to shy and pull away. Kennerly was unaware that he had inadvertently stepped into the coil of his lariat, and as the horse pulled away the rope was drawn taut. "Before I could disengage my foot," Kennerly later reminisced, "he suddenly started for the slough about fifty yards away, and I might have been the carcass of a wolf for all the horse cared. He dragged me at his best speed over prickly pears and burrs, into the water, out on the other side, down through the length of it, then recrossed to the camp side, bolting for some of his companions who were grazing there."[29]

Field describes the horror the men experienced watching the scene unfold: "We could hear gasping ejaculations of pain from our unfortunate companion, as his body violently struck here and there the uneven surface of the ground." No one knew what to do. Chasing the horse would only make him run faster. A few men grabbed their rifles, but were afraid to shoot for fear of hitting Kennerly. Finally the animal noticed the other horses staked for the night and ran toward them, halting as quickly as he had bolted. "All crowded to the spot, and little Kennerly was picked up, very faint indeed, but able to speak and declare in a gay, undaunted manner, that he was not hurt a bit. It was a curious contrast — the coolness of the boy after such a perilous adventure, and the palpitating fright into which he had thrown us all."[30]

On June 26, during a long, hot, and dusty day's ride, Matthew Field and two of his companions struck out on their own, determined to drink from a mountain stream they saw glinting at the bottom of a deep canyon. They urged their horses down the steep hill and, dismounting, ran toward the cool water. "We threw ourselves prostrate to kiss the brink of this fluid crystal, and then, with a luxurious *abandon*, we fell backward upon the grass beneath the ash trees, and shouted aloud with delight." The rest of the party had gone ahead without them, and the stragglers had just decided that it would be wise to hurry up and rejoin the group when they saw one of their companions, on horseback, gingerly making his way down the canyon toward the stream. To catch his attention they let out an imitation of an Indian yell — an imitation so accurate that the man thought they were in fact a party of Sioux and quickly hid himself among the rocks and scrub brush. The men searched for their companion until late afternoon, but finally decided he must have slipped away.[31]

As evening fell they returned to the camp to discover that the missing man was Cyprien Menard, an attorney newly admitted to the St. Louis bar. No one had seen him for most of the afternoon. As they later learned, when Menard fled what he thought was a party of Sioux he had lost his horse, but had decided that if he followed the course of the river he would sooner or later catch up with the party at that night's camp.

Darkness came, but there was no sign of the missing man. As soon as daylight permitted, Stewart sent a search party back to look for Menard, not knowing that during the night Menard had passed the camp and was actually in front of the others, hurrying (or so he thought) to catch up. With the men staying in one place, determined not to go forward without their missing comrade, the distance between them was actually increasing. After three days of fruitless searching, the party held a council at which it was decided that Menard had probably been captured or killed or perhaps had died of exposure, and that there was no course but to continue on their journey.

With heavy hearts the men set out the next day. They had been traveling only half an hour when they discovered a buffalo's skull on which was written with a charred stick, "June 28 — Evening — I have lost my horse, my feet are bare and sore — I am hungry and tired — my ammunition gone, assist me or I perish!" It was signed, "Menard." Ten men quickly grabbed meat and wine, mounted the fastest horses, and, accompanied by Father Hoecken, set off to rescue their companion. Five or six miles farther they found another skull, this one with a message reading, "June 29 — Menard is still on the Platte and will continue so — Please hasten to me, as my feet are so sore I can go no further!" Only a little beyond they found the man, "his eyes staring wide, and cheeks hollow, but with a heart as a lion." Clark Kennerly, who described Menard as one of his "intimate friends," remembered their emotional reunion. "From the physical reaction, which was natural after his long wandering, he succumbed and fell to the ground through sheer exhaustion and joy of being rescued."[32]

The party encountered a group of trappers descending the river in little bateaux on its way to St. Louis at the end of the season. One of the trappers, Alexander Chauvin, decided to turn back and join Stewart's entourage, while one of the gentlemen, John Radford, chose to join the trappers and return to St. Louis, where he was to be married to Cyprien Menard's sister. Just before Radford left the party he was involved in a contretemps with Antoine Clement that might have cost him his life. The two men had gone out buffalo hunting together.

Clement brought down a huge bull with one shot and, leaning his rifle against the carcass, was about to begin to butcher it — when the creature roared to its feet, wounded but very much alive. Without his horse and rifle Clement needed a way to keep his distance from the beast's horns, and in an instant he remembered the game he used to play, to Alfred Jacob Miller's great consternation. He grabbed the buffalo's tail, and as the animal whirled and bucked in anger, Clement was dragged along behind him, yanked and jerked but kept at a safe distance from the buffalo's lethal protrusions.

Clement shouted at Radford to shoot, but the sight of the hunter being tossed around like a rag doll convulsed Radford into spasms of uncontrollable laughter. Clement began to shout and swear in two languages, "Shoot! *Shoot! Merde!*" but Radford only doubled up, holding his sides in merriment. Finally Clement was able to shake his hunting knife free from its scabbard and onto the ground, and as he circled around once more, he grabbed the weapon and with a few quick strokes hamstrung the animal. He then turned on John Radford in a bloody rage and would have used the knife on him, if Radford had not abjectly and profusely apologized.[33]

The country the entourage was passing through was dotted with odd rock formations of stunning beauty, and the young gentlemen and the seasoned trail hands alike drew up their horses and gazed in wonder at the landscape. "When we encamped one evening at 'Chimney Rock,' in the close neighborhood of Scott's Bluff," wrote Matt Field, "a heavy storm was gathering across the sky, and all was black above us, while the level beams of the descending sun shot from an opening in the western horizon, kindling up the bluffs into burnished silver, and no sunset exhibition ever produced a more superb and sublime effect. — The whole camp paused, with exclamations of wonder and admiration at the scene, not merely those with eyes formed particularly to be attracted by grandeur and beauty, but the hunters, the drivers, everybody, were riveted in astonishment at the spectacle!"[34]

On July 3 the party traveled with care, looking for a special spot to call a halt to the day's travels. The men found a place near the river with timbered banks, luxurious grass, a splendor of wildflowers, wood enough for fires, and a spring "clear as the eye of an angel, cold as eternal snow." Here they made camp. Early the next morning most of the men were up before dawn, and as the sun shot its first rays over the glowing horizon a volley of twenty-six guns (one for each state in the Union) — and fifty-six others that went off somewhat at random — heralded the arrival of the Fourth of July. The celebration called for the raising of the American flag but no one, not even the two army officers, had thought to bring one along. With ingenuity and creative flair, the gentlemen promptly took up their needles and set to work to remedy the situation. Two red silk handkerchiefs were donated and carefully cut into strips. Dr. Tilghman reached into his medical kit and drew out several rolls of white cloth bandages. A man's blue calico shirt, a couple gilded hatbands, a few fancy tassels, and — voilà! — a proper (and unique) specimen of Old Glory. The raising of the flag was followed by a Catholic Mass celebrated by Father De Vos.

The main event of the day was a grand feast. Stewart abutted his tent with the next-largest tent in the assembly, creating one huge space, though there was still room for only half of the party (Field gives the total number of men in the entourage at ninety-three), so the group was divided, with four of the messes gathering outside on the grass. Those inside the tent sat on the ground on either side of a long strip of oilcloth that served as a table. The menu included gumbo, boudin sausages, buffalo tongue, forcemeat balls, juleps made from bourbon, mountain snow, and wild mint, and for dessert a real English plum pudding, baked with great care by A. M. Storer (who had evidently recovered from his fit of pique at having his cow claimed by another).

Sir William, who sat at the head of the oilcloth, rose as the hock was being passed around and proposed the first toast: "Prosperity to the Union." Then George Christy, a Harvard-educated lawyer from New Orleans, rose and delivered an ode written especially for the celebration. If having as his host a former British officer proved awkward for the poet on this commemoration of America's independence, Christy did not shrink from the challenge:

The days have gone past, and the dangers have vanish'd
That threatened her struggles in freedom's first hour;
The men that would slave us are fallen and banish'd —
We stand in our majesty, manhood and power.

There were more toasts and more songs, and then in honor of their host the party sang a special version of "God Save the Queen" that was carefully worded to remain appropriate for the patriotic holiday:

God save our noble land,
Long may our Union stand
God save our land!
Long may Victoria reign,
Thrice blest and blest again!
While we at peace remain,
God save our land![35]

Storer had made two large plum puddings, but it was the opinion of most of the Americans that a little plum pudding goes a very long way. At the end of the feast one of the glistening brown ovoids remained uneaten. Much alcohol was being consumed on all sides and the party was getting rather boisterous, so to prevent his marvelous creation from ending up in the role of a football, Storer spirited the pudding away, hiding it in Lt. Sidney Smith's tent.

As the afternoon wore on, the celebration became increasingly raucous. Rhine wine was flowing freely, and Stewart decided that is was perhaps wise to channel some of the exuberance into sporting contests. First, a horse race. The men jumped on their mounts bareback and tore off over the prairie, over hills and through clumps of trees as far as the river — where some of the inebriated riders lost their seat and fell into the sobering ice-cold water. Whoops and jeers, shouts of encouragement, wagers and profanity.

Lieutenant Smith, who was generally acknowledged the best horseman of the group, issued a challenge in the form of a game of Follow the Leader. He spurred his horse toward the mountains, and the others took off after him. He wheeled and darted, then galloped back to tear through the camp at top speed, followed by a train of bareback horsemen determined to keep up with him and match him feat for feat. Finally Smith announced that he was going to ride his horse right into his tent, challenging the others to follow him. This sent poor Storer scurrying, fearful for his hidden pudding. The Englishman made it to the tent just in time to scoop up the endangered dessert, but before he could exit Smith was at the tent entrance, his horse snorting and stomping. Fortunately for Storer, the horse balked at the idea of entering the tent, giving the Englishman just enough time to pull up a couple tent stakes, shove the pudding to safety, and crawl out after it.

The next day the party reached Fort John on the Laramie River, and the Independence Day feast was rivaled by a real home-style breakfast of fried dried meat, coffee, milk, crullers, fried eggs, butter, and cheese. The men spent five days at the fort and then pushed on.

They had been traveling now for forty-seven days. It had been over two months since Matt Field had left his wife, Cornelia, and their child in New Orleans, and he confided to his diary that he "rode alone all the morning thinking of Corney, baby, home and relatives — my custom often, tho' only mentioned here." He could not share with the young gentlemen his longing for the comforts of married life as he felt they would not understand, and when bouts of homesickness assailed him he found their campy banter and incessant sexual innuendoes difficult to endure. In his diary he wrote,

There are men, and in all other respects decent persons, too, who indulge in, and laugh merrily over, what they no doubt fondly fancy is wit, or, at least, smartness, while it is, in fact, merely the constant and promiscuous use of a vulgar word that they really neither know how to spell or pronounce! If one says "I want to show you something," your wit of this description will say, "O, show your ass!" (meaning arse) and this is really laughed over and honored as true attic salt, while it is in truth only a disgrace to the speaker, an offence to every person of taste, a sacrilege to star-eyed *esprit* and a thing from which genius must turn with pity and disgust. Pah! the pencil is soiled and unfitted for better use in mentioning so vile a custom![36]

A few days later Field and Sir William rode out together in advance of the camp. As they passed through a deep gully they saw signs that a flash flood had recently swept through the narrow passage to a height of thirty or forty feet, carrying away everything in its path. The object of their side trip was a visit to a natural bridge that Field estimated was thirty feet from the ground to the bottom of the arch, with an additional fifty feet to the top of the bridge. A river swept among the fragments of rock at its base, roaring and foaming at their feet. (The rock formation is now part of Ayers Natural Bridge Park in Converse County, Wyoming.)

On July 15 the party camped beside a very high range of bluffs near the banks of the Platte. No sooner had the men set up camp than they were attacked by swarms of mosquitoes and tiny toads "about the size of black beetles." When the insects invaded Stewart's tent he realized that sleeping would be impossible that evening unless something drastic was attempted, and he ordered a few of the men to build a small fire in the center of his tent, hoping that the smoke would drive the mosquitoes away. Antoine Clement set out hunting and killed eight buffalo cows; with the six that were killed by Joe Poirier, there would be food enough for a lavish banquet that evening. The day was scorching, and several of the men waded gingerly into the cold, fast-moving stream. Suddenly there was a cry of "Fire! Fire! Fire!" The campfire that had been set to smoke out the mosquitoes had gotten out of control, and part of Stewart's elegant marquee was consumed by the flames. As he stood before the smoldering remains, Sir William shrugged and observed laconically that at least they had got rid of the mosquitoes.[37]

A few days later Matthew Field wrote a letter to the *Picayune* describing the progress the party had made thus far. "The epistle was of the sunniest and liveliest kind," Field later remembered, "aiming to assure friends at home of our complete safety, and how well every thing was going with us, dwelling upon our freedom from molestation or danger . . . and our happy escape from accident or peril of any kind." He had just sealed the cheery letter with a glistening red drop of sealing wax when he heard the loud crack of a rifle discharge. A man shouted, "Good God!" and a younger voice cried out *"Mon Dieu! Mon Dieu!"* Field rushed to the scene. "The next instant all eyes were directed to the spot where the misfortune occurred, by a still louder voice calling hurriedly for *'Doctor Tilghman!'* — and there lay poor little François Clément in the arms of Sir Wm. Stewart, with the blood rushing in torrents from his left breast!"[38]

François Clement, Antoine's younger brother, was one of the young French Canadian engagés hired in St. Louis. He was about fifteen years old. "The boy was a favorite with Capt. Stewart," Field wrote, "and generally rode with him as page or *protégé*." On July 18 as François was reaching into a tent to retrieve a shotgun, the weapon accidentally discharged, sending an ounce ball through the lower lobe of his left lung, severing the pulmonary artery and exiting under his left shoulder blade. Dr. Tilghman attempted to render aid, but the wound was obviously fatal. "Laissez-moi," moaned the boy, weakly pushing the doctor away. "Laissez-moi, Monsieur le Docteur. Je suis mort! Je suis mort!" He called for his brother; Antoine leaned over, and the boy kissed him. He asked for water and lamented that he would never again see his dear mother. Father De Vos, quickly donning an alb and stole, anointed the boy with chrism for the sacrament of Extreme Unction. Dr. Tilghman, seeing that the boy was in great pain, gave him a strong sedative, and François drifted to sleep before he died.[39]

In the morning a funeral Mass was said in a tent that Charles Geyer, the German botanist on the expedition, had decorated with wildflowers, and then Antoine Clement's little brother was lowered into an unmarked grave. Matt Field read a poem:

No words to be read are over his head,
And no sculptured praise to save
The name of poor François, pale & dead
In his lonely mountain grave!

The ground was leveled and packed, and a fire was burned over the spot, "for it was necessary to hide, not mark, a Christian's grave in that far land of desolation."[40]

Antoine was deeply shaken by his brother's death.

The fine form of the sturdy, sun-burned mountaineer seemed like a figure hardened into bronze, as he knelt, speechless and immovable, beside his dying brother during the gloomy hours of that evening. He kissed the boy repeatedly, but never wept or uttered a syllable. He sat with the corpse, and never spoke. When the camp moved away from the grave, next day, there we left Antoine, all alone, and there he stood, his figure growing indistinct in distance, until all sight of him was gone; and never, during all the rest of our travel, did Antoine mention his brother, until, when on the steamboat, nearing his home, with a choking voice and eyes filling up with tears, he asked the writer of this [Matt Field] to give him on paper the dying words of François.

Although he was unable to read or write himself, Antoine must have clutched the written words as a last tangible link to his dead brother as he wondered how he could possibly break the news to their mother.[41]

By 11 o'clock the morning of the funeral the party was under way again, though gloom prevailed. Field wrote in his diary, "Great depression in camp on account of yesterday's melancholy accident — the very animals came with more docility to their harness, and every thing seemed to be more subdued." Three days later the men reached Independence Rock, where Field recorded, "A rowdy spree in the evening."[42]

About five miles from Independence Rock was another of the famous landmarks of the region: a sharp cleft in the granite ridge called Devil's Gate. Here the Sweetwater River had cut a gorge three hundred feet wide at its top but only thirty feet wide at its base, causing the pent-up river to foam and roar as it fought its way into the valley below. Twenty of the men set off from camp to explore the landmark, but for most the climb proved too strenuous. Only Matthew Field, Stedman Tilghman, and Cyprien Menard succeeded in reaching the center of the cleft. There they encountered A. M. Storer, who had entered from the other side, and they toasted each other over the deafening rush of water (beverage unspecified).

Further along they found a secluded grotto tranquil enough for bathing, and they quickly stripped and dove into the cool water. After two months on the trail the bottom half of their faces, their necks, and their hands had been burned a deep russet color but the rest of their bodies, almost always covered against the glaring sun, had remained white as marble. Perhaps it was the sight of their pale bodies that suggested it, but the men noticed that the rocky hillside above the pool appeared to be furnished with shallow niches crying out for ornamentation. The nude men clambered up to the various openings and amused one another by striking poses in imitation of Greek statues. It was a memorable afternoon, and they commemorated the event by inscribing their names on a buffalo skull that they then mounted in the secret grotto they named the Niche in the Wall.

The party reached the Continental Divide on the first day of August. Matt Field noted the event in his diary, then provided a sketchy précis of what must have been a very long private conversation with Sir William. The brief references are in some cases the only American source for information about Murthly Castle and its environs. Stewart explained about the remnants of Birnam Wood on the property and its connection to Shakespeare's *Macbeth*. He regaled Field with a story about "Cockney Deer Hunting": in 1829 a group of sportsmen from London arrived and spent the day deer hunting — though the hunters' only previous contact with the animal had been "a peep over the walls of Windsor to see noble stags appear and dart away." Having shot a dozen, they had the deer hauled to their inn, and with pleasure ordered a grand feast of the game they had brought down. The hunters were waiting with great anticipation when the landlord appeared and begged them not to shoot any more of his goats.[43]

Stewart shared stories about the mysterious "Saddle Stone" that lay on a lonely heath upon the family property, source of a prophecy: "The raven shall sit on the Saddle Stone, / And feast on the bluid of gentlemen!" There were ghost stories, discussions about the works of Sir Walter Scott, and disputations on demonology and witchcraft. Though Field does not specify the time or location of the conversation, one imagines it was in the evening around the flickering campfire.[44]

As the party made its way through the South Pass the men noticed boggy patches of soil that Field described as "quagmires." One of the servants Stewart had brought with him from Scotland was "a rollicking Scotch boy" named Tom Craig. Fascinated with the spongy ground that sprang under his feet like a trampoline, Tom commenced a vigorous demonstration of the Highland Fling. To everyone's horror, with the very first jump he broke through the topsoil and sank below the ground as far as his waist. Only his presence of mind allowed him to clamber out before being swallowed up entirely.[45]

The altitude, which had been steadily climbing, now began to evidence itself in an abrupt change in the weather. It was the third day of August, yet in the morning there was an eighth of an inch of ice on the water pail. The party bade farewell to the Jesuit priests, who headed north for Flathead country, and with the departure of the clergymen the atmosphere of the encampment shifted perceptibly. For the first time in his narrative Field mentions serious dissension among the members of the party, reporting a fight between two of Sublette's men: Jack Cromwell and Jo Smith (the latter nicknamed the Prophet because he bore the name of the Mormon leader). "Jack took up arms for little Dr. Tilghman, had the sympathy of everybody with him, and he beat Jo very severely, nearly loosing an eye by brutal gouging in the engagement." Cromwell had evidently employed tactics common among combatants in the mountain regions of Kentucky and Virginia, where men as a matter of course tried to gouge out an opponent's eyes by inserting their thumbs in the sockets. Field does not explain what offense triggered the confrontation or why Cromwell fought in Tilghman's place.[46]

Whatever pent-up tensions were being released, the men were at last able to relax and enjoy themselves the following day when, after over two months of travel, they reached their destination, a jewel-like mountain pool they christened Stewart's Lake. (It is now called Fremont Lake, after John C. Frémont, who visited it at a later date.) To Field the setting was "gorgeous beyond conceiving." The lake was deep and clear, fed by mountain falls that turned the turquoise water into dazzling silver foam. "Found a most lovely encampment on the lake," Field wrote, "every body in ecstacies with the scene. . . . [T]rout a foot long darting about in the glassy water — 20 lines were in the water in as many minutes, and as many fish were floundering in the grass immediately after."[47]

Another of the men, Richard Rowland, wrote to his sister in a similar vein: "We found beautiful lakes in the mountains delightfully situated quite enchanted places full of fine trout easily caught the water was clear as chrystal quite green on the borders the middle as blue as indigo depth unknown The water was fed from the snows which covered the tops of the mountains at the head of the Lake at the foot were falls or rapids which flowed among the framgent of Granite brought there by some convulsion of Nature It was 10 or 12 miles Long & 3 or so Wide buried in hills you could not see it before you gained the margin of the waters."[48]

On the shores of this secluded lake Sir William at last distributed the costumes he had carried across the continent, and the long-dreamed-of Renaissance pageant began. It was here that Friedrich Armand Strubberg, traveling through what he imagined to be an uninhabited wilderness, peered over the edge of a granite ridge and to his amazement saw a phantasmagorical encampment of colorful tents and velvet-clad men: "old chivalrous costumes with large plumed hats with rolled-up brims, jerkins with slit sleeves, leather leggings, tall riding boots with enormous spurs, large gauntlets . . . broad violet-blue and May-green velvet greatcoats . . . the hat of an Italian brigand captain with red cock's feathers . . . long perfumed locks."[49]

Strubberg and his party descended to the fantastic gathering and were warmly welcomed by their noble host.

The finest wines adorned our tables, which were filled with the most delicious fare by professional chefs, we smoked the best cigars and drank the finest coffee. All these things which were so sumptu-ous for us were spiced by an extremely happy mood which showed itself in every direction in the camp and was made known loudly in every conversation. One passed time shooting at a target, with racing competitions, with various games in which the dexterity of the body was made to count, with cards and dice, and the hunt, the latter of which appeared to be enjoyed by only a part of the company, while the others amused themselves more in the vicinity of the camp.[50]

No detailed description of the interior of Stewart's sumptuous marquee survives, but in *Altowan* the English nobleman Roallan travels throughout the Rockies in a tent fit for a Mughal emperor. "The lodge of Roallan had been pitched," Stewart writes, "its carpets and its buffalo robes, its tiger skins and its robes of sable; choice arms of every sort hung around; and in the center stood the censer, from which was to be lit the sacred pipe. The couches, which extended round the lodge, scarcely differed in appearance; but that one on the right hand, at the entrance, was heaped with richer furs, and spread with more scrupulous care than the others. A part of the back was raised, so that a slight breeze might be admitted, and a view obtained of the mountains and the rapid river that flowed from the melting glaciers."[51]

The pristine lake, the flamboyant costumes, the exotic decor, the untrammeled revelry had a profound effect on the imaginations of the young participants. "'The Lady of the Lake' had ever been a favorite poem in our family," remembered Clark Kennerly, "and some of its lines were now recalled to me at Loch Drummond. It seemed that one had only to step forth and blow a blast upon his hunting horn, when 'fair Ellen' would appear in her little skiff,

> 'With head upraised and look intent
> And eye and ear attentive bent,
> And locks flung back and lips apart
> Like monument of Grecian art.'

In spite of the fact that no 'chieftain's daughter' appeared, except in my fancy, the charms of the place proved so seductive that we here went into camp for several weeks."[52]

Stewart had brought with him two India-rubber boats for fording streams. These were now brought out and inflated for the men's enjoyment, and parties could soon be seen drifting lazily across the surface of the lake. Each boat was large enough to carry fifteen men, but Sir William on one occasion invited only Matt Field, George Christy, and Cyprien Menard to join him for an outing on the water. "4 men — 'Steinwein', chocolate & dried meat," Field jotted in his diary, and at the end of the memorable day he added: "Camped in a wild hollow of the rocks, and drank E. Johns imported 'Steinwein' all the evening till bed time — chatting about Egypt, the pyramids and Chartres street N[ew] O[rleans]. The pleasantest evening of the whole trip — we threw our robes and blankets together, and all slept like tops."[53]

One drowsy afternoon as the camp dozed and the men drifted listlessly in the India-rubber boats, there was suddenly a cry of "Jump! jump! get your guns! quick, for your lives!" Thirty mounted riders descended on the encampment, firing rifles and shrieking Indian war cries. There was much splashing and fumbling for rifles — until the riders were revealed to be trappers and Snake Indians from nearby Fort Bridger. Sir William had sent over a personal invitation for them to join in the festivities. The trappers and the Indians set up separate camps near the Stewart party, and for the next two weeks the gathering looked very much like an old-fashioned rendezvous, with drinking, gambling, and athletic contests that included ball games and horse races.[54]

One of the races had as it purse one dozen bottles of champagne, one dozen bottles of hock, six leather shirts, one pair of pistols, two mules, and an assortment of "Indian trinkets" — a total value at Rocky Mountain prices of around $500 (about $15,000 in current value). The entries included a bay horse named Chieftain belonging to Sir William and a sorrel owned by William Sublette but ridden by one of the engagés named Tom. "Tom, the half-breed," recorded Field in his diary, "rode naked (or three cornered breeches, made out of a red handkerchief) and bare-backed, coming in 30 yards ahead, like a bronze mercury in a state of supernatural animation! Never saw a more beautiful picture." The betting on the races was intense, and the Snakes' love of gambling led them to make reckless wagers. With a twinge of guilt Clark Kennerly remembered of the Indians, "They were sports of the first water, and would bet with a right good will, piling up their pelts, bear, buffalo and beaver skins — all articles of much moment to the Indian — while we, the civilized, educated and philanthropic Christians, would bet colored beads, the cheapest butcher knives, pieces of looking glass almost large enough to reflect one's nose, together with small packages of mean tobacco."[55]

One of the chiefs of the Snake tribe was a white man named Jack Robertson (Kennerly calls him Robinson), who had married a Flathead woman known as the Madam. The Robertson tepee rivaled Sir William's marquee as the place for the choicest entertainment, and the men soon dubbed it the St. Charles Hotel (after the fanciest hostelry in New Orleans). Madam Jack was the grande dame of the gathering. Robertson had showered his wife with gewgaws, and the bright ornaments, colorful beads, and tinkling bells that decorated her clothing and her horse were worth hundreds of dollars.

The Madam was proud of her reputation as the best seamstress in the Rockies, and Clark Kennerly decided to take advantage of her skills. Early in the trip he had shot an antelope — not for food, since at that season antelope subsisted on sagebrush, which gave their meat a foul and acrid taste — but with the intention of having a true Indian-style buckskin outfit made of the hide. He skinned the animal himself (gagging and gasping for air, so putrid did the animal smell because of its diet), and then for the next few weeks he rubbed the hide with smooth stones every evening until it was soft and pliable.

Now he asked Jack Robertson if his wife might make a buckskin suit from it. The Madam was summoned, and when her husband explained what needed to be done, she motioned for Kennerly to stand and turn around slowly. She measured him with her eyes, nodded, and, taking up a knife, cut out the pattern precisely. The next day the outfit was ready: a shirt and trousers complete with decorative fringe. They fit him exactly — until the first rain, at which point Kennerly learned the importance of the proper tanning and curing of leather. As soon as the trousers became wet they began to stretch, and to keep from tripping he needed continually to slice strips off the leg bottoms. "Then the sun

good!' or 'well! well!,'" after which Sir William distributed blankets, balls, powder, tobacco, and a horse. The formal response of the Sioux was given by Ta-tonka-Seenta (Buffalo Bull's Tail), a handsome man of about fifty-five who wore armbands of brass wire around his biceps and a pair of bracelets made from old steel trunk handles. "These ornaments upon the naked bronze of the Indian's skin produced a very fine effect," wrote Field, "and as he sat in front of Capt. Stewart, with his buffalo robe thrown in picturesque looseness around him, he formed an object for the eye to rest upon with lively satisfaction." The speeches completed, the feast formally commenced with the entry of two large steaming kettles, one filled with buffalo stew and the other with hot coffee.[60]

If at the end of his hosting duties Stewart congratulated himself on his successful foray into the field of white-Indian diplomacy he later had reason to reevaluate his efforts, for the very next evening another band of Sioux, this one led by Little Thunder, tore into camp, spewing a torrent of abuse. They had been under the impression that Stewart and his party were intending to visit *their* encampment. They had prepared a great feast, slaughtering half the dogs in the village, and had created places of honor on buffalo robes in the best lodges. All day they had waited, and yet the white men never came. Then they learned that while they had been searching the horizon expectantly for the tardy guests, the visitors were feasting a minor band of Sioux of no particular importance — and were giving out fine presents to less worthy warriors. Little Thunder threatened to take all the white men's horses and leave them to walk out of the land of the Sioux.

With a coolness that recalled his response to the Crow Indians who back in 1834 had tried to prod his trappers into landing the first blow, Sir William merely ignored their ire and welcomed the Indians with exaggerated gestures of friendship and hospitality, as though nothing untoward were happening. The charade was perhaps easier to pull off as Little Thunder bore an uncanny resemblance to Stewart's very first American friend, the New York editor James Watson Webb — if the New York newspaperman, the Apollo of the Press, had been cast in bronze.

The company pushed on. For more than a week the pleasant weather held, but then a cold wind rose and behind it came driving rain. For five days they rode through a downpour, and they struggled to keep dry in their tents at night. There was one clear, cold day, and then the rains returned. On September 29 Field wrote in his diary, "Got to an encamping place in the storm, and pitched tent drenched to the skin. Storm continued, colder and harder until midnight, when it changed to snow. Couldn't sleep a wink, and lay in the water freezing — tent flapping and tearing in the tempest — left the tent in my dripping blankets and crawled into the Captain's lodge, where I sat, Indian fashion, over the ashes until daybreak!"[61]

And that night something happened that split the company in two.

Clark Kennerly recorded in his diary that "there has been a great stir in camp on account of Captain Stewart's stopping so long when there was no necessity, therefore, there has been a division made, and all those who were able to leave, decided to do so the next morning." The disagreement over waiting for the Indian woman to recover from the birth of her baby had happened over a month earlier, so it certainly was not the immediate cause of the breach. Perhaps it was just the bad turn in the weather. Kennerly records that it snowed during the night and some of the men needed to be dug out of drifts in the morning. In a letter to the *Picayune* Field mentions that Stewart wanted to halt long enough for the hunters to replenish meat supplies before leaving buffalo country. No one relished the idea of repeating the deprivations they had experienced on the way out.[62]

Still, there was clearly a hint of mutiny in the breakup of the party, with a small group of men deciding no longer to travel under Stewart's command. The disgruntled men did not seem to belong to any one faction; the portion splitting off included the members of four "messes" — numbering twenty-two men, about a quarter of the total party. Among those leaving were Kennerly and his cousin Jeff Clark, the two army officers Graham and Smith, Cyprien Menard, brothers Theodore and Adolphus Heermann, and A. M. Storer. The two parties were never very far apart as they headed home; Field was able to visit back and forth between the two camps en route. No one involved on either side would ever specify what caused the breach — other than one group's desire to travel slightly faster than those immediately associated with Stewart.

As they neared their destination Matt Field sent ahead a letter to be printed in the *New Orleans Daily Picayune* announcing his return from the Far West and assuring the newspaper's readers that he was full of amazing tales to share in the months to come. "I seize the chance, however, to assure you of our full safety, our speedy return home, and fine and flourishing condition of health. . . . We are the fattest, greasiest set of truant rogues your liveliest imagination can call up to view. We are the merriest, raggedest — perhaps you will add, the ugliest — set of buffalo butchers that ever cracked a rifle among the big hills of Wind River." Clark Kennerly later professed to be equally pleased with the journey. "Arriving in St. Louis in the early part of November," he told his daughter, "the party was disbanded and Sir William, taking his farewell dinner at *Cote Paquemine*, departed, highly pleased with his trip, for his home in Scotland, he invited me to pay him a visit there for the shooting season. . . . Sir William was a mighty hunter and a prince among sportsmen, so I will finish this narrative with a toast to his memory, the same used in Oliver Cromwell's day as to that other royal Stuart, 'over the water.'"[63]

Matt Field and Clark Kennerly may have been reporting truthfully about the unqualified success of the "pleasure trip" — but they are at odds with many of the accounts appearing in contemporary newspapers. Only a few weeks after the journey commenced, rumors about the party began to circulate throughout the country. A Baltimore newspaper cited an article from Alabama: "The editor of the Mobile Register states, upon the authority of a gentleman of that city, that the report of the disagreement and disbanding of the party who accompanied Sir William Drummond Stewart, of Scotland, to the head waters of the Platte river is wholly incorrect. The story was invented by a servant of the expedition, who was discharged for bad conduct." A New York newspaper gave a slightly different description of the dispute: "The truth is, that a man by the name of Sarphey, who had by some mistake been allowed to join the expedition, and who, by his bad and roguish conduct, had rendered himself obnoxious and disagreeable, had been invited to leave, found upon his arrival at St. Louis, that his unexpected return would have to be accounted for. He accordingly trumped up the lie which has caused so many newspaper remarks, and so much anxiety for the safety of the gallant party." The reference is most probably to a relative of fur trader Jean Baptiste Sarpy, from one of the most socially prominent families in St. Louis, though no young member of the clan is known to have accompanied Stewart.[64]

When the members of the party began to straggle into St. Louis, a reporter for the *Missouri Republican* tried to gather the latest news of their journey, but the men were reticent about sharing details of the rupture. "A portion of Sir Wm. Stewart's party, amounting to twenty men, arrived at our landing last evening on board the steamer Omega. The portion thus arrived had for some cause quit Stewart about the 1st October, near the mouth of the Platte River, the reason we could not learn; the remainder of the party may be expected down in a few days." The *Niles Register* announced, "The rest of the sportsmen that were with Sir W. D. Stewart, have now all returned to St. Louis, except a few men left with Sir W. at Independence, from which they design to travel by land to St. Louis. The Republican says that some of the party express themselves very well pleased with their excursion, while others are very much dissatisfied."[65]

A New York newspaper under the headline "Stewart's Expedition to the Rocky Mountains. — Probable Failure" put the blame squarely on Sir William himself:

We learn from the St. Louis Gazette of the 12th instant that six more of the American Fur Companies' boats arrived at the levee on the 12th, forty-five days from the Yellow Stone, laden with buffalo robes furs, &c. Among the persons who came down with these boats were several who left St. Louis with Sir William Drummond Stewart. They describe the fatigues attending the expedition and the overbearing rudeness of Sir William as insupportable. Thirteen of the company had left him at the South Forks of the Platte; and many others were preparing to leave. Some of the company had threatened to shoot him if he persisted in his tyrannical course. . . . All were in good health, though worn down with fatigue.[66]

Stewart left St. Louis soon after his arrival, traveling to New Orleans, where he spent the winter. His original plan was to return to St. Louis in the spring and then journey overland on a return visit to Santa Fe — but he soon learned that damaging rumors and gossip had begun to circulate. It was perhaps time for him to leave America. To Robert Campbell he wrote that his affairs in Scotland had become so pressing that they required his immediate return home. With his old bachelor friend William Sublette he could admit that business concerns had little to do with his precipitous departure.

Sublette, understanding the delicate nature of the situation, wrote in sympathy and support:

Dear Friend. . . . I see Lowery Ogle Jeff Clarke Chouteau & Roland and spoak to all of them about you and with the aception of Chouteau they said you had allways treated them Like gentlemen and that they thought Greyham [Lt. Richard Graham] Greate house [either Isaac Greathouse or his son George] and Herman [either Adolphus or Theodore Heermann] (your N[ew] O[rleans] Friend) was the Whole cause of those slanderous tales your friends I think now understand the whole off the matter and are well Satisfied it was all through malice &c &c if not they shall know all the causes &c &c I was sorry you left so soon and hope to see you here in the Spring.[67]

Leo Walker was even more vigorous in professing his strong support despite the swirling controversy.

I have just learned thro our friends of the Am fur Co., that you have changed your mind and are going East, instead of West. This I regret to hear for many reasons. I was anxious to have seen you once more, and talk over mountain adventures, for altho there were scenes of an unpleasant character — so there must always be when discordant materials are collected together — But the recollections [of] your uniform kindness to me will always be cherished in grateful remembrance. I have been thinking that you may possibly have been detered from carrying out your projected[?] plans in consequence of the vile slanders that were so industriously circulated against you by your enemies. Excuse me my dear Sir for attending to a subject so revolting to the feelings of a gentleman but I thought it would be gratifying to you to learn, that this — like all other base calumnies is fast passing away, and I look forward with pleasure to the day when your traducers will blush for their conduct.

I have been particularly vexed by the want of gratitude shown by certain gentlemen in this place. It was reasonably supposed that they above all others had the best opportunities of knowing as well as myself and would feel the deepest interest in defending a friend to whom they owed so much! But when questioned on the subject an equivocal shrug of the shoulders, was the only answer given. You will of course understand whom I mean.

I together with some other *true* friends of your's will never cease our friendly services until the last shade of suspicion vanishes before the steady light of truth — then, I shall hope and expect to see you once more among us.[68]

The vile, revolting slanders, the malicious stories, the shades of suspicion are not enumerated, but the tone of the correspondence makes it unlikely that the dispute arose simply because of Stewart's authoritarian manner. A charge of "rudeness" is rarely referred to as vile slander or revolting, base calumny. The letters from Stewart's supporters suggest that something much more serious was being alleged. Given the tensions in the ill-matched party, perhaps those members who became disgusted with the campy banter of the costume party chose to suggest that Sir William had made (or tolerated) inappropriate and unwanted sexual advances. When the damaging allegations were made public, many of the friends who had shared his hospitality in St. Louis felt reluctant to rush to his defense for fear of being tarred with the same brush.

At another time or in another place, the slanderous rumors that circulated concerning the pleasure trip might have led to a duel, but such affairs of honor were uncommon among Stewart's associates. When Alexis de Tocqueville returned to France after his 1831 visit to the United States, he reported that "the duel based on extreme susceptibility to points of honour, the monarchic duel, is almost unknown in America; the laws which *oblige* a man to fight in some parts of Europe in certain defined cases do not exist at all." While duels did take place in America well into the nineteenth century, they were confined in the latter decades almost exclusively to the South, or to places — such as gold rush–era California — where large numbers of southerners had migrated. Missouri during William Drummond Stewart's visits was particularly averse to such affairs. The 1821 trial of William Bennett for the murder of Alonzo Stuart in a duel (Bennett was defended unsuccessfully by Thomas Hart Benton) "aroused such horror and bitterness as to turn the local people violently against dueling."[69]

Sir William never directly challenged his accusers — not with dueling pistols, not with suits for slander, not even with rebuttal letters to the editor. It was not that he lacked the courage to do so; from his earliest days in America Stewart enjoyed a reputation for cool fearlessness. Yet he apparently did nothing at all to contradict the damaging tales that were being circulated about him. Given the high regard in which he was held after his many exploits in the Rockies, it would not have taken much in the way of a defense to effectively counteract the undercurrent of rumor and innuendo. Why, then, did he flee the United States without issuing a word of protest?

Charles Upchurch provides a possible explanation in his analysis of the ways aristocrats in Britain during this period responded to allegations of homosexual activity:

> There were many ways to disavow same-sex desire in the face of an accusation, and officials seemed willing to accept even the most implausible of explanations. But the conscience of a respectable man would not be satisfied by an implausible explanation simply because it was accepted by others. A nineteenth-century man of character did

not gain his sense of masculine status and self-worth from the opinion of others, as he would if his reputation played a greater role in his self-image. Any excuse vigorously defended, however implausible, might get a man of otherwise good character out of a conviction for sex between men; yet in earnestly proclaiming a lie, or vigorously defending an untruth, a man would no longer be respectable in his own eyes. His peers might never know, his reputation might remain intact, but he would know that he had compromised his character.

Stewart had enjoyed a long sojourn in a land where for the first time he could pursue his desires without censure. That period of dispensation was now clearly ending, and it is likely that he did not want to sully the experience by refuting everything that the American West had come to represent for him.[70]

One of the participants in the journey who was grateful for the attention shown to him was H. Brubaker (who appears in Clark Kennerly's remembrances as "Bluebecker"). Stewart left his mules with the young man in Independence, with instructions for him to care for the animals until Stewart needed them the following spring. Brubaker, on learning that the captain would not be returning after all, wrote with a proposition. "What I halve got is fifty Dollars," the lad explained,

> as I bought a suit of Cloath. Dear Sir if you will assist a poor boy as you partley stated you would by saying I may trade thoas mules for a part of a store and get a start in this world as you wold not feel this small sum and it would be glorious to me and make me a happy young man for ever and think I could do a good buisness if I should be so luckeye as to reseive a letter from you favourable I would pay it as quick as posable could make it and would thank you kindley and be your umble servant for Ever as I think I was as true a servant as you had on the Mountains at Least I tryed to be so, as I stood a good many blunts for your sake.[71]

Blunts were short, thick needles used to sew heavy fabrics, suggesting that Brubaker had been teased for his association with the captain. Stewart assented to the sale of the mules, and Brubaker replied with an effusive letter of thanks and the news that he would use part of the money to benefit his mother, who lived in Lancaster County, Pennsylvania. "My intentions to use it is to go home and buy a small home for her as I will never for sake My Dear Moather and with the ballans I will go to Philadelphia and buy cloths and casanetts and start a cloathing store to pay back as kind a man as you." Brubaker's familiarity with needles would have lasting benefits for him.[72]

When Stewart departed St. Louis for New Orleans he left Antoine Clement behind, and sometime before April of the following year, Clement married. Stewart sent him a letter congratulating him and inviting him and his new wife to visit in Scotland. The illiterate Clement brought the letter to Robert Campbell to read, asking Campbell to advance him the money for the journey, with the understanding that Sir William would eventually reimburse the amount. "I am very much at a loss to determine how to act in order to carry out your wishes," Campbell wrote to Stewart, "from your note to Antoine and from what I have learned from enquiries of Thomas I am led to believe that you wish to have him go to Murthly, but I confess I have some fear that Antoine might be led to squander the money in dissipation and that you might regret his having started." Stewart had deposited money with Campbell with the understanding that Clement could draw on the funds as needed, but through drinking and gambling he had quickly run through the money and was asking for more. Campbell wrote that he would attempt to keep Clement in St. Louis until a letter from Stewart could arrive giving further instructions.[73]

Stewart replied outlining strict conditions under which Campbell should entrust Clement with the necessary funds for the journey, and Clement agreed to the conditions in full. Unfortunately, as soon as the money was in his hands, he headed for the Market House tavern and went on a weeklong "drinking frolic." William Sublette wrote with a discouraging report: "I am Enclined to think that Antuon Clemon is doing Very Little Good."[74]

Antoine Clement did not return to Scotland. In 1846 he joined one of the two regiments of Missouri volunteers under the command of

Col. Stephen W. Kearny that marched on Santa Fe at the beginning of the Mexican-American War. He was with Kearny's volunteers when they invaded Mexico to join forces with troops under the commands of Zachary Taylor and John E. Wool. In 1848 Sir William received a letter from Alexander Chauvin giving news of Clement's whereabouts: "Antoine behaved very well in all the Mexican War he fought bravely in several battles, and received very high wages, so soon as he landed in St. Louis, he got in his old way of drinking and came near killing himself. [H]e is now in the mountains with his brother Bazil, they are to winter amongst the Black Feet indians." Chauvin concluded his letter with the news that young Brubaker, though he had not achieved his dream of opening a haberdashery with the funds he had realized from the sale of Stewart's mules, was now a clerk in a clothing store, and was "Married and doing well."[75]

Stewart opens *Edward Warren* with a rueful, nostalgic chapter in which the narrator looks back fondly on his time in America — an America that has since completely vanished because of the irresistible tide of greed and commerce. "But the pedlar and the 'mover' came," laments the narrator, "and Antoine, after visiting Paris, Constantinople, and Cairo, has gone to the Blackfoot village." Nothing the wealthy laird could buy him was enough to capture the wild child of the prairie. William Drummond Stewart and Antoine Clement were never to meet again.[76]

12

In nineteenth-century America if discussions about the private habits of a lifelong bachelor moved from smirking innuendo to pointed accusation, he had only two options: to marry or to move on. When rumors and allegations began to circulate concerning what exactly had happened on the Rocky Mountain pleasure tour, Sir William Drummond Stewart was able to make a strategic exit, first to New Orleans and then home to Scotland. His co-captain William Sublette was not so fortunate. Sublette's roots ran deep in the Missouri soil and he could not easily relocate. His poor health had not been improved by the trip to the mountains, and his personal finances, always complicated by too much property and too few liquid assets, had become worrisome. For Sublette, remaining in St. Louis appeared to be the only viable option.

In 1842 Sublette had sought to improve his cash flow problems by leasing out his beloved Sulphur Springs estate to Dr. Thomas Hereford of Tuscumbia, Alabama. While most of the Hereford family remained temporarily in Alabama, the doctor moved into the Sulphur Springs estate with his eldest daughter, Frances, known to everyone as Frank. Frank Hereford was described as a southern beauty with a temper "equal to brimstone," and though she could be intractable at times, she was open to the influence of friends who advised her to "catch some good amiable and rich man . . . as a full purse is very useful." She had left a beau at home in Alabama, but in St. Louis she soon became romantically involved with William Sublette's younger brother, Solomon.[1]

After the return of Stewart's pleasure tour, it was quickly arranged that Frank should marry William instead. The two were married on March 21, 1844, in the Presbyterian church in St. Louis, and a little over a year later William Sublette was dead, succumbing to consumption in Pittsburgh while on a business trip east with his new wife and his old friend Robert Campbell. Campbell chose not to interrupt the business trip to accompany Sublette's body on the return trip to St. Louis, or to attend his partner's funeral. "Robert was not particularly solicitous towards Sublette's widow," reports a Campbell descendent. "He shipped Frances back to St. Louis with a note to his Buchanan cousin in Pittsburgh asking him to help her on her way home." Frank inherited the bulk of William's property and later married Solomon Sublette, as she had originally planned.[2]

Sir William Drummond Stewart returned to his estate in Perthshire on August 10, 1844. Without a partner living with him, he no longer needed to be discreet about his sleeping arrangements; though he at first resumed his residence in Dalpowie Lodge, he soon moved into the castle itself (confounding those who believed that he would never spend another night under Murthly's roof). In advance of his arrival, the local newspapers reported that the London steamer to Dundee had brought down several large cages containing a few of the American antelope that Sir William had captured in his latest trip to the Rocky Mountains. The animals were accompanied on the journey by "a Yankee Keeper, who is conversant with their habits." The identity of the keeper is unknown.[3]

In December of 1845 a fire destroyed part of the castle; the damage to the structure was extensive, but everyone escaped unharmed. "I write chiefly to ask you to tell me how I can be useful to you," wrote his neighbor Lord Breadalbane when he heard of the fire, "and to say that I trust you will make this house your home, and that if your boy is with you that you will bring him too." Major repairs were required, and Sir William used the opportunity to add an entire new wing that included a billiards room on the ground floor with a master bedroom suite on the level above. After years of staying in the finest hotels of Europe and America, he had grown accustomed to creature comforts that the old castle had sadly lacked.[4]

Stewart's son, Will, was now fifteen. Though they had never had a close relationship — for nearly half of the boy's life his father was traveling on a different continent — father and son now began to establish an intimacy, and when Will turned eighteen his father sent him on the requisite Grand Tour under the watchful eye of a tutor, Bonamy Mansell Power. Power wrote regular reports on the progress of his young charge, praising him for his growing grasp of German, for his sophisticated manners, and for his sturdy good looks. From Vienna Will wrote to his father describing a ball given by the Russian ambassador that he had attended in the company of the comte Pálffy. Like his father and his uncles before him, the young man was moving in very high society.

Both son and tutor seemed disposed to cater to Sir William's penchant for young men, as their correspondence with him from the Continent includes several references to new acquaintances they were sending to Murthly Castle with letters of introduction to the laird. Will dispatched a young friend named Mariasky, later closing a letter to his father (in French) hoping "that you are in good health and that you are enjoying yourself well with your young companion." Mariasky's visit was evidently a success, for Power wrote,

> There is a certain young friend of his and ours (Mr. Udvarnoky) who is become so jealous of Mariasky's good fortune that he is now absolutely en route for Orleans to pick up French so that he may too go and see you. I have given him the Encouragement that I thought you would give him a welcome, and particularly told him to go to Orleans, for I know that if he went to Paris he would throw himself into the vortex of gaiety and that there he would find so many persons who spoke his language [Hungarian] that he could never learn French. He is an excellent fellow with as much simplicity as Mariasky but more dignified, he is a gentle and handsome person — if you will invite him he will visit you in July.

A few weeks later Power wrote again: "We have this moment received a letter from dear Jami who writes on the Eve of his departure for Edinburgh his visit to Murthly will be something to look back upon. I am sure you must have been charmed with him what an admirable character for a Romance. Romance is it not, his character was certainly very much allied to that of Antoine."[5]

For his own part Sir William continued to pursue relationships with young working-class men who were eager to take monetary advantage of his interest. J. Pittman wrote him from London, "I should much like to come and see you this Christmas but that I will leave for your permission. I have a kind invite to spend the Christmas with some friends, near Liverpool were I did last year but if you come to town I shall not think of going. [H]oping Dear Sr W you will pardon me in the liberty in wich I am asking to send me ten pounds to enable me to pay a few Bills wich I owe and would greatly oblige."[6]

When Will Stewart returned from his Grand Tour, he decided to pursue a career in the army. His father purchased a commission for him, and on June 2, 1847, he became an ensign in the Ninety-third Sutherland Highlanders. For the next six years his regiment was stationed at home, and without the distraction of a deployment abroad the handsome young soldier pursued a number of romantic liaisons, taking full advantage of the seductive power of both a dashing uniform and the promise of a baronetcy. Unlike his father Will was attracted to women, but like his father he preferred sexual partners outside his social class. In 1853 a woman named Mary, the unmarried daughter of a Southampton merchant, bore him twin boys. She herself died in childbirth. Christie Stewart is believed to have taken responsibility for the twins, sending them to a Catholic boarding school near Southampton. Family tradition suggests that the boys, George and Herbert, were all their lives unaware of the identity of their father.[7]

During this period Sir William took the unusual step of attempting to break the entails on both Grandtully Castle and Murthly Castle so that he would not be legally required to pass the estates on to his son. Although the House of Lords had allowed him to sell Logiealmond because (after prolonged investigation) it was determined that the entail was no longer in force, the legal status of the other two castles was fairly clear: they could not be easily alienated from the Stewart family. The original documents for this litigation have not been located, and information about the attempt comes only from references found in later legal proceedings — these documents contain the information that the 1851 effort was unsuccessful, but do not explain Sir William's reasons for attempting it.

His motivation may have been simply financial. From time to time he appears to have moved into one of the lodges on his estate in order to rent out Murthly Castle, presumably because he was periodically short of funds. Selling one or both of the properties would, as with the sale of Logiealmond, provide much-needed cash. Or perhaps he was beginning to note the flaws in Will's character and he questioned the young man's ability to be a good steward of the family property. (In this he would be prescient.) Given the events surrounding the end of Sir William's life, there is a very real possibility that during the 1850s he became enamored with yet another young man and that he wished to have him designated heir in place of his disappointing son. Absent further documentation, we can only speculate. In any event, the attempt ended in failure.

With the outbreak of the Crimean War, the Ninety-third Sutherland Highlanders were dispatched to the front. Will, now Lieutenant Stewart, was thrown into some of the fiercest fighting of the war, including the battle of Balaclava, where his regiment formed part of the legendary "Thin Red Line" that held out against the Russian onslaught. He was promoted to captain and sent to India, where he took part in the relief of Lucknow. Six Victoria Crosses were awarded to the Ninety-third Highlanders for heroism at that battle. Sir Colin Campbell decided that five of the medals should go to enlisted men, and he asked the officers to chose among themselves which man of their rank would be the sole recipient of the honor. When the votes were tallied, Captain Stewart was the choice of his brother officers by a large majority. He was described as "an officer of remarkable coolness in action, nothing ever appearing to disturb his equanimity in the very slightest degree." On May 6, 1859, he was promoted to major, and the following year he separated himself from the service.[8]

Unfortunately, with Major Stewart's departure from the army the happiest period of his life was behind him. Unable to find anything that gave him the personal satisfaction of his years as an officer, Will spent much of his time carousing in taverns on inebriated sprees that only increased in duration and debauchery as his anomie became ever more difficult to overcome. His post-military life was one long record of drunkenness and decline. While Sir William was himself no stranger to a life of sybaritic extravagance, he had always maintained a certain degree of dignity and self-possession, rarely deviating from the manly decorum expected of an officer and a gentleman. Will's behavior in the years after he left the army degenerated from spirited hijinks to pugnacious aggression to morose stupors, and though Sir William had always displayed a patient indulgence for young men who required a high level of maintenance from those who loved them, with his own son he found the tearful mea culpas and inevitable relapses far less endearing. Will ran up debts he could not pay, quarreled with his father over money, drank, and womanized.

In the spring of 1865 Will was living at Rampling's Waterloo Hotel in Edinburgh when he met Margaret Wilson, the seventeen-year-old daughter of a fishing tackle shop owner. He began courting the young girl, showering her with presents he could ill afford. By the end of the summer his money was gone, and with no replenishing funds expected from home, he was kicked out of his hotel room for failure to pay his bill. Mr. Wilson proved eager to promote the union of his daughter with the son of a baronet, offering Major Stewart a room in his own home, a small house on a street renowned for hosting no fewer than five brothels in the same block. Margaret's father was a confirmed alcoholic and her mother was described as coarse and profane, but Major Stewart apparently fit happily into their decidedly louche household.

That December Will descended on Murthly Castle with both Margaret Wilson and her father in tow, evidently planning some sort of confrontation with his father. Whether his intention was to force Sir William to welcome and accept his disreputable companions or to shame him into providing better financial support for his indigent son is unclear. Finding the laird away and the castle locked up, Will barged in and spent several hours pouring out his father's expensive brandy for his already-inebriated guests. When Sir William returned after the holidays to learn of the outrage, he went to court to obtain a formal interdict against his son and the Wilsons, prohibiting them from ever entering the property again without his permission.

In February Major Stewart announced to the Wilsons that he wanted to throw a party to celebrate his thirty-fourth birthday. Expensive champagne, brandy, and port flowed freely in the home of the tackle shop owner, and the guests soon became uproariously drunk. In the morning Will awoke to find himself in bed with young Margaret, with no memory of what had happened the night before. Margaret's father was happy to fill him in. According to public testimony later published in the *Times* of London,

> Major Steuart filled the wine-glasses all round. He then went down on his knees, and for the purpose of carrying through a marriage between himself and the pursuer, he said to the pursuer: — "Maggie, will you be my wife?" The pursuer replied, "Yes;" and then and there accepted Major Steuart as her husband, and they became married persons. He then took a plain gold marriage-ring from his vest pocket, and placed it on the third finger of her left hand, after which he held up his right hand, and while still on his knees said: — "I swear by the Almighty God that I take you for my wife." The health of the married couple was proposed by Mr. Wilson, and drunk by all present.[9]

The event (if it ever occurred) constituted a legally binding "Scotch Marriage" by which a couple could be wed without benefit of clergy simply by announcing their intentions before family and friends. "Afterwards the couple were bedded after the old Scotch fashion, and stockings, pillows, and other articles thrown at them," Mr. Wilson assured the court. Will never acknowledged that a marriage had taken place that night, and Margaret continued to use her maiden name, so Wilson's account of the evening cannot be taken at face value. On April 2, 1867, Margaret gave birth to a son while Will was in Birnam fishing. Her father sent a letter to Will notifying him of the birth, but his only reply was a complaint about how poorly the fishing trip was turning out.[10]

Sir William experienced a series of blows and disappointments beyond the troubling conduct of his wayward son. In 1846 he received word that his younger brother Thomas had been murdered in Italy. As a young man Thomas Stewart had associated himself with the sexually scandalous coterie of the famous French dandy Count d'Orsay, but while at Oxford he converted to Catholicism, and in time the siren song of fashionable society was muted by a growing call to the religious life. Thomas moved to Italy and there joined the Benedictine Order, eventually rising to the rank of abbé.

On July 17, 1846, he was visiting Case Brugiate, near Ancona on the Adriatic. According to a story published in the *Times*, Abbé Stewart had withdrawn to a secluded beach and was preparing to undress when a nineteen-year-old peasant approached and offered to hold his umbrella. Stewart consented and tipped the young man for his services. Later stories reported that the young man was a "ruffian" who had been released from prison just the day before. After accepting the coins, the young man asked the abbé if he would be bathing alone again later that day, to which Stewart replied that he would be there but that he would not need assistance.

When Stewart returned to the same secluded spot between four and five in the afternoon, the ruffian was waiting for him. Thomas began to undress. "He took advantage of the moment that Stewart was passing his shirt over his head, and inflicted three stabs, which Stewart received on his left arm, and at once faced his murderer, without weapon or covering to his body, and demanded his intentions. The wretch replied 'Plunder.' . . . The monster hesitated for a moment, and then rushed again upon Stewart, and stabbed him eight times more, two of which wounds extended to the whole length of the stiletto." All the contemporary reports suggest that the motive for the attack must have been robbery — ignoring the obvious fact that the thief had only to wait until Stewart had undressed completely and swum out to sea to scoop up all his belongings and flee without effort or resistance.[11]

Stewart staggered to a cottage about half a mile away, where he later died. The British consul had the body embalmed and placed in the church of Santa Maria, where it lay in repose until arrangements could be made to return it to Scotland. According to the *Times*, while the body lay in the church a young child, crippled from birth, climbed over the coffin and was miraculously cured. "The fame of this miracle spread and [the] halt flocked in from all sides. Numerous other miracles are said to have been performed, — offerings of wax began to drop in to the Church, — scores of children were brought in to be cured of all kinds of diseases." The press of believers descending on the church became so alarming that the British consul, fearing that the coffin might be damaged, called in the gendarmes to block the entrance while the body was spirited out the back way. When the church reopened pilgrims surged forward to kiss the ground where the coffin had once rested.[12]

A different possible scenario for the murder later emerged. In 1855 Richard Robert Madden published *The Literary Life and Correspondence of the Countess of Blessington* (the woman involved in the ménage à trois with Count d'Orsay). In a footnote about Abbé Thomas Stewart (whose name the countess mentions in one of her letters), Madden relates the story of Thomas's murder and of the subsequent fate of his valet, an Italian named Luigi Baranelli. In his will Thomas left his valet an annuity of £20. Madden became aware of the legacy when Baranelli came to London and took a job as a waiter while attempting to collect the money. The two men met through a mutual acquaintance, and Madden advised Baranelli to write to William Drummond Stewart directly about the matter. When Madden quizzed the waiter about the circumstances of the murder, he was told that the abbé was killed by "desperadoes." "I could not understand from him," Madden later wrote, "what had brought him to the spot where he found his wounded master, or whether he had accompanied him to the place, and had fled when the brigands made their appearance." Although he found Baranelli's account to be confused and contradictory, Madden merely dismissed him at the time as "a half-witted sort of fellow."[13]

In 1854 Luigi Baranelli was arrested in London for the murder of Joseph Lambert, who had rented a room to the troubled young man. Baranelli shot Lambert point-blank in the head while he was sleeping, also wounding Lambert's common-law wife, and then turned the gun on himself in an unsuccessful suicide attempt. When the police arrested him, he kept murmuring to himself, "I am a murderer, I am an assassin." One of the doctors who examined Baranelli concluded that he was "of unsound mind," but two other doctors ruled that he was mentally competent. He was hanged on May 1, 1855, at Newgate Prison. Madden suggested that Baranelli murdered Thomas Stewart in order to obtain the legacy his employer had promised him.[14]

The murder of his brother had a profound and disturbing impact on Sir William. He wrote to James Watson Webb that Thomas was murdered "while bathing poor fellow his assassin who had been employed to hold an umbrella over him while he undressed attacked him when naked for the sake of his trinkets we suppose there was a struggle as my brother fell with eleven stabs of a stiletto & lingered only eight hours." Stewart confided to Webb that he was unable now to sleep, disturbed by nightmares of his brother's murder. Sir William had reason to worry. He knew that his own penchant for unruly working-class men left him as vulnerable as his brother had been. Abbé Stewart's Requiem Mass was the first funeral conducted in the newly restored chapel on the Murthly estate.[15]

In 1847 Sir William's brother George Stewart also died. A lifelong bachelor, George had been living alone in Braco Castle since the death of his last remaining elderly aunt. It seemed now that their sister's dire warning was coming true — the Stewart family was going the way of the "Dull Gooses," blessed with many male heirs but all of them unwilling or unable to produce further male heirs. Of the original five Stewart brothers only William and Archibald were left. The relationship between the two remaining brothers, never close, had by the 1840s disintegrated into barely concealed hostility. Archibald was a staunch Calvinist who was viscerally repulsed by both his brother's Catholicism and his homosexuality. Many Protestants in Great Britain at the height of the Oxford Movement considered the two failings inextricably linked.[16]

On October 1, 1856, Christian Battersby Stewart also died, perhaps of pulmonary consumption. The details of her death are as sketchy as those of her life. She and Sir William had never lived together as husband and wife and for decades had communicated primarily through their son and other third parties, so her death — while perhaps lamented — had no substantial impact on Stewart. Porter and Davenport pass along a local legend that Mae Reed Porter heard while researching in Dunkeld in 1952: "She lingered for several weeks, slowly losing strength. A woman relative who came to attend her, suggested, 'Think of your family and make a financial request.' Christina is said to have replied, 'I brought nothing to the estate and I will take nothing from it.'" The story may be apocryphal, but it is consistent with her behavior throughout their very long and odd connection. Lady Stewart was buried in the Catholic chapel at Grandtully Castle.[17]

In the following years the relationship between Sir William and his son, Will, became increasingly strained. One source of contention was a legacy left by Will's uncle, the murdered abbé. Believing that his eldest nephew would already be well provided for under the terms of the entailed estate, Thomas attempted to pass along his personal wealth in a way that would provide for other members of the family's next generation. He left the majority of his estate to any children who might eventually be born to his brother George. If George died without issue, the inheritance was to be awarded to any children of his youngest brother, Archibald — and if Archibald was childless, the full amount would be divided among any children of his eldest brother, William. George died unmarried and Archibald, while yet living, was a middle-aged bachelor with no prospect of heirs. Sir William controlled the distribution of Thomas's estate and, perhaps concerned about how Will might squander the inheritance, sequestered the funds with the specious argument that Archibald might still eventually marry and produce children who would then inherit in place of Will. For twenty-two years following the abbé's death Sir William refused to release the inheritance, and so in 1868 Will sued his father. The court interpreted the instructions in the abbé's will to mean that the money should pass to any children living at the time of Thomas Stewart's death. Though it was theoretically possible that Archibald Douglas Stewart might at the age of sixty marry and produce children, that point was irrelevant. The court awarded the entire inheritance to Will.[18]

Sir William retained a passionate interest in the United States. He followed closely the unfolding of presidential elections, the fluctuations in the American economy, and other events making headlines in newspapers. In 1857 he wrote to James Watson Webb concerning the struggle between the federal government and the Mormon pioneers who were in open rebellion in the so-called Utah War. Though it had been thirteen years since he had traveled through the Rockies, he retained an almost photographic memory of the region. "I have been much interested in the accts from the Rocky Mts," he wrote to Webb.

> I suppose your government think it necessary to assert their authority. Though the wise plan would have been to have let the thing go on at Utah until it fell to pieces of itself or the tyranny[?] of some Prophet drove his subjects to rebellion. The expedition could not have been worse planned or conducted — to reach the salt lake with an expedition to impose a military force upon the Mormons, it would be necessary to take two years for the march. The grass fails after August & at last becomes without nourishment for the greater part of the route beyond Sweet water. The place to winter must be an object of importance. Laramé has not sufficient quantity of grass for winter hay nor fuel for a considerable force. Some days further on among the streams that flow from the Fort Butte into the Platte at the cataracts or cut rocks as they are called, there are many meadows where large quantities of hay might be made & stacked for the

winter use of the expedition, so that they might not touch the hay from the states brought up in pressed bales of one hundred weight each so as to be transportable by beasts of burthen in case of wheel carriage failing it is to be observed that a large circle of enclosure must be made & guarded to surround the winter supply & protect it from ignited arrows. There is also a place some two days further on called Deer creek where I do not know that there is so much grass but where there is Coal on the surface of the creek. I have burned some of it — perhaps it might be best to send out hay making parties to different places where there is possibility of carting to a general depot, where the horses & cattle for the next years expedition must be kept ready for the earliest practicable start in the spring. The main difficulty being provisions. The Indians might be induced to bring in dried meat by sending traders that is the Chyennes & Crows perhaps others, but strict economy & care are necessary. Perhaps a strong *avant garde* should be sent on fully ten days before the main body which by halting & sending back might give information by which an occupied pass might be turned by the main body. Perhaps you may think of mentioning these hints to the President [James Buchanan] if so offer my respectful regards to his Excellency.[19]

Except in his memories and in his dreams, Sir William would never again see America, but in 1856 America came to him in a strange and unexpected way that would have lasting consequences for Murthly Castle. From Texas, Ebenezer Nichols wrote of his enthusiasm for a project to link Galveston, Houston, and Henderson by a railroad line. His chief obstacle was finances, which were becoming increasingly problematic as the nation rumbled with a dispute over the future of slavery. So intemperate was some of the rhetoric that he feared it might lead to open civil war. Sir William replied with a suggestion: British investors were positively obsessed with the idea of railroad building and it might be possible to sell enough stock in Britain to launch this Texas dream. Since a prolonged stay might be necessary to assure a successful trip, and since the question of war at home was ever present, he suggested that Nichols bring with him his wife and three sons — William, Franc, and Fred.

Sir William met the Nichols family when it arrived in London and proposed that the boys return with him to Scotland, freeing their parents to enjoy the city without the entanglement of children. The eldest son declined, but the two younger boys eagerly agreed to spend their summer in a real castle. Once in Scotland, Fred quickly became homesick for his parents and was dispatched back to London to rejoin them, but Franc fell in love with the aristocratic life. Ebenezer Nichols's business trip was extremely successful, but when he came to gather his family together to return to Texas, Franc refused to leave. Sir William offered to provide a home and education for the ten-year-old, and the Nicholses, after some hesitation, agreed to the arrangement and sailed for the United States, leaving one of their young sons behind. Francis Rice Nichols would spend the next fifteen years at Murthly Castle, in time becoming Sir William's adopted son.

For Sir William, the arrival of Franc Nichols provided a new and unexpected opportunity. It is most likely that as the laird entered his sixties he began to regret what he had missed by spending so much time abroad. In Franc he was being given a second chance at fatherhood. The young American, so enthusiastic, independent, and headstrong, would allow him in his golden years to experience at last the role of wise but doting parent.

The problem, of course, was that Sir William already *had* a son. It is not surprising to read that between Will the actual son and Franc the surrogate there developed an open and undisguised antagonism. Franc quickly slipped into the role of the favored child, while Will continued to alienate himself further from his father's affections through his dissolute behavior. The cause and the effect were intertwined. Nor was the ill will toward Franc confined to the Stewart family. "The people of the estate and the villagers living in Dunkeld never liked Franc," Porter and Davenport report, "and their animosity toward him grew as the lord of the castle more and more accorded to this 'interloper' the position of a son. The youth responded to this attitude with mischievous, annoying, and sometimes cruel retaliations which, as he grew older, became more serious." The negative impression that the young American created during his years at Murthly Castle was to have a long and lasting legacy. Descendants of William Drummond Stewart today still refer to the Texan by the sardonic epithet "Franc the Yank."[20]

In September 1867 Will severed his last remaining tie with the army, selling his commission for about £10,000, and with the profits he paid off all his debts. The following February he brought Margaret once again to Birnam, where they occupied separate hotel lodgings — she under the name Miss Wilson. Alone, he attempted to gain entrance to Murthly Castle but was again sent away. When he protested he was warned by his solicitor, Melville Jameson, that if he persisted he could be arrested for breach of the interdict. Turned away from his family home for the last time, Will abandoned Margaret and his son, never to return to Scotland. The boy later died, still an infant, and Margaret eventually married another man.

Will traveled for a time throughout England and on the Continent, continuing his excessive drinking until he began to suffer from severe delirium tremens. At Hythe near Southampton on the evening of October 18, 1868, while profoundly drunk, he attempted to give a demonstration of the exotic sword swallowing he had witnessed in India. It all went terribly wrong. The stick he inserted down his throat in place of a sword caused internal injuries, resulting in a fatal inflammation of the lungs. The deputy coroner ruled that he died "whilst in an unsound state of mind." His body was returned to Scotland, and he was buried next to his mother in St. Mary's Chapel at Grandtully.[21]

When Will died Franc Nichols was twenty-three. He and Sir William were living together in Dalpowie Lodge, where the baronet and Antoine Clement had once been happy. Murthly Castle was rented to a man named James Graham, a merchant with residences in Manchester and Glasgow, who used the property as a vacation home. The elderly baronet and his adopted son traveled on the Continent together, and the Nichols family visited from Texas on several occasions, but the negative feelings that Franc engendered among Sir William's family, friends, and tenants necessarily limited their social contacts. In 1869 Sir William drew up a will leaving all of his inheritable and movable property "to my beloved adopted son, Francis Nichols Stewart." The most important of his possessions — the estates of Murthly and Grandtully — were beyond his power to bequeath, being protected by the law of entail. Without a "son of the body" to become the next baronet, the estates would in due course pass to Sir William's much-despised youngest brother, Archibald Douglas Stewart, the last surviving of Sir George Stewart's five sons.

In 1870 Sir William began to experience severe and recurring bronchial problems. Realizing that his health was failing and that he had but a little time left, he became determined to alter the line of inheritance — perhaps motivated equally by a wish to provide for Franc and by an intense desire to block Archibald from inheriting. He decided once again to challenge the entailment. The action was likely to be contentious, expensive, and protracted, and he faced the likelihood that there would not be time to resolve the matter before his death. The suit could continue after his passing, but Franc himself would not be able to lead the effort. Under Scottish law, foreigners were barred from bringing lawsuits in the courts of Scotland; they were required to "sist a mandatory," or appoint a Scottish surrogate to represent their interests and accept liability for court costs. Given Franc's intense unpopularity, finding a local champion would be a challenge.[22]

As a last resort Sir William devised a scheme that would utilize a most effective weapon: greed. He sold both Murthly and Grandtully to a man named Henry Padwick for the sum of £350,000 — perhaps £150,000 below the market value for the properties — the sale to be accomplished six months after the entail was judged invalid. The arrangement made Padwick a party of interest in the suit, providing him with ample motivation to spare no effort in pursuing a favorable judgment, as he would be acquiring two extremely valuable properties at a rock-bottom price. The money realized by the sale would become part of Sir William's estate and therefore pass to Franc Nichols Stewart — and Archibald would be prevented from inheriting the properties.

If the scheme worked, Archibald would still become a baronet, but one without a castle to live in.

In April 1871 Sir William's bronchial condition developed into pneumonia, and on the 28th he died. With his passing, life at Murthly entered a strange period of suspended animation. Franc Nichols Stewart was either unwilling or unable to take the necessary steps to proceed with a funeral, opting instead to telegraph Sir William's solicitors, Jamieson and Moncrieffe, to inform them of the laird's passing. When the two men arrived from Perth they found that nothing had been done to prepare for the service, so by default they stepped in and took control of the situation.

Archibald Douglas Stewart had not yet been notified of his brother's death; Franc had no idea of how to contact him. With some difficulty Jamieson and Moncrieffe uncovered the address and sent a telegram notifying Sir Archibald of the death and suggesting that they would wait until the following Thursday and then proceed with the burial. Franc would take no part in the funeral arrangements beyond passing along the information that Sir William had expressed a wish that his funeral not be a public one. As the surviving brother and the new head of the family, Sir Archibald was the person who should be giving directions, and the solicitors informed him that they wished to give him every opportunity to express his desires concerning the funeral arrangements for his deceased brother — but they could not decently delay the interment more than one week. Their telegram was polite but urgent. It received no response. When it became clear that arrangements could not be completed before the planned Thursday interment, the funeral was delayed one day (it was now a full week after Sir William's death) and Sir Archibald was alerted via telegram of the change in schedule. There was still no response.

Jamieson and Moncrieffe, with the assistance of an undertaker, opened the family crypt in the chapel at Murthly. There they discovered that there was no room for another coffin, finding it necessary to shift the coffin containing the remains of Sir William's grandfather in order to create sufficient space. Not until the evening of Thursday, May 4 (the day before the funeral service), did they receive a response from Sir Archibald — one that forbade them from proceeding with the burial as planned.

Rumors concerning the circumstances of Sir William's death began to circulate almost immediately after it was announced. Local newspapers reported that Sir William might have been a victim of foul play: scratches found on his face suggested a violent struggle. Sir Archibald demanded an autopsy, suspecting that his brother had been murdered by his adopted American son. An autopsy was quickly performed, and the coroner pronounced the cause of death to be congestion of the lungs arising from bronchitis. On the day of the funeral, as the mourners began to gather for the service, Jamieson and Moncrieffe received a telegram instructing them that Sir Archibald wanted his brother to be entombed in the new addition to the chapel, away from the old family crypt. Sir Archibald himself chose not to attend his brother's funeral.

On Friday, May 5, Sir William Drummond Stewart's body was at last carried to the chapel on the Murthly estate down the long dismal archway of trees known as the Dead Walk, a passage by tradition taken only once by each laird — at the time of his funeral procession. His coffin was placed temporarily in the old family crypt while the new space was prepared as his final resting place.

For reasons that are not clear, Franc Nichols Stewart now decided that there should be a second autopsy. The corpse was therefore disinterred and examined by two professors from Edinburgh, who concluded that the results of the initial autopsy were correct. The passionate traveler was then at long last laid to rest.

The tussle over the body was merely the opening salvo in what became a prolonged and unseemly battle over the estate. Fearing that Franc would immediately begin to empty the contents of the castle, Sir Archibald, as the new laird, and James Graham, as the current tenant, sought an injunction preventing him from entering the premises. The sheriff granted an interim interdict, but the measure was immediately challenged by Franc's solicitor. The owner and the tenant agreed to allow the heir to retrieve the movable property that he had inherited but insisted that he be prevented from removing any "fixtures" attached to the building, or from taking up residence in the castle even on an interim basis.

Franc had clearly inherited all the "movables" associated with the castle and since no one was contesting that particular point, he decided to construe very liberally the meaning of the word. He proceeded to strip Murthly Castle so quickly and so completely that Sir Archibald was compelled to go to Perth Sheriff Court in an attempt to block the plunder. A report published in the *Scotsman* described the proceedings:

> At the Perth Sheriff Court, yesterday, the report by Mr. Rhind, architect, Edinburgh, as to what were fixtures and what movables in Murthly Castle and grounds was taken into consideration. Mr. Rhind was of the opinion that the pictures and tapestry forming or in place of panels of the rooms, the mirrors in the music room, gas brackets in the dining-room, the wainscot chimney piece, the bookcase in the library, vases in the garden-grounds to be fixtures. He had no hesitation in saying that the pictures in the music-room were fixtures on the ground (1) that the mouldings all round them are a portion of the plaster work of the room; and (2) because, if removed, there would be nothing left but the bare stone wall behind. He knew no law, and it certainly was not the practice, that anything fixed "by screw nails only" was movable. If everything fixed with screw-nails only was movable, without reference to any other peculiarities of its construction, it would include the whole doors and window shutters of the house, which were never removed, or looked on as movable.[23]

The castle itself was not the only victim of Franc Nichols Stewart's depredations. The *Scotsman* reported that "Sheriff Barclay has also this week granted interim interdict, until further orders of the Court, against Mr. Nichols Steuart removing the altar, railing, pictures and clock within or connected with the chapel at Murthly, and also the vases on the grounds of Murthly or adjoining the Castle, and the thrashing-mill at Ardoch."[24]

Everything that was not screwed down — and a few things that were — was transported to Edinburgh, where Franc held a giant jumble sale. According to the *Scotsman*, the paintings brought "upwards of £2000" and the tapestries and furniture "upwards of £1700." (The entirety of the personal property inherited by Franc was estimated to have a value of about £40,000, or roughly £2.75 million in current value, about $4.5 million.)[25]

While no dispute was raised on the question of the contents of the two castles (beyond defining what "movables" meant), the question of the entails on Murthly and Grandtully was still very much in contention. Unfortunately for would-be owner Henry Padwick (and eventually for Franc Nichols Stewart), avarice came to the forefront. Padwick had not yet initiated the suit to break the entail, but realizing that the struggle might drag on for months — even years — he requested a court-appointed judicial factor, or neutral agent, to collect the rents owing from the various Stewart properties and to hold them out of Sir Archibald's control until the question of the entail was settled. The House of Lords viewed the entire matter with a very jaundiced eye.

"One great peculiarity in the present application," observed the Lords,

> is that there is no judicial competition; for no proceedings have as yet been taken to set aside the deed of entail. The case therefore is out of the category of a pending judicial conflict. What then is there else before us? We have here a deed of entail which has been a title of possession for a century and a half, and under which there is now existing an apparent heir of entail [Archibald Douglas Stewart] legally entitled to the full possession of the estate. Undoubtedly he has not acquired the actual possession; but in the eye of the law he is entitled to the full possession of the estate. It is sought to deprive him of this possession at the instance of a gentleman who comes forward and says, and it is all that he says, "I mean to raise proceedings in Court in order to challenge the right of the heir on entail."

With his unseemly rush to protect his rents, Padwick had fatally prejudiced his case. The court evinced no inclination to overturn the 1851 holding that the entails on Murthly and Grandtully were valid. Sir Archibald Douglas Stewart eventually inherited the properties, though the interloping American had stripped them to the walls of most their valuable contents.[26]

"While this was taking place," write Porter and Davenport, "Franc became virtually a prisoner at Dalpowie, because of the hatred felt toward him by tenantry on the estate. They declared he had made a practice of skulking through the woods at night, shooting at them when they used their ferrets to get rabbits for food. After Sir William's death Franc dared not go beyond the 300-yard long driveway that extended from Dalpowie to the main road leading to Dunkeld, for fear he would be set upon by these enraged farmers and killed. When he left Murthly for the last time, Padwick accompanied him as a sort of body-guard."[27]

Franc the Yank as a child had been determined to leave Texas and all it represented far behind him, but he now fled to Galveston. There he married Ella Hutchings, the daughter of a prominent and wealthy Houston family. The marriage soon ended in divorce, and Nichols Stewart spent the remainder of his life at Nicholstone, the family home in Dickinson, in the company of handsome young cowboys who were eager to be taken under the wing of a cultured gentleman of aristocratic upbringing. Franc died of a stroke on November 23, 1913, at the age of sixty-seven.

William Drummond Stewart, whose movements had once been chronicled in major newspapers throughout America, soon slipped into obscurity. For anyone studying the American fur trade of the 1830s his was a name frequently encountered, as he is mentioned in the diaries, memoirs, and correspondence of most of the key figures, but because he remained an outsider — the gentleman on a pleasure tour — he was easily marginalized. Not until Porter and Davenport's biography was published in 1963 was much known about his life, but that book was so flawed that it lent little sheen to his reputation.

Stewart's role in the story of the Rocky Mountains in the early nineteenth century is insignificant when compared to that of William Ashley,

William Sublette, Jim Bridger, or Jedediah Smith, yet his story is important because so very little is known about what life was like in America for homosexuals during this period. His was in many ways a unique life, yet it encompassed a wide range of personae — the fashionable dandy, the skilled hunter, the patron of the arts, the fearless explorer, the youth-obsessed lover, the military martinet, the inept novelist, the aristocratic laird. In a sense his life provides a window into the many ways of being gay in early nineteenth-century America.

At the center of his story — as at the center of his life — stand the majestic Rocky Mountains. It was the Rockies that made him the man he was, and they became for him a symbol of all that was splendid and challenging and liberating about America. His life in the Far West changed William Drummond Stewart so profoundly that he found it difficult to assume the inherited mantle of a Scottish laird. Instead he lived out the remainder of his life in an uneasy liminal space that was far from the Wind River Mountains and yet not quite Scotland, encircled by Perthshire but cocooned in a dreamscape of the limitless prairie. To the best that his fortune and his imagination could conjure, he re-created the American West on the banks of the Tay, surrounding himself with paintings and animals and plants and artifacts — and people — that had an almost talismanic power for him. He need only grasp in one hand Jim Bridger's arrowhead and close his eyes to be transported to the place where for the first time in his life he had experienced profound and astonishing joy.

Notes

INTRODUCTION

1. Ron Tyler to William Johnston, February 28, 1980, William Johnston Research Files, Walters Art Museum, Baltimore MD.

2. Bernard DeVoto, *Across the Wide Missouri* (1947; repr., Boston: Houghton Mifflin, 1998), xiv.

3. Marshall Sprague, *A Gallery of Dudes* (Boston: Little, Brown, 1967), 32.

4. Claude Courouve, *Les assemblées de la manchette: Documents sur l'amour masculin au XVIIIe siècle* (Paris: Courouve, 1987), 17. For examples of community building before the coining of the word *homosexual*, see, among others, Judy Grahn, *Another Mother Tongue: Gay Words, Gay Worlds* (Boston: Beacon, 1984); Jonathan Ned Katz, *Love Stories: Sex between Men Before Stonewall* (Chicago: University of Chicago Press, 2001); Christian, Graf von Krockow, *Die Preußischen Brüder, Prinz Heinrich und Friedrich der Große: Ein Doppelportrait* (Stuttgart: Deutsche Verlags-Anstalt, 1996); Thomas A. Foster, ed., *Long Before Stonewall: Histories of Same-Sex Sexuality in Early America* (New York: New York University Press, 2007); Clare Lyons, "Mapping an Atlantic Sexual Culture: Homoeroticism in Eighteenth-Century Philadelphia," *William and Mary Quarterly* 60, no. 1 (July–September 2003): 119–54; Jeffrey Merrick, "Sodomitical Inclinations in Early Eighteenth-Century Paris," *Eighteenth-Century Studies* 30, no. 3 (1997): 289–95; Rictor Norton, *Mother Clap's Molly House: The Gay Subculture in England, 1700–1830* (London: GMP, 1992); Kent Gerard and Gert Hekma, eds., *The Pursuit of Sodomy: Male Homosexuality in Renaissance and Enlightenment Europe* (Binghamton NY: Harrington Park, 1989); Michel Rey, "Parisian Homosexuals Create a Lifestyle, 1700–1750: The Police Archives," in "Unauthorized Sexual Behavior during the Enlightenment," ed. Robert P. Maccubbin, special issue, *Eighteenth Century Life*, n.s., 9, no. 3 (May 1985): 179–91; Simon Richter, "Winckelmann's Progeny: Homosocial Networking in the Eighteenth Century," in *Outing Goethe and His Age*, ed. Alice A. Kuzniar (Stanford: Stanford University Press, 1996), 33–36; Randolph Trumbach, "Sex, Gender, and Sexual Identity in Modern Culture: Male Sodomy and Female Prostitution in Enlightenment London," *Journal of the History of Sexuality* 2, no. 2 (1991): 186–203; Charles Upchurch, *Before Wilde: Sex between Men in Britain's Age of Reform* (Berkeley: University of California Press, 2009).

5. Alfred Kinsey, Wardell B. Pomeroy, and Clyde E. Martin, *Sexual Behavior in the Human Male* (Philadelphia: W. B. Saunders, 1948), 638–47.

6. *100 Years of Marriage and Divorce Statistics, United States, 1867–1967* (Rockville MD: Health Resources Administration, National Center for Health Statistics, 1973), 4. The most concise analysis of this phenomenon can be found in Michael R. Haines, *Long Term Marriage Patterns in the United States from Colonial Times to the Present* (Cambridge MA: National Bureau of Economic Research, 1996). Chevalier Félix de Beaujour, *Sketch of the United States of America, at the Commencement of the Nineteenth Century, from 1800 to 1810* (London: J. Booth, 1814), 74.

7. Arthur W. Calhoun, *A Social History of the American Family*, vol. 1, *Colonial Period* (Cleveland: Arthur H. Clark, 1917), 52; William Benemann, *Male-Male Intimacy in Early America: Beyond Romantic Friendships* (New York: Harrington Park, 2006), 14; Haines, *Long Term Marriage Patterns*, 3, [26].

8. Richard J. Fehrman, "The Mountain Men — A Statistical View," in *The Mountain Men and the Fur Trade of the Far West*, ed. LeRoy R. Hafen (Glendale CA: A. H. Clark, 1972), 10:16. William R. Swagerty later built on Fehrman's study, adding twenty more men to the statistical analysis. Swagerty's study lowers the percentage of lifelong bachelors, but since his figures extend further into the 1840s and 1850s than Fehrman's it may be that as the fur trade faded and the Rockies became more populated, the attraction for homosexual men lessened. William R. Swagerty, "Marriage and Settlement Patterns of Rocky Mountain Trappers and Traders," *Western Historical Quarterly* 11, no. 2 (April 1980).

9. See also Michael Lansing, "Plains Indian Women and Interracial Marriage in the Upper Missouri Trade, 1804–1868," *Western Historical Quarterly* 31, no. 4 (Winter 2000): 413–33; Bruce M. White, "The Woman Who Married a Beaver: Trade Patterns and Gender Roles in the Ojibwa Fur Trade," *Ethnohistory* 46, no. 1 (Winter 1999): 109–47. Many men retired from the trade and settled into more populous areas where white women were available, or married Mexican women in the West.

CHAPTER 1

1. Friedrich Armand Strubberg, *Amerikanische Jagd-und Reisenabenteuer* (Stuttgart: Cotta, 1858), 335. All translations from German into English are by Kevin Jewell.

2. Strubberg, *Amerikanische Jagd-und Reisenabenteuer*, 336.

3. Strubberg, *Amerikanische Jagd-und Reisenabenteuer*, 338–39.

4. Strubberg, *Amerikanische Jagd-und Reisenabenteuer*, 336–37.

5. Mae Reed Porter and Odessa Davenport, *Scotsman in Buckskin: Sir William Drummond Stewart and the Rocky Mountain Fur Trade* (New York: Hastings House, 1963), 9; Charles Dalton, *The Waterloo Roll Call: With Biographical Notes and Anecdotes* (London: Eyre and Spottiswoode, 1904), 82.

6. *Historical Record of the Fifteenth, or the King's Regiment of Light Dragoons,*

Hussars: *Containing an Account of the Formation of the Regiment in 1759, and of Its Subsequent Services to 1841* (London: John W. Parker, 1841), 92–97.

7. Stuart Reid, *Wellington's Army in the Peninsula, 1809–14* (Oxford: Osprey, 2004), 77.

8. Mae Reed Porter and Clyde Porter Papers, 1839–1970, box 47, American Heritage Center, University of Wyoming, Laramie. Though Porter records the ribbon as being "red and black" when she viewed it in Texas in 1956, it is likely that the colors had darkened, and that the medal retained its standard-issue scarlet and blue ribbon. The medal is still in the possession of Franc Nichols Stewart's descendants in Dickinson, Texas.

9. *Historical Record of the Fifteenth*, 103; Porter and Davenport, *Scotsman in Buckskin*, 15.

10. Bertram Lord Ashburnham to William Drummond Stewart, August 19, 1832, GD121/1/box 101/bundle 21, Grandtully Muniments, National Archives of Scotland, Edinburgh.

11. Ashburnham to Stewart, August 19, 1832. There was no member of Parliament named Driver during this period, so the reference is not to a "safe" parliamentary seat.

12. Ashburnham to Stewart, August 19, 1832.

13. Nick Foulkes, *Last of the Dandies: The Scandalous Life and Escapades of Count d'Orsay* (London: Little, Brown, 2003), 151–59.

14. Foulkes, *Last of the Dandies*, 344–45.

15. Benjamin Disraeli, *Henrietta Temple, a Love Story* (London: Henry Colburn, 1837), 3:147.

16. Louis Crompton, "Homophobia in Georgian England," in *Among Men, Among Women: Sociological and Historical Recognition of Homosocial Arrangements*, ed. Mattias Duyves et al. (Amsterdam: Sociologisch Instituut, 1983), 236; A. D. Harvey, "Prosecutions for Sodomy in England at the Beginning of the Nineteenth Century," *Historical Journal* 21, no. 4 (December 1978): 939.

17. William Drummond Stewart, *Edward Warren*, ed. Bart Barbour (Missoula MT: Mountain Press, 1986), 88. Copies of the original edition of Stewart's second novel are difficult to obtain, so for ease of reference I will cite to the 1986 paperback reprint. Quotations have been checked against the original edition for accuracy and completeness. See, for example, the experience of British diplomat Augustus John Foster, who became enamored with an American Indian who was visiting Washington City, in Benemann, *Male-Male Intimacy*, 168–83.

18. Harry Cocks, "Abominable Crimes: Sodomy Trials in English Law and Culture, 1830–1889" (PhD diss., University of Manchester, Faculty of Arts, 1998), 68–69; Louis Crompton, *Byron and Greek Love: Homophobia in 19th-Century England* (Berkeley: University of California Press, 1985), 229; *Times* (London), April 7, 1830, 6.

19. Cocks, "Abominable Crimes," 253.

20. For accounts of arrests for "indecent assault," see the *Times* (London), March 31, 1830; April 2, 1830; April 5, 1830; April 7, 1830; April 12, 1830; April 20, 1830; May 21, 1830; June 21, 1830; August 14, 1830.

21. Upchurch, *Before Wilde*, 16.

22. In the early 1830s two women — both coincidentally named Christian Stewart — became involved in litigation. One was a housekeeper who sued her former employer for child support when he failed to keep his promise to marry her if she became pregnant after consenting to have sex with him. The second suit concerned the division of an estate inherited by the widow of a brewery operator in the county of Lanark.

Porter misidentifies three letters in the collection, which she contends are from Christie. The signature on the letters that Porter transcribes as "C. S. Stewart" is admittedly obscure, but on a fourth letter in the same handwriting the signature is very clearly C. S. Steuart. There are none of the epistolary conventions for letters exchanged between Victorian spouses ("My dearest husband" or "I remain / Your loving wife"). Internal evidence in the letters, including one from May 12, 1848, in which the writer describes landing "a fine fish 1500 weight after half an hour's work," suggests that C. S. was a man, perhaps an agent on the estate. In any case, there would be no reason for Christie to adopt a different spelling of the last name, nor to use S as her middle initial. She would either have used M for Marie (her middle name) or B for Battersby (her maiden name).

23. William George Stewart to Christian Battersby, November 10, 1841, GD/121/1/box 101/bundle 22, Grandtully Muniments, National Archives of Scotland; James Gillespie Graham to John Stewart, April 18, 1832, GD/121/1/box 101/bundle 21, Grandtully Muniments.

24. The portrait published in *Scotsman in Buckskin* and identified as "Lady Stewart — the beautiful laundress" cannot be identified by Stewart's current descendants. Charles Augustus Murray, *The Prairie-bird* (New York: Harper and Brothers, 1849), 4, 155.

25. Crompton, *Byron and Greek Love*, 197–98; Fiona MacCarthy, *Byron: Life and Legend* (New York: Farrar, Straus and Giroux, 2002), 75; William Drummond Stewart, *Altowan; or, Incidents of Life and Adventure in the Rocky Mountains* (New York: Harper and Brother, 1846), 2:152.

26. Walker, Richardson, and Melville to John Stewart, May 18, 1832, GD121/1/box 101/bundle 21, Grandtully Muniments.

27. Joseph M. Melville to John Stewart, February 2, 1832, GD121/1/box 101/bundle 21, Grandtully Muniments.

28. "America," *Edinburgh Review*, July 1824, 433.

29. "America," 429–30.

30. "Travellers in America," *Edinburgh Review*, December 1818, 143.

31. "Travellers in America," 142.

32. "America," 441; see also "Birkbeck's Notes on America," *Edinburgh Review*, June 1818, 140.

33. For a discussion of sexuality among Native Americans as viewed by the thinkers of the Scottish Enlightenment, see Pat Moloney, "Savages in the Scottish Enlightenment's History of Desire," *Journal of the History of Sexuality* 14, no. 3 (2005): 237–65. William Robertson, *The History of America* (London: A. Strahan, 1788), 4:62–63, 65–66.

34. "The Americans and Their Detractors," *Edinburgh Review*, July 1832, 521.

35. "Birkbeck's Notes on America," 122, 137.

36. Leslie A. Fiedler, *Love and Death in the American Novel* (Normal IL: Dalkey Archive, 1997), 192.

37. Fiedler, *Love and Death in the American Novel*, 212–13.

CHAPTER 2

1. Stewart, *Edward Warren*, xiii.

2. Stewart, *Altowan*, 1:unnumbered preliminary page; DeVoto, *Across the Wide Missouri*, 27.

3. Stewart, *Altowan*, 2:112.

4. Stewart, *Altowan*, 2:80.

5. Stewart, *Altowan*, 1:242–43.

6. Stewart, *Altowan*, 2:98.

7. Stewart, *Edward Warren*, 1.

8. Stewart, *Edward Warren*, 8.

9. Stewart, *Edward Warren*, 10.

10. A. Farenholt, "Some Statistical Observations concerning Tattooing as Seen by a Recruiting Surgeon," *U.S. Naval Medical Bulletin* 7, no. 1 (January 1913), cited in Albert Parry, *Tattoo: Secrets of a Strange Art as Practised among the Natives of the United States* (New York: Simon and Schuster, 1933), 86; Hanns Ebensten, *Pierced Hearts and True Love: An Illustrated History of the Origin and Development of European Tattooing and a Survey of Its Present State* (London: Derek Verschoyle, 1953), 48. For an exploration of the homoerotic use of tattoos in the twentieth century, see Samuel M. Steward, *Bad Boys and Tough Tattoos: A Social History of the Tattoo with Gangs, Sailors, and Street-corner Punks, 1950–1965* (New York: Haworth, 1990). Nineteenth-century criminologist Cesare Lombroso recorded at least two tattoos that were linked to homosexuality: an image of linked hands on the chest and the words "Entra Tutto" (It enters everywhere) tattooed on the penis. Cesare Lombroso, *Criminal Man* (Durham NC: Duke University Press, 2006), 60.

11. Stewart, *Edward Warren*, 10–11.

12. Stewart, *Edward Warren*, 12–13.

13. Stewart, *Edward Warren*, 14–15.

14. Stewart, *Edward Warren*, 22.

15. Stewart, *Edward Warren*, 29.

16. Stewart, *Edward Warren*, 425.

17. Stewart, *Edward Warren*, 35.

18. Stewart, *Edward Warren*, 75–76.

19. Stewart, *Edward Warren*, 39–40. Ned (like Stewart himself) sails to America in 1832. In the novel Ned is a passenger on a ship named the *Sesostris*. There was in the 1830s a ship named *Sesostris* based in London (Alexander Yates, captain), a cargo ship with "first-rate accommodations for passengers," but at the time Stewart sailed for America the *Sesostris* was on a voyage to India, so it could not have been the ship on which Stewart himself traveled. Stewart may have been familiar with that ship because of his later dealings in the cotton trade (cotton being one of the chief cargos of the *Sesostris*), or — more likely — he may have chosen the name for the fictional voyage because of his familiarity with another ship also named *Sesostris*, this one a French steamer. Stewart was perhaps a passenger on that later *Sesostris* when it sailed from London in 1839. In that year Stewart is known to have visited Constantinople, and the *Times* of September 27, 1839, announced the arrival of the *Sesostris* in that exotic port, with Mustafa Rashid Pasha, the Ottoman ambassador to France, its most distinguished passenger. It was the type of accommodations and the class of fellow passengers that Stewart would seek at that later stage in his life. *Times* (London), October 4, 1833; September 27, 1839.

20. Stewart, *Edward Warren*, 51.

21. Stewart, *Edward Warren*, 168.

22. Stewart, *Edward Warren*, 169.

23. Stewart, *Edward Warren*, 238–39.

24. Stewart, *Edward Warren*, 239.

CHAPTER 3

1. Stewart, *Altowan*, 1:25.

2. Herman Melville, *Moby Dick* (New York: Columbia University Press, [1999]), 2; E. Porter Belden, *New-York: Past, Present, and Future* (New York: G. P. Putnam, 1849), 31; visitor from Maryland, quoted in Rodman Gilder, *The Battery: The Story of the Adventurers, Artists* . . . (Boston: Houghton Mifflin, 1936), 54; *Flash*, June 23, 1842, 1.

3. For an in-depth analysis of the flash newspapers, see Patricia Cline Cohen, Timothy J. Gilfoyle, and Helen Lefkowitz Horowitz, *The Flash Press: Sporting Male Weeklies in 1840s New York* (Chicago: University of Chicago Press, 2008).

4. *Whip*, January 29, 1842, 2.

5. *Whip*, February 12, 1842, 2; *Flash*, March 5, 1842, no. 2.

6. *Flash*, August 14, 1842, quoted in Cohen, Gilfoyle, and Horowitz, *The Flash Press*, 197.

7. *Picture of New York in 1846* (New York: C. S. Francis, 1846), 116; *Sportsman*, July 22, 1843, 2; Walt Whitman, *Leaves of Grass* (New York: [s.n.], 1855), 78.

8. *New York Courier*, September 25, 1832, 1.

9. For an extended exploration of the topic of young rural men moving to New York City, see Allan Stanley Horlick, *Country Boys and Merchant Princes: The Social Control of Young Men in New York* (Lewisburg PA: Bucknell University Press, 1975).

10. Sean Wilentz, *Chants Democratic: New York City and the Rise of the American Working Class, 1788–1850* (Oxford: Oxford University Press, 2004), 110, 403; Brian P. Luskey, "Jumping Counters in White Collars: Manliness, Respectability, and Work in the Antebellum City," *Journal of the Early Republic* 26, no. 2 (2006): 176; Howard P. Chudacoff, *The Age of the Bachelor: Creating an American Subculture* (Princeton: Princeton University Press, 1999), 33. In 1985 historian Michael Lynch delivered a paper at New York University titled "New York City Sodomy, 1796–1873." The paper, a preliminary report on his research into the records of the Court of General Sessions for the City of New York, detailed several sodomy prosecution cases. Lynch's untimely death unfortunately prevented the completion of this important research; his paper and a possible recording made of the presentation have now been lost. Lynch's papers were deposited with the Canadian Gay and Lesbian Archives, but his research on early New York City sodomy cases cannot be found in the collection (e-mail message from G. P. King, librarian, November 15, 2006). NYU's Institute for the Humanities believes that Lynch's lecture was tape-recorded, but it is unable to locate the recording (e-mail message from Molly Sullivan, January 2, 2007). In 2007 I spent an entire day at the New York City Municipal Archives searching the microfilmed court reports for only one year — 1846 (a date cited by Lynch) — but was unable to locate a sodomy case. I determined it would take many months to replicate Lynch's lost research. My thanks to Timothy J. Gilfoyle for his assistance in trying to locate Michael Lynch's research. Gilfoyle's *City of Eros: New York City, Prostitution, and the Commercialization of Sex, 1820–1920* (New York: Norton, 1992) first alerted me to Lynch's work.

11. *Vanity Fair*, February 4, 1860, 84.

12. *Vanity Fair*, January 18, 1860, 72.

13. Stewart, *Altowan*, 1:25–26.

14. Stewart, *Altowan*, 2:133.

15. James Watson Webb, introduction to Stewart, *Altowan*, 1:vii.

16. Webb, introduction to Stewart, *Altowan*, 1:xi.

17. Webb, introduction to Stewart, *Altowan*, 1:viii.

18. William Drummond Stewart to James Watson Webb, October 9, 1832, James Watson Webb Papers, Yale University Manuscripts and Archives, New Haven CT.

19. Stewart, *Edward Warren*, 43.

20. See, for example, Washington Irving, *The Adventures of Captain Bonneville, U.S.A., in the Rocky Mountains and the Far West* (New York: G. P. Putnam, 1857), 51, 68; Hiram Martin Chittenden, *The American Fur Trade of the Far West* (New York: Francis P. Harper, 1902), 1:255–56.

21. William R. Nester, *From Mountain Man to Millionaire: The "Bold and Dashing Life" of Robert Campbell* (Columbia: University of Missouri Press, 1999), 19; LeRoy R. Hafen, ed., *Trappers of the Far West: Sixteen Biographical Sketches* (Lincoln: University of Nebraska Press, 1983), 308.

22. Chittenden, *The American Fur Trade of the Far West*, 1:255.

23. File of *The State of Missouri v. P. A. Sublette and Morgan Swope*, Court Files November Term 1819 to February Term 1821, quoted in John E. Sunder, *Bill Sublette, Mountain Man* (Norman: University of Oklahoma Press, 1959), 25.

24. Sunder, *Bill Sublette*, 66, 115.

25. Quoted in Patrick C. MacCulloch, *The Campbell Quest: A Saga of Family and Fortune* (St. Louis: Missouri History Museum, 2009), 103–4.

26. MacCulloch, *The Campbell Quest*, 81.

CHAPTER 4

1. Stewart, *Edward Warren*, 45.

2. Ann Raney Thomas Coleman Papers, 3:13, Duke University Library, Durham NC; Harbert Davenport, "Dr. Benjamin Harrison," typescript, Harbert Davenport Collection, Archives Division, Texas State Library, Austin; Charles Larpenteur, *Forty Years a Fur Trader on the Upper Missouri* (New York: Francis P. Harper, 1898), 1:16; William Henry Harrison, quoted in Pat Ireland Nixon, "Dr. Benjamin Harrison, Temporary Texan," *Journal of the History of Medicine and Allied Sciences* 1 (1946): 109.

3. *Maximilian, Prince of Wied's Travels in the Interior of North America, 1832–1834,* vol. 22, part 1 of *Early Western Travels, 1748–1846,* ed. Reuben Gold Thwaites (Cleveland: Arthur H. Clark, 1906), 231.

4. Swagerty, "Marriage and Settlement Patterns," 163; Chittenden, *The American Fur Trade,* 1:55; Susan Lee Johnson, *Roaring Camp: The Social World of the California Gold Rush* (New York: Norton, 2000), 170.

5. Irving, *Adventures of Captain Bonneville,* 86.

6. Chittenden, *The American Fur Trade,* 1:60–61.

7. Quoted in William Marshall Anderson, *The Rocky Mountain Journals of William Marshall Anderson,* ed. Dale L. Morgan and Eleanor Towles Harris (San Marino CA: Huntington Library, 1967), 32.

8. Alexis de Tocqueville, *Democracy in America* (Cambridge: Sever and Francis, 1864), 2:259. For an exploration of bear culture, see Les Wright, *The Bear Book:*

Readings in the History and Evolution of a Gay Male Subculture (Binghampton NY: Haworth, 2001).

9. Kerry R. Oman, "Winter in the Rockies: Winter Quarters of the Mountain Men," *Montana: The Magazine of Western History* 52, no. 1 (Spring 2002): 38–40; Frances Fuller Victor, *The River of the West: Life and Adventures in the Rocky Mountains and Oregon* (Hartford CT: Columbian Book, 1870), 1:137.

10. Augustus John Foster, Diary, 1806, 12, Augustus John Foster Papers, Library of Congress, Washington DC; for more about Foster, see Benemann, *Male-Male Intimacy*, 168–83.

11. Warren A. Ferris, *Life in the Rocky Mountains: A Diary of Wanderings on the Sources of the Rivers Missouri, Columbia, and Colorado from February, 1830, to November, 1835* (Denver: Old West, 1940), 40–41.

12. Swagerty, "Marriage and Settlement Patterns," 171, 173; Alexander Barclay, quoted in George P. Hammond, *The Adventures of Alexander Barclay, Mountain Man: From London Corsetier to Pioneer Farmer* . . . (Denver: Old West, 1976), 42.

13. DeVoto, *Across the Wide Missouri*, 34.

14. George Frederick Ruxton, *Life in the Far West* (New York: Harper and Brothers, 1849), 18.

15. Victor, *The River of the West*, 1:142.

16. Irving, *Adventures of Captain Bonneville*, 200, 181.

17. Irving, *Adventures of Captain Bonneville*, 182.

18. Stewart, *Edward Warren*, 428; with minor corrections in punctuation to correspond with the 1854 London edition.

19. Stewart, *Edward Warren*, 428.

20. Larpenteur, *Forty Years a Fur Trader*, 1:36–37.

21. Ferris, *Life in the Rocky Mountains*, 265–66.

22. Stewart, *Edward Warren*, 429.

23. Larpenteur, *Forty Years a Fur Trader*, 1:40–41.

24. Stewart, *Edward Warren*, 429; Larpenteur, *Forty Years a Fur Trader*, 1:40–41.

25. Victor, *The River of the West*, 1:143.

26. Stewart, *Edward Warren*, 429.

CHAPTER 5

1. Marvin C. Ross, ed., *The West of Alfred Jacob Miller (1837): From the Notes and Water Colors in the Walters Art Gallery* (1951; repr., Norman: University of Oklahoma Press, 1969), opposite 37.

2. Stewart, *Edward Warren*, 225, 230.

3. Stewart, *Edward Warren*, 226.

4. Stewart, *Edward Warren*, 425, 253; DeVoto, *Across the Wide Missouri*, 309.

5. Stewart, *Edward Warren*, 88.

6. Stewart, *Edward Warren*, 90–91.

7. Monica Rico, "Sir William Drummond Stewart: Aristocratic Masculinity in the American West," *Pacific Historical Review* 76, no. 2 (2007): 176.

8. Stewart, *Edward Warren*, 123.

9. Stewart, *Edward Warren*, 91.

10. Stewart, *Altowan*, 2:155.

11. Irving, *Adventures of Captain Bonneville*, 204.

12. Nester, *From Mountain Man to Millionaire*, 108.

13. Sunder, *Bill Sublette*, 154.

14. Larpenteur, *Forty Years a Fur Trader*, 1:10, 11–12.

15. For an extended discussion of this phenomenon, see Horlick, *Country Boys and Merchant Princes*; Wilentz, *Chants Democratic*; Michael Zakim, "The Business Clerk as Social Revolutionary; or, A Labor History of the Nonproducing Classes," *Journal of the Early Republic* 26, no. 4 (2006): 563–603.

16. Jesse A. Applegate, "Views of Oregon History, ms., Yoncalla, Oregon," 1878, BANC MSS P-A 2, Bancroft Library, University of California, Berkeley.

17. Hammond, *The Adventures of Alexander Barclay*, 12, 14.

18. William Drummond Stewart to William Sublette, December 17, 1838, William L. Sublette Papers, Missouri Historical Society, St. Louis; DeVoto, *Across the Wide Missouri*, 360. Stewart's penmanship is unusually neat for a nineteenth-century correspondent. Anyone looking at the sentence as it is written in the original letter would be hard pressed to interpret the word as anything other than "Fairy." The slang meaning of the word — an effeminate homosexual — was current in America from at least the late nineteenth century, as in 1896 the *American Journal of Psychology* reported the existence in New York City of a secret homosexual organization called the Fairies. Given the usual lag time from the adoption of a term by an underground society and its appearance in the text of a scholarly publication (lengthened in this case by society's reluctance to discuss the unspeakable), it is extremely likely that when in 1836 Stewart and Sublette used the term *Fairy* they indeed meant the type of effeminate homosexual that at that time was associated with the pejorative term *counter-jumper*.

19. Quoted in Nester, *From Mountain Man to Millionaire*, 110.

20. Quoted in Nester, *From Mountain Man to Millionaire*, 120.

21. Robert Campbell to William Sublette, January 25, 1838, Sublette Papers.

22. Hugh Campbell to William Sublette, December 5, 1836, Sublette Papers; William Sublette to Hugh Campbell, January 1, 1837, Sublette Papers.

23. Nester, *From Mountain Man to Millionaire*, 132.

24. Quoted in MacCulloch, *The Campbell Quest*, 176.

25. William Sublette to William Drummond Stewart, June 16, 1841, Sublette Papers; William Sublette to William Drummond Stewart, January 5, 1842, Sublette Papers.

26. William Sublette to William Drummond Stewart, St. Louis, June 16, 1841, William Drummond Stewart Papers, Missouri Historical Society, St. Louis; William Sublette to William Drummond Stewart, undated, but circa April 1842, Stewart Papers.

27. Robert Campbell to William Drummond Stewart, February 3, 1842, Stewart Papers.

28. Mary A. Town to William Sublette, October 31, 1836, Sublette Papers.

29. Mary A. Town to William Sublette, March 14, 1837, Sublette Papers.

30. Albert G. Boone to William Sublette, May 5, 1843, Sublette Papers.

CHAPTER 6

1. Frederick E. Hoxie, *Parading through History: The Making of the Crow Nation in America, 1805–1935* (Cambridge: Cambridge University Press, 1995), 55; Ned Blackhawk, *Violence over the Land: Indians and Empires in the Early American West* (Cambridge MA: Harvard University Press, 2006), 10.

2. For more on the impressive physical display presented by the Plains Indians, see Max Carocci, *Ritual and Honour: Warriors of the North American Plains* (London: British Museum Press, 2011), and *Warriors of the Plains: The Arts of Plains Indian Warfare* (London: British Museum Press, 2012).

3. Edwin Thompson Denig, *Five Indian Tribes of the Upper Missouri: Sioux, Arickaras, Assiniboines, Crees, Crows,* ed. John C. Ewers (Norman: University of Oklahoma Press, 1961), 154–55.

4. Denig, *Five Indian Tribes of the Upper Missouri,* 155–56.

5. DeVoto, *Across the Wide Missouri,* 123, 124; Henry Angelino and Charles L. Shedd, "A Note on Berdache," *American Anthropologist,* n.s., 57, no. 1, pt. 1 (February 1955): 121–26.

6. Angelino and Shedd, "A Note on Berdache," 125. Because of the overarching topic of this book, this discussion will concentrate on biologically male berdaches who assumed the gender roles of women. There were also women who cross-dressed and assumed the roles of men, though their numbers were considerably smaller, and they often had very different reasons for switching genders. Evelyn Blackwood, "Sexuality and Gender in Certain Native American Tribes: The Case of Cross-Gender Females," *Signs* 10, no. 1 (Autumn 1984): 27–42.

7. Sue-Ellen Jacobs and Wesley Thomas, "Native American Two-Spirits," *Anthropology Newsletter* 35, no. 8 (1994): 7; Richard C. Trexler, "Making the American Berdache: Choice or Constraint?" *Journal of Social History* 35, no. 3 (Spring 2002): 630. For a less contentious exploration of this linguistic dilemma, see Carolyn Epple, "Coming to Terms with Navajo 'Nádleehí': A Critique of 'Berdache,' 'Gay,' 'Alternate Gender,' and 'Two-Spirit,'" *American Ethnologist* 25, no. 2 (May 1998): 267–90.

8. Sue-Ellen Jacobs, Wesley Thomas, and Sabine Lang, eds., *Two-Spirit People:*

Native American Gender Identity, Sexuality, and Spirituality (Urbana: University of Illinois Press, 1997), 3.

9. Sabine Lang, *Men as Women, Women as Men: Changing Gender in Native American Cultures* (Austin: University of Texas Press, 1998), xv.

10. Charles Callender and Lee M. Kochems, "The North American Berdache," *Current Anthropology* 24, no. 4 (August–October 1983): 443–70; Lang, *Men as Women, Women as Men.*

11. Will Roscoe, "'That Is My Road': The Life and Times of a Crow Berdache," *Montana: The Magazine of Western History* 40, no. 1 (Winter 1990): 49.

12. S. C. Simms, "Crow Indian Hermaphrodites," *American Anthropology*, n.s., 5 (1903): 581.

13. Maximilian, Prince zu Wied, *Reise in das innere Nord-America in den Jahren 1832 bis 1834* (Coblenz: J. Hoelscher, 1839–41), 1:401. "Sie haben viele Bardaches oder Mannweiber unter sich, und sind vor den übringen Nationen Meister in unnatürlichen Gebräuchen."

14. Denig, *Five Indian Tribes*, 187.

15. Quoted in Simms, "Crow Indian Hermaphrodites," 580.

16. Robert H. Lowie, "Social Life of the Crow Indians," *Anthropological Papers of the American Museum of Natural History* 9, pt. 2 (1912): 226.

17. Robert H. Lowie, "Myths and Traditions of the Crow Indians," *Anthropological Papers of the American Museum of Natural History* 25 (1918): 28–30.

18. Alfred L. Kroeber, "Psychosis or Social Sanction," *Character and Personality* 8, no. 3 (1940): 209.

19. Walter L. Williams, *The Spirit and the Flesh: Sexual Diversity in American Indian Culture* (Boston: Beacon, 1986), 36–37; Will Roscoe, *Changing Ones: Third and Fourth Genders in Native North America* (New York: St. Martin's, 1998), 26; Robert H. Lowie, *The Sun Dance of the Crow Indians* (New York: American Museum of Natural History, 1915), 31–32.

20. Demitri Boris Shimkin, "Some Interactions of Culture, Needs, and Personalities among the Wind River Shoshone" (PhD diss., University of California, Berkeley, 1939), 90.

21. George A. Dorsey, *The Arapaho Sun Dance* (Chicago: Field Columbian Museum, 1903), 173–76; Clark Wissler, *Societies and Dance Associations of the Blackfoot Indians* (New York: American Museum of Natural History, 1913), 415. Following the quaint practice of nineteenth-century ethnologists, Wissler lapses into Latin whenever he writes something graphically sexual. My thanks to Jennifer Nelson for her translations into English.

22. Alice B. Kehoe, "The Function of Ceremonial Sexual Intercourse among the Northern Plains Indians," *Plains Anthropologist* 15 (1970): 99–103. For a contrary view, see Harriet Whitehead, "The Bow and the Burden Strap: A New Look at

Institutionalized Homosexuality in Native North America," in *Sexual Meanings: The Cultural Construction of Gender and Sexuality*, ed. Sherry B. Ortner and Harriet Whitehead (Cambridge: Cambridge University Press, 1981). Whitehead would seem to argue against the symbolic significance of the root transfer when she maintains that "American Indians were not given to using semen as a reification of manhood" (87), though she does not address this particular ceremony.

23. A. B. Holder, "The Bote: Description of a Peculiar Sexual Perversion Found among North American Indians," *New York Medical Journal* 50 (1889): 623–25. Williams reports that among the berdaches of the Southwest, receptive anal intercourse is the preferred sexual act (*The Spirit and the Flesh*, 97–99).

24. Eve Kosofsky Sedgwick, *Between Men: English Literature and Male Homosocial Desire* (New York: Columbia University Press, 1985).

25. Claude E. Schaeffer, "The Kutenai Female Berdache: Courier, Guide, Prophetess, and Warrior," *Ethnohistory* 12, no. 3 (Summer 1965): 200. Shaeffer's article, with its references to "deviates," "bizarre behavior," and "sexual aberrancy" — in an article that otherwise reads as a positive, even admiring, description of the woman in question — is a powerful indication of the revolution in language that has taken place since 1965.

26. Quoted in Schaeffer, "The Kutenai Female Berdache," 214–15.

27. Stewart, *Edward Warren*, 209.

28. Francis Parkman, *Sketches of Prairie and Rocky-Mountain Life* (Boston: Little, Brown, 1892), 283; Victor Tixier, *Tixier's Travels on the Osage Prairies*, ed. John Francis McDermott (Norman: University of Oklahoma Press, 1940), 215.

29. George A. Dorsey and James R. Murie, *Notes on Skidi Pawnee Society* (Chicago: Field Museum of Natural History, 1940), 107; Leslie Spier, *Yuman Tribes of the Gila River* (Chicago: University of Chicago Press, 1933), 330–31; Ernest Beaglehole and Pearl Beaglehole, *Hopi of the Second Mesa* (Millwood NY: Kraus, 1976), 65; David G. Mandelbaum, *The Plains Cree* (New York: American Museum of Natural History, 1940), 244.

30. Lowie, "Social Life of the Crow Indians," 212; Robert H. Lowie, "Notes on the Social Organization and Customs of the Mandan, Hidatsa, and Crow Indians," *Anthropological Papers of the American Museum of Natural History* 21, pt. 1 (1917): 92.

31. Ross, *The West of Alfred Jacob Miller*, 179.

32. Irving, *Adventures of Captain Bonneville*, 939.

33. James P. Beckwourth, *The Life and Adventures of James P. Beckwourth*, ed. T. D. Bonner (New York: Knopf, 1931), 184.

34. Beckwourth, *The Life and Adventures of James P. Beckwourth*, 185.

35. Beckwourth, *The Life and Adventures of James P. Beckwourth*, 186.

36. Stewart, *Edward Warren*, 429n.

37. Stewart, *Edward Warren*, 429n.

38. Stewart, *Edward Warren*, 430n.

39. Stewart, *Edward Warren*, 158.

40. Stewart, *Edward Warren*, 158–60.

CHAPTER 7

1. Anderson, *Rocky Mountain Journals*, 144.

2. Porter and Davenport, *Scotsman in Buckskin*, 81. I am grateful to Charles Howard Ashworth's descendant Jan Wood for bringing this article to my attention (e-mail message to author, December 19, 2008).

3. "Extraordinary Instance of Youthful Enterprize," *Manchester Herald*, September 12, 1835.

4. "Extraordinary Instance of Youthful Enterprize."

5. "Charles Howard Ashworth," *Army and Navy Chronicle*, n.s., 2 (July 1–June 30, 1836): 316. Again, I am grateful to Ms. Wood for later bringing this second article to my attention.

6. Larpenteur, *Forty Years a Fur Trader*, 70–71.

7. Ray H. Mattison, "James A. Hamilton (Palmer)," in Hafen, *The Mountain Men and the Fur Trade*, 3:165.

8. DeVoto, *Across the Wide Missouri*, 120.

9. Quoted in DeVoto, *Across the Wide Missouri*, 402.

10. Anderson, *Rocky Mountain Journals*, 27–28.

11. Jason Lee, "Diary of Rev. Jason Lee," *Quarterly of the Oregon Historical Society* 17, no. 2 (June 1916): 123–24.

12. Lee, "Diary," 138.

13. Lee, "Diary," 138.

14. William Marshall Anderson, "Anderson's Narrative of a Ride to the Rocky Mountains in 1834," ed. Albert J. Partoll, *Frontier and Midland* 19, no. 1 (Autumn 1938): 62.

15. Quoted in Susan M. Colby, *Sacagawea's Child: The Life and Times of Jean-Baptiste (Pomp) Charbonneau* (Spokane WA: Arthur H. Clark, 2005), 104.

16. Colby, *Sacagawea's Child*, 107.

17. For an analysis of the evidence, see Colby, *Sacagawea's Child*, 110–11.

18. Clyde Porter to Eleanor W. Towles, July 5, 1957, reel 16, Dale Lowell Morgan Papers, Bancroft Library, University of California, Berkeley.

19. Anderson, *Rocky Mountain Journals*, 142–43; Lee, "Diary," 140; see also Colby, *Sacagawea's Child*, 136–37.

20. John K. Townsend, *Narrative of a Journey across the Rocky Mountains, 1834*, vol. 21 of *Early Western Travels, 1748–1846*, ed. Reuben Gold Thwaites (Cleveland: Arthur H. Clark, 1905), 197.

21. Townsend, *Narrative*, 198; Nathaniel Wyeth, *The Journals of Captain Nathaniel J. Wyeth* (Fairfield WA: Ye Galleon, 1969), 71.

22. Townsend, *Narrative*, 203–4.

23. Townsend, *Narrative*, 211.

24. Townsend, *Narrative*, 216.

25. Townsend, *Narrative*, 219.

26. Townsend, *Narrative*, 221.

27. Townsend, *Narrative*, 218–19.

28. Townsend, *Narrative*, 224–25.

29. Jason Lee, "Diary of Rev. Jason Lee," *Quarterly of the Oregon Historical Society* 17, no. 3 (September 1916): 244–45.

30. Lord Byron, George Gordon, *The Works of Lord Byron, Complete in One Volume* (Frankfurt am Main: H. L. Brœnner, 1826), 474. There are only a few possibilities for the volume of Byron that Stewart carried with him to America in 1832. *Sardanapalus* was first published in 1821 by John Murray in London, issued with two other plays, *The Two Forscari* and *Cain, a Mystery*. It is unlikely, however, that Stewart burdened himself with a volume of only three of Byron's minor works. A more probable choice would be an edition of the complete or collected works. John Murray also published *The Works of Lord Byron* in 1821, in an octodecimo edition perfect for traveling — though in five volumes. Unfortunately, that edition does not include *Sardanapalus*. Perhaps the most likely edition therefore is the one-volume *Works* published in Frankfurt am Main in 1826, which includes the play. Lee, "Diary" (September 1916), 254. The Sardanapalus story was evoked in the early twentieth century by the gay poet Federico García Lorca in his unfinished poem "Oda y burla de Sesostris y Sardanápalo" ("Ode and Mockery of Sesostris and Sardanapalus"), published posthumously by Miguel García-Posada from manuscript drafts (Ferrol: Esquio-Ferrol, 1985). The poem links Byron's king of Ninevah with a legendary Egyptian pharaoh. While there are no overt homosexual references in the Sesostris story as it was handed down — other than his role as world conqueror, making him a proto–Alexander the Great (see Martin Braun, *History and Romance in Graeco-Oriental Literature* [Oxford: Basil Blackwell, 1938], 13–18) — it is intriguing that when Stewart chose a name for the ship that would take the fictional hero Edward Warren to America, he chose to call it the *Sesostris*.

31. Townsend, *Narrative*, 231.

32. Wyeth, *Journals*, 73; Townsend, *Narrative*, 232–33.

33. Townsend, *Narrative*, 255–56.

34. Townsend, *Narrative*, 256.

35. Wyeth, *Journals*, 76.

36. Lee, "Diary" (September 1916), 258; Townsend, *Narrative*, 264.

37. Townsend, *Narrative*, 277.

38. Townsend, *Narrative*, 292.

39. Lee, "Diary" (September 1916), 262.

40. Frederick V. Holman, *Dr. John McLoughlin, the Father of Oregon* (Cleveland: Arthur H. Clark, 1907), 29–30.

41. Adele Perry, *On the Edge of Empire: Gender, Race, and the Making of British Columbia, 1849–1871* (Toronto: University of Toronto Press, 2001), 29–30.

42. *Columbia District Correspondence Book*, B.223/b/9, 1833–1834, November 18, 1834 (microfilm IM229), Hudson's Bay Company Archives, Winnipeg.

43. *Columbia District Correspondence Book*.

44. Burt Brown Barker, *The McLoughlin Empire and Its Rulers* (Glendale CA: Arthur H. Clark, 1959), 219.

45. Barker, *The McLoughlin Empire*.

46. Barker, *The McLoughlin Empire*, 222.

47. Barker, *The McLoughlin Empire*, 219–20.

48. Barker, *The McLoughlin Empire*, 220.

49. Barker, *The McLoughlin Empire*, 249.

50. William H. Gray, *A History of Oregon, 1792–1849* (Portland OR: Harris and Holman, 1870), 46–54.

51. Gray, *A History of Oregon*, 54.

CHAPTER 8

1. Wyeth, *Journals*, 96; Osborne Russell, *Journal of a Trapper; or, Nine Years in the Rocky Mountains, 1834–1843* (Boise ID: Syms-York, 1921), 20.

2. DeVoto, *Across the Wide Missouri*, 220.

3. Quoted in DeVoto, *Across the Wide Missouri*, 230.

4. Frances Fuller Victor, *The River of the West: Life and Adventure in the Rocky Mountains and Oregon* (Hartford CT: Bliss, 1879), 187.

5. Stewart, *Edward Warren*, 230.

6. William Drummond Stewart to James Watson Webb, November 15, 1835, Webb Papers.

7. Stewart, *Edward Warren*, 3.

8. John I. Merritt, *Baronets and Buffalo: The British Sportsman in the American West, 1833–1881* (Missoula MT: Mountain Press, 1985), 18.

9. For the identification of Sillem and biographical information about him, I am indebted to Hans-Wolff Sillem of Hamburg, who is the senior genealogist for the Sillem family and who was generous in sharing information about his family's history. In *Baronets and Buffalo* John I. Merritt misidentifies the young man accompanying Murray as "Vernunft." A German of that name (spelled "Vernunfft" in Porter and Davenport and "Vernufft" in DeVoto — first name unknown) enters into the picture two years later, living in England and serving as a business party for some cotton speculation that Stewart engaged in with the British consul at New Orleans, John Crawford. I can find no documentation that this man was Murray's traveling partner, or even that he ever visited the United States.

10. Charles Augustus Murray, *Travels in North America* (London: Richard Bentley, 1839), 1:289–90.

11. Murray, *Travels in North America*, 2:167.

12. Stewart, *Edward Warren*, 47.

13. Murray, *Travels in North America*, 2:183–84.

14. Murray, *Travels in North America*, 2:185–86.

15. James Stuart, *Three Years in North America* (Edinburgh: R. Cadell, 1833), 2:246–47.

16. *Scotsman* (Edinburgh), November 25, 1835.

17. *Scotsman* (Edinburgh), November 25, 1835.

18. For an extensive discussion of the cotton industry in New Orleans, see Edward L. Miller, *New Orleans and the Texas Revolution* (College Station: Texas A&M, 2004), 6–18; James E. Winson, "Notes on the Economic History of New Orleans, 1803–1836," *Mississippi Valley Historical Review* 11, no. 2 (September 1924): 200–226; Peter Temin, "The Causes of the Cotton-price Fluctuations in the 1830's," *Review of Economics and Statistics* 49, no. 4 (November 1967): 463–70.

19. Temin, "Causes of the Cotton-price Fluctuations," 464; Winston, "Notes of the Economic History of New Orleans," 206.

20. Murray, *Travels in North America*, 2:192, 203.

21. William Drummond Stewart to William Sublette, Charleston, February 28, 1836, Sublette Papers.

22. DeVoto, *Across the Wide Missouri*, 244, 246; Sprague, *A Gallery of Dudes*, 32.

23. Quoted in Clifford Merrill Drury, ed., *Where Wagons Could Go: Narcissa Whitman and Eliza Spalding* (Lincoln: University of Nebraska Press, 1997), 36, 30.

24. For an extended discussion of the life of Eliza Spalding, see Deborah Lynn Dawson, "Laboring in My Savior's Vineyard: The Mission of Eliza Hart Spalding" (PhD diss., Bowling Green State University, 1988).

25. Stewart, *Edward Warren*, 427.

26. DeVoto, *Across the Wide Missouri*, 249; Clifford Merrill Drury, *Henry Harmon Spalding* (Caldwell ID: Caxton, 1936), 38.

27. Gray, *A History of Oregon*, 115.

28. Gray, *A History of Oregon*, 116.

29. Clifford Merrill Drury, ed., *First White Women over the Rockies: Diaries, Letters, and Biographical Sketches of the Six Women of the Oregon Mission Who Made the Overland Journey in 1836 and 1838* (Glendale CA: A. H. Clark, 1963–66), 1:51–52.

30. Drury, *First White Women over the Rockies*, 1:52–53.

31. John E. Sunder, *Joshua Pilcher, Fur Trader and Indian Agent* (Norman: University of Oklahoma Press, 1968), 56–57.

32. Gray, *A History of Oregon*, 117.

33. Gray, *A History of Oregon*, 117–18.

34. Victor, *The River of the West*, 202.

35. Gray, *A History of Oregon*, 122–23.

36. *National Intelligencer*, October 26, 1836.

37. Gray, *A History of Oregon*, 123.

38. Victor, *The River of the West*, 207.

39. *Times* (London), June 22, 1849.

40. George Frederick Ruxton, "Life in the 'Far West,' Part IV," *Blackwood's Edinburgh Magazine*, September 1848, 304.

41. Ruxton, "Life in the 'Far West,'" 306.

CHAPTER 9

1. Quoted in Porter and Davenport, *Scotsman in Buckskin*, 131.

2. Ron Tyler, "Alfred Jacob Miller and Sir William Drummond Stewart," in *Alfred Jacob Miller: Artist on the Oregon Trail*, ed. Ron Tyler (Fort Worth TX: Amon Carter Museum, 1982), 19. Tyler corrects Miller's assertion that the address was 132 Chartres, taking the address from a city directory of the period. Notebook of Alfred Jacob Miller, owned by L. Vernon Miller, quoted in Ross, *The West of Alfred Jacob Miller*, xvi–xvii.

3. No detailed study has yet been done of the artist colony that Miller joined in Italy, but there are hints, reading between the lines of nineteenth-century biographers, that these men were for the most part homosexual in their orientations. Eugene Plon, *Thorvaldsen: His Life and Works* (Boston: Roberts Brothers, 1873), relates several romances Thorvaldsen had with women and suggests that he fathered an illegitimate child with a woman named Anna Maria, but Plon can find no evidence of his subject's emotional attachments after the age of forty-nine. "From this time (1819) Thorvaldsen seems to have been free from all entanglements. Anna Maria herself no longer appears in his life" (70–71). Thorvaldsen never married. With Victorian delicacy Lady Eastlake in *Life of John Gibson, R.A., Sculptor* (London: Longmans, Green, 1870) wrote: "But though capable of ardent affection, his love for his art asserted its supremacy, and (not altogether perhaps without an occasional struggle) took the place of all other sources of happiness. He passed through life therefore with few cares, and, beyond his two brothers, with no domestic ties; though no man was ever the object of truer friendships and purer attachments" (4). His companion during his final years was the painter Penry Williams (see T. Matthews, *The Biography of John Gibson, R.A., Sculptor, Rome* [London: Heinemann, 1911]). Horatio Greenough eventually married, but the marriage contract specified that he and his wife maintain separate estates. Horatio Greenough, *Letters of Horatio Greenough, American Sculptor*, ed. Nathalia Wright (Madison: University of Wisconsin Press, 1972), 220n; William R. Johnston, "The Early Years in Baltimore and Abroad," in Tyler, *Alfred Jacob Miller*, 16.

4. Quoted in Sandra Tome, "Restyling an Old World: Nathaniel Parker Willis and Metropolitan Fashion in the Antebellum United States," *Representations*, no. 85 (Winter 2004): 103, 104; Alfred Jacob Miller, Journal, undated entry, 21, Walters Art Museum; Greenough, *Letters*, 130, 142.

5. For a detailed discussion of Miller's youth, see Johnston, "The Early Years in Baltimore and Abroad," 7–18.

6. Miller notebook, quoted in Ross, *The West of Alfred Jacob Miller*, xvi.

7. Lisa Strong, *Sentimental Journey: The Art of Alfred Jacob Miller* (Fort Worth TX: Amon Carter Museum, 2008), 23.

8. Ross, *The West of Alfred Jacob Miller*, xviii. William Johnston of the Walters Art Museum in Baltimore, perhaps the foremost expert on Alfred Jacob Miller, believes that Miller may have been gay, though he has uncovered no definitive documentation (e-mail exchange with the author, September 1, 2009).

9. Alfred Jacob Miller to Brantz Mayer, St. Louis, April 3, 1837, quoted in Robert C. Warner, *The Fort Laramie of Alfred Jacob Miller* (Laramie: University of Wyoming Press, 1979), 144.

10. Alfred Jacob Miller to Brantz Meyer, Murthly Castle, October 18, 1840, quoted in Warner, *The Fort Laramie of Alfred Jacob Miller*, 54.

11. Warner, *The Fort Laramie of Alfred Jacob Miller*, 144.

12. David L. Brown, *Three Years in the Rocky Mountains* (Cincinnati: Eberstadt and Sons, 1950), 5, originally published in *Cincinnati Daily Morning Atlas, 1840*.

13. Stewart, *Edward Warren*, 97, 98, 286, 433.

14. Miller, Journal, 45.

15. Ross, *The West of Alfred Jacob Miller*, opposite 139.

16. Quoted in DeVoto, *Across the Wide Missouri*, 314.

17. Ross, *The West of Alfred Jacob Miller*, opposite 52.

18. Ross, *The West of Alfred Jacob Miller*, opposite 36.

19. Ross, *The West of Alfred Jacob Miller*, opposite 51.

20. Ross, *The West of Alfred Jacob Miller*, opposite 52.

21. Ross, *The West of Alfred Jacob Miller*, opposite 147.

22. Ross, *The West of Alfred Jacob Miller*, opposite 132.

23. Ross, *The West of Alfred Jacob Miller*, opposite 120.

24. Ross, *The West of Alfred Jacob Miller*, opposite 155.

25. Ross, *The West of Alfred Jacob Miller*, opposite 151.

26. Ross, *The West of Alfred Jacob Miller*, opposite 64.

27. Strong, *Sentimental Journey*, 45. In Strong's book see, for example, the paintings on 47, 48, 107, 110, 111.

28. Brown, *Three Years in the Rocky Mountains*, 6.

29. Brown, *Three Years in the Rocky Mountains*, 7.

30. Brown, *Three Years in the Rocky Mountains*, 8.

31. Brown, *Three Years in the Rocky Mountains*, 8.

32. Brown, *Three Years in the Rocky Mountains*, 11.

33. DeVoto, *Across the Wide Missouri*, 322.

34. Brown, *Three Years in the Rocky Mountains*, 11.

35. Brown, *Three Years in the Rocky Mountains*, 12.

36. Quoted in Fred R. Gowans, *Rocky Mountain Rendezvous: A History of the Fur Trade Rendezvous, 1825–1840* (Layton UT: Peregrine Smith Books, 1985), 153–54.

37. Ross, *The West of Alfred Jacob Miller*, opposite 146.

38. Quoted in Porter and Davenport, *Scotsman in Buckskin*, 163.

39. Sir Alexander Muir Mackenzie, "Bygone Perthshire; or, Social Life Fifty Years Ago," *Chambers's Journal*, December 1905–November 1906, 115.

40. Porter and Davenport, *Scotsman in Buckskin*, 162.

41. *Register of the Basilica of St. Louis, King of France (Old Cathedral)*, roll 172, no. 3, Archdiocesan Archives, St. Louis, Missouri.

42. Bishop Bruté's letters (in French) to Bishop Rosati are held by the Archives and Records Office of the Archdiocese of St. Louis. They are extensive and easily legible. Rosati's letters to Bruté are also part of the collection, but I encountered difficulties in obtaining access to them. According to Sister Mary Salesia Godecker, Bruté's first biographer, "The bishop returned home on Saturday, November 25, [1837] after an absence of five or six weeks" (*Simon Bruté de Rémur, First Bishop of Vincennes* [St. Meinrad IN: St. Meinrad Historical Essay, 1931], 333). Part of the time Bishop Bruté was traveling he was in the company of Bishop Rosati, so it is likely that he was actually present for Stewart's baptism on November 20.

CHAPTER 10

1. William Drummond Stewart to Bishop Joseph Rosati, April 29, 1838, S-RG1B4.3, Bishop Joseph Rosati Papers, Archives and Records Office of the Archdiocese of St. Louis.

2. Quoted in Drury, *Where Wagons Could Go*, 240.

3. Clifford Merrill Drury, ed., *On to Oregon: The Diaries of Mary Walker and Myra Eells* (Lincoln: University of Nebraska Press, 1998), 73.

4. Drury, *On to Oregon*, 80.

5. DeVoto, *Across the Wide Missouri*, 352.

6. Jabondis, Esq., to William Drummond Stewart, November 30, 1838, bundle 21, Grandtully Muniments.

7. James Gillespie Graham to William Drummond Stewart, November 12, 1838, bundle 21, Grandtully Muniments.

8. Will of Sir John Archibald Drummond Stewart, December 5, 1838, PROB 11/1904, Records of the Prerogative Court of Canterbury, National Archives, London.

9. James Gillespie Graham to William Drummond Stewart, November 12, 1838, bundle 21, Grandtully Muniments.

10. Graham to Stewart, November 12, 1838.

11. William Drummond Stewart to James Watson Webb, April 4, 1839, Webb Papers.

12. *New York Morning Herald*, May 11, 1839, quoted in Ron Tyler, "Alfred Jacob Miller and Sir William Drummond Stewart," in *Alfred Jacob Miller*, 37; Augustus Greele to William Drummond Stewart, May 17, 1839, quoted in Tyler, "Alfred Jacob Miller and Sir William Drummond Stewart," 37–38.

13. *Times* (London), June 4, 1839; Caroline LeRoy Webster, *Mr W. and I: Being the Authentic Diary of Caroline LeRoy Webster* (Binghamton NY: Ives Washburn, 1942).

14. *Times* (London), June 17, 1839; W. M. Acworth, *The Railways of Scotland: Their Present Position* (London: John Murray, 1890), 106–7.

15. Catherine Stewart Bastide to William Drummond Stewart, Dept. de l'Averiron, France, August 15, 1839, bundle 21, Grandtully Muniments; Douglas Murray, *Bosie: A Biography of Lord Alfred Douglas* (New York: Hyperion, 2000), 5–11.

16. Catherine Stewart Bastide to William Drummond Stewart, Dept. de l'Averiron, France, August 15, 1839, bundle 21, Grandtully Muniments.

17. Quoted in Warner, *The Fort Laramie of Alfred Jacob Miller*, 158.

18. Stewart, *Altowan*, 2:111–12.

19. Strong, *Sentimental Journey*, 41–42. Strong first presented these ideas in "American Indian and Scottish Identity in Sir William Drummond Stewart's Collection," *Winterthur Portfolio* 35, nos. 2–3 (Summer–Autumn 2000): 127–55. While the article makes many very perceptive points, I am less convinced by her argument that "his collecting [of Indian artifacts] answered his desire to articulate for himself and his peers an authentic Scottish identity in the wake of serious challenges to the Highland way of life from which that identity derived" (129). While Murthly Castle was, according to Miller, decorated with ancient Scottish artifacts (almost certainly installed before Stewart assumed the baronetcy), these were excluded from Stewart's personal space in Dalpowie Lodge. If there were a connection between the two cultural identities (in Stewart's perception), one would expect an intermingling of decors. For a similar discussion of Stewart's rooms, see Rico, "Sir William Drummond Stewart," 177–80.

20. Rudolph Ulrich to William Drummond Stewart, St. Louis, July 17, 1839, bundle 21, Grandtully Muniments.

21. In the Mae Reed Porter and Clyde Porter Papers at the University of Wyoming are handwritten transcriptions of these letters. They are apparently the letters referred to in the bibliography of *Scotsman in Buckskin* as "original letters to his immediate family while living in Murthly Castle and in London. Courtesy of the owner, L. Vernon Miller, of Baltimore." However, the current members of the Miller family were unaware of the existence of the letters when contacted at my request by William Johnston of the Walters Art Museum. I had made photocopies

of the transcripts during my research at the University of Wyoming, and so recopied them for the Miller family. The whereabouts of the originals is now unknown. Many appear in transcription in Warner's *The Fort Laramie of Alfred Jacob Miller*. Alfred Jacob Miller to Family, Murthly Castle, October 6, 1840, box 45, Porter and Porter Papers; Warner, *The Fort Laramie of Alfred Jacob Miller*, 157.

22. Alfred Jacob Miller to Decatur Miller, Murthly Castle, October 31, 1840, box 45, Porter and Porter Papers.

23. Alfred Jacob Miller to Decatur Miller, Murthly Castle, October 2, 1841, box 45, Porter and Porter Papers.

24. Alfred Jacob Miller to Decatur Miller, Murthly Castle, June 24, 1841, box 45, Porter and Porter Papers.

25. Alfred Jacob Miller to Decatur Miller, Murthly Castle, July 26, 1841, box 45, Porter and Porter Papers.

26. Alfred Jacob Miller to Decatur Miller, London, February 10, 1842, box 45, Porter and Porter Papers.

27. J. E. Handie to William Drummond Stewart, New York, October 29, 1841, bundle 22, Grandtully Muniments.

28. J. E. Handie to William Drummond Stewart, New York, November 20, 1841, bundle 22, Grandtully Muniments.

29. Handie to Stewart, November 20, 1841.

30. William Sublette to William Drummond Stewart, St. Louis, June 16, 1841, bundle 22, Grandtully Muniments.

31. Catharine Stewart Bastide to William Drummond Stewart, La Moque, France, January 19, 1842, buddle 22, Grandtully Muniments.

32. George Stewart to William Drummond Stewart, Logiealmond, July 15, 1841, bundle 22. Grandtully Muniments.

33. *George Drummond Stewart and William David Earl of Mansfield v. William Drummond Steward*, 18 *Scottish Law Reporter* 508 (1846).

34. *Mansfield et al. v. Stewart*, 9th and 10th Victoria, 1846, pp. 148–49. A postcard of Grandtully Castle mailed sometime between 1912 and 1924 (based on the penny stamp depicting George V) includes a message: "My most cherished memory of this place is Lady Stewart's garden party & the six bottles of lime juice & soda I succeeded in drinking!" (collection of the author).

CHAPTER 11

1. *Evening Courant*, September 8, 1842, reprinted in *Times* (London), September 13, 1842.

2. Queen Victoria, *Leaves from the Journal of Our Life in the Highlands*, ed. Arthur Helps (London: Smith, Elder, 1868), 20–22, 26.

3. Hammond, *The Adventures of Alexander Barclay*, 41.

4. Harrison C. Dale, "A Fragmentary Journal of William L. Sublette," *Mississippi Valley Historical Review* 6, no. 1 (June 1919): 102; Richard H. Graham and Sidney Smith, "Report of Journey to the Rocky Mountains," ed. John E. Sunder, *Bulletin, Missouri Historical Society*, October 1954, 52n40.

5. Porter and Davenport, *Scotsman in Buckskin*, 211–12.

6. Dale, "A Fragmentary Journal of William L. Sublette," 108; *Missouri Republican*, May 27, 1843, quoted in Matthew C. Field, *Prairie and Mountain Sketches*, collected by Clyde Porter and Mae Reed Porter, ed. Kate L. Gregg and John Francis McDermott (Norman: University of Oklahoma Press, 1957), xxi–xxii.

7. Quoted in Edward Harris, *Up the Missouri with Audubon: The Journal of Edward Harris*, ed. John Francis McDermott (Norman: University of Oklahoma Press, 1951), 6; William Drummond Stewart to John James Audubon, Baltimore, November 16, 1842, John James Audubon Papers, Beinecke Library, Yale University, New Haven CT.

8. John James Audubon to Friends, St. Louis, April 2, 1843, quoted in *Audubon in the West*, ed. John Francis McDermott (Norman: University of Oklahoma Press, 1965), 47–48.

9. John James Audubon to Lucy Audubon, quoted in Stanley Clisby Arthur, *Audubon: An Intimate Life of the American Woodsman* (New Orleans: Harmanson, 1937), 454–55; John James Audubon to Friends, St. Louis, April 2, 1843, quoted in McDermott, *Audubon in the West*, 47; John James Audubon to Friends, St. Louis, April 17, 1843, quoted in McDermott, *Audubon in the West*, 57.

10. John James Audubon to Lucy Audubon, quoted in Arthur, *Audubon*, 454.

11. Field, *Prairie and Mountain Sketches*, xxv.

12. William Clark Kennerly, as told to Elizabeth Russell, *Persimmon Hill: A Narrative of Old St. Louis and the Far West* (Norman: University of Oklahoma Press, 1949), 143.

13. Matt Field to Cornelia Ludlow Field, Camp William, Shawnee Country, Missouri Territory, May 18, 1843, quoted in Field, *Prairie and Mountain Sketches*, xxvi.

14. *Daily Picayune*, July 8, 1843.

15. *Daily Picayune*, May 30, 1843.

16. Kennerly, *Persimmon Hill*, 144.

17. *Daily Picayune*, June 1, 1843. The reference is to Henry Russell's "The Fine Old English Gentleman" (1836).

18. Theodore Talbot, *The Journals of Theodore Talbot, 1843 and 1849–53*, ed. Charles H. Carey (Portland OR: Metropolitan, 1931), 5–6.

19. Matthew Field to N. M. Ludlow, Shawnee Land, May 14, 1843, quoted in Field, *Prairie and Mountain Sketches*, 17. The most likely candidate for Miss Power is Maurice Henry Anthony O'Reilly Power (1821–49), who studied law but left the profession to pursue a career in acting. He died in poverty at the age of twenty-eight. He would have been twenty-two at the time of Stewart's last western journey.

20. Dale, "A Fragmentary Journal of William L. Sublette," 107.

21. Graham and Smith, "Report of Journey to the Rocky Mountains," 46. It is also possible that Field mistakenly switched the identities of the tribes, and that it was three Osages who sought refuge with the party.

22. Field, *Prairie and Mountain Sketches*, 42–43.

23. Field, *Prairie and Mountain Sketches*, 45.

24. *Daily Picayune*, December 5, 1843.

25. *Daily Picayune*, December 5, 1843.

26. *Daily Picayune*, November 25, 1843.

27. *Daily Picayune*, November 25 1843.

28. *Daily Picayune*, November 26, 1843.

29. Kennerly, *Persimmon Hill*, 151; Field, *Prairie and Mountain Sketches*, 55.

30. *Daily Picayune*, November 28, 1843.

31. Field, *Prairie and Mountain Sketches*, 58.

32. Field, *Prairie and Mountain Sketches*, 59–62; Kennerly, *Persimmon Hill*, 147.

33. *Daily Picayune*, February 6, 1844.

34. *Daily Picayune*, February 6, 1844.

35. *Daily Picayune*, February 9, 1844.

36. Matthew Field, Journal, July 9 and 11, 1843, Missouri Historical Society, St. Louis.

37. Field, *Prairie and Mountain Sketches*, 104.

38. *Daily Picayune*, November 16, 1843. See also Matthew Field, "Death in the Wilderness," *Rover, a Weekly Magazine* 2 (1844): 393.

39. Field, *Prairie and Mountain Sketches*, 111; Field, "Death in the Wilderness," 394.

40. Field, *Prairie and Mountain Sketches*, 111; Field, "Death in the Wilderness," 394.

41. *Daily Picayune*, November 16, 1843. See also Field, "Death in the Wilderness," 394.

42. Field, *Prairie and Mountain Sketches*, 112, 114.

43. Field, *Prairie and Mountain Sketches*, 131–33.

44. Field, *Prairie and Mountain Sketches*, 131–33.

45. Field, *Prairie and Mountain Sketches*, 133.

46. Field, *Prairie and Mountain Sketches*, 133. For gouging and castrating as common fighting techniques, see Isaac Weld, *Travels through the States of North America and the Provinces of Upper and Lower Canada, during the Years 1765, 1796 and 1797* (London: J. Stockdale, 1799), 192–93; Nicole Etcheson, "Manliness and the Political Culture of the Old Northwest, 1790–1860," *Journal of the Early Republic* 15, no. 1 (Spring 1995): 64; Elliott J. Gorn, "'Gouge and Bite, Pull Hair and Scratch': The Social Significance of Fighting in the Southern Backcountry," *American Historical Review* 90, no. 1 (February 1985): 18–43.

47. Field, *Prairie and Mountain Sketches*, 135.

48. Richard Rowland to his Sister, St. Louis, January 9, 1944, Richard Rowland Letters, 1840, 1844, Oregon Historical Society, Portland.

49. Strubberg, *Amerikanische Jagd-und Reisenabenteuer*, 338.

50. Strubberg, *Amerikanische Jagd-und Reisenabenteuer*, 339.

51. Stewart, *Altowan*, 1:117–18.

52. William Clark Kennerly, as told to Bessie K. Russell, "My Hunting Trip to the Rockies in 1843," *Colorado Magazine*, January 1945, 33.

53. Field, *Prairie and Mountain Sketches*, 135–36.

54. Field, *Prairie and Mountain Sketches*, 150.

55. Field, *Prairie and Mountain Sketches*; Kennerly, "My Hunting Trip to the Rockies in 1843," 34.

56. Kennerly, "My Hunting Trip to the Rockies in 1843," 34.

57. Kennerly, *Persimmon Hill*, 157.

58. Field, *Prairie and Mountain Sketches*, 163.

59. *Daily Picayune*, December 13, 1843.

60. *Daily Picayune*, December 13, 1843.

61. Field, *Prairie and Mountain Sketches*, 204.

62. Kennerly, "My Hunting Trip to the Rockies in 1843," 37.

63. *Daily Picayune*, November 7, 1843; Kennerly, "My Hunting Trip to the Rockies in 1843," 38.

64. *American, and Commercial Daily Advertiser* (Baltimore), August 15, 1843; *Brother Jonathan: A Weekly Compend of Belles Lettres and the Fine Arts* (New York), August 19, 1843.

65. *Missouri Republican*, October 24, 1843; *Niles Register*, November 18, 1843.

66. *Brother Jonathan*, July 29, 1843.

67. William Sublette to William Drummond Stewart, St. Louis, November 22, 1843, bundle 22, Grandtully Muniments.

68. Leonidas Walker to William Drummond Stewart, St. Louis, April 20, 1844, bundle 22, Grandtully Muniments.

69. Stephen Banks, "Killing with Courtesy: The English Duelist, 1785–1845," *Journal of British Studies* 47 (July 2008): 539; Alexis de Tocqueville, quoted in Robert Baldick, *The Duel: A History of Duelling* (London: Chapman and Hall, 1965), 115, 124. In his book *Duels and the Roots of Violence in Missouri* (Columbia: University of Missouri Press, 2000), Dick Steward writes extensively about "dueling" in Missouri but admits that "the Missouri duel paled in comparison to its counterpart in the Deep South," and that it was in any case a rare occurrence. Steward describes as a "duel" any act of violence committed by one person seeking revenge upon another. "Brawling, assault and battery, and other forms of mayhem were attributed to 'hot blood' and noble courage. Consequently, when gentlemen from Missouri dueled,

they were less inclined to pay respects to all of the formal trappings of the code duello and more likely to concentrate on the matter at hand, namely, the elimination of an adversary" (11). I would contend that without "all of the formal trappings," no true duel has taken place.

70. Upchurch, *Before Wilde*, 184.

71. H. Brubaker to William Drummond Stewart, Independence, Missouri, November 29, 1843, bundle 22, Grandtully Muniments.

72. *Oxford English Dictionary*, 2nd ed. (Oxford: Clarendon, 1989), 2:333; H. Brubaker to William Drummond Stewart, Independence, Missouri, April 24, 1844, bundle 22, Grandtully Muniments.

73. Robert Campbell to William Drummond Stewart, St. Louis, April 22, 1844, bundle 22, Grandtully Muniments.

74. William Sublette to William Drummond Stewart, St. Louis, April 20, 1844, bundle 22, Grandtully Muniments.

75. Alexander Chauvin to William Drummond Stewart, St. Charles, Missouri, November 20, 1848, bundle 22, Grandtully Muniments.

76. Stewart, *Edward Warren*, 4.

CHAPTER 12

1. Sunder, *Bill Sublette*, 194–95; MacCulloch, *The Campbell Quest*, 202.

2. MacCulloch, *The Campbell Quest*, 202.

3. *Dundee, Perth and Cupar Advertiser*, June 28, 1844.

4. Lord Breadalbane to Sir William Drummond Stewart, Taymouth, Scotland, December 5, 1845, bundle 22, Grandtully Muniments.

5. William George Drummond Stewart to Sir William Drummond Stewart, Vienna, August 2, 1847, bundle 22, Grandtully Muniments: "Esperant que vous [êtes] en bonne santé et que vous vous amusez bien avec votre jeune compagnon." Bonamy Mansell Power to Sir William Drummond Stewart, Vienna, August 2, 1847, bundle 22, Grandtully Muniments; Bonamy Mansell Power to William Drummond Stewart, Vienna, August 29, 1847, bundle 22, Grandtully Muniments.

6. J. Pittman to William Drummond Stewart, London, December 11, 1845, bundle 22, Grandtully Muniments.

7. For this information I am indebted to Brian Best of the Victoria Cross Society, who forwarded information from Edward Hayter, a descendant of Herbert John Stewart (correspondence dated August 11, 2009).

8. Quoted in Leslie Southwick, "The Sword Presented to Major William George Drummond Stewart, VC, in Recognition of His Services in the Crimean War and Indian Mutiny Campaign," *Arms and Armour* 5, no. 2 (2008): 124.

9. "Peculiarities of the Scotch Marriage Law," *Times* (London), May 7, 1872, 11.

10. "Peculiarities of the Scotch Marriage Law."

11. *Times* (London), September 1, 1846.

12. *Times* (London), September 1, 1846. For a fictional account of the murder written by a descendent of the tenants of the cottage and drawing upon family stories concerning the crime, see Carlo Brunelli, *Il prete scozzese* (N.p.: Orecchio di Van Gogh, 2008).

13. R. R. Madden, ed., *The Literary Life and Correspondence of the Countess of Blessington* (London: T. C. Newby, 1855), 105–6.

14. *The Annual Register; or, A View of the History and Politics of the Year 1855* (London: F. and J. Rivington, 1856), 4–10.

15. William Drummond Stewart to James Watson Webb, Murthly Castle, August 4, 1846, Webb Papers.

16. Evelyn Waugh captures this lingering prejudice in his Oxford novel *Brideshead Revisted* when Charles Ryder's cousin Jasper warns him, "Beware of Anglo-Catholics — they're all sodomites with unpleasant accents."

17. Porter and Davenport, *Scotsman in Buckskin*, 265.

18. *David Wedderspoon et al. (Stewart's Trustees) v. Sir William Drummond Stewart*, 41 *Scottish Jurist* 5 (1868).

19. William Drummond Stewart to James Watson Webb, Grantley Hall, December 19, 1857, Webb Papers.

20. Porter and Davenport, *Scotsman in Buckskin*, 269; interview with Thomas Steuart Fothringham, May 1, 2007.

21. Brian Best, "The Strange Death of the Laird's Son — William Drummond Steuart vc," *Journal of the Victoria Cross Society*, October 2007, 19–20.

22. William Spink, *Hand-book of Procedure and Redress of Law* (Edinburgh: W. Patterson, 1879), 12.

23. *Scotsman*, June 16, 1871.

24. *Scotsman*, June 17, 1871.

25. *Scotsman*, June 17, 1871; June 19, 1871.

26. *Henry Padwick and Another v. Sir Archibald Douglas Steuart*, 43 *Scottish Jurist* 454 (1871).

27. Porter and Davenport, *Scotsman in Buckskin*, 272.

Index

Edward Warren (W. D. Stewart)
(*continued*)
  novel, 35; cross-dressing woman in,
  115–16; description in, of life of
  mountain men, 159; description in,
  of travel, 60–61; as homoerotic text,
  20, 42–43, 46–48, 89–90, 118; Kit
  Carson in, 124; Louis Phillipson
  as character in, 190–91; Marcus
  Whitman as character in, 162–63;
  murder of Marshall in, 122–23; plot
  summary of, 39–48; reprint edition
  of, 37
Eells, Cushing, 210
Eells, Myra Fairbanks, 210, 211
Ermatinger, Francis, 115, 155, 212,
  213
Ewing, F. Y., 211, 212

The Far West (ship), 163
Ferris, Warren, 74, 81
Fiedler, Leslie A.: *Love and Death in
  the American Novel*, 32–33
Field, Matthew: and amateur
  theatricals, 249–50; and Cyprien
  Menard, 256–57; descriptions of
  food by, 251–52; and Devil's Gate,
  264–65, 272; and homosexual
  banter, 261–62; recruitment of,
  245–46
Fielding, Henry: *Tom Jones*, 17
Fitzpatrick, Sublette & Bridger, 155
Fitzpatrick, Tom: encounter of, with
  Crows, 119–20, 122; as leader
  of expeditions, 91–92, 103, 123,
  156, 158, 168–69, 177, 182, 190;
  and Narcissa Whitman, 174; and
  William Drummond Stewart, 33
flash newspapers, 51–54
Flathead Indians, 64, 107, 115, 131,
  156, 178, 179, 206, 266, 270

Fontenelle, Lucien, 83, 155–56, 211
Fort Bonneville WY, 67
Fort Bridger, 269
Fort Hall ID, 134, 136, 140–41
Fort Independence MO, 189
Fort John. *See* Fort Laramie WY
Fort Laramie WY, 197, 212, 261, 272,
  294
Fort Saint Vrain CO, 238
Fort Stikine AK, 150
Fort Union MT, 128–30, 133
Fort Vancouver WA, 138, 145–48, 155,
  158, 180
Fort Walla Walla WA, 139, 143–44,
  155
Fort William WY, 156, 175, 182, 197
Foster, Augustus John, 73
Foucault, Michel, 4–5
Fraeb, Henry, 103
Fraser, Simon, 148–50, 153
free trappers, 69–72
Frémont, John C., 2, 239, 248–49, 266
Fremont Lake, 266–67
Froissart, Jean, 200

Gallatin, Albert, 73
A Gallery of Dudes (Sprague), 4
Galveston TX, 237, 295, 303
Geyer, Charles, 263
Gibson, John, 186, 322n3
Gillespie Graham, James, 17, 125,
  214–16
Graham, James, 297, 300
Graham, Richard Hill, 243–44, 251,
  274, 277
Grand Tetons, 203
Grandtully Castle, 221, 233, 286–87,
  293, 297
Gray, Mary Augusta Dix, 210
Gray, William, 115, 172–73, 174,
  176–77, 178–79, 202, 210, 211

orientation of, 323n8; at Sulphur
Springs, 93; visits of William
Drummond Stewart to, 185–86,
216–17, 237
Mississippi River, 162–63, 220, 239
Missouri Historical Society, 3, 96, 101
Missouri River, 92, 109, 133
Mitchell, David, 130
Moby Dick (Melville), 51
Mojave Indians, 107
Mono Indians, 107
Mormons, 294–95
Morse, Samuel F. B., 186
Murie, James R., 116
Murray, Charles Augustus, 36, 160–
63, 167, 206; *The Prairie-bird*, 26
Murthly Castle: art collection at, 18; as
birthplace of William Drummond
Stewart, 14; and construction of
New Murthly, 125, 159, 183;
decoration of, 21; entail of, 286–87,
298–99; and fire of 1844, 284–85;
Queen Victoria's visit to, 235–37;
Ron Tyler's visit to, 1; stories about,
265; and William Drummond
Stewart's death, 300–303; William
Drummond Stewart's inheritance of,
213, 220–22

Napoleon Bonaparte, 14–15, 28
National Archives of Scotland, 24
Navajo Indians, 107
Newman, John Henry, 206
New Orleans Daily Picayune, 245,
246, 247, 253, 262, 274, 275
New Orleans LA, 96, 162, 163–67,
185–86, 216–17, 237, 246, 277
New York City NY, 50–60, 160
Nez Percé Indians, 64, 131, 138, 168,
170, 179, 180, 206
Niagara Falls, 60, 160

Nichols, Ebenezer B., 166, 237–38,
295–96
Nichols, Franc, 296–303
North Bend OH, 67
Northern Paiute Indians, 107
North Platte River, 11
Nuttall, Thomas, 130, 139, 143–45

O'Fallon, John, 62, 93
Ogle, James, 277
Ojibwa Indians, 107
Old Green Tree Tavern, 95
Omaha Indians, 176
Omega (ship), 276
Order of St. Benedict. *See*
Benedictines
Osage Indians, 107, 116, 250–51
Ottoman Empire, 21

Padwick, Henry, 298–99, 302–3
Palais-Royal, 52
Palmer, James Archdale Hamilton,
128–30
Panic of 1837, 202–3
Parker, Samuel, 156–67, 170, 180, 210
Parkman, Francis, 116
Paul Wilhelm of Württemberg, Duke,
132–34, 247
Pawnee Indians, 116, 160–62,
250–51, 252
Philadelphia PA, 62
Phillipson, Louis, 190–91
Phillipson, Miranda, 191
Phillipson, Philippe, 190–91
Pierre's Hole, battle of, 64–65, 156
Pilcher, Joshua, 175–77, 179, 182
Pima Indians, 107
Pittman, J., 286
Platte River, 253, 257, 262, 275, 276,
277, 294
Poe, Edgar Allan, 186

St. Louis Jockey Club, 92
St. Louis MO, 67, 93–96
Storer, A. M., 255, 259–61, 264–65, 274
Strong, Lisa, 187, 223
Strubberg, Friedrich Armand, 11–13, 267–68
Stuart, Alonzo, 279
Stuart, James, 164
Sublette, Milton, 92, 130, 169
Sublette, Philip, 63
Sublette, Solomon, 284
Sublette, William: death of, 284; 1833 trip of, to Rockies, 75, 78; 1834 trip of, to Rockies, 132; 1843 trip of, to Rockies, 238–39; marriage of, 283–84; relationship of, with Robert Campbell, 61–65; and Robert Campbell's courtship of Virginia Kyle, 96–102; and Robert Campbell's marriage, 230; and sexual orientation of clerk, 3, 96; and William Drummond Stewart, 33, 67–68, 277; youth of, 63–64
Sublette & Campbell, 69, 81, 92–94, 99–100
Sulphur Springs, 64, 92–93, 99–100, 101, 130, 283
Sun Dance, 112–14, 316n22
Sutter, John Augustus, 211
Sweetwater River, 177, 264, 272, 294

Talbot, Theodore, 248–49
The Taming of the Shrew (Shakespeare), 249
Taos NM, 122, 123
Ta-tonka-Seenta (Sioux), 273
tattooing, 41
Taylor, Hubert, 16
Taylor, Zachary, 282
Taymouth Castle, 125, 185

Tay River, 185, 220, 236–37
Tewa Indians, 107
Thing, Joseph, 130
Thorvaldsen, Bertel, 186, 322n3
Three Forks, 103
Tilghman, Stedman, 249, 259, 263, 264–65, 266, 272
Times of London, 23, 180, 218, 289, 290–91
Tixier, Victor, 116
Tocqueville, Alexis de, 35–36, 71, 279
Tom Jones (Fielding), 17
Tongue River, 92
Town, Mary A., 101
Townsend, John, 126, 128, 130, 135–39, 141–45
Trollope, Fanny, 36
Tyler, Ron, 1–2

Ulrich, Rudolph, 224
Upchurch, Charles, 279

Vérendrye, François, 104
Vérendrye, Louis-Joseph, 104
Victoria, Queen, 19, 160, 196, 199, 225, 236–37

Waiilatpu WA, 180
Waldren, George T., 54
Walker, Elkanah, 210, 212
Walker, Joe, 199, 211
Walker, Leo, 271, 277–78
Walker, Mary Richardson, 210, 211
Walters Art Museum, 87
Warfield, Charles A., 121
Waterloo Medal, 15–16, 307n8
Webb, James Watson: and Altowan, 36; biography of, 58–60; resemblance of, to Little Thunder, 273; and William Drummond Stewart, 158–59, 165, 217, 218, 237, 292, 294–95

11-12

9↑